The publisher and the University of California Press Foundation gratefully acknowledge the generous support of the Atkinson Family Foundation Imprint in Higher Education.

Seeing Race Again

Seeing Race Again

COUNTERING COLORBLINDNESS
ACROSS THE DISCIPLINES

Edited by Kimberlé Williams Crenshaw,
Luke Charles Harris, Daniel Martinez HoSang,
and George Lipsitz

UNIVERSITY OF CALIFORNIA PRESS

University of California Press, one of the most distinguished university presses in the United States, enriches lives around the world by advancing scholarship in the humanities, social sciences, and natural sciences. Its activities are supported by the UC Press Foundation and by philanthropic contributions from individuals and institutions. For more information, visit www.ucpress.edu.

University of California Press
Oakland, California

Library of Congress Cataloging-in-Publication Data

Names: Crenshaw, Kimberlé, editor. | Harris, Luke Charles, 1950– editor. | HoSang, Daniel, editor. | Lipsitz, George, editor.
Title: Seeing race again : countering colorblindness across the disciplines / edited by Kimberlé Williams Crenshaw, Luke Charles Harris, Daniel Martinez HoSang, and George Lipsitz.
Description: Oakland, California : University of California Press, [2019] | Includes bibliographical references and index. |
Identifiers: LCCN 2018035602 (print) | LCCN 2018041744 (ebook) | ISBN 9780520972148 (epub and ePDF) | ISBN 9780520300972 (cloth : alk. paper) | ISBN 9780520300996 (pbk. : alk. paper)
Subjects: LCSH: Racism in higher education—United States. | Multicultural education—United States. | Post-racialism—United States. | Race discrimination—United States. | United States—Race relations.
Classification: LCC LC212.42 (ebook) | LCC LC212.42 .S44 2019 (print) | DDC 344/.0798—dc23
LC record available at https://lccn.loc.gov/2018035602

Manufactured in the United States of America

26   25   24   23   22   21   20   19
10   9   8   7   6   5   4   3   2   1

CONTENTS

PREFACE AND ACKNOWLEDGMENTS

PRAYING TO THE DISCIPLINARY GODS
WITH ONE EYE OPEN

This volume is the culmination of more than a decade of shared inquiry involving dozens of scholars investigating the origins, evolution, and consequences of racial colorblindness as a metaphor for social relations across the academic disciplines. Its genealogy, however, reaches beyond the academy both to the Civil Rights Movement, which briefly shook the foundations of American social life, and to the demobilizing campaigns within the legal and political arena to restabilize the American social order in its aftermath. Anchoring the slowed pace of race reform in the 1980s, and the dismantling of the civil rights infrastructure throughout the 1990s, colorblind rhetoric crossed over into popular culture to provide ideological cover for ballot initiatives and other efforts to neutralize affirmative action and other antisubordination measures.

Despite its solidly conservative deployment in the post–civil rights era, colorblindness received an unexpected rebranding in 2008 as the ideological standard-bearer for the country's postracial future. This was a remarkable ride for a concept that defied definition, measurement, or theorization. Indeed, the work that colorblindness does across so many sectors and issues is stunning given the utter lack of consensus as to what it really is. Unanswered questions about whether it is a social theory, a moral imperative, or merely a rhetorical prophylactic have not significantly undermined its uptake by institutions and pundits ranging from liberals who hold it as a transcendent ideal to organizations whose assault on university policy marches under this banner. Descriptive questions about whether human beings can actually choose to be colorblind or whether it is a cognitive impossibility only complicate the more fundamental question about whether it can produce a more just and legitimate social world. The feeble justification for colorblindness seems incongruous with its ubiquitous presence in public discourse pertaining to race and the social world.

This anomalous reality formed the centerpiece of a research initiative that moved from the affirmative action battlefields of California, Michigan, and Washington to the Center for Advanced Study in the Behavioral Sciences (CASBS) and the Center for Comparative Studies in Race and Ethnicity (CSRE) at Stanford. The African American Policy Forum (AAPF) had been involved in campaigns in multiple states to preserve race-conscious policies, working together with the American Civil Liberties Union (ACLU) and other organizations to bring cross-disciplinary research to bear on the enduring nature of racial inequality in American society. The dominance of colorblindness as the embodiment of racial justice underscored the need for a powerful counternarrative that could convey an alternative vision of racial equity, one tied to the historical and contemporary ways that race actually worked as opposed to the fantasies of racial transcendence peddled by critics such as Ward Connerly and organizations like the Center for Individual Rights. The idea that the commonsense appeal of colorblindness could not be directly countered to defeat popular initiatives to undermine equal opportunity policies was underscored by the conventional messaging experts who encouraged a version of a "mend it, don't end it" approach. Campaign messaging in defense of affirmative action largely sidestepped racial matters to foreground the presumably more palatable case of gender equity.

With the exception of Colorado, the campaigns designed to defend racial justice and affirmative action without acknowledging racial injustice went down to withering defeat. Without a powerful counternarrative, the easily inflated rhetoric of colorblindness proved to be a trap for liberals. For critics of civil rights, colorblindness served as a battle-tested Trojan horse, one that could deliver easy reversals of the painstaking victories that courageous Americans had risked everything to secure. Under the magic of the colorblind trope, historically marginalized communities were reframed as illegitimate beneficiaries of reverse discrimination while those who inherited the advantages of a society built, as Justice Harlan approvingly observed in *Plessy v. Ferguson,* on the superiority of whites were lifted up as victims. As Luke Charles Harris notes, through this classic misdirection the diminished overrepresentation of whites became the critical civil rights issue of the post–civil rights era.[1]

The yawning losses sustained by civil rights constituencies and the troubling future that lay ahead prompted the editors of this collection, both individually and collectively, to mobilize knowledge to reveal the contemporary workings of racial power. Daniel Martinez HoSang's *Racial Propositions: Ballot Initiatives and the Making of Postwar California,* for example, uncovered the connections between California's anti–affirmative action and anti-immigrant campaigns and midcentury efforts to use popular initiatives to reverse civil rights victories. HoSang reveals how California's long history of subjecting minoritized racial groups has long been rationalized by appeals to race-neutral values like "freedom" and "choice." George Lipsitz's work interrogating power and resistance stretched across sociology, history, and Black Studies. Luke Charles Harris's trenchant critiques of both constitutional jurisprudence and political science revealed the otherworldly dimensions of a constitutional and political theory of equality that failed to center white supremacy as its starting proposition. And Kimberlé Williams Crenshaw's work as a founder of Critical Race Theory took up the ways that the racial revolt against white supremacy had been depoliticized and tamed by liberal legalism. The common denominator in all of these projects was their focused interrogation of the profound contradiction between abstract American ideals of equality divorced from social reality and the messier story of how racial power is constituted and reproduced through colorblind tropes and stealth performances.

These projects, like so many others pursued across the academy, set forth powerful frameworks that revealed the illegitimate hold of colorblindness as either a descriptive prism or a normative analytic. Yet a powerful counternarrative to colorblindness had yet to emerge. Thus, the Countering Colorblindness across the Disciplines project grew out of an effort to aggregate knowledge about our racial past to illuminate how the legacy of white supremacy continued to shape contemporary racial disparities.

Although information gaps between researchers and advocates were not new, the more surprising but equally important chasm between academics dedicated to race scholarship across disciplines had yet to be addressed. Indeed, even as the need for cross-institutional collaboration between academics and policy advocates was frequently acknowledged in the efforts to defend civil rights, opportunities for the collective targeting of the colorblind gloss on racial hierarchies across academic disciplines were rare. Disciplinary boundaries and research practices threatened to deepen rather than disrupt the tenacious hold of colorblind ideology. Evidence that revealed the unwarranted prominence of colorblind discourse remained in disaggregated disarray across the academic disciplines.

A particularly powerful illustration of the way that colorblindness remained uncontested absent intentional cross-disciplinary efforts lies in the interface between social psychology and law. Claude Steele, the leading researcher in the discovery of stereotype threat, brought a new and compelling viewpoint into AAPF's summits and interventions on affirmative action. His breakthrough work on stereotype threat revealed the demonstrable instability of the baselines on which so much of the constitutional debate about "preferential treatment" and "reverse discrimination" was predicated. As Justice Powell had observed in the 1978 decision *Regents of University of California v. Bakke:* "Racial Classifications in admissions conceivably could serve [another] purpose, one which petitioner does not articulate: fair appraisal of each individual's academic promise in light of some cultural bias in grading or testing procedures" (438 U.S. 265, fn. 43).

Steele's work seemed to provide direct evidence that could, if taken up by legal theorists and judges, disrupt the meritocratic baseline on which the constitutional presumption against affirmative action was predicated. Of course, the fact that disruption was possible did not automatically reshape the contours of legal doctrine. What it did do, however, was reveal that doctrinal rules that framed colorblindness as the constitutional embodiment of race neutrality were nothing but a policy choice of judges that could just as convincingly go a different way.

This critical race encounter between law and social psychology prompted important insights that eventually come together as central themes of the Countering Colorblindness project. First among them was the recognition that a comprehensive understanding of colorblindness's many implications required multiple opportunities for participants to understand the history and methods of the disciplines and how developments in one discipline bear implications for another. Notwithstanding the promise of an interdisciplinary approach to colorblindness, it is clear that targeted opportunities for scholars to engage these questions of colorblindness across disciplines were rare. AAPF then convened short working-group meetings around the world, including in the United States, India, Italy, and Brazil. Yet there were no fully sustainable opportunities to stage a multilayered exchange among scholars who were in some way engaging colorblindness.

The Countering Colorblindness project finally came to fruition in 2008 when a critical mass of thinkers met together at Stanford for a yearlong effort to build a sustainable initiative around colorblindness and its consequences. Luke Charles Harris and George Lipsitz, along with Kimberlé Crenshaw (a fellow at CASBS) and director Claude Steele, formed the initial group, which several CASBS scholars subsequently joined.

The working group set about to challenge colorblind ideology and to bring disciplinary knowledge to bear against the unchecked growth of this framework in all discourses pertaining to race. As we framed the missions at the time, the goal was to

> examine how the idea of colorblindness influences the dominant sensibilities of an array of academic disciplines, shaping knowledge production and other institutional practices. Here our goal will be not only to create an interdisciplinary genealogy of colorblindness as an idea. More provocatively, we will seek to understand colorblindness as an institutional practice that reproduces its own appeal by limiting the means by which countervailing information is legitimately produced.

These were not simply academic questions but were central to our effort to build a stronger research-based foundation for racial justice advocacy in the civil and political sectors.

On paper, the plan was a good one. In reality, the early stages of dialogue proved tough going. While the interrogation of colorblindness across the disciplines bore the illusion of a common point of departure, the constraints of disciplinary allegiances, distinct terminologies, and analytic conventions made it difficult to agree on a clear agenda or language. Still, we labored on with our hit-or-miss experiments in framing what we would interrogate and how.

Eventually, we would learn just how significant disciplinary barriers can be, and how the agnosticism that helped to facilitate meaningful exchange among some of us was discomforting to others. We learned as well that disciplinary methods could contain useful avenues into various ways of conceiving and managing information and that there was, to paraphrase an adage, "a method to the disciplinary madness." Specifically, there were insights that might be drawn from our respective paradigms notwithstanding their sometimes troubling histories.

Those who navigated a space between unmitigated endorsement and utter abandonment of their disciplinary paradigms seem to be most suited for our exchange. Claude Steele, in his characteristically succinct display of conceptual profundity, described how the project attracted three kinds of scholar. The first (and largest) group were the "true believers," those who consider the norms and commitments of their discipline to be sacred and beyond reproach. A second group, the "heretics," remain deeply suspicious and skeptical of disciplinary norms, logics, and knowledge, often altogether fleeing the disciplines in which they were originally trained. Only the last group—"those that pray to their disciplinary gods with one eye open"—contributed to and gained the most from this transdisciplinary encounter. We were all, by that time, focused on bringing our tool set to the common problematic: colorblindness. But we did so with an agnosticism about what was workable.

The scholars who have contributed to this volume and who have otherwise supported this project understand and can utilize the conventions, methodological norms, and theoretical commitments that structure our respective disciplines. But we also deploy them to challenge, rather than simply enforce, ways of producing officially recognized knowledge. We seek to subvert, redeploy, and marshal the particular insights of disciplinary formations to address the structural dimensions of racial domination.

Across the year at Stanford, during weekly dialogues, we taught ourselves to become "transdisciplinary," a product of listening and dialogue to understand how academic disciplines contributed to the contemporary legitimacy of racial hierarchies. Guided by the convening strategies out of which the Critical Race Theory movement emerged, we were intentional about establishing a practice across disciplines that would allow us to better grasp the contours of colorblindness and to peel away its ability to mask illegitimate racial power. We catalogued particular institutional practices and beliefs that suppress intellectual projects that challenge such hierarchies and explored why exclusionary practices in knowledge-building institutions escaped the kinds of critiques and reforms deemed appropriate for other realms of society. In stepping out of comfort zones, we uncovered insights we hadn't known we were looking for. Our meanderings produced surprising insights derived from sustained dialogues; yet once identified, they were foundational to our work moving ahead.

Eventually, participants began to see race and colorblindness through a polysynthetic gaze forged from our multiple prisms. Colorblindness, after all, constitutes a core orientation and presumption in most academic disciplines, shaping research methodologies and channeling resources in a way that marginalizes and sometimes entirely precludes critical work on race-related topics. To counter it is to confront many of the most enduring shibboleths of the academic disciplines, particularly constructions of research objectivity, neutrality, and authority. In so doing, we acquired an inventory of exemplary interdisciplinary works, methods, and theories, along with the tropes intended to disguise race, such as merit, market, and choice. We learned to recognize affinities between the role of precedent in law and history; the stance of neutrality in science and musicology; and the tendencies toward disaggregation in epidemiology, education, and sociology. We sought to identify critical intersections wherein studying race from more than one disciplinary perspective might illuminate previously taken for granted aspects of a problem. For example, in the law the idea of the "intent" to discriminate has become the primary touchstone of a constitutional claim for racial discrimination, attenuating more nuanced possibilities of understanding racial power. These developments reflect and parallel trends in social psychology in which, in the 1950s and '60s, racism was often conceptualized as an intentional phenomenon and associated with particular personality types. Similarly, in sociology, institutional and structural accounts of racism and political economy are often displaced by a race relations paradigm that trivializes attention to the material distribution of resources and power across disparate sectors of society. Philosophy, history, literary studies, and other fields in the humanities have often foreclosed an understanding of the ways in which race, as an optic of power and a mode of social formation, has served as a structuring force within these disciplines.

The exchanges and conversations helped us to open up the radical contestations that emerge within particular disciplines that sometimes shape and inform practices and critiques in other fields. For instance, legal scholars have been able to be better prepared to assess the colorblind scholarship of social science when it is used in legal cases to indemnify racist laws. At the same time, scholars in the social sciences can be more conversant in the ways in which a colorblind constitutionalism travels outside the law. Legal thinkers and social scientists can learn about the nature of textualization, narrative, and argument from humanists, while scholars of expressive culture in the humanities can learn from social scientists and legal scholars about the ways in which cultural texts emerge from and speak to social and historical contexts.

We also developed a heightened awareness of the migration of concepts across academic disciplines into the realms of journalism, philanthropy, public policy, and popular culture. These questions matter not just to the academy but also to the broader arena of public policy in which colorblindness functions as a laissez-faire intervention against the redistribution of resources and reform efforts.

Our initial group met weekly for eight months, culminating in a weeklong seminar at Stanford in which we doubled our number by recruiting colleagues who were similarly "one eye open." Together we represented scholars from diverse disciplines, including psychology, sociology, education, economics, philosophy, law, political science, comparative literature, English, history, and musicology. The success of this first weeklong seminar propelled the project forward in a number of directions. We have since convened multiple Countering Colorblindness seminars and meetings, and have collectively offered several undergraduate and graduate courses. Many of the essays in this volume were first presented at a weeklong seminar in 2015 at the University of Oregon organized by Daniel Martinez HoSang.

Countering Colorblindness is predicated on the fact that knowledge production in the academy is intimately linked to policy development in civil society. Academics, teachers, and researchers possess substantial resources that can be better mobilized to advance socially just policies and practices. Moreover, within each discipline there have been efforts for antiracist thought and practice that have faced resistance and suppression. A nuanced understanding of disciplinary norms, methodologies, and registers is essential if we are not only to identify what happened to suppress those currents but also to comprehend the ways that considerations of race have been excluded at the broadest levels of epistemic investigations within the traditional disciplines.

Having turned our critical lens onto the academy itself to understand how colorblind paradigms shape the production of knowledge, the faculty seminars, workshops, and research that have unfolded within the first decade of the Countering Colorblindness project have culminated in this volume. The implications of these pieces, however, constitute the case for disciplinary practices that go beyond the superficial appeal of diversity.

The historical conditions of conquest, slavery, Indigenous dispossession, apartheid, and attempted genocide from which every traditional academic discipline emerged require a thorough vetting of these legacies. For these established disciplines to be revitalized, we must reckon with these histories. One cannot simply diversify the existing disciplines without such a reckoning. And while we believe the disciplines possess modes of analysis and methods of inquiry that can allow us to understand and mobilize against racial subordination and hierarchy, we know that the university is once again becoming a central site of social and political struggle. Conservative forces have renewed their attacks on the academy in ways that undermine critical work and widen the gap between conventional race management and the deeper interrogation that Countering Colorblindness represents. A path forward, we hope, will come by garnering the strength to fight back with tools to enhance our own capacity, and through projects that keep the university from being a silent partner in—and a promoter of—social injustice rather than an institution that interrogates the most challenging questions about racial equity.

Almost all of the essays in this volume were authored or coauthored by participants in the Countering Colorblindness project. The inaugural seminar at Stanford in 2009 was convened by CASBS fellow Kimberlé Williams Crenshaw and sponsored by the African American Policy Forum. CASBS director Claude Steele and CSRE director Dorothy Steele provided support for cofacilitators George Lipsitz and Luke Charles Harris. Glenn Adams and Alfredo Artiles rounded out the CASBS planning team. Subsequent convenings were hosted in 2013 at the UCLA School of Law in partnership with Devon Carbado, Cheryl Harris, and the Critical Race Studies program, and in 2015 at the University of Oregon, organized by Daniel Martinez HoSang and the Department of Ethnic Studies with funding provided by the College of Arts and Sciences, the Office of Academic Affairs, and the Wayne Morse Center for Law and Politics, led by Margaret Hallock.

In addition to the aforementioned coordinators, scholars who contributed to these seminars include Carol Anderson, Felice Blake, Eduardo Bonilla-Silva, Bryan Brayboy, Jordan Camp, Justine Cassell, Jean-Claude Croizet, William Darity, Jennifer Eberhardt, Lynn Fujiwara, Alison Gash, Leah Gordon, Lani Guinier, Kris Gutiérrez, Michael Hames-García, Craig Haney, Paula Ioanide, Loren Kajikawa, Claire Jean Kim, Brian Klopotek, Joseph Lowndes, Sharon Luk, Zakiya Luna, Hazel Markus, Ernesto Martínez, Marzia Milazzo, Charles Mills, Natalia Molina, Chandan Reddy, Milton Reynolds, Dwanna Robertson, Nikhil Pal Singh, Sandra Smith, Lani Teves, Barbara Tomlinson, Kimberly West-Faulcon, Priscilla Yamin, and Tukufu Zuberi.

Following the 2015 seminar, Daniel Martinez HoSang coordinated the effort with coeditors and contributors to bring this volume to fruition. Many more people whose work does not appear in this volume contributed to its formation. Their ideas and scholarship shaped the contours and content of this volume in myriad ways. Various staff affiliated with CASBS, the University of Oregon, the UCLA School of Law, CSRE, and AAPF provided important assistance in the planning and hosting of these seminars. The efforts of AAPF's Camila Morse were vital in this respect for the

2009 CASBS seminar. Ever Osorio Ruiz at Yale and Anna Titus at the University of Oregon provided critical editorial assistance toward the end of the project.

Finally, we thank Niels Hooper, Bradley Depew, and the wonderful production team at the University of California Press for their diligent work in bringing this volume to fruition, along with four anonymous reviewers whose comments strengthened many of the individual essays and the volume as a whole.

Kimberlé Williams Crenshaw
Luke Charles Harris
Daniel Martinez HoSang
George Lipsitz

NOTE

1. Luke Charles Harris, "Beyond the Best Black: The Making of a Critical Race Theorist at Yale Law School," *Connecticut Law Review* 43, no. 5 (July 2011), http://uconn.lawreviewnetwork.com/files/2011/12/Harris.pdf.

ONE

Introduction

Kimberlé Williams Crenshaw, Luke Charles Harris,
Daniel Martinez HoSang, and George Lipsitz

The essays in this volume reflect and engage the profoundly contradictory role of the university in constructing, naturalizing, and reproducing racial stratification and domination. Stretching from the racially specific projects of the past to the colorblind conventions of academic performance today, leading scholars in the social sciences, law, and humanities reveal in this book how disciplinary frameworks, research methodologies, and pedagogical strategies have both facilitated and obscured the social reproduction of racial hierarchy. The indictment of the knowledge-producing industry contained in these pages uncovers the chapters of racial history that remain undisturbed behind the walls of disciplinary convention and colorblind ideology. At the same time, the conditions of possibility out of which these essays were produced situate the university as a site in which antiracist projects can be seeded and developed. The disciplines not only produce racial power and inhibit racial knowledge, they also offer discursive tools and analytic moves that, properly contextualized, enable and enhance the telling of race and the reimagination of racial justice. In grappling with this duality, this collection embodies the twin objectives of the Countering Colorblindness project: to unpack and disrupt the racial foundations of the disciplines, and to aggregate and repurpose disciplinary insights into an alternative understanding of the social world.

This volume amplifies the methods and challenges that are foundational to critical race projects that interrogate the epistemic parameters of racial power in order to enable emancipatory possibilities both within the academy and in the social world beyond. Countering Colorblindness transcends the institutional and discursive boundaries that contain racial knowledge in multiple ways. The project is first and foremost transdisciplinary. The story it tells about the foundations of racial hierarchy and its contemporary disavowals across the university—in particular the traveling and uptake of particular orientations toward race between disciplines—can only become fully legible through the aggregated sum of its disciplinary parts. One cannot, for example, understand the narrowed ways in which racism has come to be imagined within law as the bigotry of specific individuals without engaging similar containments within sociology, social psychology, and the like.

Countering Colorblindness, however, transcends not only boundaries within the university, but boundaries between the university and civil society more broadly. The contemporary social conditions shaped by histories of white supremacy—education, health, criminal justice, employment, housing—are linked to the construction and disavowal of race within the academic disciplines themselves. Most institutions are now formally organized around the untested assumption that colorblindness is the exclusive measure of a fair and just organizational practice, an assumption that is predicated on and enabled by the privileging of colorblind solutions to color-bound problems within scholarly disciplines. Questions of racial discrimination, inequity, and injustice are typically framed as problematic only to the extent that the troubling conditions can be attributed to contraventions against the colorblind ideal. This resort to colorblindness is not solely an institutional-level response. As Eduardo Bonilla-Silva's work has long documented, individuals now defend themselves against the slightest intimation that their preferences or decisions might be racially inflected with the all-purpose disclaimer that they neither see race nor take it into account.[1]

As a political project, colorblindness derives from a seeming naturalness and inevitability. It resonates with time-honored practices and ideals in Western thought and social relations. A long history of artistic expression and humanities scholarship has grounded aspirations for social justice in the elision of difference. The market subject of classical capitalist theory, the citizen subject of liberalism—and even the universal worker of Marxism and the universal woman of feminism—all rest upon an ideal of interchangeability wherein differences are said not to matter. These traditions teach that similarity should trump difference; that beneath the surface the appearance of "otherness" masks a common human condition.

Although many humane and egalitarian projects in history have been based on humanist concepts of liberal interchangeability, contemporary scholars have raised questions about the dangers of ignoring fundamental differences, particularly distinctions linked to social position, vulnerability, and power. While conceding that all of our fates are linked and acknowledging the sordid histories of parochial particularism, these scholars contend that some important differences do not disappear simply by affirming sameness. Furthermore, the identities celebrated as universal by the standards of humanism and liberalism are almost always actually dominant particulars masquerading as universals. Indeed, the abstract assertions of human interchangeability in law, economics, and politics tend to serve as mechanisms for occluding the seemingly endless differentiations, inequalities, and injustices of existing social relations.

In postulating a common human experience, many great traditions in art, law, and politics celebrate the symbolic transcendence of difference without offering or even suggesting the need for access to equitable opportunities or conditions. In these settings, differences become contaminated with a menacing otherness, an otherness that threatens the promise of an ideal egalitarian future. People *with* problems thus become identified *as* problems; and the members of groups who object to social inequality then become castigated for calling attention to differences that matter in their lives.

These perspectives make colorblindness seem a laudable goal. They make it appear as though the solution to vexing problems of difference is to simply stop acknowledging such differences. In this way, they cover over embodied inequalities with a disembodied universalism. Perhaps most importantly, they locate questions of social justice in a stark choice between egalitarian universalism on the one hand and a putatively parochial and prejudiced particularism on the other.

Against this deep philosophical background, today's colorblindness easily trumps race-conscious interventions as more appealing and ultimately morally just. As a consequence, efforts to sustain investment in race-conscious research and policy face an uphill battle. A telling example of the malaise that exists in social justice discourse can be found in the ineffective efforts of social justice advocates to push back against colorblindness with concepts and strategies that are at best anachronistic. Moreover, much of the policy that is the object of policy debates bows to the colorblind imperative in the final analysis. As the legal scholar Mark Golub explains, "Anti-racist criticism too often has been defined by the object of its critique, and so offers inadequate tools for resisting it. Even when it is rejected, that is, color-blindness discourse sets the terms of debate, defines normative goals, and limits the scope of legitimacy for alternative formulations of racial justice."[2] In his exemplary research, however, Golub deploys careful, critical, and detailed analyses of landmark Supreme Court cases to reveal how the ideal of colorblindness as the default position for social justice actually functions as a color-conscious tool crafted to protect white preferences and privileges.

As colorblindness becomes increasingly entrenched as the common denominator in efforts to deny and transcend racial power, the parameters of racial discourse between the university and the general public reveal an interdependent relationship that is far closer than scholars often acknowledge. Colorblindness operates as the default intellectual and ethical position for racial justice in many corners of the academy and in public policy, imposing profound limitations on scholars, students, and the wider public. The compromised capacity of disciplines to respond effectively to the wide set of political, economic, and social problems that mark public life today demand new strategies that situate a critical understanding of race and racism at the center of knowledge production and public engagement.

Despite colorblindness's appearance as a commonsense value and practice, it is an idea sustained more by the repetition of its use and by the power of those who invoke it than by a firm basis in reality, research, theory, or for that matter, the Constitution. Indeed, scholars from a variety of disciplines have produced powerful studies that contest its viability as a definitive determinant of social justice. This research disproves some of the central claims made for colorblindness, and casts considerable doubt about how a future wrapped around this ideal will unfold.

Yet even apart from this research, colorblindness at the most basic level mobilizes a metaphor of visual impairment to embrace a simplistic and misleading affirmation of racial egalitarianism. Its emphasis on color imagines racism to be an individualistic aversion to another person's pigment rather than a systemic skewing of opportunities, resources, and life chances along racial lines. The blindness part of the metaphor presumes that visually impaired people are incapable of racial recognition and that recognition itself is the problem that racism presents. Yet as the research of Osagie K. Obasogie establishes, visually impaired people hold the same understandings of race that sighted people possess. They are neither more nor less likely to engage in racist judgments.[3] Moreover, visually impaired people who are white enjoy the unfair gains, unjust enrichments, and unearned status of whiteness, while those who are people of color experience the artificial, arbitrary, and irrational impediments caused by racism and social prejudices against disability. Not only must the logic and salience of colorblindness as a metaphor be rejected, but so must the presumptions about normativity and disability that underwrite it.

Given the slender reed upon which the weighty denial of racial power rests, one might think that a powerful antidote to the widespread use of colorblindness might arise fully activated from the knowledge-producing industry. But despite the depth of scholarly understanding about the inadequacies of colorblindness as a theory, policy, cognitive possibility, or constitutional principle, this canon has gained little traction in efforts to draw attention to the racist realities that the colorblind perspective works to obscure. Consequently, the wealth of information produced in the academy pertaining to race—historical, economic, sociological, psychological, literary, and legal—has yet to converge into a coherent commonsense understanding of the world that we live in. Indeed, far from countering colorblindness, the prevailing practices around which privileged knowledge is produced and authorized operate to enhance the stabilizing dimensions of colorblind discourse. Thus, countering colorblindness requires an interrogation into the disciplinary, cultural, and historical dynamics that sustain a disaggregated, partial, and parochial knowledge base about one of the most vexing societal problems of our time.

The failure of the disciplines to produce a collective accounting of the realities of race in contemporary society occludes the more fundamental indictment upon which countering colorblindness rests. Behind the colorblind façade of the existing disciplines is the historical role that knowledge production has played in creating and fortifying racial projects ranging from slavery and segregation to imperialism and genocide. Historically situated against this backdrop, colorblindness thus becomes a series of moves and investments that conceal the fingerprints of the university in constructing the very conditions that colorblind frameworks refuse to name.

SEEING AND UNSEEING RACE IN THE ACADEMY

Every established discipline in the academy has an origin that entails engagement and complicity with white supremacy. In the age of conquest, colonization, Indigenous dispossession, and empire, Europeans' vexed confrontations with peoples from Africa, Asia, and Latin America whom they perceived to be "other" gave rise to anthropology's interest in "primitive" civilizations and geography's impetus to map the world.[4] Scholars of philosophy, history, sociology, political science, and economics turned to biology in explaining how and why European empires came to dominate the world, attributing that dominance to evolution and "the survival of the fittest" instead of systematically investigating the brutality of conquest and the cruelties of expropriation and exploitation.[5] Invocations of biological difference imbued racism with a seemingly scientific inevitability, positioning whites as the winners in a fair struggle while displacing people of color from the realm of history and positioning them in the domain of nature.[6] This displacement provided the organizing logic for the seemingly endless depictions of monstrous uncivilized primitives in Euro-American literature, painting, theater, and film.[7]

The social sciences took form as nomothetic enterprises committed to discovering general scientific laws governing social structure and organization. This search for general laws through discrete and particular methods of study tended to disaggregate the unified totality of social relations into detached and disconnected practices. The binary opposition between race and class, for example, presumes a racial system that is not classed and a class system that is not raced. Moreover, this search for "universal" principles in sociology, political science, history, and economics was conducted almost exclusively in just five nations—Germany, France, Italy, Great Britain, and the United States—and the practices dominant in those places were judged to be applicable to all of humanity.[8] The search for a putatively authentic human culture in populations presumed to be previously untouched by European contact led ethnographers to position the Indigenous and colonized people they studied in Africa, Asia, and the Americas as "people without history" rather than coinhabitants of the modern world.[9] This denial positioned Europe as the center of modern progress while viewing inhabitants of the global south as premodern and therefore rationally and ontologically deficient.[10] Political science and sociology came into being as managerial sciences promising to promote the efficient and orderly administration of nations and empires while providing mechanisms for controlling the social discontent and discord that they attributed to people characterized as different, deviant, delinquent, defective, or dependent.[11]

For example, Robert Vitalis demonstrates that the formation of International Relations as a scholarly field in the early twentieth century was intimately tied to U.S. expansion and imperialism.[12] Columbia's John Burgess, considered one of the founders of the field, stated plainly that "American Indians, Asiatics and Africans cannot properly form any active, directive part of the political population which shall be able to produce modern political institutions." After the U.S. military helped to overthrow the Hawaiian monarchy in 1894, the new provisional government appealed to

Burgess seeking his counsel in establishing a new "republican government." Burgess replied: "I understand your problem to be the construction of a constitution which will place the government in the hands of the Teutons, and preserve it there, at least for the present." Burgess then offered a series of recommendations related to representation and voting requirements in order to sustain white rule in Hawaii.[13] Perhaps not surprisingly, the discipline's first scholarly journal was titled the *Journal of Race Development*. Published continuously since 1910, it was renamed *Foreign Affairs* in 1922, the title it carries today.[14] Academics like Burgess and many of his contemporaries, including historian Lothrop Stoddard and naturalist Madison Grant, played central roles in elaborating the white supremacist commitments of U.S. immigration and foreign policy across the twentieth century.[15]

Perceptions of innate human difference led scholars in the emerging physical and natural sciences in the eighteenth and nineteenth centuries to labor tirelessly to generate scientific theories of racial difference and hierarchy. Physical and cultural anthropologists continued to pursue and publish such studies well into the 1960s.[16] Many of the key tools of the social sciences were developed in the early twentieth century by sociologists, psychologists, and other social scientists as methods of statistical evaluation that were designed to measure innate and hereditary group-based differences in cognitive abilities.[17] Despite centuries of devastating critiques of the core premises and presumptions of this research, some contemporary social statisticians remain trapped in the underlying logic of racial reason by treating race as a biological category rather than a social construct and by attributing life outcomes to the racial identities of individuals rather than to the racist practices of systems and structures.[18] While some antiracist scholars make excellent use of statistical methods, the seeming neutrality of statistical research design often masks unacknowledged ideological predispositions.[19] As Leah Gordon, a contributor to this volume, demonstrates in her insightful book *From Power to Prejudice,* a commitment to methodological individualism has often functioned to render racism a private matter rather than a public concern. She shows how seemingly neutral decisions about research design skewed scholarship on race to privilege the idea of prejudice over power. Gordon argues that because the validity of statistical findings depends on submitting significant numbers (n) to analysis, researchers came to privilege surveys of the attitudes of individuals which contained a large "n" (as many numbers as there were individuals) over the study of groups where each group could consist of only one "n." This provided a methodological impetus to focus on individual prejudice rather than collective power, not because prejudice was more important, but merely because it was easier to measure.[20]

The emergence of economics as a discipline separate from its previous locus inside moral philosophy suppressed the study of socially constructed institutions. Economic activity would be assessed as simply the sum total of autonomous actions by universally interchangeable rational and self-interested acquisitive subjects.[21] Moreover, as Nancy MacLean has shown, particular subfields of economics, such as the "public choice" paradigm developed at the University of Virginia in the 1950s and 1960s, linked attacks on a broad range of public institutions (especially public education) with the preservation of American apartheid. Here, the core logic of an entire academic subfield was implicitly constituted around assumptions of white supremacy, even as it disavowed any racial intent and animus.[22]

The humanistic disciplines coalesced around idiographic inquiries focused on the particularities of difference. Yet by presuming that the dominant particulars of Europe represented the apex of human achievement and aspiration through what Sylvia Wynter terms the project of man, the humanities falsely aggregated all of humanity into a disembodied universalism said to be the only alternative to parochial particularisms. This legacy has structured the study of difference largely on axes of margins and centers rather than axes of domination and oppression, leaving the humanities ill-suited in respect to race to discern which differences make a difference and why.[23]

Within the humanities, since the Renaissance, scholars of religion, ethics, philosophy, history, literature, and the arts have shaped their inquiries around what Walter Mignolo describes as the *"humanitas"* model of the bourgeois Western subject—the self-possessed individual uniquely capable of logic, rationality, and contemplation.[24] A clear racial bias governed the ways in which the disciplines studied the civilizations of antiquity. Classics departments venerated the literature, history, and philosophy of ancient Greece and Rome as part of a continuous history that culminated in modern Europe. Great civilizations in China, India, and Egypt, however, were studied separately in disciplines like Oriental Studies. They were presumed to have no influence on the modern world.[25] The Maya-Aztec, Tawantin-suyo, and Nok, Nri, and Oyo Benin societies were not studied as civilizations, but rather as parts of a premodern primitivism that belonged more to nature than to history. Anthropologists might have been expected to engage in nomothetic generalizations, but their study of allegedly primitive peoples led them to emphasize particularity and difference through idiographic epistemologies.

Humanitas lives in opposition to the *"anthropos,"* embodied in the range of colonized peoples alleged to stand outside of modern history and whose labor, land, and bodies become resources for the advancement of civilization itself. Like the prodigious theorists of scientific racism, humanists also played a central role in justifying the modern epoch of colonization, slavery, and genocide. Europe's most prominent theorist of human freedom, John Locke, not only justified chattel slavery, but invested in the slave trade himself and helped South Carolina's slave owners write the constitution that secured their control over the humans they held in bondage. Immanuel Kant constructed philosophical arguments about morality from the vantage point of a person who believed that "humanity is at its perfection in the race of the whites." He argued that only white Europeans were capable of mastering the arts and sciences, and advised that administering beatings to Black servants required a split cane rather than a whip because of the thick skin of the Negro. Kant dismissed a statement made by an African on the grounds that "the fellow was quite black from head to foot, a clear proof that what he said was stupid."[26] Similarly, G. W. F. Hegel constructed a theory of change over time in which the "true theatre of history" existed only in the temperate zone in which he lived, leaving Africa as "no historical part of the world" because that continent allegedly lacked any "movement or development."[27]

The canonization of national literatures and efforts at purification of national languages in Europe functioned as instruments of class rule at home and of imperial domination abroad. In his *Essay Concerning Human Understanding,* John Locke took time out from savoring the profits he made from the slave trade to advance the idea of purified national languages as the key to modernity. Locke considered "impure" speech as the domain of the peoples of Asia and the Americas, laborers, the poor, and women. Unregulated discourse led to factionalism, conflict, and disorder, in his view. He argued that language had to be separated from society, purified of ties to social positions and interests. Just as he had done for the subject of the contract in law, Locke emphasized the abstraction, decontextualization, and generalization of language, imagining that each individual needed to be trained to speak from within an autonomous self. This concept of language represented knowledge as monologic, rational, individual, and universal and replicated in expressive culture a preference for the self-regulating autonomous individual of contract law and economic theory.[28] Yet the autonomous individual posited by Locke always remained haunted by the enslaved "other" whose bondage made possible the profits garnered by contracting free subjects. The novel became a key mechanism for universalizing this individual subject, not by depicting unfettered agency but instead by constituting the subject as besieged and frightened, always on the verge of engulfment by the social aggregate, an aggregate often made up of dark faces from the global south and their surrogates in the metropolis, rendered through depictions of nightmares, hallucinations, and incidents of horror.[29]

In her innovative, insightful, and enormously generative research on the discursive construction of colorblindness in essays and literary works created in Panama, South Africa, Brazil, and the United States, Marzia Milazzo demonstrates how even intellectuals from the colonized global south came to embrace the epistemology of disavowal in regard to race. Milazzo reveals how Olmedo Alfaro, for example, deployed racist attacks against West Indians in Panama as a means of advancing nationalist ideals about that nation as a paragon of Iberian-American civilization while disavowing any racist intent. Alfaro celebrated Panama as a multiracial democracy threatened by the presence of West Indian immigrants through a series of subterfuges central to the toolkit of colorblind racism. He used the Spanish language and Latin civilization as proxies for Panamanian whiteness while asserting that because West Indian Blacks were indistinguishable (to him) from American Blacks they were carriers of the U.S. imperial project suppressing Panamanian nationalism. Milazzo notes that this kind of white nationalism, now ascendant in Europe, the United States, and beyond, requires demonization of racial others, even while it purports to be about national culture, religion, language, citizenship, and virtually anything but race.[30]

In short, during their emergence and initial development, most academic disciplines had no difficulty "seeing" race. The logic of racial hierarchy and colonialism structured the very foundations of their research and teaching paradigms. Their development was coextensive with the emergence of imperialism, slavery, and modern racism. These institutional relationships have surfaced explicitly in the recent wave of campus protests at universities—including Yale, Princeton, Brown, and others—over the participation by those institutions in various parts of the slave economy and their continued veneration of the champions of slavery and genocide in the naming of buildings.

Contemporary humanists and social scientists generally believe that the disciplines have come a long way since their origins in the era when Europe was solidifying its colonial empires. Most humanists would not endorse the claims about Africa and Africans that Hegel and Kant declared. Very few social scientists openly embrace eugenics, even as academic efforts to claim a biological or genetic foundation for race in some quarters remains stubbornly persistent.[31] Yet changes in the disciplines with respect to race have been more cosmetic than substantive. The history of the disciplines leaves them suffused with unacknowledged and uninterrogated premises and practices that preserve the patterns of the past and impede progress in the present and future.

Disciplinary knowledge, then, is more than the sum of separate inquiries in discrete areas of knowledge. It is part of a historically specific body of knowledge, an episteme, that contains premises, presumptions, and practices that work together to hide the workings of racialized power.

RESISTANCE AND DISAVOWAL

Beginning in the early twentieth century, the academy's complicity with racial domination faced rising opposition, evident in the interventions of scholars such as W. E. B. Du Bois, Anna Julia Cooper, Ida B. Wells, Zora Neale Hurston, and Carter G. Woodson. Du Bois's magisterial *Black Reconstruction in America,* for example, took specific aim at historiographical narratives depicting Reconstruction and the postbellum period as a disastrous experiment in multiracial democracy. Du Bois understood that the imperative to upend and remake such paradigms of scholarship was central to the broader task of antiracist freedom movements.[32]

As these challenges became linked to broadening social movements in the mid-twentieth century, higher education itself became a central locus in the struggle for racial justice. The academy could no longer claim to be a neutral observer of the problem of the color line. As Roderick Ferguson explains, the Third World students that marched on the halls of San Francisco State, Cornell, UCLA, and hundreds of other campuses during the 1960s and 1970s carried a vision of education and knowledge production based on the "idea that everything could be rewritten, knowledge could be reorganized, and institutions could be changed for the good of minoritized communities."[33] These conflicts fueled critical institutional transformations, evident in the establishment of Black Studies, ethnic studies, and women's and gender studies programs and the arrival of a new generation of students from groups that had long been excluded from the academy. Children of the *anthropos* found places in the halls of *humanitas.*[34]

While this period of insurgency discredited some of the more odious intellectual defenses of white supremacy, the disciplines and their keepers remained unwilling to interrogate many of the foundational commitments of their fields. Mainstream disciplines largely abandoned the explicit use of racist language, referents, and claims in favor of a discourse of racial color-blindness. Paralleling what Neil Gotanda calls the "racial non-recognition" that was unfolding within the broader legal and political culture, this modality of racial performance in academia became the implicit norm and standard of antiracism.

In the main, disciplines replaced their investments in flagrantly racist modes of inquiry and knowledge production with a refusal to apprehend and engage racialized histories, structures, identities, and contexts. An alternative that stopped short of outright denial of race was to assign such projects to marginalized subfields—for example, "Racial and Ethnic Politics." Incorporating race as a bounded and peripheral topic that may be relevant only in some situations or for some people left the white supremacist origins of the disciplines undisturbed. The emergence of a subfield paradigm—dominant across the social sciences and humanities—depoliticizes the meaning and implications of racialized difference through putative strategies of inclusion. In this way, it reproduces the colorblind framework by treating minoritized scholarship as an object of disciplinary study (e.g., the study of Black political participation) rather than as a foundational framework for the disciplines as a whole. Race and racism are rendered as marginal to the fundamental intellectual concerns of research and pedagogy, reproducing the notion of the white subject as the normative standard or "reasonable person" in academic, legal, and public policy discourse. As the groundbreaking Trinidadian theorist C. L. R. James explained in an interview in 1970 to *The Black Scholar*—one of the first academic journals explicitly oriented toward antiracist scholarship—emerging fields such as Black Studies had a far-reaching intellectual imperative: "Black Studies require[s] the complete reorganization of the intellectual life and the historical outlook of the United States, and world civilization as a whole." Yet while James believed that the institutional autonomy of formations like Black Studies was important, he did not imagine it as a disciplinary subfield. Instead he argued that for scholars it was "a chance to penetrate more into the fundamentals of Western civilization, which cannot be understood unless Black studies is involved."[35]

Thus, during a period of growing intellectual and activist insurgency, disciplines that for more than a century had explicitly recognized race and utilized it to justify the legitimacy of racial hierarchy decided to resist the implications of their racial investments in terms of a sensory limitation: colorblindness. By thoroughly disclaiming the racial contours of the disciplinary project in response to the insurgency, they sought to describe their preferred mode of inquiry in a way that valorized their capacity to ignore race and racism. Yet colorblindness is inadequate to the task at hand, not only to repudiate the racial projects around which the disciplines were built, but also to make plain the contemporary practices that continue to discipline knowledge about racial power and contain resistance to it. The challenge is not simply to disrupt the discourse of colorblindness. It is also to comprehend and critique how contemporary disciplinary practices enable racial structures and inhibit the means to dismantle them.

Colorblindness is a wide-ranging technology of power, fundamental to all disciplinary formations, that functions within the prevailing university structure to sustain a disaggregated knowledge base about one of the most troubling societal problems of our time. Disciplinary knowledge exudes epistemic whiteness, thus refusing to assess and transform relationships of domination and inequality across the social field. One dimension of contemporary practice can be seen in the way that the separation of knowledge inquiries into discrete disciplines produces both unjust aggregation and destructive disaggregation. When we need to account for the particularities of individual and collective experience, prevailing patterns of research design falsely aggregate antagonistic populations into seemingly harmonious universal totalities. At the same time, a facile aggregation appears in the embrace by psychologists and economists of the experimental techniques that rule research in biology, physiology, physics, and math. This dynamic promotes proclamations of putatively universal principles about psychic and economic life that ignore the crucial specificities of time and place. Similarly, the market subject of capitalism, the individual interior subject of psychology, and the rights-bearing subject of law are all presumed to embody universal human traits, rather than being the products of a particular history in one part of the world.

When we need to see the interconnectedness and totality of human relationships, prevailing patterns of research design study them separately and often incommensurably. A destructive disaggregation emerges when historians focus on specialized monographs about discrete times and places that ignore larger patterns of social history. Scholarship premised on the specialized tasks of biology, psychology, and physiology that assess human life in isolation from the social forces that shape it results in laws that treat social institutions as unconnected atomized entities. In this setting, discriminatory acts by school boards, real estate agents, corporate polluters, employers, and urban planners can only be adjudicated separately, rather than interactively and dynamically, rendering their aggregated racial costs as curious societal disparities having no legal consequence. In both the social sciences and humanities, colorblindness relies on an interrelated process of abstraction and decontextualization, emphasizing the ontological priority and primacy of the private interiority of the individual (and individual feeling) detached from context. Methodologically, many disciplines conceptualize social relations as merely the sum of many different and easily identifiable actions, imagining universality as something that can only be structured on solidarities of sameness rather than dynamics of difference. [36]

The task of countering colorblindness is thus not merely to see race again, but to reenvision how disciplinary tools, conventions, and knowledge-producing practices that erase the social dynamics that produce race can be critically engaged and selectively repurposed toward emancipatory ends.

SEEING RACE AGAIN

A generation after the passage of landmark civil rights legislation, scholars from numerous fields documented the ways in which the reproduction of racial power and domination required particular forms of disavowal and denial. In the 1980s, legal scholars in the field of Critical Race Theory (CRT), such as Kimberlé Crenshaw, Mari Matsuda, Neil Gotanda, Charles Lawrence, Cheryl Harris, and Gary Peller, interrogated the doctrinal basis of "racial nonrecognition," which transforms race into a matter of skin color and then demands formal symmetry as the embodiment of equal treatment under the law. Having thus reduced the ways in which racism takes place to the use of racial classifications, a broad range of social, economic, and political asymmetries become sequestered from legal review, essentially constitutionalizing relationships of racial domination. CRT scholars charted the Supreme Court's deployment of this impoverished conception of "equal protection," which is now utilized by the Court to restrict the remedial uses of race while maintaining a very high bar against challenges to a wide array of practices that burden and disempower minoritized communities.

Thus, equal protection protects unequally, strictly scrutinizing race classifications that limit the constitutionality of race-conscious remedies, yet utilizing exceedingly narrow interpretations of what constitutes discriminatory effects against racialized minorities. As a result, untold numbers of discriminatory practices against historically aggrieved communities are allowed to continue unabated.

Critical race scholarship has also articulated the need to use racial position as an epistemological perspective from which to better apprehend the reality of all topics, not just "race-relevant" ones. Similar interventions have emerged across the numerous disciplines. In the 1990s, influential work by sociologists Eduardo Bonilla-Silva, Leslie Carr, Stephen Steinberg, Tukufu Zuberi, Ruth Frankenberg, and others revealed the ways that white subjects evaded their complicity with racism by invoking colorblind tropes. In the humanities, scholars including Toni Morrison, Gayatri Spivak, and Edward Said similarly recognized the foundational imperative to remake the conventions and frameworks of disciplinary knowledge production in order to unfetter the possibilities for more widespread political transformations.

The academic resistance to the conventional modes of racial disavowal stretched into the early decades of the twenty-first century as generative work has explored the deployment of colorblindness within criminal justice, genetics and medicine, education, political history, media studies, visual arts, literature, public policy, and many other fields. These and other critical interventions reveal that disciplinary knowledge is more than the sum of separate inquiries in discrete areas of knowledge. It is part of a historically constituted episteme that contains premises, presumptions, and practices that together hide the workings of racial power.

The chapters in this volume build upon an important body of scholarship on the emergence of racial colorblindness within and outside the academy. The demand that underscores this volume challenges scholars and the disciplines to see race again. The task it urges is to confront the underlying logic and assumptions of the colorblind paradigm that dominates so many disciplines today. It describes, analyzes, and interprets exemplary efforts by researchers and teachers to contest commitments to colorblindness within their respective fields. In the process, it identifies an array of methodologies, pedagogies, and theoretical approaches that use race as a central analytic and framework to reimagine and invigorate their disciplines, their research, their teaching, and their public engagement. As Kimberlé Crenshaw has observed, there is an opportunity now for "scholars across the disciplines not only to reveal how disciplinary conventions themselves constitute racial power, but also to provide an inventory of the critical tools developed over time to weaken and potentially dismantle them." Indeed, because the conventions of colorblindness enacted within the university have far-reaching effects, Crenshaw argues that an unprecedented opportunity exists "to present a counter-narrative to the premature societal settlement that marches under the banner of post-racialism."[37] The Countering Colorblindness project could not be a more timely answer to this call.

RECLAIMING THE UNIVERSITY

In an essay in 1971 describing the "vocation" of the Black scholar in a moment of political and social upheaval, the writer and political strategist Vincent Harding noted the ways in which the "American university" has become "so regularly filled with misleading calls to the mystic, universal fellowship of objective, unpigmented scholarship (or with more crassly formulated invitations to respectability and a certain safety, in exchange for the abandonment of our real question)." Like the many scholar activists working from the frameworks of feminists of color, Indigenous studies, and other critical fields, Harding argued that scholarship and pedagogy must always be responsive to the political, social, and economic conditions that constitute the university and its conditions of possibility. As with Harding, for us the answers to the "real question" must "emerge hard and thorny out of the ancient, ever-present struggles of our community towards freedom, equality, self-determination, liberation" in an effort to secure "the essential reality we seek."[38]

Following Harding, Roderick Ferguson has argued that critical interdisciplinary work attending to race must acknowledge and pursue opportunities afforded by not only the *formalization* of such programs (e.g., the departmentalization of programs such as Ethnic Studies, Chicano/a Studies, etc.) but also the *informalization* of critical strategies that aspire to "redraft and reclaim the university" around principles of social and epistemological redistribution. For Ferguson such strategies must activate and deploy the critical insights and energies of race-conscious modes of scholarship "without presuming that we need formal authorization and certification to do so."[39]

This volume and the broader Countering Colorblindness project aspire to the interventions framed by Ferguson. Challenging disciplinary adherence to colorblind strategies must take place in an array of formalized and institutionally recognized spaces: new courses, pedagogy, and syllabi; publication projects; and initiatives within disciplinary organizations and conferences.

But institutional recognition and incorporation is not the ultimate horizon of possibility. As Ferguson explains, the broader imperative is to produce "institutional spaces within and outside the academy that can disrupt the various economies that attempt to narrow the possibilities of minority existence."[40]

Thus, in the process of challenging and destabilizing various disciplinary iterations of the colorblind paradigm, we must also, in Ferguson's words, "remake and remobilize energies for the reorganization of knowledge and the transformation of institutions."[41] To counter colorblindness is to contribute to the urgent task of reorienting the contemporary university to engage a wider set of social crises, taking seriously the forms of hierarchy, violence, and dispossession that mark our world. This project accompanies a broader effort in which scholarship and teaching that explicitly engage issues of racial power, domination, and resistance form the groundwork for new possibilities and imaginaries that can make contemporary academic disciplines relevant rather than cynical, democratizing rather than constraining.

NOTES

1. E.g., Eduardo Bonilla-Silva, *Racism without Racists: Color-Blind Racism and Racial Inequality in Contemporary America,* 3rd ed. (New York: Rowman & Littlefield, 2009).

2. Mark Golub, *Is Racial Equality Unconstitutional?* (Oxford: Oxford University Press, 2018), 5.

3. Osagie K. Obasogie, *Blinded by Sight: Seeing Race through the Eyes of the Blind* (Stanford: Stanford University Press, 2014), esp. 3, 124, and 126.

4. Emmanuel Chukwudi Eze, "The Color of Reason: The Idea of 'Race' in Kant's Anthropology," in *Postcolonial African Philosophy,* ed. Emmanuel Chukwudi Eze (Oxford: Blackwell, 1997), 105, 107. In *Black Marxism: The Making of the Black Radical Tradition* (London: Zed Books, 1983), Cedric Robinson demonstrated that this stratification had already been racialized in Europe even before its colonial contacts with Asia, Africa, and Latin America.

5. Immanuel Wallerstein et al., *Open the Social Sciences: Report of the Gulbenkian Commission on the Restructuring of the Social Sciences* (Stanford: Stanford University Press, 1996), 29.

6. George Stocking, *Race, Culture, and Evolution: Essays on the History of Anthropology* (Chicago: University of Chicago Press, 1968).

7. Esther Lezra, *The Colonial Art of Demonizing Others: A Global Perspective* (New York: Routledge, 2014); Nathan Irvin Huggins, *Harlem Renaissance* (New York: Oxford University Press, 1971); Ella Shohat and Robert Stam, *Unthinking Eurocentrism: Multiculturalism and the Media* (London and New York: Routledge,

1994); Darcy Grimaldo Grigsby, *Extremities: Painting Empire in Post-Revolutionary France* (New Haven, CT: Yale University Press, 2002); Laura Wexler, *Tender Violence: Domestic Visions in an Age of U.S. Imperialism* (Chapel Hill: University of North Carolina Press, 2000); Nancy Armstrong, *Fiction in the Age of Photography: The Legacy of British Realism* (Cambridge, MA: Harvard University Press, 1999).

8. Wallerstein et al., *Open the Social Sciences*, 20.

9. Eric R. Wolff, *Europe and the People without History* (Berkeley: University of California Press, 2010).

10. Wallerstein et al., *Open the Social Sciences*, 22.

11. Khalil Gibran Muhammad, *The Condemnation of Blackness: Race, Crime, and the Making of Modern Urban America* (Cambridge, MA: Harvard University Press, 2010), 46; Wallerstein et al., *Open the Social Sciences*, 19, 20.

12. Robert Vitalis, *White World Order, Black Power Politics: The Birth of American International Relations* (Ithaca, NY: Cornell University Press, 2015).

13. Cited ibid., 36.

14. Ibid., 18–20.

15. Lothrop Stoddard, *The Rising Tide of Color: The Threat against White World-Supremacy* (New York: Scribner, 1920); and Madison Grant, *The Passing of the Great Race*, 4th ed. (New York: Scribner, 1936).

16. Audrey Smedley, *Race in North America: Origin and Evolution of a Worldview* (Boulder, CO: Westview Press, 1993), 269–91.

17. Tukufu Zuberi and Eduardo Bonilla-Silva, "Toward a Definition of White Logic and White Methods," in *White Logic, White Methods: Racism and Methodology,* ed. Tukufu Zuberi and Eduardo Bonilla-Silva (Lanham, MD: Rowman & Littlefield, 2008), 5–12.

18. Politically influential scholarship by James Q. Wilson, Charles Murray, and the late Samuel P. Huntington retains many of the racist premises and presumptions of eugenics research. Yet even scholars who understand the illegitimacy of treating race as a biological concept still deploy it as causal explanation. See Tukufu Zuberi, "Deracializing Social Statistics: Problems in the Quantification of Race," in Zuberi and Bonilla-Silva (eds.), *White Logic, White Methods,* 127–34.

19. William P. Darity and Patrick L. Mason, "Evidence on Discrimination in Employment: Codes of Color, Codes of Gender," in *African American Urban Experience: Perspectives from the Colonial Period to the Present,* ed. Joe Trotter, Earl Lewis, and Tera Hunter (New York: Palgrave Macmillan, 2004), 156–86; Shelley Lundberg and Richard Startz, "Private Discrimination and Social Intervention in Competitive Labor Markets," *American Economic Review* 73, no. 3 (June 1983): 340–47; Gary A. Dymski, "Racial Exclusion and the Political Economy of the Subprime Crisis," *Historical Materialism* 17, no. 2 (2009): 149–79.

20. Leah Gordon, *From Power to Prejudice: The Rise of Racial Individualism in Midcentury America* (Chicago: University of Chicago Press, 2015), 53–77.

21. Wallerstein et al., *Open the Social Sciences,* 17.

22. Nancy MacLean, *Democracy in Chains: The Deep History of the Radical Right's Stealth Plan for America* (New York: Penguin Random House, 2017).

23. Sylvia Wynter, "Unsettling the Coloniality of Being/Power/Truth/ Freedom: Towards the Human, after Man, Its Overrepresentation—an Argument," *CR: The New Centennial Review* 3, no. 3 (2003): 257–37.

24. Walter Mignolo, *The Darker Side of Western Modernity: Global Futures, Decolonial Options* (Durham, NC: Duke University Press, 2011), 81–86.

25. Wallerstein et al., *Open the Social Sciences,* 23.

26. Immanuel Kant, "Of the Different Races of Man," in *Race and the Enlightenment: A Reader,* ed. Emmanuel Chukwudi Eze (Cambridge, MA: Wiley-Blackwell, 1997), 138–40; Eze, "The Color of Reason," 116, 117, 119.

27. G. W. F. Hegel, *Philosophy of History* (Mineola, NY: Dover, 1956), 90.

28. Richard Bauman and Charles Briggs, *Voices of Modernity: Language Ideologies and the Politics of Inequality* (Cambridge: Cambridge University Press, 2003), 29, 31, 35, 38.

29. Nancy Armstrong, *How Novels Think: The Limits of Individualism from 1719–1900* (New York: Columbia University Press, 2005), 11.

30. Marzia Milazzo, "White Supremacy, White Knowledge, and Anti–West Indian Discourse in Panama: Olmedo Alfaro's *El peligro antillano en la América Central,"* *Global South* 6, no. 2 (2012): 65–86.

31. For an example of a recent argument for race as a biologically grounded concept, see Jiannbin Lee Shiao, Thomas Bode, Amber Beyer, and Daniel Selvig, "The Genomic Challenge to the Social Construction of Race," *Sociological Theory* 30, no. 2 (2012): 67–88. For a critique of this work, see Daniel HoSang, "On Racial Speculation and Racial Science: A Reply to Shiao et al.," *Sociological Theory* 32, no. 3 (2014): 228–43.

32. W. E. B. Du Bois, *Black Reconstruction in America: An Essay toward a History of the Part Which Black Folk Played in an Attempt to Reconstruct Democracy in America, 1860–1880* (New York: Harcourt, Brace, 1935).

33. Roderick A. Ferguson, "University," *Critical Ethnic Studies* 1, no. 1 (2015): 49.

34. See, e.g., Asafa Jalata, "Revisiting the Black Struggle: Lessons for the 21st Century," *Journal of Black Studies* 33, no. 1 (2002): 86, 94; and Ibram X Kendi, *The Black Campus Movement: Black Students and the Racial Reconstitution of Higher Education, 1965–1972* (New York: Palgrave, 2012).

35. C. L. R. James, "Interviews: C. L. R. James," *The Black Scholar* 2, no. 1 (1970): 41–43.

36. Wallerstein et al., *Open the Social Sciences.*

37. Kimberlé Williams Crenshaw, "Twenty Years of Critical Race Theory: Looking Back to Move Forward," *Connecticut Law Review* 43, no. 5 (July 2011): 1262.

38. Vincent Harding, "The Vocation of the Black Scholar and the Struggles of the Black Community," in *Education and the Black Struggle: Notes from a Colonized World,* ed. Institute of the Black World (Atlanta: Institute of the Black World, 1974), 5, 9.

39. Ferguson, "University," 51.

40. Ibid., 50.

41. Ibid., 51.

PART ONE

———

Masks

The essays in this section address words, tropes, and concepts used within the disciplines to occlude race privilege via colorblind approaches. The authors examine popular tropes that hide colorbound conditions, such as merit, market, choice, neutrality, and innocence, as well as the different modes of racialization (i.e., through Indigeneity, blackness, foreignness, white victimhood) that mask and sustain racial domination. We urge readers to consider the insights produced when reading these essays together, shedding different perspectives on the shared process through which racial power becomes cloaked and expelled from critical examination or critique.

In the opening essay, George Lipsitz shows that colorblind racism is not new—not the product of a late-twentieth-century "post–civil rights" era, but instead one of the oldest technologies of racial domination, a long-standing practice rooted in slavery and Indigenous dispossession. This essay reveals the long legacy of colorblind policy formations and formulations in politics, public policy, and law. It chronicles a record of legal measures dating to the Colonial Era that deployed colorblindness to achieve racist effects without having to declare racial intent. This juridical framework provided the political and ethical groundings for pervasive patterns of private discrimination that prevail today whereby businesses enact racially targeted policies without expressly mentioning race, as in the operation of credit scoring and the siting of environmental hazards.

Lipsitz's essay can be read productively with Kimberlé Williams Crenshaw's chapter reviewing the political and intellectual currents that fueled the emergence of Critical Race Theory (CRT) in the late 1980s and early 1990s. In response to the histories and forces documented by Lipsitz, the Civil Rights Movement advanced a series of insurgent demands for structural transformation. Crenshaw demonstrates how, following these demands, a politically broad range of institutional actors within legal scholarship and legal education "embraced a gradualist strategy of integration premised on the assumption that colorblind meritocracy stood outside the economy of racial power." Meritocracy, then, became one of the central tropes deployed to demobilize and disavow challenges to racialized structures of power within the law.

Sociologist Dwanna McKay of the Muscogee nation attends to the ordinary ways that racial power becomes naturalized across a variety of sites, such as sports mascots, children's songs, and cultural celebrations. But Robertson argues that the practices of disavowal central to some forms of colorblindness often operate differently for Indigenous groups, for whom racist stereotypes, representations, and narratives, including celebrations of genocide, are often quite explicit. Robertson describes the processes and consequences of the racialized invisibility of Indigenous peoples in an era of colorblind rhetoric that works to produce a legitimized form of racism. Marzia Milazzo then demonstrates the malleability and transportability of colorblind discourse in contemporary Brazil and South Africa. Within a range of genres and settings, Milazzo reveals that when racial disparities and differences are represented as aberrational rather than structural, long histories of white supremacy become disavowed and naturalized. Her work confirms what scholars in the social sciences have also found, that colorblindness gives a liberal veneer to decidedly illiberal policies.

Finally, Kimberlé Crenshaw's chapter "How Colorblindness Flourished in the Age of Obama" connects to the other essays in the section by demonstrating the ways in which a symbol of hyperracial visibility (Obama) paradoxically facilitated the further disavowal of racist structures and outcomes. Viewed from this perspective, we can understand Obama's election and presidency as the culmination of the long history of disavowals documented by Robertson and Lipsitz, rather than their negation. Similarly, the insights of Lipsitz and Robertson about the latent and everyday forms of white racial resentment are crucial to understanding Crenshaw's argument about the links between Obama's tenure and the white nationalist impulses that animated the Trump campaign. Crenshaw shows how the ascendency of postracialism under Obama served to accelerate the invisible and disavowed racism chronicled by Robertson. By denying and foreclosing the need for any systemic efforts to address racial disparities and hierarchies, Obama's postracialism offered fertile grounds for those resentments to flourish.

TWO

The Sounds of Silence

HOW RACE NEUTRALITY PRESERVES
WHITE SUPREMACY

George Lipsitz

How precisely does the issue of color remain so powerfully determinative of everything from life circumstance to manner of
death, in a world that is, by and large, officially "color-blind"?

PATRICIA WILLIAMS[1]

While appearing to be color blind and power evasive, patriarchal
whiteness is a system that protects the privileges of whites
through diminishing Indigenous entitlements.

AILEEN MORETON-ROBINSON[2]

Colorblind talk furthers racial power not through the direct
articulation of racial differences but rather by obscuring the
operation of racial power, protecting it from challenge, and permitting ongoing racialization through racially coded methods.

CLAIRE JEAN KIM[3]

Very few problems can be solved by pretending that they do not exist. In a
society plagued by pervasive racial stratification and subordination, race-
bound problems require race-based remedies. Yet the idea that we can and
should be colorblind has emerged as the preferred response to racism in both
public policy and private life in the United States. Despite continuing residential, school, and job segregation, a growing racial wealth gap, severe racial
health disparities, and diametrically divergent racialized relationships to
criminal justice institutions, we are told that it is dangerous and divisive to
enforce fully the laws that ban discrimination in housing, schools, jobs,
and business opportunities, to invest in asset-building programs and educa-
tional-enhancement initiatives, or to utilize affirmative action in hiring,

contracting, and college admissions. A series of Supreme Court decisions, state laws, and presidential proclamations dating back to the 1970s have severely limited the ability of government to craft race-based remedies for race-bound problems. In popular culture and everyday discourse, purporting *not* to see color is considered a virtue. Whites who live in mostly white neighborhoods replete with advantages and amenities where children attend well-funded fully equipped schools with experienced and credentialed teachers boast that they "don't see race." They express dismay that Latina/o, Black, Asian, and Indigenous people living in impoverished ghettos, barrios, and isolated rural enclaves plagued by inadequate housing, disproportionate exposure to toxic hazards, and inferior educational opportunities seem unduly, and improperly, focused on racial identity. We should not even mention race, we are told, because that only strengthens racism. Yet as David Theo Goldberg explains, the formula that requires us to give up the mention of race asks us to reject "the word, the concept, the category, at most the categorization. But not, pointedly not, the conditions for which those terms stand."[4]

Colorblindness pretends that racial recognition rather than racist rule is the problem to be solved. Colorblindness does not do away with color, but rather reinforces whiteness as the unmarked norm against which difference is measured. Moreover, the appeal to colorblindness is a claim with no content. It is a proclamation without a program, a pronouncement without a plan of action. Even its most zealous proponents cannot explain how simply not noticing and not mentioning the decidedly unequal distribution of opportunities and life chances in U.S. society can possibly lead to closing the racial wealth gap or the racial health gap. As Kimberlé Crenshaw has repeatedly argued, expecting social institutions to redress racial injuries without referring to race is like having to ask directions to a destination you are not allowed to name. Colorblindness thus survives and thrives not because of what it produces, but because of what it prevents: that is, exposure, analysis, and remediation of the skewing of social opportunities and life chances by race. Rather than a recipe for a just society, colorblindness constitutes a core component of a long-standing historical whiteness protection program.

Colorblindness is a one-way street. It is invoked as an ideal and an imperative only when color consciousness is used to address and redress the unearned privileges of whiteness, when it could lead to accountability and action in response to conditions created by centuries of structural and personal racism. It holds that whites are all individuals who can never be held accountable for the enrichments they enjoy as a group. Yet the very collective color consciousness that is marked as illegitimate when it comes to explaining white advantage is deployed relentlessly as an explanation for the disadvantages experienced by communities of color. The most enthusiastic proponents of colorblindness as public policy routinely notice the existence of races and in fact harp on the purported collective flaws in the genes, chromosomes, and cultures of aggrieved racial groups as causal factors that "explain" and justify unequal educational and economic outcomes.

The political and cultural legitimacy of colorblindness rests on a series of deliberate and debilitating lies about history. Colorblindness purports to be a recent invention, an imputed product of the success of the civil rights movement, civil rights laws, and the political and legal gains they envisioned and enacted. Yet in fact it is merely a present-day manifestation of a long-standing political project emanating from Indigenous dispossession, colonial conquest, slavery, segregation, and immigrant exclusion. Its invocations of the egalitarian aims of the freedom movements of the mid-1960s hide an enduring allegiance to the evasions of accountability and practices of denial and disavowal at the heart of white supremacy.

The falsifications of history central to colorblindness attribute conquest, colonization, slavery, segregation, and immigrant exclusion to the mere fact of racial recognition rather than to carefully constructed structures of racial rule. For this stance to be credible, we would have to believe that the mere shock of seeing differently pigmented people, rather than desire for unjust enrichments, led European Americans to kill indigenous people and seize their lands, kidnap Africans and work them as slaves in America, conquer Mexico and make its former citizens second-class subjects, bar immigration from Asia, and ban intermarriage. Yet the actual historical record demonstrates that the structures of white supremacy stemmed less from the color differences that Euro-Americans *did* see than from their refusal *to* see the humanity of people of color. Aileen Moreton-Robinson notes that Indigenous dispossession around the world depended on an act of *not seeing*, on the fiction of *terra nullius*. This legal principle proclaimed that lands inhabited by Indigenous people, held in common and with no recognizable state claiming sovereignty over them, were in fact empty and available for white possession.[5] This refusal to see the history, dignity, and humanity of the people Europeans conquered did not require direct reference to race, but it produced a form of racism that established, solidified, and regulated legal and economic structures premised on white patriarchal possession that endure to this day.[6]

Attributing racist subordination to the mere act of racial recognition reverses cause and effect. As the scholarship of Ian Haney Lopez establishes, describing racist legal categories as *responses* to differences in color occludes the ways in which legislation and litigation *produced* the very differences they purported to police. Laws banning immigration from Asia, reserving naturalized citizenship only for whites, and outlawing racial intermarriage created the different complexions and phenotypes that became understood as constitutive of nonwhiteness and whiteness.[7] Explicit racial recognition has never been a necessary prerequisite for racial subordination. Nationalities and continents served as proxies for race when Congress enacted the Chinese Exclusion Act of 1882 and the Asiatic Barred Zone provisions of the Johnson-Reed immigration act of 1924. No law naming Mexican Americans was needed to justify state and federal authorities working in concert to round up and deport hundreds of thousands of people of Mexican ancestry in the 1930s and 1950s. Race never needed to be mentioned in legislative acts and administrative actions in the 1970s and 1980s that encouraged immigration from Ireland but produced backlogs of applicants from Asia.[8]

Many of the key mechanisms of white racial rule in U.S. history achieved determinate racist effects without ever having to declare racial intent. These include the three-fifths clause and the fugitive slave provisions in the Constitution, state "grandfather" clauses, poll taxes and "understanding clauses," alien land laws, the Wagner Act, Social Security, and, more recently, the sentencing differential between powder and rock cocaine in the war on drugs, the requirement for picture identification cards in order to vote, placing the governments of economically depressed municipalities under state control, the use of high-stakes testing as a guide to allocating educational resources, and the use of measures of credit worthiness that do not mention race but work to disqualify worthy minority borrowers. Social welfare provisions routinely accessed by whites are belittled as racial entitlements when accessed by Latino/as, Native Americans, Asian Americans, or Blacks. To focus only on overt uses of race by the state in the past or present hides from scrutiny most of the actions that produce, preserve, and protect racial stratification. In the past, employment, housing, and educational discrimination thrived in both the north and south with and without overt state endorsement. Both the historical record and present practices expose the faulty premises and assumptions that purport to fight racism by requiring the state to dispense with any direct reference to race but not to challenge the racist practices that make such references necessary.

The practice of producing racist effects without having to declare racial intent informed the drafting of key provisions of the United States Constitution. A possessive investment in whiteness was inscribed early in the document in the three-fifths clause that appears in article 1, section 2, paragraph 3. This provision gave slave-holding states preferential representation in Congress (and consequently a quota of extra influence over the federal government) by allowing slaves to be counted as three-fifths of a person for purposes of representation. Yet neither slavery nor race is mentioned explicitly. Instead, representation is described as determined by the numbers of "free Persons," "those bound to Service for a Term of Years" (indentured servants), and "three fifths of all other Persons." Everyone knew that those "other persons" were African Americans held in bondage, who were not considered citizens or even humans in many other senses but whose enslavement added to the political power of the states in which they were held. Thus the first constitutional support for the slave system was articulated in a colorblind frame.

Similar colorblind language characterized article 4, section 2, paragraph 3 of the Constitution, which put the full force of the federal government behind returning runaway slaves to their owners. This provision provided the foundation for subsequent legislation that essentially compelled every person under the jurisdiction of the government to serve as a slave catcher. Yet once again, neither slavery nor race was mentioned. The wording in this section describes the obligation of all to return to bondage a "Person held to Service or Labour in one State, under the Laws thereof, escaping into another." In similar fashion, article 1, section 9, paragraph 1 did not need to refer to race to protect the interests of white supremacy. It stipulated that Congress could not prohibit the "Migration or Importation of such Persons as any of the States now existing shall think proper to admit" until at least 1808. Thus the slave trade was given constitutional protection for at least one generation. The three-fifths clause, the fugitive slave clause, and the clause protecting the slave trade all secured racial advantages for whites, achieving racist effects without having to declare racial intent. Legal scholar Robert Williams discerns a similar pattern in systematic violations by the U.S. government of treaties with Indigenous peoples. These actions required no explicit mention of race but rather rested on stated and unstated assumptions about civilization and savagery.[9]

The era of Jim Crow segregation provides the key points of reference for proponents of colorblindness. They allege that in these years, overt, direct, and referential uses of race created injustices that were corrected by the putatively colorblind remedies of the modern civil rights era. Yet colorblindness was also a tool of racial tyranny in the era of Jim Crow. Because the 15th Amendment expressly prevented denying Black men the right to vote, segregationists resorted to ruses steeped in colorblindness to preserve the franchise for whites. State grandfather clauses that stayed in place for much of the nineteenth century deployed colorblind language in restricting the right to vote to people whose grandfathers had been voters. This provision was colorblind, in that it made no mention of race; yet because the grandfathers of Blacks had been slaves or otherwise disenfranchised, they could not qualify to vote by this colorblind standard. Many whites who qualified also did not have grandfathers who voted; poor whites only got the franchise in the south because coalitions of Blacks and whites in the era of Reconstruction instituted the universal franchise. But in a racially stratified society in the Jim Crow era, poor whites could be welcomed as voters by local registrars without needing to account for their grandparents' status as Blacks did. When grandfather clauses fell out of favor with the courts, they were replaced with other colorblind ruses: literacy tests given to Blacks but not whites and made so difficult that no one could pass them; poll taxes pegged at exorbitantly high amounts when Blacks tried to vote; and selective enforcement of laws against vagrancy and loitering to force Blacks to labor for whites under oppressive slavery-like conditions or be sent to jail where they did similar labor for the state, effectively removing them from voting.

While these colorblind laws functioned to augment and extend white supremacy, a law containing express recognition of race provided a key resource in the fight *against* racism. The 1866 Civil Rights Act affirmed that all people under the jurisdiction of the United States—citizen and noncitizen, ex-slave and never enslaved—had the same right to make contracts and pursue business opportunities "as is enjoyed by white citizens."[10] Never repealed and never invalidated by the courts, this act remains statute law as it was in 1866. Its express color consciousness reveals how race-based remedies often mischaracterized as inventions of the 1970s have a long and honorable history of legal standing and precedent.

Before the Civil War, the full force and power of the federal government worked to support and sustain the system of racialized, permanent, and hereditary chattel slavery. In his famous address at Gettysburg, Abraham Lincoln called for a new birth of freedom designed to give the nation the first real democracy it had ever known. The 13th, 14th, and 15th Amendments to the Constitution and the 1866 Civil Rights Act gave tangible form to this new freedom by placing the power of the federal government behind Black freedom to the exact dimension and degree that it had previously backed the slave system. In a very short time, however, the racial regime of white supremacy reasserted itself, and it did so through the ruse of colorblindness. Laws intended to dismantle *racial subordination* were interpreted maliciously by the courts as merely bans against *racial recognition* by the state, giving judicial impetus and approval to private discrimination. Actions by the state to protect Black rights were portrayed as intolerant incursions on the liberty and traditional privileges of whites. The 1875 Civil Rights Act that mandated equal access to public accommodations for all races was ruled unconstitutional by the Supreme Court in 1883 on the grounds that it constituted reverse racism against whites. Even though section 2 of the 13th Amendment empowered Congress to pass laws eliminating the "badges and incidents of slavery," i.e., the racial stigmas pervading public and private policy in the afterlife of slavery, the Court claimed that Congress had no right to regulate racial exclusion from public accommodations because this exclusion was implemented through private individual behavior rather than state statutes. Civil rights laws were not seen as a guarantee of equal rights for Blacks, but instead only a temporary punishment for whites found guilty of discriminating in too overt a fashion. Speaking for the Court majority in the 1883 *Civil Rights Cases,* Justice Joseph Bradley stated that the public accommodations law passed in 1875, only ten years after the adoption of the 13th Amendment and seven years after the 14th, bore no relevance to the enduring legacy of slavery. Belittling Black people and the alleged special favors he saw being given to them by civil rights laws, Justice Bradley stated with exasperation about the Negro that "there must be some stage in the progress of his elevation when he takes the rank of a mere citizen and ceases to be the special favorite of the laws, and when his rights as a citizen or a man are to be protected by the ordinary modes by which other men's rights are protected."[11] Few Blacks could have imagined themselves as special favorites of the law in 1883 in the face of vigilante and state violence, unprosecuted rapes and killings, theft of property, mass incarceration, and debt peonage. The Court took no notice of these conditions. Instead, its decision went so far as to claim that the 13th Amendment only banned slavery itself, that it was far-fetched to think that pervasive racial discrimination in the 1860s and 1870s was a badge or incident of slavery.

The case of *Plessy v. Ferguson* looms large in the discursive politics of colorblindness, but in a way that distorts its true history and enduring meaning. Justice John Harlan, in his dissent against the ruling for the majority by Justice Henry Brown that upheld a Louisiana law requiring Blacks and whites to ride in separate railroad cars, argued that "our constitution is colorblind and neither knows nor tolerates classes among its citizens." This passage is often cited in support of colorblindness as the antidote to racial segregation. Yet when placed in the context of the rest of the paragraph authored by Harlan and his subsequent record, it becomes clear that for him, declaring the Constitution to be colorblind was a way of making white supremacy *more* powerful and more effective rather than less so. In the sentence that precedes his description of the Constitution as colorblind, Harlan observes: "The white race deems itself to be the dominant race in this country. And so it is in prestige, in achievements, in education, in wealth and in power. So, I doubt not, it will continue to be for all time if it remains true to its great heritage and holds fast to the principles of constitutional liberty."[12] Here, colorblindness becomes a means for preserving the dominance of the white race, of allowing custom and vigilante violence to do the work of racial suppression without relying on formal intervention by the state. Yet even Harlan supported segregation by the state in some cases. In 1899, he authored the Supreme Court's unanimous opinion in the case of *Cumming v. Board of Education,* which upheld as consistent with the "colorblind" Constitution the legality of Jim Crow segregation in public schools.[13] The disagreement between Harlan and the other justices about colorblindness was not a disagreement about whether whites would rule, but rather about whether colorbound or colorblind policies worked best to secure white rule and the concomitant unfair gains and unjust enrichments of white supremacy.

Proponents of the colorblind approach to law and social policy often identify themselves as heirs to Harlan's dissent and as opponents of the racial recognition allowed by *Plessy.* In fact, however, they share with both sides in the *Plessy* decision its key ruse: treating differently situated people as if they are equal. *Plessy* justified segregation not because it claimed Blacks were inferior, but rather by purporting that the Louisiana Separate Car Act enacted no racial injury because while Blacks were prohibited from riding in the clean, well-appointed, safe cars reserved for whites, whites were equally prohibited from riding in the dirty, shabby, dangerous cars reserved for Blacks. The pretense that justified Jim Crow segregation for the next sixty years was that separate was equal, that Blacks and whites were treated alike. This is the same rationale, as we shall see later in this chapter, that the Roberts Court would employ in the first decade of the twenty-first century in dissolving desegregation programs in Seattle and Louisville, fair hiring and promotions standards in New Haven, and legal protections for voting rights in Shelby County, Alabama. Striking down these policies and programs, in the Court's view, now extends the presumption that differently situated Blacks and whites are treated equally. The Jim Crow segregation that *Plessy* promoted as the law of the land may now be unconstitutional, but the logic of formal equivalence at its heart remains in place. As Kimberlé Crenshaw explains, "The same interpretive strategy deployed to legitimize segregation is now being deployed to immunize the racial status quo against any substantive redistribution."[14]

Achieving colorbound ends through colorblind means persisted in public policy throughout the Jim Crow era. Race did not need to be mentioned expressly because legislators could always find proxies for race such as eligibility for naturalized citizenship (denied to Asians) or labor market segment (farmworkers and domestics were predominantly Latino, Asian, and Black).

In the first two decades of the twentieth century, the alien land laws passed in fifteen states made it illegal for Asian immigrants to own land. These acts proceeded from expressly racist and nativist campaigns against Asians as unassimilable, unwelcome, and forever foreign. Yet the laws carefully avoided any overt mention of race or nationality, denying these property rights only to "aliens ineligible for citizenship." This phrase comes from the openly and expressly racist immigration and nationality act of 1790 restricting naturalized citizenship to "free white males." As Ian Haney Lopez demonstrates in *White by Law,* the courts never came to a definitive conclusion about who was white or what constituted whiteness, finally declaring in *United States v. Bhagat Singh Thind* that whiteness was essentially whatever white people thought it was.[15] Yet there was no ambiguity or confusion about who was *not* white in respect to the alien land laws that deprived immigrants from Asia of the opportunity to own assets that appreciated in value and could be passed down to subsequent generations, precisely because of their perceived race. This created an indirect yet real and lucrative subsidy to whiteness.[16] White privilege became more secure rather than less by not being named specifically.

Legislation passed as part of President Franklin Roosevelt's New Deal in the 1930s also achieved colorbound ends through colorblind means. No expressly racial language appeared in the Wagner Act, which established the National Labor Relations Board and helped workers form unions to bargain for better wages and working conditions; in the Social Security Act, which established government-supported old age pensions and survivor benefits policies; or in the Federal Housing Act (FHA), which saved the homebuilding and lending industries by putting the full faith of the federal government behind private mortgages. Yet each of these laws contained covert and coded colorbound clauses. The Wagner Act and Social Security did not cover farmworkers and domestics, occupations with large numbers of workers of color. The Federal Housing Act set up the Home Owners Loan Corporation, which relied on "secret city survey files" that channeled loans with favorable terms to whites while virtually shutting Blacks out of the private housing market.[17] The appraisal manuals used by the Home Owners Loan Corporation in assessing worthiness for FHA loans redlined Black neighborhoods, making them ineligible for loans, while designating white neighborhoods—especially those with deed restrictions banning residency by Blacks in perpetuity—as good credit risks.

The Jim Crow segregation that prevailed mostly in southern and border states entailed express references to race that resulted in dual school systems for Black and white students and in laws relegating whites and Blacks to different water fountains, bathrooms, and sections of buses. Proponents of colorblind policies envision these practices and policies as the real racism. Yet even in the age of Jim Crow, racial subordination and oppression were not confined to the south. Blacks who came from the southern states to the cities of the north discovered that Jim Crow laws and signs reading "Whites Only" were not necessary to produce segregated schools, jobs, and neighborhoods. At the 1963 March on Washington, Martin Luther King declared that in the south the Negro cannot vote, but in the north the Negro has nothing to vote for. Malcolm X repeatedly counseled his followers not to think of racism as a peculiarly southern problem. "Stop talking about the South. Long as you're south of the Canadian border, you're south," he quipped. Kwame Ture, who challenged Jim Crow segregation directly and fiercely in Mississippi in his work with the Student Nonviolent Coordinating Committee, wrote in 1967 that the key to racial justice resided in the north, where "the core problem within the ghetto is the vicious circle created by the lack of decent housing, decent jobs, and adequate education."[18] In his last book, *Where Do We Go from Here? Chaos or Community,* Dr. King argued that the Black freedom movement could never be content with simply taking down the Jim Crow signs but leaving in place the racial stratification that prevented a real sharing of rights, responsibilities, and resources.

COLORBLINDNESS IN THE AGE OF CIVIL RIGHTS: GETTING AROUND *BROWN*

The foundational fictions of colorblindness portray the historical struggle for Black freedom as a struggle to be free from racial recognition rather than from racial subordination. Their adherents assume that colorblindness is the antithesis of racism despite its long history as an effective tool of racial subordination. In attacks on civil rights laws and affirmative action policies they cite Dr. King's wish expressed at the 1963 March on Washington—that one day his children might be judged by the content of their character rather than by the color of their skin—as proof that he opposed the very affirmative action and restorative justice measures that he in fact emphatically and expressly supported. Perhaps most tellingly, proponents of colorblindness tell a story of where the struggle for civil rights went wrong that ignores the depths, dimensions, and duration of white resistance and refusal. They focus instead on the myth that Blacks proved unfit for freedom and sought special preferences that they had not earned. These accounts conveniently omit that the most ferocious (and most effective) arguments against *Brown v. Board of Education of Topeka,* the Civil Rights Act, the Voting Rights Act, and the Fair Housing Act were phrased in colorblind terms that did not openly defend the privileges of whiteness but instead couched their claims as defenses of states' rights and property rights, as well as efforts at "saving" putatively innocent white women and children from the predations of Black criminality and disease.

The massive and largely successful resistance to *Brown v. Board* in both the north and south rarely proclaimed white supremacy overtly. Instead it used the language of neighborhood schools, property rights, and child protection. Just as the grandfather clause was necessary to get around the 15th Amendment's prohibition against denying the right to vote to Blacks, opponents of *Brown* who could not openly argue for the supremacy of whites could depict Blacks as unfit for freedom. They depicted Black children as unruly, as riddled with disease, as products of indecent and immoral conjugal relations.[19] Anticipating subsequent manipulation of the words of Dr. King, the segregationists could claim they were not objecting to Black students because of the color of their skin, but because of what they alleged to be the content of their character. As a footnote to the ruling opinion in *Brown v. Board* noted acerbically, they were attempting to cite the effectiveness of segregation in harming Black communities as a rationale for continuing to segregate them.

In the north, widespread residential segregation enabled resistance to school integration to masquerade as a defense of neighborhood schools, small government, and local control. Opponents of desegregation found succor in the Supreme Court's 1974 *Milliken v. Bradley* decision.[20] In this case, the district court found that officials in Detroit created illegally segregated schools by locating new schools in neighborhoods that were either all white or all Black, and by allowing white students to transfer out of predominately Black schools while forbidding Black students to transfer. Judge Stephen A. Roth ruled that private sector decisions in real estate and home lending businesses shaped and reflected expectations that white schools would have more resources and more experienced and better teachers. He ordered a cross-district transfer program throughout the city and its suburbs as the proper remedy to create integrated and equitable education. Opponents did not openly ask for the perpetuation of white and Black schools. Instead they used district lines as a proxy for race and promoted the ideal of local autonomy as a colorblind principle that had to be upheld. This claim was clearly a pretext for discrimination. Drawing school district lines in Michigan had always been a state rather than a local responsibility. The eighty-five districts in the Detroit region did not conform to neighborhood or municipal boundaries. The opponents of desegregation bemoaned the uses of buses for the purpose of integration, even though some three hundred thousand children in the region already rode to schools (most of them segregated) in buses that crossed a variety of boundaries. Some suburbs were served by as many as six different school districts. One district extended over five cities, two districts sprawled over three counties, and seventeen districts served two counties. When the case came to the Supreme Court, the majority opinion banned busing across district lines in deference to the newly invented but piously invoked principle of local autonomy. Speaking for the majority, Justice Potter Stewart declared that segregation in Detroit and its suburbs stemmed from "unknown and unknowable causes," ignoring the enormous volume of evidence presented in the case. The decision instructed white parents that they could escape the mandates of *Brown v. Board* by moving to all-white suburbs where they could hoard resources for their children and deny them to Blacks by invoking the colorblind principle of local control. The concept was upheld by the Court as sacred when it benefited white interests in *Milliken v. Bradley,* yet it would be dismissed out of hand by the Roberts Court in 2007 when respect for local decision-making and control of schools served the interests of desegregation and Blacks in *Parents Involved in Community Schools v. Seattle School District No. 1,* despite long-standing claims by each of the conservative justices that they respected judicial precedent, honored settled law, and opposed activism from the bench.[21]

Twenty years after the *Milliken* decision, proponents of desegregation in Kansas City attempted to take advantage of the one loophole that case offered them. While *Milliken* forbade interdistrict busing, it did allow school boards to provide enhanced educational opportunities for victims of racial exclusion. After seeing city school officials resist implementation of *Brown v. Board* for twenty-three years, the federal courts ordered Kansas City to desegregate its schools in 1977. Yet city and state officials did all they could to evade their responsibilities. They did not produce even a plan for desegregation until instructed to do so by the courts in 1985, and did not implement the plan until 1988. Consistent with *Milliken v. Bradley,* the plan included expenditures on educational enrichments for inner city schools attended mostly by Blacks. Preposterously but effectively, opponents complained that the educational "sweeteners" provided by the plan were too good—so good, in fact, that they *might* provide an incentive for suburban white students to attend inner city schools, which would promote the cross-district busing banned by *Milliken.* Echoing the language deployed in the *Civil Rights Cases* in 1883, the Court ruled that these benefits allocated to Blacks constituted unfair impositions on whites, that after seven years of desegregation educational inequity in Kansas City no longer had anything to do with the past. The Court declared that innocent and individual decisions by home seekers caused segregation in Kansas City and the attendant quality of well-funded schools in the suburbs but dilapidated and underfunded schools in the city. Once again, the Court decided that Blacks could no longer be the "special favorite" of the law because seven years of limited desegregation had wiped out the effects of slavery, state laws banning Blacks from public schools, mandatory Jim Crow segregation, and thirty-four years of resistance to *Brown.*[22]

As Kimberlé Crenshaw has demonstrated repeatedly, colorblindness is not a valid legal principle, nor a viable social theory. It is essentially a rhetorical prophylactic, a device designed to prevent color-conscious responses to colorbound conditions. Coaching by the federal courts has encouraged its deployment in organized campaigns against affirmative action, school desegregation, fair housing, and fair hiring. Both private and public actors have learned that colorblindness provides a language that legitimates the pursuit of white racial advantage without having to admit racist intent. This process is exemplified in a report written by the Los Angeles consulting firm Cerrell Associates for the California Waste Management Board in 1984. The report advised the state to locate waste incinerators and toxic dumps in Mexican communities, but it did so covertly through carefully coded language. The report's profile of places suitable for these nuisances and hazards described them as sites with large numbers of low-income working-class Catholics with a high school education or less and generally employed in farming or ranching.[23] As with the Constitution's three-fifths clause, state grandfather clauses, and alien land laws, no one was actually fooled by this kind of circumlocution; everyone knew it targeted people of Mexican ancestry, but its colorblind language provided protective cover for color-based suppression and oppression. The use of education, income, and place as a proxy for race enables and excuses the systematic poisoning of communities of color, as evidenced by the crises caused by environmental racism in areas inhabited primarily by Asians in Richmond, California, by Native Americans in northern Wisconsin, and by Blacks in Flint, Michigan.[24]

THE ROBERTS COURT AND CONTEMPORARY COLORBLINDNESS

In the *Parents Involved in Community Schools* case of 2007, the Supreme Court abandoned more than fifty years of precedent in ruling that the successful, popular, and voluntary school desegregation programs that were adopted in Louisville, Kentucky, and Seattle, Washington, in accord with the mandates of *Brown v. Board* violated the Constitution. The Court objected to the practice of taking race into account in assigning students to schools for the purpose of integration. Chief Justice Roberts declared that race-based remedies for segregation are impermissible. "The way to stop discrimination on the basis of race," he announced, "is to stop discriminating on the basis of race."[25] Roberts's carefully crafted rhetoric elevated colorblindness into a constitutional principle fabricated to protect, preserve, augment, and lock in the distinctly colorbound privileges, advantages, and enrichments secured by whites through long histories of both de jure and de facto segregation in housing, education, and employment. With an indifference to reality worthy of the totalitarian state described by George Orwell in *1984,* the Court declared in this case that integration is discrimination, that segregation is colorblindness, that racial subordination is fine but racial recognition is prohibited, and that the best way to make racism disappear is to pretend that it does not exist.[26]

The Court's ruling in *Parents Involved* invalidated *as discrimination* the only practical and feasible means of reducing discrimination. The remedies outlawed by the Court had been developed democratically by local school boards and communities in order to address and redress de jure segregation in Louisville and de facto segregation in Seattle. These legacies of school segregation coupled with systemic housing discrimination in the two cities relegated Black students to overcrowded and underfunded schools with limited course offerings, inadequate instructional equipment, and fewer experienced and credentialed teachers compared to the schools attended by white students in more affluent neighborhoods. Yet the collective, cumulative, and continuing material injuries inflicted on Black students by segregation did not interest the Court. The case did not reveal one single actual injury suffered by any white student because of the desegregation programs. Yet the ruling and concurring opinions of the conservative justices focused on the largely imagined potential injuries that white students *might* suffer in the future if school board assignments by race would ever put them in a position where they lost a desired place in a school to a Black competitor.

Prohibiting state agencies from recognizing race makes it impossible to craft effective remedies for racial discrimination, not just in schooling, but in employment and voting as well. The Roberts Court went on to expand the specious rationale of colorblindness that it placed at the heart of the *Parents Involved* case in a series of subsequent decisions about employment discrimination and voting rights. In the 2009 *Ricci v. DeStefano* case, the Court thwarted enforcement of fair employment law by city officials in New Haven, Connecticut.[27] That municipality's fire department administered a test to firefighters seeking promotion. No Black test takers attained the scores needed for promotion. As they were obligated to do by Title VII of the Civil Rights Act, city administrators checked to see if the test contained biases that imposed unfair impediments to Blacks seeking promotion. They discovered that the test was flawed, that there was no legitimate merit rationale for giving the written portion of the test 60 percent of the final grade. The city decided to devise a new exam, one consistent with long-standing race-neutral best practices in psychometric testing. The lower courts supported this decision as a matter of equity and fairness, but the Supreme Court overturned their rulings, ordering the fire department to honor the results of tests shown to be both defective and racially biased, simply because promotion applicants who were not Black and did well on those tests *might* feel that not counting those results would constitute being disadvantaged because of their race.

In his dissenting opinion in the 2012 case *Arizona v. U.S.,* Antonin Scalia put the contradictions of colorblindness on clear display.[28] Scalia claimed the state had the right to require local law enforcement officials to engage in profiling of potential violators of immigration law, a statute that the majority of the Court recognized to be both an improper preemption of federal law and a promotion of racial profiling practices. Scalia had long opposed civil rights remedies because he claimed that racial recognition and assertions of group identities violate the Constitution. Yet in order to justify a law that placed all Latino/as in Arizona under suspicion, he cited as legal precedent the laws passed in southern states before the Civil War to ban entry into the state of free Blacks. In essence, Scalia held that Blacks and Latino/as could not be treated as members of aggrieved groups when they petitioned the courts for civil rights, but they could be condemned as a collective racial menace when states felt doing so would protect the interests and settled expectations of whites.

In the 2013 *Shelby County v. Holder* case, the Court invalidated the "preclearance" clause crucial to the enforcement of the 1965 Voting Rights Act (as renewed and amended in 1975, 1982, and 2006) on the grounds that it stigmatized the states and counties with long histories of racially motivated voter suppression in the past and present by treating them differently from jurisdictions with clean records.[29] Writing for the majority once again, Justice Roberts claimed that these states and counties were being punished for practices of voter suppression from 1965 that no longer applied. He compared voter registration numbers by race in 1965 and 2013, found relative parity, and declared the problem solved. Yet as Roberts knew well, the Voting Rights Act was designed to do more than make it possible to register to vote. Over four decades, the preclearance provision was used to prevent a proliferation of new forms of discrimination once the right to register to vote had been won. The record before the Court revealed that there had been more than seven hundred overtly discriminatory actions in the covered jurisdictions between 1982 and 2006. These actions included continuing efforts at suppressing and diluting Black votes in the areas covered by the act through measures that included canceling or delaying elections when it appeared Blacks would win elective office, gerrymandering district lines, curtailing early voting, moving polling places to inaccessible locations outside Black neighborhoods, purging voter rolls, and responding to victories by Blacks in district elections by requiring all offices to be voted on at-large. During oral arguments in the case, Justice Scalia described the protection of Black voting rights as a "racial entitlement," that is, a special privilege given to Blacks by recognizing them as an aggrieved racial group. Scalia attributed the overwhelming votes in favor of the act by Congress in 1965, 1975, 1982, and 2006 not to the workings of representative democracy and the accountability of representatives to their constituents, but rather to the fears among legislators that they would be seen as racist if they did not vote to protect Black rights. Thus saving them from this imagined injury, in Scalia's judgment, justified dispensing with a provision needed to address and redress the documented record of extensive actual injuries to Blacks by racist voter-suppression schemes.

The ruling by the Roberts Court in *Shelby v. Holder* had its desired effect. In some 165 out of 381 counties surveyed that were previously covered by the preclearance provisions of the Voting Rights Act, the numbers of polling places in segregated minority neighborhoods during the 2016 elections were reduced. At least 868 polling places were closed outright. In others, new voting restrictions such as requiring picture identification were put in place. These no longer needed Department of Justice clearance because of the *Shelby v. Holder* decision. They depressed minority voter turnout, especially in Arizona, Texas, Wisconsin, Michigan, and North Carolina. Cochise County, Arizona, an area near the Mexican border that has a 30 percent Latino/a population, opened only eighteen polling places for its 130,000 residents in 2016, compared to the forty-nine polling venues in place in 2012 before the *Shelby v. Holder* decision.[30]

In a society suffused with systematic school segregation, employment discrimination, and voting suppression, the Roberts Court thus finds race-based remedies to be objectionable, but not the race-bound realities that make them necessary. Justice Roberts argues that he is stopping discrimination on the basis of race by banning the use of race as a factor in making school assignments, preventing city officials from discarding the results of a fundamentally flawed test that produced a racially biased result, and ending the federal government's ability to require states and counties with records of racially discriminatory behavior to clear in advance changes in voting procedures that could damage minority voters.

In the *Parents Involved, Ricci,* and *Shelby* cases, the Roberts Court deployed the rhetoric of colorblindness to terminate the very remedies that Congress and previous courts found to be most effective in combating unjust colorbound conditions in school segregation, employment discrimination, and voting suppression. The Roberts Court, however, discovered inequality not in the differently situated positions of Black and white students in Louisville and Seattle, of Black and non-Black applicants for promotion in the fire department in New Haven, or of Black and white voters in Shelby County, but in remedies that recognized that long histories of discrimination leave Black people differentially situated from whites. In their zeal to promote an illusion of colorblindness and to cloak their claims in universal interchangeability, the conservative justices responsible for the decisions in these three cases abandoned principles they had long claimed to be central to their judicial philosophy: (1) *stare decisis* (the legal principle of determining points in litigation according to precedent), (2) deference to decisions by local authorities and Congress, (3) insistence that civil rights claimants demonstrate actual injuries, and (4) requiring overt declarations of racist intent before finding a policy with disparate impact to be racist. In these cases, however, the Roberts Court overturned the settled law that *stare decisis* would require them to let stand. They overruled the judgment of local school boards, municipal authorities, and Congress. They required no proof of anyone actually being injured by the policies in place, nor did they find or even look for any evidence of overt racist intent. Yet while contradicting what they had long claimed to be their core beliefs, they acted in accord with obligations to something much greater than their often-stated judicial philosophy: the racial regime of white supremacy.

The linguistic and logical inversions needed to justify decisions in these cases did not stem from inconsistency or hypocrisy on the part of individual judges. They were instead part and parcel of the workings of what Cedric Robinson describes as a racial regime, which he defines as a constructed social system "in which race is proposed as a justification for the relations of power."[31] Racial regimes make racial stratification appear natural, necessary, and inevitable by hiding their history, by refusing to reveal their origins or expose to scrutiny their enduring mechanisms. Analyzing the decisions of the Roberts Court from this perspective reveals that its invocation of colorblindness was not, as claimed, a good-faith effort to implement the ideals of the mid-twentieth-century civil rights movement, but rather an expression and extension of the consistent, continuing, cumulative, and collective machinations of the racial regime that has always been central to the legal, social, and cultural order of the U.S. nation. Patricia Williams attributes "racism's hardy persistence and immense adaptability" to habits "of human imagination, deflective rhetoric and hidden license."[32] When placed in historical context, the decisions of the Roberts Court reveal the precise imagination, rhetoric, and license behind what Robinson terms the "discernible origins and mechanisms of assembly" of an ongoing and poisonous racial regime that remains "unrelentingly hostile" to its exposure as racist.[33]

In banning school desegregation in Seattle and Louisville, undermining fair hiring in New Haven, and ending protection of voting rights in Shelby County, the Roberts Court followed the pattern of denial and disavowal that permeated Justice Bradley's ruling opinion in the nineteenth-century *Civil Rights Cases*. Antidiscrimination law becomes portrayed as race discrimination. Measures designed to secure rights for Blacks are caricatured as making Black people into special favorites of the law. Whites asked to obey the law, conversely, are represented as victims of reverse racism. In the *Parents Involved* and *Shelby* cases, the very success of school desegregation policies and laws protecting voting rights were cited as reasons for dismantling them. As Justice Ginsberg noted in her dissent in *Shelby*, this is like throwing away your umbrella because it is not raining today.

Devon Carbado and Cheryl Harris note the link between this revival of nineteenth-century racist arguments and attacks on affirmative action in the post–civil rights era. *Parents Involved, Ricci,* and *Shelby* were not affirmative action cases, but the Roberts Court treated them as if they were, as if educational equity, fair hiring, and voting rights are what Justice Scalia called "racial entitlements" to be belittled and discarded.[34] Decades of mean-spirited and mendacious attacks on affirmative action as a special preference for undeserving minorities and women stands at the center of the Court's logic on cases that are not about affirmative action at all, revealing that the campaign against affirmative action has in fact been a campaign all along against antidiscrimination law in general. Colorblindness is useful as a trope in this discursive battle because it relies on a widely believed but completely false historical fiction: that racial subordination by law has been simply a matter of overt racial recognition, that colorblind policies prevent color-bound practices. This view fails to acknowledge the long history of colorblind racism embodied in a wide range of laws and practices that secured racist ends without having to declare racist intent. By separating recognition of difference from differential power it presents the inaccurate and even implausible claim that the harm done by de jure segregation in schools, jobs, public accommodations, and housing rested solely on the state's recognition of race. By this measure, whites and Blacks would have suffered equally from Jim Crow segregation. Yet the racial recognition attached to Blackness created a racial caste system rooted in social subordination, economic exploitation, and barriers against asset accumulation and education. Racial recognition by the state posed no problem for whites until the Civil War amendments and the 1866 Civil Rights Act directed the federal government to support Black freedom to the same dimension and degree that it had supported slavery and segregation. The problem with "whites only" water fountains, bathrooms, railway cars, shopping and recreation venues, and deed restrictions was not that they made people think about race, but rather that they functioned as visible manifestations of a racist caste system that relegated people of different races to distinctly different opportunities, life chances, rights, and resources. The signs and symbols of Jim Crow, the laws that mandated separate schools and public accommodations, and the statutes prohibiting interracial marriages were only the most obvious manifestations of a system of racial subordination that could function quite successfully without ever having to make direct mention of race.

In the era of the Roberts Court, new proxies have emerged. Race can be identified—but not named—by policing residents of particular neighborhoods differently, by making voting eligibility dependent on possessing the kinds of photo identity cards Blacks are least likely to have, by judging credit worthiness on the basis of criteria that whites are most likely to possess, by giving tax abatements and subsidies for the kinds of property white people are most likely to own.

The long history of focusing on racism as color hides its identity as a condition. Racism today is less a matter of interpersonal recognition than of social organization. It manifests itself as displacement and dispossession, deportability and disproportionate vulnerability, as eviction and incarceration, predatory lending and premature death. A society suffused with commitments to colorblindness is not a *less racist* society; it is merely a *more effectively racist* society. As Ian Haney Lopez explains, "Colorblindness is . . . not a prescription but an ideology, a set of understandings that delimits how people comprehend, rationalize, and act in the world."[35] Colorblindness creates an ever-increasing list of proxies for race that function as pretexts for discrimination. Seemingly race-neutral policies will have disparate effects on differentially situated individuals and groups. As Kimberlé Crenshaw notes with acerbic insight, "Treating different things the same can generate as much inequality as treating the same things differently."[36] Fighting nonexistent "voter fraud" by requiring prospective voters to have the forms of photo identification that Blacks are least likely to have suppresses Black voters without having to admit doing so. Tax-cutting measures that are really just tax-shifting mechanisms provide tax abatements and subsidies for the property most likely to be owned by whites (income, property, capital gains, and inheritance), while increasing the payroll taxes, user fees, and fines that are likely to be levied on Blacks, to create a covert form of racial wealth redistribution away from Blacks and toward whites. Reductions in federal and state support for cities coupled with demands that municipalities conduct themselves like capitalist enterprises lead to privatization of public services with attendant increases in fees, shutoffs of service, indebtedness, and municipal bankruptcies that disproportionately affect Blacks.[37] In Michigan, the cities placed under state emergency management contain 9 percent of the state's residents, but 50 percent of Michigan's Black population.[38]

In private transactions, qualities associated with whiteness are used to determine merit. In mortgage lending, for example, the FICO 4 score is used to measure qualifications for home purchasers. Yet this scoring system revolves around the experiences of whites and their historically open access to credit. People of color who are capable money managers and thoroughly good credit risks get disqualified by this scoring system precisely because discrimination has prevented them and their families from securing loans in the past. If lenders used the FICO 9 or Vantage 3.0 credit scoring systems, an estimated nine and half million more Blacks and Latinos would qualify for loans.[39] Yet even the best credit scoring systems contain biases against borrowers of color, as Lisa Rice, Deidre Swesnik, James Carr, and other fair housing advocates have long argued.[40] When mortgage loans were channeled almost exclusively to whites, credit scoring did not exist. Like standardized tests in education and literacy tests in voting, credit scoring came into existence largely to provide a seemingly colorblind way to make colorbound distinctions.

Cedric Robinson teaches us that racial regimes are unrelentingly hostile to their exposure as racist. They discourage inquiries about their history, their "discernible origins and mechanisms of assembly."[41] The history of white supremacy in the United States reveals that colorblindness is not new, not fair, and not even feasible. As Malcolm X observed, when it comes to racial subordination, the names change but the game's the same. The persistence of colorblind rhetoric binds us to colorbound conditions. Symmetrical treatment under decidedly unequal circumstances perpetuates injustice. Eduardo Bonilla-Silva reminds us that rhetorical frames like colorblindness are diversions designed to direct attention away from differential incomes, wages, and wealth, from occupational stratification and segmentation, from residential segregation and educational inequality, from environmental racism and health inequities, and from differential treatment inside the criminal justice system.[42] Colorblindness is a tawdry part of the present, not a noble ideal for the future. It is part of a political program that elevates white vanity over Black humanity. It leaves unrefuted W. E. B. Du Bois's answer nearly a century ago to the question, What is whiteness and why do people desire it? "Then always," Du Bois wrote, "somehow, some way, silently but clearly, I am given to understand that whiteness is the ownership of the earth forever and ever. Amen!"[43]

COLORBLINDNESS AND THE DISCIPLINES

The uncritical acceptance of colorblindness as the pervasively preferred response to racism perpetuates a long-standing history of failure by the legal and political systems to offer equal opportunity and equal protection of the law to all. It also demonstrates, however, a tremendous failure of the ways of knowing institutionalized in disciplinary research and teaching. The fundamentally false renderings of history and law at the core of appeals to colorblindness are not aberrant and isolated mistakes, but rather evidence of an epistemic regime inscribed in the disciplines that is designed to preserve, protect, and defend the privileges and powers of whiteness. As philosopher Charles Mills explains, the knowledge traditions of the Enlightenment entail "an agreement to misinterpret the world" through "a particular pattern of localized and global cognitive dysfunctions (which are psychologically and socially functional), producing the ironic outcome that whites will in general be unable to understand the world they themselves have made."[44] The historical archive about slavery and reconstruction has been structured in dominance by primary source documents placed in archives by people with power and by secondary sources that reflect the perspectives of the narrow range of people in society with sufficient wealth (and whiteness) to secure credentials from elite institutions. Oppositional scholars able to tap into alternative archives and knowledge traditions are tolerated but most often treated as witnesses whose testimony can be ruled inadmissible even before they speak.[45]

Legal scholarship has consistently perpetuated the errors and misjudgments of the past by relying on precedents set by slave owners and white supremacists in the *Civil Rights Cases* of the 1870s and 1880s, rather than the New Birth constitution announced by President Lincoln at Gettysburg and inscribed in law in the 13th, 14th, and 15th Amendments and the 1866 Civil Rights Act.[46]

Although the disciplines of history and the law bear significant culpability for the uncritical embrace of colorblindness as public policy and popular common sense, disciplines do not exist in isolation. Fabrications and falsifications of history and law take place within an episteme created across the disciplines. The facile assumptions by nineteenth-century social scientists that human experience is governed by the boundaries of the sovereign territories on the world map took the existence and the legitimacy of the nation for granted, erasing the dispossession of Indigenous people as the foundational fact of nationalism and empire.[47] John Locke's arguments placing the autonomous contracting subject at the center of the social world provide the organizing logic for political and legal theories of rights and responsibilities. Yet Locke had the leisure and luxury to contemplate the free contracting subject only because of the profits made from the labor of Black humans held in bondage in South Carolina by his patron the Earl of Shaftesbury. Locke invested in the slave trade, proclaimed the legitimacy of chattel slavery as the fruits of victory in a just war, and created rationales for slavery that proved extremely useful to slave owners in North America, especially key framers of the U.S. Constitution.[48] This history has an enduring influence in the present, when the property of investors, owners, and high-end consumers is considered sacred while the possessions of homeless people are confiscated routinely, when protecting the lives of police officers is the state's highest responsibility while the lives of unarmed Black men and women taken by those officers are considered disposable and their deaths beyond accountability. As Charles Mills observes, "The representative political figure of the modern period remains the White contractor of social contract theory—not the Red aborigine whose land has been taken for the contractual construction of the White settler state or the Black slave who has been contracted over by being bought and sold by the White Atlantic."[49]

The migration of concepts across the disciplines has played a fundamental role in creating epistemic whiteness. The early anthropological and later philosophical writings of Immanuel Kant sowed the seeds of what would become modernization theory and state of nature anthropology in political science and economics. Charles Darwin's theories about evolution as a biological phenomenon became appropriated for white supremacist purposes in economics and sociology. Psychology's emphasis on the individual sociobiological subject, law's concern for the autonomous rights-bearing subject, and the emphasis on the self-interested market subject in economics cohered around a methodological individualism that constructed social relations as simply the sum of easily identifiable actions by individuals. Within that framework, structural racism and race as a sense of group position disappear, denying the collective agency central to white supremacy and precluding recognition of collective injuries and remedies. In the humanities, creative work and criticism of novels, paintings, symphonies, theater, and dance privileged the cultivation of interiority rather than social connections. The narrative arc, tensions, and closures of these creative works called into being an interior psychic subject characterized by a fear of engulfment by a threatening social aggregate, a sensibility easily adaptable to forging monstrous depictions of presumably primitive people at home and abroad. In the ages of conquest, colonization, and empire, these phobic investments projected white guilt about the violence of empire onto its victims, portraying aggression as frontier defense.[50]

The division of research into disciplinary specialties took place under historically specific conditions. The disciplines constitute part of a pattern from the past that shapes both the problems and the possibilities of the present. The core premise of disciplinary inquiry is that productive research takes place through concentrated study of separate and seemingly discrete aspects of our shared social existence. This practice of allocating different research objects and different research questions to distinct fields has been, and continues to be, a generative source of important evidence, ideas, and arguments. It has enabled disciplinary scholars to conduct worthy work on all aspects of human existence, including the practices and processes of racialization. The disciplines will not disappear anytime soon, and important work remains to be done inside each of them. Yet in scholarship, as in most aspects of life, everything that can enable can also inhibit. Yesterday's solutions can become today's problems. As David Marshall quips about the humanities, in universities we often have "twenty-first century students, a twentieth-century curriculum, and a nineteenth-century bureaucracy."[51] On campuses, each discipline generally has its own floor or building. Libraries place books from different disciplines on different shelves. In the world outside these institutional spaces, however, the concerns of the disciplines meet, meld, clash, conflict, converge, and diverge. We need to rethink the disciplines and go beyond them. The self-reflexive criticisms of the disciplines and the interdisciplinary inquiries that emerge from the Countering Colorblindness across the Disciplines project and that appear in this book are efforts in that direction.

When it comes to the reckoning with disciplinary complicity in past and present racisms, however, it will not be enough to change the practices of research, reading, writing, and teaching. The academy is a product of the society it studies, and it is structured to serve managerial ends, to make the existing unjust and unacceptable allocations of dignity, wealth, and power function more smoothly. It should not be a surprise that the pervasive patterns of segregation and subordination that shape society are evaded, ignored, or disavowed by colorblind constructs in history, law, education, economics, psychology, sociology, and urban planning. It is not just what Mills calls "the epistemology of ignorance" that produces this neglect; it is also the effects of societal segregation on the demography of the academy. More than a half century after the passage of important civil rights laws, academic disciplines and the professions they serve remain disproportionately the preserve of whites. Nearly 70 percent of mathematicians and life scientists are white. Whites account for 70 percent of health care professionals and more than 80 percent of social scientists. Seventy-four percent of all college and university faculty members are white, as are 84 percent of full-time professors and 89 percent of college and university presidents. As Jennifer Hamer and Clarence Lang inquire, "How, then, can we legitimately criticize the overwhelmingly white character of, say, the Ferguson Police Department when the dean's, provost's and chancellor's offices of many four-year public universities are virtually all white, even as state demographics have become more racially diverse?"[52]

Attempting to counter colorblindness reveals the systemic and structural nature of racist subordination. It punctures the illusions of innocence and objectivity that scholars use to deny and disavow the academy's culpability in the indecent and unjust social order of our society. It means that we have to examine, critique, and revise old ways of knowing and develop new ones. These are daunting obligations. Yet countering colorblindness also offers an opportunity to do our work better, to do it decently and with dignity, to become cocreators of a new society rather than apologists for the one that now exists.

NOTES

1. Patricia J. Williams, *Seeing a Color-Blind Future: The Paradox of Race* (New York: Farrar, Straus & Giroux, 1997), 15.

2. Aileen Moreton-Robinson, *The White Possessive: Property, Power, and Indigenous Sovereignty* (Minneapolis: University of Minnesota Press, 2015), 77.

3. Claire Jean Kim, *Bitter Fruit: The Politics of Black-Korean Conflict in New York City* (New Haven, CT: Yale University Press, 2000), 17.

4. David Theo Goldberg, *The Threat of Race: Reflections on Racial Neoliberalism* (Malden, MA: Wiley-Blackwell, 2009), 21.

5. Moreton-Robinson, *White Possessive,* 5.

6. Ibid., 193.

7. Ian Haney Lopez, *White by Law: The Legal Construction of Race* (New York: NYU Press, 2006), 10–11.

8. Ibid., 27–28.

9. Robert Williams Jr., *Savage Anxieties: The Invention of Western Civilization* (New York: Palgrave Macmillan, 2012); also idem, *Like a Loaded Weapon: The Rehnquist Court, Indian Rights, and the Legal History of Racism in America* (Minneapolis: University of Minnesota Press, 2005).

10. 1866 Civil Rights Act, 14 Stat. 27–30, enacted April 9, 1866.

11. Bradley, J., Opinion of the Court, *Civil Rights Cases* 109 U.S. 3 (1883), 25, https://supreme.justia.com/cases/federal/us/109/3/case.html.

12. Quoted in Lopez, *White by Law,* 218.

13. Ibid.

14. Kimberlé Crenshaw, "Color Blindness, History, and the Law," in *The House That Race Built: Original Essays by Toni Morrison, Angela Y. Davis, Cornel West, and Others on Black Americans and Politics Today,* ed. Wahneema Lubiano (New York: Vintage, 1998), 282.

15. 261 U.S. 204 (1923), https://supreme.justia.com/cases/federal/us/261/204/case.html.

16. Lopez, *White by Law,* 90, 91.

17. George Lipsitz, *The Possessive Investment in Whiteness: How White People Profit from Identity Politics* (Philadelphia: Temple University Press, 2006), 24–47.

18. Kwame Ture and Charles Hamilton, *Black Power: The Politics of Liberation* (New York: Vintage, 1967), 155.

19. Anders Walker, "Legislating Virtue: How Segregationists Disguised Racial Discrimination as Moral Reform following *Brown v. Board of Education,*" *Duke Law Journal* 47 (1997): 399, 418; Kenneth J. Neubeck and Noel A. Cazenave,

Welfare Racism: Playing the Race Card against America's Poor (New York: Routledge, 2001), 71–72; Phoebe Godfrey, "Brainwashing and Bathrooms: The Discourse of Race, Gender, and Sexuality in the Desegregation of Little Rock's Central High," *Arkansas Historical Quarterly* 42 (2003): 42–67.

20. 418 U.S. 717, www.oyez.org/cases/1973/73-434.

21. 551 U.S. 701, www.oyez.org/cases/2006/05–908. George Lipsitz, "Separate and Unequal: Big Government Conservatism and the Racial State," in *State of White Supremacy: Racism, Governance, and the United States,* ed. Moon-kie Jung, Joao Costa Vargas, and Eduardo Bonilla-Silva (Stanford: Stanford University Press, 2011), 110–29.

22. Theodore M. Shaw, "Equality and Educational Excellence: Legal Challenges in the 1990s," in *In Pursuit of a Dream Deferred: Linking Housing and Education Policy,* ed. john a. powell, Gavin Kearney, and Vina Kay (New York: Peter Lang, 2001), 263. Justice Ginsberg dissenting, Ruth Bader Ginsburg, *Missouri et al. Petitioners v. Kalima Jenkins et al., Certiorari to the United States Court of Appeals for the Eighth Circuit,* No. 93–1823, 1995, 53.

23. Cerrell Associates, Inc., "Political Difficulties Facing Waste-to-Energy Conversion Plant Siting," Los Angeles, 1984, www.ejnet.org/ej/cerrell.pdf. Thanks to Sarah Rios for calling this report to my attention.

24. George Lipsitz, "Unexpected Affiliations: Environmental Justice and the New Social Movements," *Works and Days* 24, no. 47/48 (2006): 25–44; Bindi V. Shah, *Laotian Daughters: Working toward Community, Belonging, and Environmental Justice* (Philadelphia: Temple University Press, 2012); Rick Whaley and Walter Bresette, *Walleye Warriors: An Effective Alliance against Racism and for the Earth* (Philadelphia: New Society Publishers, 1994); Andrew Highsmith, *Demolition Means Progress: Flint, Michigan, and the Fate of the American Metropolis* (Chicago: University of Chicago Press, 2015), 254.

25. Opinion of Roberts, C.J., *Parents Involved in Community Schools v. Seattle School Dist. No. 1,* 551 U.S. 701 (2007), 41, https://supreme.justia.com/cases/federal /us/551/701.

26. Lipsitz, "Separate and Unequal."

27. 557 U.S. 557, www.oyez.org/cases/2008/07–1428.

28. Opinion of Scalia, J., *Arizona v. United States,* 567 U.S. 387 (2012), 4, https:// supreme.justia.com/cases/federal/us/567/387.

29. 570 U.S. 2 (2013), www.oyez.org/cases/2012/12–96. The preclearance clause required Justice Department approval before changes could be made in voting procedures in designated districts.

30. Ari Berman, "There Are 868 Fewer Places to Vote in 2016 because the Supreme Court Gutted the Voting Rights Act," *Nation,* November 4, 2016, www.thenation .com/article/there-are-868-fewer-places-to-vote-in-2016-because-the-supreme -court-gutted-the-voting-rights-act.

31. Cedric Robinson, *Forgeries of Memory and Meaning: Blacks and the Regimes of Race in American Theater and Film before World War II* (Chapel Hill: University of North Carolina Press, 2007), v–vi.

32. Williams, *Seeing a Color-Blind Future,* 16.

33. Robinson, *Forgeries of Memory and Meaning,* v–vi.

34. Devon W. Carbado and Cheryl I. Harris, "The New Racial Preferences," *California Law Review* 95 (2008): 118.

35. Lopez, *White by Law,* 157.

36. Crenshaw, "Color Blindness, History, and the Law," 285.

37. Jennifer F. Hamer and Clarence Lang, "Race, Structural Violence, and the Neoliberal University: The Challenges of Inhabitation," *Critical Sociology* 41, no. 6 (2015): 900–901.

38. Chris Lewis, "Does Michigan's Emergency-Manager Law Disenfranchise Black Citizens?" *Atlantic,* May 9, 2013, www.theatlantic.com/politics/archive/2013 /05/does-michigans-emergency-manager-law-disenfranchise-black-citizens/275639.

39. Kenneth Harney, "Flexible Rules Could Extend Mortgages to Millions," *The Real Deal: New York City Real Estate News,* September 26, 2014, https://therealdeal .com/2014/09/26/flexible-rules-could-extend-mortgages-to-millions.

40. Lisa Rice and Deidre Swesnik, "Discriminatory Effects of Credit Scoring on Communities of Color," *Suffolk University Law Review* 46 (2013): 935–66; James H. Carr, "Outdated Credit Scoring Models Shut Minorities Out of Housing Market," *Forbes,* April 9, 2015, www.forbes.com/sites/janetnovack/2015/04/09/outdated -credit-scoring-models-shut-minorities-out-of-housing-market.

41. Robinson, *Forgeries of Memory and Meaning,* v–vi.

42. Eduardo Bonilla-Silva, *Racism without Racists: Color-Blind Racism and the Persistence of Racial Inequality in America* (Lanham, MD: Rowman & Littlefield, 2014), passim but esp. 25–72.

43. W. E. B. Du Bois, *Darkwater: Voices from within the Veil* (1920; New York: Oxford University Press, 2007), 18.

44. Charles Mills, *The Racial Contract* (Ithaca, NY: Cornell University Press, 1997), 18.

45. Cedric Robinson, George Rawick, W. E. B. Du Bois, and Cheryl Harris among others are scholars who have successfully established a body of scholarship that, if taken seriously, would render colorblindness unthinkable. For the silencing of voices that challenge epistemic whiteness, see Charles Mills, "White Ignorance," in *Race and Epistemologies of Ignorance,* ed. Shannon Sullivan and Nancy Tuana (Albany, NY: SUNY Press, 2007), 11–38.

46. Nathan Newman and J. J. Gass, A New Birth of Freedom: The Forgotten History of the 13th, 14th, and 15th Amendments (New York: Brennan Center for Justice at NYU School of Law, 2004); Thurgood Marshall, "Reflections on the Bicentennial of the United States Constitution," *Harvard Law Review* 101, no. 1 (November 1987): 1–5.

47. Immanuel Wallerstein et al., *Open the Social Sciences: Report of the Gulbenkian Commission on the Restructuring of the Social Sciences* (Stanford: Stanford University Press, 1996), 26.

48. Robin Blackburn, *The Making of New World Slavery: From the Baroque to the Modern, 1492–1800* (London: Verso, 1998), 216–60; John Quiggin, "John

Locke against Freedom," *Jacobin,* June 28, 2015, www.jacobinmag.com/2015/06 /locke-treatise-slavery-private-property.

49. Charles Mills, "White Time: The Chronic Injustice of Ideal Theory," *Du Bois Review* 11, no. 1 (2014): 33.

50. Donald Lowe, *History of Bourgeois Perception* (Chicago: University of Chicago Press, 1983); Nancy Armstrong, *How Novels Think: The Limits of Individualism from 1719–1900* (New York: Columbia University Press, 2005); Esther Lezra, *The Colonial Art of Demonizing Others* (New York: Routledge, 2014); Walter Mignolo, *The Darker Side of Western Modernity* (Durham, NC: Duke University Press, 2011); Susan McClary, *Bizet's Carmen* (Cambridge: Cambridge University Press, 1992), 15–43; Edward Said, *Orientalism* (New York: Vintage, 1979).

51. David Marshall, "The Places of the Humanities: Thinking through Bureaucracy," *Liberal Education* 93, no. 2 (Spring 2007), www.aacu.org/publications -research/periodicals/places-humanities-thinking-through-bureaucracy.

52. Jennifer Hamer and Clarence Lang, "Race, Structural Violence, and the Neoliberal University: The Challenges of Inhabitation," *Critical Sociology* 41, no. 6 (2015): 898.

THREE

Unmasking Colorblindness in the Law

LESSONS FROM THE FORMATION OF CRITICAL RACE THEORY

Kimberlé Williams Crenshaw

This essay revisits the history of how Critical Race Theory (CRT) emerged as an intellectual response to colorblindness in the context of institutional struggles over the scope of equality and the content of legal education. It exemplifies how in the aftermath of a groundbreaking challenge to the social order, institutional actors from across the political spectrum embraced a gradualist strategy of integration premised on the assumption that color-blind meritocracy stood outside the economy of racial power. The emergence and continuing significance of CRT in relation to colorblind ideology is a reflection of the cross-institutional traveling of resistance, the conditions of possibility that seed insurgent knowledge, and the continuity of these dialectics in the contemporary era.

The multiple and politically inconsistent articulations of colorblindness would seem to challenge the coherence of any narrative in which it was centered. Yet its various articulations across the historical and political terrain give testament both to its endurance and to its generative role as a point of critical interrogation in the rationalization of racial inequality. While celebrated as the ultimate objective of the Civil Rights Movement, its original articulation in constitutional law revealed that formal colorblindness and white supremacy are far less antagonistic to one another than the faithful would otherwise believe.

Portions of this article were originally published as Kimberlé Williams Crenshaw, "Twenty Years of Critical Race Theory: Looking Back to Move Forward," *Connecticut Law Review* 43, no. 5 (July 2011): 1253–352.

Colorblindness is further entrenched by the fact that opponents and true believers are not easily positioned along a conventional liberal/conservative divide. As the struggles over faculty hiring and curricular content would ultimately reveal, colorblindness, in some way or another, carried purchase within liberal, conservative, and radical conceptions of law. Liberals—including academics and powerful allies within the civil rights establishment—would embrace its norms but argue for exceptions in order to diversify institutions that had been historically constituted as white. Conservatives, many of whom once opposed integration and resisted the legitimacy of *Brown v. Board of Education* (1954), eventually changed their rhetorical strategies. Reinterpreting *Brown* as a constitutional commandment imposing colorblindness, conservatives mobilized the landmark case to justify race-blind limits on the scope of race reform. In some ways, colorblindness was also adopted by left-leaning theorists and activists, including some adherents within critical legal studies, a progressive-leaning field of scholarship whose foundation was to challenge the notions of law's neutrality and show how the rule of law was highly politicized to reinforce structures of power. Even within those spaces there were those who resisted the legitimacy of race as a point of departure for any intellectual project or discursive claim.

CRT emerged out of concrete institutional struggles over how these ideological investments would converge in the prevailing battles over the production of legal knowledge. The struggles revealed an ambivalence among mainstream civil rights advocates over the content and contours of the revolt against white supremacy as it moved from lunch counters in the South to elite institutions of the North. The gradualism that so many lawyers had resisted when mobilized by southern elites to defend de jure segregation became a fuzzier target when mobilized in the context of elite academic institutions. De jure and de facto distinctions had been contested by civil rights advocates. They recognized that patterns of segregation and racial power were built not simply on formal rules and "White Only" signs, but also on practices, networks, and other social interactions that predictably reproduced white dominance across the social terrain. Yet something was different when it came to higher education, especially as it pertained to teaching jobs in the legal profession. More pointedly, the civil rights establishment, never fully on board with ethnic studies and other demands from activist students on college campuses, was even less inclined to endorse conceptions of knowledge that contravened basic ideologies about law and legal education. As the controversy exposed a generational and ideological rupture over race and law, it deepened the tension between those who understood "bias" as the touchstone of illegitimate hierarchy and those who spoke the language of power. When it became clear that the debate was less about the pace of reform and more about its substantive content, the conceptual divide among elites and their critics about the relationship between racial power and colorblind merit sharpened.

Those who eventually gravitated to a more critical perspective understood the remedial challenge in terms of dismantling particular regimes of epistemic power. Among those who understood the challenge solely from a vantage point of integrating colored bodies into previously white spaces, the constitutionally permissible use of race to enhance "diversity" was defended as a race-conscious exception to colorblindness. Yet this liberal investment in colorblind merit revealed a contradiction that undercut the most powerful arguments to sustain race-conscious projects within the law and society as a whole. The same proponents who supported "diversity" when it came to students in the classroom argued against any substantive valuation of race in the context of recruiting faculty. This liberal ambivalence would come back to undercut affirmative action, creating a confusing rhetorical agenda that decried the absence of fully integrated professions but failed to interrogate the meritocratic baselines that naturalized this maldistribution of opportunity. The baselines that remained uninterrogated figured prominently in the conservative critique of "reverse discrimination," rendering the remedial exception to colorblindness vulnerable to constitutional assault.

The scope of the conflict, however, extended beyond the more immediate controversy about courses and faculty recruitment. The contestation about the contours of legal education—what it constituted and who was authorized to engage in it—exposed a mode of rationalizing racial dominance that was also being deployed in the courts and across society. The rhetorics of institutional defense that were playing out in legal education were of a piece with judicial rule-making that was actively reversing the momentum toward racial reform.

The struggle about racial power and its relationship to colorblindness helped to clarify exactly what was at stake in both legal education and law more broadly. The sharpening of the conflict not only exposed tensions between the emerging critics and discursive formations that were left, centrist, and conservative, but it also clarified the boundaries between opposition, accommodation, or agnosticism. Critical Race Theory was the embodiment of a race-conscious and justice-oriented intellectual project within and outside the institutional spaces of the discipline.

The first question of "why law?" is seldom asked, notwithstanding the contemporary trajectory of CRT's travels across disciplines. Today, CRT can claim a presence in education,[1] psychology,[2] cultural studies,[3] political science,[4] and even philosophy.[5] The way that CRT is received and mobilized in other disciplines varies, but it is clear that CRT has occupied a space in the canon of recognized intellectual movements that few other race-oriented formations have achieved. Given that many of the basic insights of CRT grew out of other disciplinary traditions, one wonders whether there is a temporal, disciplinary, or institutional explanation from which to understand how and why CRT emerged where and when it did.

The question takes on added significance when one considers the long if disjointed tradition of scholars, students, and other actors setting forth trenchant critiques of how the various disciplines framed and legitimized racial power within the academy and in society at large. W. E. B. Du Bois, for example, critiqued the disciplinary practices of history in his seminal *Black Reconstruction in America*.[6] Sociologist Oliver Cox exposed the whiteness of sociology by the mid-twentieth century.[7] Joyce Ladner delivered yet another salvo against the disciplinary practices of sociology in the 1970s with her provocatively titled collection *The Death of White Sociology*.[8] Robert Guthrie published a scathing critique of psychology in 1998 with *Even the Rat Was White*.[9] More recently, the sociologists Tukufu Zuberi and Eduardo Bonilla-Silva have challenged empirical methodologies.[10] And the incomparable Toni Morrison's *Playing in the Dark* became an instant classic in literary criticism.[11] These and other texts from a variety of fields have contested the terms by which the academy has disciplined knowledge about race. Indeed, critiques of the academy's role in establishing the epistemic foundation and political legitimacy for racial hierarchy have circulated within the academy for years.[12] Although these critiques smoldered, it is perhaps fair to say they never quite caught fire as intellectual movements within their respective disciplines.[13] What was it that ignited CRT as a movement in law? How is it that certain preconditions for a critical intellectual movement actually developed into one? I want to explore these questions through various angles, taking up the possibility that a unique confluence of temporal, institutional, and political factors set the stage out of which CRT emerged.

The question raised herein is one that has been asked of social movements more broadly, particularly the Civil Rights Movement. An important overarching factor that historian Aldon Morris examines is "frame align-ment," the notion that the movement was buoyed and pushed forward by a rhetoric that created a broad consensus on the relevant frame.[14] Through this frame, Morris argued that the Civil Rights Movement was able to overthrow the southern Jim Crow regime because its organized, rational, and successful use of mass nonviolent direct action persuasively shifted previous notions of movements as spontaneous, nonrational, and unstructured. Morris's concept of frame alignment can be used to understand how, why, and when CRT emerged as an intellectual movement, but with nuance that stands the con-cept on its head. One might say that what nourished CRT and facilitated its growth from a collection of institutional and discursive interventions into a sustained intellectual project was a certain dialectical misalignment. Within the context of particular institutional and discursive struggles over the scope of race and racism in the 1980s, significant divergences between allies concerning their descriptive, normative, and political accounts of racial power began to crystallize. This misalignment became evident in a series of encounters—institutional and political—that brought into play a set of "mis-understandings" between a range of individual actors and groups. Although all of the players would have seen themselves as fully embracing the norma-tive commitment to "racial equality," institutional conflicts over issues such as the integration of elite law faculties, the prevailing construction of merit, and the viability of intellectual projects centered on race brought what might have otherwise been viewed as marginal differences between allies into sharp relief. Early CRT was occupied by efforts to create an inventory of these "sharp reliefs," theorizing the tensions between competing frames as well as interrogating the different interventions and rhetorical claims that they pro-duced. This process in turn created the conditions for the emergence of a particular articulation of racial power, one that eschewed the reigning frames that worked to reduce racism to matters of individual prejudice or a by-product of class.

CRT was not, however, simply a product of a philosophical critique of the dominant frames on racial power. It was also a product of activists' engage-ment with the material manifestations of liberal reform. Indeed, one might say that CRT was the offspring of a post–civil rights institutional activism that was generated and informed by an oppositionalist orientation toward racial power. Activists' demands that elite institutions rethink and transform their conceptions of "race neutrality" in the face of functionally exclusionary practices engendered a particularly concrete defense of the status quo. These defenses in turn produced precisely the apologia for institutionalized racial dominance that critics of the dominant thinking on "race relations" had voiced both historically and in more recent struggles over the terms of knowledge production in the academy. These institutional struggles presented postreform critics with the hands-on opportunity to create an affirmative account of racial power and to mark the limits of liberal reform. How the first generation of Race Crits came to understand these limits and to create space to generate a fuller account of racial power in law and society are key dimensions of the CRT story.

This movement dimension of CRT is probably the least engaged aspect of its original formation and perhaps the most at risk in efforts to define, brand, and market CRT. Specifically, the view of CRT as a stable project sometimes denies the extent to which CRT was and continues to be constituted through a series of dynamic engagements situated within specific institutions over the terms by which their racial logics would be engaged. Thus, what is in play here is less of a definitive articulation of CRT and more of a sociocultural narrative of CRT.[15] CRT is not so much an intellectual unit filled with natural stuff—theories, themes, practices, and the like—but one that is dynamically constituted by a series of contestations and convergences pertaining to the ways that racial power is understood and articulated in the post–civil rights era. In the same way that Kendall Thomas reasoned that race was better thought of as a verb than a noun,[16] I want to suggest that shifting the frame of CRT toward a dynamic rather than static reference would be a productive means by which we can link CRT's past to the contemporary moment.

So, was there something special about law as a discursive field that made it a particularly fertile ground for the synthesis of the ideas that would become "critical race theory"? As I will argue, I think the answer is a qualified "yes." In short, the key feature of the story rests not on the uniqueness of the critiques themselves, but on the rapid unraveling of liberal reform and the rule of law as guarantor of racial progress.

MOVEMENT ORIGINS AND POLITICAL FORMATION

In the summer of 1989, twenty-four faculty of color answered a call to attend a "New Developments in CRT" workshop at the University of Wisconsin. Meeting oddly enough in a convent, they all had agreed to submit something written as a ticket for admission. It was not at all clear, however, that this would be an event worth lining up to attend. After all, the title was a bit misleading. The "New Developments in CRT" was premised on the assumption that there was already something old. But prior to the moment that the invitation was drafted, there really was no CRT as such. The name was made up by this author. It represented more of a possibility than a definitive project.[17] Although the terms did make sense in light of the group's aspirations, the billing suggested that there was a "there there" that wasn't really there yet.

The committee that sent that letter and the invitees whom they solicited represented a motley crew of minority scholars who populated the backdoor speakeasies at the American Association of Law Schools (AALS) and Critical Legal Studies (CLS) annual gatherings. These speakeasies were usually hotel rooms and other small enclaves where a certain cohort congregated, drawn by word of mouth, to discuss the events and dynamics transpiring on the main stage. The group might be described as intellectual nomads, folks who were attracted to both liberal antidiscrimination and Critical Legal Theory discourses at a time when the two traditions were connected only at the margins. The organizers had all gravitated in some way or another toward the environs of CLS: among them was an Asian American law professor who had attended the very first CLS conference about a decade earlier, and three others who had first approached CLS as students at Harvard Law School during the late 1970s and 1980s. That group was, respectively, Neil Gotanda, Stephanie Phillips, Terri Miller, and this author. Joining this group were Richard Delgado and, later, Linda Greene, both linked to the project through earlier integration struggles at Harvard, and who were by then professors at the host site, Wisconsin Law School.

We were all veterans, in one way or another, of particular institutional conflicts over the nature of colorblind space in American law schools. Among the twenty-four participants who attended the first workshop, fully a third had been directly involved in a protracted and very public protest over race, curriculum, and faculty hiring at Harvard Law School six years earlier.[18] Adding to that number were several others who had gravitated toward CLS conferences and summer camps, attracted by its critical stance against hierarchy, but often frustrated by the currency of arguments that cast doubt on the viability of race as a unit of analysis or the utility of race consciousness in deconstructing hierarchy. The workshop was, metaphorically speaking, a clearing at which we had arrived, each bearing something of a travelogue of a journey through the uncharted terrain of the post–civil rights landscape. Partly because of our struggles within liberal environments like law schools and within radical environments like CLS, we sought like-minded souls who wanted to begin the conversation beyond the points where we so often got stuck. We did not know exactly where the project would go, but we did know that we wanted to move beyond the noncritical liberalism that often cabined civil rights discourses and a nonracial radicalism that was a line of debate within CLS.

This gathering was thus underwritten by specific institutional and organizational struggles over how racial power would be articulated in a post–civil rights America. There were by this time many fights, both within the academy and in society at large, over how far and to what ends the aftershocks of white supremacy's formal collapse would travel. These tensions were evident in struggles ranging from the raw contestations over schools and public resources in the public sphere to the more refined debates about "diversity" in the walled-off worlds of the nation's editorial rooms and faculty lounges. Among the many tremors at the fault lines of race reform and retrenchment were contestations that stand out as defining moments because of their unique role in both synthesizing the multiple strains of racial politics of that moment, and serving as a point of departure for series of related events. The eruption that served as a point of departure in CRT's trajectory was the institutional struggle over race, pedagogy, and affirmative action at America's elite law schools.

SETTING THE STAGE OF AN ALTERNATIVE COURSE

The time was 1982. The setting was Dean James Vorenberg's office at Harvard Law School. Dean Vorenberg, a man with solid civil rights credentials, and longtime member of the NAACP's Legal Defense Fund's (LDF) National Board of Directors,[19] sat face-to-face with a small delegation representing Harvard's Black Law Student Association (BLSA). Years had passed since the Civil Rights Movement brought down the "White Only" signs across America's formally segregated institutions. Any remaining battles over segregation and white supremacy seemed worlds away from the genteel environs of Harvard Law School. The ship that the dean captained had sailed smoothly through the unrest that had disrupted other institutions, and there was no immediate reason to assume that anything but calm seas lay ahead. The dean had one problem though: the school over which he presided had a faculty of more than sixty, yet only one tenured faculty member was a person of color.[20]

The virtual shutout of people of color had not always been quite so extreme at Harvard. The school had suffered a 100 percent reduction in its tenured minority faculty when Derrick Bell left the school the preceding spring, frustrated that the school had not managed to hire additional people of color.[21] Regrettably, from the school's perspective, the pool of minority candidates who were qualified to join the Harvard club was just too shallow to pluck out minority professors on demand. The dean had his eye on a couple of potential candidates, but recruiting these few highly successful lawyers was a long-term strategy at best. The dilemma was simply put: those who were able were not willing, and apparently those who were willing were not able.[22] Gradualism was thus dictated by the circumstance. The dismal number of minority faculty would eventually increase as the growing number of elite law graduates acquired the requisite credentials to compete for positions at Harvard and other elite law schools.

Across from the dean sat several students who, like him, also had a problem. Many had come to the law school in hopes of pursuing careers in social justice advocacy, a trajectory that was in keeping with their histories of community activism and social protest. Some had also been exposed to ethnic studies and other disciplines in which the basic premises of institutional authority were open to critique, especially in contexts in which racial marginality seemed at play. They had hoped to resume such studies in Derrick Bell's courses, especially Constitutional Law and Minority Issues. From the students' perspective, then, Bell's departure left the school with gaping holes in the curriculum.[23] Constitutional Law and Minority Issues, for one, had simply been dropped from the curriculum, and efforts to encourage the school to offer the course and to recruit scholars of color to fill this and other curricular gaps had gained little traction.[24]

As the students saw it, the course was an essential component of a basic legal education that Harvard was failing to deliver.[25] Equally urgent for the students was the dearth of minority law professors at the school and the inadequate attention given to the legal problems facing racial minorities more broadly. For the students, the problems were linked: greater minority representation on the faculty would likely increase the attention to a range of issues that were currently marginal in the school's curriculum.[26]

Moreover, as students entering into a profession in which race was likely to play a significant role in their career trajectories, exposure to lawyers who not only had acquired legal expertise in fighting racism but who had also experienced its dynamics individually and institutionally was a critical component of any meaningful preparation for the careers they hoped to pursue.[27] The students thus urged the dean to schedule the course and to use the search for someone to teach it as an initial step in recruiting full-time professors to integrate the law school.

As they faced each other, it was apparent that the dean had a real dilemma on his hands. The students were clearly articulate, comfortable, and confident. The dean could at least be satisfied that Harvard was creating a strong cohort of minority students primed for entry into the corporate machinery of America. With the brass ring so close at hand, surely these students could be captured by basic reason. The truth of the matter was that the course they sought quite simply was not part of the core mission of the law school and there was no sense of urgency to staff it. More importantly, given the perpetual "pool problem," very few people of color were qualified to teach at Harvard Law School. Those were the basic facts as Dean Vorenberg saw them. But given that they were law students, perhaps he mused that it would be far more effective to lead them to these conclusions through Socratic dialogue rather than to declare these facts outright. Thus inspired, he methodically interrogated the group at the conclusion of their presentation with a series of lawyerly challenges. He began his curricular inquiry by asking what was "so special" about a course on constitutional law and minority issues that it could not be learned through the basic course in constitutional law in combination with perhaps a placement in legal services.[28] On the question of recruitment, the dean parried with a reference to a white civil rights attorney and queried, "Wouldn't you prefer an excellent white professor over a mediocre Black one?"[29]

For a moment, both the students and the dean sat in silence as the students tried to make sense of what had just happened. The dean may well have taken the students' momentary speechlessness to signal that his point had struck a chord, but he would have been wrong. It was merely the calm before the storm.

The dean's Socratic efforts notwithstanding, all hell broke loose at Harvard Law School. Over the next two years, Harvard would become the scene of acrimony unlike any time since the student takeovers during the Vietnam War. The long, carpeted halls with conspicuous "Quiet" signs would be taken over by chanting students; the sacred faculty library would be invaded by a sea of "Desegregate Now!" t-shirts; and even the dean's inner sanctum would suffer the indignity of students standing on his desk. Worse still for an elite institution where even a hiccup finds its way into the mainstream press, this embarrassing "scene" would be broadcast for the entire nation to witness. The students were acting out, it seemed, and the spark seemed to be a battle over an obscure course and the departure of one African American professor.

The dean surely would have had no reason to predict that his conversation with students would spin so far outside the walls of Harvard Law School. First, he clearly had the upper hand in framing the debate. The dominant discourse on race and merit at the time was completely consistent with the notion that the standards for entry into law teaching were indeed colorblind, and that the so-called pool problem was simply the unfortunate consequence of meritocratic and fully defensible academic standards.[30] Few scholars and advocates questioned the blanket assertion of a null set of qualified minority law professors.[31] Given how shallow the pool was, the absence of minority law professors at elite institutions such as Harvard failed to trigger a serious internal dialogue about the possibility of unfair exclusion.[32]

If the school's institutional reliance on qualifications and merit was not enough to naturalize the nearly complete absence of minority law professors in the building, then no doubt the fact that the winds of racial retrenchment were beginning to blow in the direction of less rather than more "diversity" would have reinforced the conclusion that Harvard risked little in refusing to compromise its standards in order to increase the number of minority faculty. Institutions like Harvard had never been viewed as the bastions of discrimination like other law schools that were on the frontlines in the segregation wars.[33] In fact, by that point in time, Harvard typically enrolled a large class of students of color, a fact that demonstrated to some its willingness to bend the rules of meritocracy enough to diversify its student body.[34]

Notwithstanding its robust policies to advance student diversity, the school drew a line in the sand when it came to faculty, maintaining a firm commitment to "merit."[35] Yet as the students saw things, there was nothing magical or intrinsically compelling about the typical standards offered to justify the virtual absence of faculty of color. A degree from an elite law school, membership on a law review, and a Supreme Court clerkship were not the exclusive criteria for identifying candidates who were likely to make substantial contributions both to the educational mission of the school and to the broader goals of advancing legal knowledge. Instead, the traditional criteria were increasingly viewed as an informal and unjustified preference for the social cohort to whom these opportunities were overwhelmingly distributed: white and male candidates.[36] This perception was reinforced when the law school hired ten white males in the midst of the escalating crisis over hiring and curricular reform.

While standing firm in resisting the students' affirmative action demands, the school apparently conceded that Harvard's failure to teach any discrimination course at all was untenable. Thus, at the very end of the spring term and in the midst of the fallout over the all-white, all-male hires, the dean finally announced that a three-week minicourse on civil rights litigation would be offered in the January intersession.[37] Although the offering came in response to student demand for Bell's course, the staffing of the course would not provide an avenue for integrating professors of color into the full-time faculty at Harvard. Instead, the minicourse would be taught by two respected and very busy civil rights lawyers—Julius Chambers, a well-known civil rights attorney, and Jack Greenberg, executive director of the NAACP-LDF.[38]

The students rejected the dean's resolution as an inadequate response on a number of fronts.[39] First and foremost, the recruitment of two civil rights lawyers for a three-week course did nothing to desegregate Harvard's faculty, but instead merely confirmed the dean's provocative framing of the pool problem. As Derrick Bell subsequently argued, many students may have agreed that an "excellent white" was preferable to a "mediocre Black," but they decisively repudiated the implicit message that none of the thirty law professors whose names were forwarded to the dean were sufficiently qualified to be lifted out of the ghetto of mediocrity.[40]

On the curricular front, the students were utterly dissatisfied with both the length and scope of the course. A three-week minicourse did not provide the sustained consideration of the issues the students had hoped to address, nor did packing the entire treatment into a concentrated and exclusive time slot provide a wide enough footprint to thoroughly engage and integrate the lessons of the course into their learning and advocacy. Bell's course had invited students into a semester-long exploration of the subject matter, and the students were not prepared to settle for anything less.

This objection led somewhat naturally into a more substantive one: the course that the dean offered and the course that the students sought were simply not the same. While civil rights litigation was indeed an important addition to the curriculum, it was no substitute for an analysis of how law helped constitute the very racial structure that antidiscrimination law aimed to regulate.

The students' insistence on hiring faculty who had lived the life they would teach about was ostensibly framed as a demand for role models, but on a more fundamental level it raised epistemological questions about "perspective" that would constitute central themes in the subsequent articulation of CRT.[41] Some critics of the students understood these demands to be contrary to the notion that knowledge is objectively discoverable apart from the self, and thus they argued that the demand for a professor of color to teach the course was intellectually flawed.

Perhaps surprisingly, commentators who considered themselves civil rights traditionalists weighed in—not to critique the law school's failure to rethink its reliance on exclusionary practices but to critique the law students for reintroducing race as a criterion of merit. Reflected in their failure to question whether the criteria were functionally fair and race neutral was a narrow understanding of the institutional arrangements that were destined to reproduce racially disparate outcomes. BLSA, La Alianza, American Indian Law Students, Asian Law Students Association, and Arab Law Students collectively, as the Third World Coalition (TWC), argued that the standard, and arguably arbitrary, criteria that the law school endorsed— attendance at elite law schools, admission to the law review, and clerkships for a prestigious judge—were grossly maldistributed along racial lines. It was entirely unsurprising that candidates of color would not readily emerge from a pool they had largely been prohibited from entering.

What was predictable was that that "pool problem" would be readily accepted outside Harvard's walls without a serious interrogation of how and to what ends the pool was constituted. Absent in the public discourse was any caution against relying on the same processes for defining merit that helped to create the nearly all-white law school in the first place. In the aftermath of what was, in some sense, a social revolution against the previous racial order, it might be expected that a critical review of the practices and institutional values that had made the institution virtually all white before the collapse of white supremacy would have been more than appropriate. But Harvard administrators adopted an evolutionary approach to pool-watching. Their commitment to integrating the faculty was realized by remaining ever vigilant to see what unlikely candidates might crawl out of the pool rather than rethinking the fundamental question of how the pool was populated in the first place.

Part of that reluctance to rethink criteria for faculty recruitment was premised on a firm conviction about what the school did and did not do, a conviction that seemed to change little in the face of the social transformation that the Civil Rights Movement had underwritten. The very fact that there were no standard courses on discrimination, immigration, Indian law, and women and the law well into the 1980s indicated how sluggish legal education had been to address the seismic shifts that had taken place in the preceding decades. The fact that law was a major site of contestation around these issues, yet they remained marginal within legal education, only underscored how deeply elite legal training was tied to intellectual regimes that rewarded continuity with a troubled past rather than innovative thinking about new legal issues and constituencies. This preference, reflected in the administration's specialized vision of elite education, changed relatively little as the school began to recruit growing numbers of students from historically underrepresented groups. Nontraditional students—Black, Latino, Asian, and Native American students, female students, students interested in legal aid/legal services, and others—organized to pressure the school to think beyond the limited menu of educational options that failed to address the social transformation that had prompted many of them to study law in the first place.

Their expectations were not groundless. There was reason to think that in the context of a new social regime, Harvard might thoroughly reevaluate the content of the curriculum and the new communities and values it might serve. After all, as noted above, the school was far from a bastion of conservative resistance to integration; it had stepped up its recruiting of minority students in the 1970s, and some of its faculty were engaged in efforts to bring about social change elsewhere. The dean himself was on the board of the premier civil rights litigation organization, the Legal Defense Fund. Yet underlying the school's inability to think beyond the pool problem was a failure to bring these commitments inside the institution's everyday practices and norms, a failure to reevaluate the givens and nonnegotiables with an eye toward rethinking those dimensions of law school practice that were forged in, consistent with, and facilitated by formalized inequality.

It was at least remotely possible to imagine that aspects of legal education that had easily coexisted with and even normalized racial subordination might be reviewed with a skeptical eye whether or not the institution itself formally practiced segregation. The wholesale failure to consider the interests of underserved communities, the failure to interrogate the gaping contradictions between the formal commitment to the rule of law and the realities of racial dictatorship through much of the nation's history, the failure to reward innovative legal theories or to explore the reformist potential of legal advocacy—all these features of pre–civil rights elite legal education might have been viewed from a position of skepticism given their collaborative role in normalizing broadscale societal stratification. That "excellence" and "merit" could be attached to legal thinking that consistently failed to take up some of the most complex legal problems in society was troubling enough during segregation's tenure, but to effortlessly reproduce these values in a postsegregation world seemed to undermine rather than enhance the claims of social progress.

Obviously, a different conception of the interests and constituencies that the law school would serve would have created a different "pool" of people qualified to teach there. The school, however, was stubbornly attached to its traditional view of merit and its particular mission. Its insistence on viewing the crisis through the prism of the pool was a repudiation of the students' larger demands that it rethink its foundational assumptions about how to prepare a new generation of students for the careers that they there were planning to pursue. Indeed, the law school's commitment to preparing students for elite service in America's corporate apparatus was sometimes defended by faculty as a badge of personal honor. For instance, in one of several student-faculty fora on faculty integration, students demanded that the school revise its curriculum to offer more in the field of legal aid/legal services. A distinguished faculty member analogized such demands to asking the men at Massachusetts Institute of Technology to teach students how to fix toasters.[42]

All together, these themes established the parameters of the conflict between liberal notions of discrimination, framed around bias and colorblindness, and an emerging sensibility that comprehended such problems in terms of institutionalized racial power. If bias and discrimination constituted the lingua franca of liberal conceptions of the race problem, then objectivity and colorblindness were its natural—if not immediate—goals. Liberals and conservatives may have disagreed about the scope and defensibility of exceptions to this conception of equality, and as the case at Harvard shows, even liberals might draw lines differently depending on the context (for example, student admissions versus faculty recruitment). At the end, they shared a notion that a world free of race "bias" constituted the promised land rather than any substantive measure of racial participation in institutions across the social terrain. Colorblind merit was thus presumptively race neutral, and it was the students' demand for an affirmative effort to recruit and hire professors of color at Harvard that was framed as discriminatory.

As events unfolded, it became apparent that the struggle was not solely between the students and the administration, but between the students and the media as well. The media's framing of the controversy was not simply a product of sloppy reporting, but a marker of the preexisting tropes in mainstream civil rights discourse that were readily mobilized to narrate the students' race consciousness as racism pure and simple. The protest was initially framed by Dean Vorenberg in a letter informing the student community about the new course and the fact that BLSA and the TWC were boycotting it. Framing the students' response to the school's failure to recruit a full-time minority scholar to teach the course, the dean put the matter thus: "To boycott a course on racial discrimination because part of it is taught by a white lawyer, is wrong in principle and works against, not for, shared goals of racial and social justice."[43] The frame of reverse discrimination, intimated in the dean's letter, became increasingly shrill as the media amplified the story.[44] The progression began with stories that highlighted race as the primary but not exclusive reason for the students' boycott and soon dispensed with the underlying battle over integration altogether. Pundits—including civil rights luminaries—joined the chorus of critics to declare the student actions to be racist, pure and simple.[45]

Despite the students' disappointment over the dean's response and the subsequent conflation of a complex political contestation into a simple narrative of reverse discrimination, this sequence of events proved to be enormously meaningful in the development of the intellectual project that the controversy helped spawn. Specifically, the dean's decision and the narrowed parameters in which the ensuing controversy was framed helped to sharpen awareness of how conceptions such as colorblind merit operated to obscure the continuing patterns of racial power in presumptively race-neutral institutions. It also set in motion a chain of events that would provide fertile ground for the emergence of CRT.

In the early 1980s, the codes by which the gradual retrenchment of race reform would be articulated were not easily decipherable. It was clear that the pace of reform had slowed, and ominous clouds were gathering. While *Regents of University of California v. Bakke* (1978) effectively took racial justice off the table as the foundation for affirmative action, diversity emerged as the vehicle that would effectively integrate people of color into institutions from which they had been excluded. Hope thus prevailed within the civil rights community that significant victories could still be squeezed out of a receding reformist agenda. Yet entire bastions of entrenched racial power were rendered off-limits, clothed in the magical discourse of "merit" and "qualification." Like the scene in *The Wizard of Oz* where the omnipotent voice warns, "Pay no attention to the man behind the curtain," meritocratic discourse often blinded racial justice constituencies to its role as a mechanism of racial power. Thus it might have remained were it not for the dean's artless juxtaposition of the mediocre Black professor against the excellent white professor, and his challenge to students to recite what they might have learned had the very course that lay at the center of the controversy been offered.

The "Toto" that pulled the curtain to reveal the racial dynamics of this purportedly race-neutral claim was the Alternative Course, organized by the TWC to present an "affirmative vision of what a course which purports to address the needs of their communities can and should be."[46] The Alternative Course brought together the representational and substantive demands of the students in a vehicle that illustrated the twin goals of recruiting minority professors who were not merely "duplicates" of current faculty members and amplifying their deepening critique of American legal education. Countering the orientation of traditional legal education, the course would advance a concept of law as fundamentally political, not a set of abstract, neutral principles about which one can have purely "technical" expertise divorced from one's social and political views and values. The latter image of the law is the one upon which the status and prestige of Harvard's faculty (as all other law faculties) is built; it is also the image that legitimizes the American legal system's consistent perpetration of injustices against people of color— which is the more important reason for the Third World Coalition's rejection of it.[47]

Within this framework, the law would not be taken for granted as a technocratic institutional discourse in which lawyerly competence was being developed. Instead, the course would diverge from traditional offerings in the area by placing litigation-oriented strategies in conversation with the broader political and social struggles of racially defined communities. Organizers similarly promised that the course would explore "how racism touches peoples that are both unified by their status as minority groups and diverse in their interests and goals."[48] This signaled not only an interest in exploring race outside the context of the Civil Rights Movement, but also a commitment to interrogate the legal infrastructure of foreign policy that touched the lives of Third World people around the world. The Alternative Course thus set the stage for a broader inquiry into the relationship between race and law, and for a critical interrogation of traditional legal education more broadly. These themes would be taken up and further developed by Critical Race Theorists.

From the TWC perspective, the course was a stunning success. It drew more than one hundred participants and provided students with frameworks to understand and articulate the complex context of the current institutional struggle and its relationship to broader dynamics pertaining to race and law. Not only did the Alternative Course make the effects of the gate-keeping real (the illustrative cover on our booklet featured Harvard law professors piling desks and bookshelves against people of color pushing in from the outside), the course also provided the opportunity for a cohort of existing and future race scholars to become collectively immersed in a developing canon of critical discourses and scholarly texts.

The long-term traction the course generated was partly grounded in the collective engagement with particular texts that became part of the CRT canon. Central among them was the principal textbook for the course, *Race, Racism, and American Law* by Derrick Bell.[49] The textbook and Bell's overall product were especially important in setting the foundation upon which CRT was built. Bell's scholarship encouraged an emerging cohort of critical thinkers to place race at the center of scholarly inquiry, a license that had not yet been granted by the legal academy.

Along with Bell's foundational text, the course was informed by other works that eventually became part of the CRT canon, such as Richard Delgado's "The Imperial Scholar"[50] and an early iteration of Charles Lawrence's "The Id, the Ego, and Equal Protection: Reckoning with Unconscious Racism."[51]

Delgado had shaken up the constitutional law establishment by framing their internal conversations about race as imperialistic and white, conducted as though scholars of color had made no contributions to the discourse that merited engagement.[52] Denise Carty-Bennia, one of the first female African American law professors, provided a compelling vision of the rhetorical politics surrounding minority scholarship that circulated within the legal professoriate. In both her presentation in the course and her advice "off-line,"

Carty-Bennia decoded the various "raps" on minority scholarship that framed the work as nontraditional (which much of it was) and presumptively disqualifying (which was the crux of the debate).

For young scholars, Bell, Delgado, Lawrence, and Carty-Bennia modeled an orientation toward race work that transcended then-current paradigms in search of new discourses and possibilities. Their articulation of such critical frames within the traditional parameters of legal education linked up with the academic and activist traditions out of which many students in the Third World Coalition emerged. These formative engagements reinforced the possibility that race projects need not be contained and constrained by conventional expectations and that, indeed, the authorized points of departure in legal analysis often imported with them a rationalizing orientation toward racial domination rather than a critical one. This intimate exposure to groundbreaking scholarship reinforced and deepened a sense that a new and more integrated sensibility was emerging, one in which the regulatory frames of "race relations" and "racial prejudice" were being overwritten by the mutually constitutive frames of law and racial power.

The terms of the institutional conflict between the students and the administration were relatively easy to comprehend, but the conflict between the students and those members of the civil rights "old guard" who denounced the boycott reflects an important "misalignment" out of which CRT emerged. From the vantage point of the civil rights establishment, it was possible to frame the controversy as an intergenerational conflict between cool strategic reformism versus hot-headed youthful posturing. In this telling, the controversy boiled down to basic differences between those who favored a lawyerly stance of deliberate, reasoned demands, backed up when necessary by litigation, and those who were more interested in elevating and interrogating race and racism as an ideological project. At the most reductionist level, the tension was framed in terms of a certain pragmatism, a notion of learning the game in order to play the game, versus an identity-driven performance of racial pride, a posturing that was reckless, immature, and ultimately counterproductive. The former vision was the hallmark of orderly integration, best achieved through the selection of students who would master the institutional expectations of the rarified environment to which they had gained access and careful management of their racial particularities so as to affirm the possibility of a fully assimilated future. What Harvard students had done had triggered the nightmarish alternative that the old guard's hard work and sacrifice would turn to naught through the "bad behavior" of irresponsible youth demanding unreasonable accommodation to their special needs.[53]

The controversy revealed a realm of racial power that lay outside the regulatory boundaries of antidiscrimination law and the broader liberal repertoire on race. This "remainder" of racial power was located not at the margins of traditional forms of racial subordination but in some ways at the very center of liberal institutions that were otherwise lined up in favor of "racial reform." Within this recognition lay a font of contradictions and unrecognized convergences. For example, although liberals and conservatives tended to differ in their support of "affirmative action," there was less daylight between them on their fundamental commitment to notions of merit. While liberals may have differed with conservatives on whether these notions should be modestly revised to advance the pace of change, they were in some senses closer to each other than they were to the emerging cohort of racial justice advocates who contested the very terms on which "merit" was defined. For critics, framing such criteria as "objective" merely sanitized the racial power that was at play in determining what counted, whose interests would be privileged, and what mechanisms would serve them.

A different institutional history—one in which the legal facilitation of Jim Crow would have been recognized as one of the most significant legal problems of the twentieth century—would have widened the parameters of its institutional mission, thus inviting an alternative baseline for defining merit. This broader sense of the relevance of race would have challenged the "off-limits" question about whether and how experience shapes intellectual work and whether race should matter or simply be regarded as an unfortunate fact of social life that would eventually just "wither away." This wider prism reflected the idea that no institution was untouched by racial power.

Merit, therefore, couldn't be interrogated without attending to its social construction, and social construction could not in turn render social identity meaningless. In sum, one could not sustain an argument for affirmative action against the reverse discrimination/lowering standards line without at the same time addressing the racial preferences built into the existing standards. Liberal defenders of affirmative action seemed caught in the contradiction of defending a race-blind notion of merit alongside a color-conscious departure from it. This contradiction was the Achilles' heel of affirmative action advocacy that would weaken the rationale for such programs as the attack on affirmative action metastasized into a full-on assault by conservatives.

Why did CRT emerge out of law, and not some other discipline where similar pressures were percolating? CRT came to life in the cracks between alignment and misalignment with liberals and the civil rights establishment, as reflected in the struggle over faculty hiring, and also in relation to the progressive left in legal education—Critical Legal Studies. Early Race Crits were thus situated in a dialectical loop, attracted to and repelled by certain elements of liberal civil rights discourses, and at the same time, attracted to and repelled by certain discursive elements within CLS. CRT grew as a repertoire of discursive moves and projects that marked specific engagements over race in both liberal and radical spaces. Emerging from the anteroom of both discourses, the CRT workshop became the drawing room where the further development of these ideas took place.[54]

The opportunity to occupy a dedicated collaborative space finally came when a critical mass of minority scholars who had been active in CLS came together for an extended time period at the University of Wisconsin. CLS veterans Stephanie Phillips, Terri Miller, Neil Gotanda, and this author joined with the recently hired Richard Delgado to form an organizing committee to plan a convening initially titled "New Developments in Minority Scholarship."[55] David Trubek, at the time director of the Institute for Legal Studies at Wisconsin and a cofounder of CLS, was amenable to the proposal and agreed to provide institutional support for a four-day summer retreat. With the alignment of a working concept and institutional resources, the first CRT workshop became a reality.[56]

How, then, did we arrive at a convent with the twenty-four people who attended the first CRT workshop?[57] First, we reached out to the usual suspects—the folks who had organized and been key players in the unfolding discourse on race within CLS. Added to this core group was another set of scholars who occasionally turned up at CLS events, and a slightly larger group of scholars whose scholarship suggested an ideological and epistemological relation to the project. To identify others, we asked a question that by today's lights seems almost incomprehensible, namely, which scholars were demonstrably open to engaging a race project that was left of the liberal center? Some characters we knew personally, and others we simply cold-called after reading their work.

We borrowed a lot of different strategies to create the workshop. This author had traveled with CLS to Germany and returned with ideas about how to facilitate a certain kind of intellectual exchange designed to draw out specific connections and common themes among potentially congruent projects. Also influential were Martha Fineman's feminist workshops that sought to develop a methodology oriented toward building the field of feminist legal theory. As organizers, we wanted to get beyond the standard conference model of participants presenting their current works-in-progress. The point was to identify common threads that ran through all of the work and to synthesize those into a mosaic of ideas that would constitute an initial mapping of CRT. Recognizing that authors may be too close to their work to make such links themselves, we assigned others the task of presenting the argument and integrating the various themes into a broader frame. This strategy produced three different levels of analysis for any given work that in turn broadened the content that was available to synthesize into a whole. Not only did the participants receive direct feedback on their conceptualization and methodologies, but as a group we were able to link our projects together within an emerging ideological frame. The project thus grew into its name: Critical Race Theory.

It might be easy to underestimate the learning process and group negotiation that engaged the early participants in CRT. Forging connections into something greater than the sum of its parts involved exceptional labor, intellectual creativity, and considerable patience. In our second workshop, for example, it was clear that there was a critical, theoretical backdrop that some participants had mastered and that others wanted to learn.[58] Patricia Williams and Kendall Thomas created seminars with titles such as Liberalism and Its Critics; Poststructuralism and the Concept of Race; Race and Political Economy; and Intellectuals, Race, and Power. The topics of our sessions reveal our efforts to become conversant with a large set of critical texts and a range of analytical tools. We became students of each other and learned to respond to, and sometimes fight against, the concepts that were being mobilized to discipline or deflate the CRT project.[59]

REASSESSING THE CONDITIONS OF POSSIBILITY FOR CRT'S FORMATION

These were the formative years of CRT, a period of uncertainty, excitement, and contestation. There are, of course, other important chapters to be told about the CRT workshops, including the emergence of internal debates concerning the intersections of race with other systems of oppression; struggles over substance or identity in defining the parameters of participation; debates about the role of whites in the project; tensions about the politics and scope of the "white over black paradigm"; and questions about whether subsequent formations such as LatCrit or QueerCrit are turns, spinoffs, or splinterings of CRT. While a fuller exploration of these developments is outside the scope of this essay, it is important to note that these are ongoing debates with new chapters still to be written. The principal inquiry in this chapter highlights its key conditions of possibility in relationship to the dominant parameters in the discipline, specifically, its institutional, temporal, and epistemological dimensions.

Institutional Infrastructure

As noted above, many of the critiques of racial power that were amplified and integrated within CRT had been generated by leading race scholars for nearly a century.[60] Yet this history of critical race critiques outside law actually heightens the question of why the CRT movement emerged in law. First, although the tradition of critical thinking about race was alive for decades, numerous factors clearly suppressed the viability of a collective project organized around counterdisciplinary practices within the established disciplines. The small number of racial minorities in the academy also militated against any organized contestation at any level, but more tellingly, the consequences of foregrounding conceptions of race that were at odds with prevailing thinking were tragically debilitating for academics of color.[61] Even intellectual giants like Du Bois were stymied by rank racial gatekeeping within an academic power structure that tightly regulated the boundaries of disciplinary inquiry.[62] When Black and Ethnic Studies programs finally did become a force, it was through transcending traditional disciplinary boundaries rather than by setting up house within the confines of any specific discipline.[63] Given the transdisciplinary nature of Ethnic Studies—certainly a condition of its possibility—the emergence CRT in one of the more conservative disciplines is all the more interesting.

Unlikely as it initially seems, it is the particularly conservative character of the legal discipline that allowed a series of counterdisciplinary projects to be spawned, thus creating a possibility for CRT. The possibilities that a radical race project would emerge within a conservative discipline such as law were bolstered by the fact that the discipline had already been challenged by a series of critiques over its foundational claims. Well-respected scholars from elite institutions had famously set about the project of deconstructing core legitimizing principles, setting in motion a genealogy of critical engagement that included Legal Realism, the Law and Society movement, and eventually Critical Legal Studies. It is not exactly a straight line, ideologically speaking, and the underdeveloped engagement with race in each of these projects hints at their limitations; but the presence of organized, dissenting voices not only created cracks in the façade of law, but also established institutional beach-heads upon which subsequent mobilizations could be launched.

Casting the genealogy in this direction does not suggest that there was a critical race sensibility hidden in the DNA of these projects that naturally evolved into CRT. Yet what this history of disciplinary contestation did provide was discursive spaces—both organizational and institutional—in which these sensibilities would be articulated and further refined in the context of law. Race discourse was a "moving target" in the 1980s. The courts, the public arena, our law schools, and colleagues in CLS provided a constant flow of texts against which our developing critiques were pitched. We were both inside and outside the communities we were struggling alongside and against, trying to theorize what we were living with and embattled within. These engagements highlighted the ways in which shared frames helped define and normalize various dimensions of CRT while various misalignments helped fine-tune its contours.[64]

Temporal Opportunity

An equally important factor in the emergence of CRT was the gravitational force of the centrist projects of liberal legalism that were unfolding in the 1980s. As I have set forth above, when CRT came into existence, the spirit of insurgency still hung in the air. Sociologists might call this a period of continuously rising expectations. Affirmative action was still permissible. Racism remained speakable. Few people had ever heard of Clarence Thomas. Yet the consequences of the civil rights retreat and the limited scope of racial reform were becoming increasingly apparent.

The ideological terms upon which this slowed course of legalized reform would be rationalized were being hashed out at the same time that the unrest that rocked the university system in the late 1960s and 1970s was shaping the experiences and expectations of a new generation of students in American colleges and universities. This new cohort included activist students of color emerging from academic programs and community-organizing campaigns with intellectual and political sensibilities that were at odds with the status quo–oriented logics of mainstream institutions.

Many of the students and young faculty entering legal education in the late 1970s and early 1980s shared not only a common background in student and community activism, but also an orientation toward racial power and inequality shaped by Ethnic Studies programs that the generation before them struggled to establish. Beyond the earlier battles over mere entry into white institutions, struggles over the terms of knowledge production had become a new frontier in the academic debates on racial justice.

Legal education attracted many of these students who had come of age in the years after the Civil Rights Movement. Law students in this cohort entered academia with the notion that sit-ins and other modes of protest were appropriate avenues of action to challenge the foot dragging of recalcitrant institutions. Those who cut their activist and intellectual teeth in the universities of the 1970s and early 1980s emerged from these experiences with histories of contesting the institutional terms of higher education through direct action as well as through intellectual critique.

Given the unraveling of the reformist movement that would soon be in full swing as the Reagan courts came online, entry into law schools at this point was somewhat akin to being in the officers' club in a war zone. As the process of retrenchment gathered speed in the courts, the rationalizing dimension of legal discourse became especially visible in law schools. Battles were raging just over the wall, it seemed, but the business at hand was to achieve technocratic competence in manipulating legal rules. This in turn required shuttering the mind to pretty much everything that the activist cohort had learned.[65] Exposure to these routinized dimensions of legal training not only pointed to the self-referential and, in some ways, bankrupt notions of merit; they also revealed how the discipline of law underwrote a highly contestable status quo.

The Politics of Law

What remains to be added to this temporal explanation is what precisely it was about law that proved to be an exceptionally fertile medium for this kind of project to take root. Of course, law is not the only discipline that shores up racial hierarchy. Other disciplines certainly contribute epistemic authority to the naturalized structures of thought and action that constitute racial hierarchy. However, at least during the 1980s, law seemed to be on the frontlines of retrenchment, in part because the relationship between losing a legal battle and suffering a particular material loss was readily visible. While other disciplines do enable racial power, the connections between disciplines such as sociology, political science, and philosophy, and the social practices they authorize appear to be far more attenuated. No sophisticated theory is needed to see law operating to constitute and insulate racial hierarchies in American society.

Students and faculty of color entering this arena were thus drawn to challenging the institutional practices of legal education that in their view generated the narrow conceptions of discrimination and equality that underwrote the retrenchment. While it was certainly true that by this time the frontlines of the conservative pushback were in the courts, the White House, and Congress, the terms under which the rollback of civil rights was legally rationalized implicated legal education's own limitations. While law was far from the only discipline contributing to the narrowed possibility of reforms, it was the place that many who oversaw the collapse of race reform called home.

These factors come together to suggest a partial answer to the question "Why law?" The qualified "yes" to the question of whether there was something special about law can now be linked to the institutional, temporal, and disciplinary narrative that I have set forth. The prevailing understanding of race and law that came to a head in the 1980s had premised racial liberation on the enlightened terms of rationality. As such, racial power was understood as discriminatory racial attitudes and behavior, that is to say, a deviation from reason that was remediable through the operation of legal principles. Rationality would prevail over the bias of racial thinking through the application of neutral principles. And although civil rights lawyers and liberal allies may have differed to varying degrees on the need for targeted interventions to achieve a state in which the universalist repudiation of racial distinction might prevail, confidence that law, properly deployed, could deliver on such promises was widely shared. Yet by the 1980s and 1990s, this liberal equation of the rule of law and racial liberation was ripe for reconsideration. At the same time that hopes for continuous racial reform were unraveling, certain modes of thinking that were far more skeptical of the rule of law began to take root.[66] The critique of the ways that legal discourse rationalized dismal limits to race reform provided a window into seeing something more than a failure of legal reform. Indeed, one was able to see how the claim to rationality itself—"the rule of law" rather than to the "politics of the mob"—helped to rationalize existing racial power.[67]

The problem was not simply the takeover of the judiciary by right-wing judges, but the limits of "reason" itself. Of course, this particular critique of the dominant sensibilities in law was analogous to critiques made by a generation of scholars in other disciplines who unmasked how notions of "objectivity" and "science" shored up rather than disrupted the racial order.[68] Yet the critique in law was perhaps more explosive because of law's putatively apolitical status and the corresponding claims that reason more generally could distinguish truth from ideology. Thus, the critique of the apolitical character of law merged with a concrete critique of the epistemological claims of the Enlightenment tradition more generally.[69] In other words, the epistemological critique was not simply a "philosophical" one; it was also a practical component of claims that no neutral concept of merit justified the lack of minority law professors at elite law schools, or that no neutral process of principled, legal reasoning could justify the racialized distribution of power, prestige, and wealth in America.

My sense here is that breaking down the concept of "knowledge" that seemed necessary to contest the claims of law's neutrality in the late 1980s and 1990s migrated well across disciplines. In one way or another, every discipline faced a core problem that its very constitution as a "discipline" might be related to legitimating scholarly assumptions that have their roots in political, cultural, and racial domination.[70] The claims to nonracial disciplinary neutrality were contested to varying degrees in all disciplines, but law's apparent intimacy with the prevailing racial order presented a unique site for an intellectual sit-in. This window into the constructed nature of the racial order presented an acutely legible nexus between knowledge and power. Its legibility was facilitated as well by the temporal dimension of the post–civil rights reform in which the crack in the external façade of the status quo provided a fuller vision of a social order "caught in the act" of reforming. CRT was thus built on a platform made up of the intellectual and activist traditions that had come before. This plateau facilitated glaring scrutiny of racial order at a time when certain questions were up for grabs in a way they were not before, and probably have not been since.

CONCLUSION

Critical Race Theory came to be as one discursive response to the integrationist retreat and postreform normalization of institutional practices that produced grossly unequal distributional outcomes. A close examination of the conditions of its possibility revealed that students and faculty of color synthesized their collective encounters with liberal institutions and progressive allies into a new school of thinking about race and law. CRT's articulation in the context of specific ideological encounters was not limited to the specific institutional setting or to law writ large. It was a sustained interrogation about how the contemporary terms of racial normalization were articulated within law and increasingly insulated by it. Extending the story to contemporary developments would take up the rebranding of colorblind discourse by the terms of postracialism and the eclipse of that brief historical epoch with white nationalist investments that travel under the mantra of Trumpism. Today, critical race theories both inside and apart from the university are being primed to map the continuing significance of race despite the rhetorics of denial that are now commonplace within the societal order. The challenge is now to interrogate the limitations of contemporary race discourse in terms of both its popular embodiment and its epistemic foundations.

This is indeed the task of a broadened, interdisciplinary Critical Race Theory: to remap the racial contours of the way racial power is observed and denied—not simply to better understand and to navigate it, but to nullify and ultimately transform it.

NOTES

1. See, generally, Gloria Ladson-Billings and William F. Tate IV, "Toward a Critical Race Theory of Education," in *Critical Race Theory in Education: All God's Children Got a Song,* ed. Adrienne D. Dixson and Celia K. Rousseau (New York: Routledge, 2006), 11, 18.

2. See Glenn Adams and Phia S. Salter, "A Critical Race Psychology Is Not Yet Born," *Connecticut Law Review* 43 (2011): 1355. And, generally, Gregory S. Parks, Shayne Edward Jones, and W. Jonathan Cardi, eds., *Critical Race Realism: Intersections of Psychology, Race, and Law* (New York: New Press, 2008); and "Symposium on Behavioral Realism," special edition, *California Law Review* 94, no. 4 (July 2006), in particular Anthony G. Greenwald and Linda Hamilton Krieger, "Implicit Bias: Scientific Foundations," 945–68.

3. See Imani Perry, "Cultural Studies, Critical Race Theory, and Some Reflection on Methods," *Villanova Law Review* 50, no. 11 (2005): 915, 918–19.

4. See Barbara Luck Graham, "Toward a Critical Race Theory in Political Science: A New Synthesis for Understanding Race, Law, and Politics," in *African*

American Perspectives on Political Science, ed. Wilbur C. Rich (Philadelphia: Temple University Press, 2007), 212.

5. See, generally, Charles W. Mills, *Blackness Visible: Essays on Philosophy and Race* (Ithaca, NY: Cornell University Press, 1998); and idem, "White Ignorance," in *Race and Epistemologies of Ignorance,* ed. Shannon Sullivan and Nancy Tuana (Albany, NY: SUNY Press, 2007), 11, 13, 15, and 19.

6. See, e.g., W. E. B. Du Bois, "The Propaganda of History," in *Black Reconstruction in America: 1860–1880* (1935; New York: Free Press, 1998).

7. See, generally, Oliver Cromwell Cox, *Caste, Class, and Race: A Study in Social Dynamics* (New York: Doubleday, 1948).

8. Joyce Ann Ladner, *The Death of White Sociology* (New York: Random House, 1973).

9. Robert V. Guthrie, *Even the Rat Was White: A Historical View of Psychology,* 2d ed. (Boston: Allyn & Bacon, 1998).

10. Tukufu Zuberi and Eduardo Bonilla-Silva, eds., *White Logic, White Methods: Racism and Methodology* (Lanham, MD: Rowman & Littlefield, 2008).

11. Toni Morrison, *Playing in the Dark: Whiteness and the Literary Imagination* (New York: Vintage Books, 1993), 9.

12. See, generally, Stanford M. Lyman, "Race Relations as Social Process: Sociology's Resistance to a Civil Rights Orientation," in *Race in America: The Struggle for Equality,* ed. Herbert Hill and James E. Jones Jr. (Madison: University of Wisconsin Press, 1993); Charles W. Mills, *The Racial Contract* (Ithaca, NY: Cornell University Press, 1997), 3; idem, *Blackness Visible;* Sandra Harding, ed., *The "Racial" Economy of Science: Toward a Democratic Future* (Bloomington: Indiana University Press, 1993); George W. Stocking Jr., *Race, Culture, and Evolution: Essays in the History of Anthropology* (New York: Free Press, 1968); Charles A. Valentine, *Culture and Poverty* (1968); William Darity Jr., "Stratification Economics: Context versus Culture and the Reparations Controversy," *University of Kansas Law Review* 57, no. 4 (2008–9): 795; Laura Pulido, "Reflections on a White Discipline," *Professional Geographer* 54, no. 1 (2002): 49.

13. This is not to say that these projects had no traction. Many of these critiques—and the scholars articulating them—influenced thinking about race within disciplines and within society at large. W. E. B. Du Bois, for example, made significant inroads both within traditional disciplines and within public discourse. See, e.g., Elijah Anderson, "Introduction," in W. E. B. Du Bois, *The Philadelphia Negro* (Philadelphia: University of Pennsylvania Press, 1996).

14. Aldon Morris, "A Retrospective on the Civil Rights Movement: Political and Intellectual Landmarks," *Annual Review of Sociology* 25 (1999): 517, 524–25.

15. I build here on the sociocultural perspective as articulated, for example, by Hazel Rose Markus and Shinobu Kitayama, "The Cultural Psychology of Personality," *Journal of Cross-Cultural Psychology* 29 (1998): 63.

16. Kendall Thomas, comments at a panel on Critical Race Theory, Conference on Frontiers of Legal Thought, Duke Law School, Jan. 26, 1990, quoted in Charles

Lawrence, "Unconscious Racism Revisited: Reflections on the Impact and Origins of 'The Id, the Ego, and Equal Protection,'" *Connecticut Law Review* 40 (2008): 943.

17. Kimberlé Williams Crenshaw, "The First Decade: Critical Reflections, or 'A Foot in the Closing Door,'" *UCLA Law Review* 49 (2002): 1343, 1364.

18. While this protest was one of the first, protests such as this were confined neither to Harvard nor to the 1980s. See Wendy Leo Moore, *Reproducing Racism: White Space, Elite Law Schools, and Racial Inequality* (Lanham, MD: Rowman & Littlefield, 2008), 13.

19. Dean Vorenberg was a member of the National Board of Directors of the NAACP's Legal Defense Fund for twenty-eight years. See his obituary, *New York Times,* Apr. 15, 2000, A13. Jack Greenberg notes that he worked with Dean Vorenberg on civil rights matters and persuaded him to join the LDF's board. Jack Greenberg, "In Memoriam: James Vorenberg," *Harvard Law Review* 114, no. 1 (2000): 1, 3.

20. Adam S. Cohen, "Law School Dispute: Blacks' Boycott Creates Press Frenzy," *Harvard Crimson,* Sept. 13, 1982.

21. Derrick A. Bell, *Confronting Authority: Reflections of an Ardent Protester* (Boston: Beacon Press, 1994), 42, 44–46.

22. See Abby D. Phillip, "Race Sparked HLS Tension," *Harvard Crimson,* June 1, 2008, www.thecrimson.com/article/2008/6/1/race-sparked-hls-tension-a -battle/.

23. See Wanda Payne, "Bell Toasted by 200 at Farewell Tribute Dinner," *Harvard Law Record,* Nov. 26, 1980, 13.

24. Laura Taylor, "Prof. Bell Named U. of Oregon Law Dean," *Harvard Legal Record,* Mar. 14, 1980, 1, 14; Dave Horn, "Third World Coalition Renews Support for Course Boycott," *Harvard Law Record,* Sept. 17, 1982, 1.

25. The dissatisfaction with the scope and content of legal education was not at all limited to the TWC groups but was shared across a range of student groups. Many of these sentiments were reflected in what came to be called "The Little Red Book," otherwise known as *Legal Education and the Reproduction of Hierarchy,* self-published by Duncan Kennedy in 1983.

26. Letter from Ibrahim Gassama and Cecelie Counts to *Washington Post,* July 29, 1982 (on file with author).

27. Letter from Irma Tyler Wood to Dean James Vorenberg, Harvard Law School, Mar. 9, 1982 (on file with author).

28. Crenshaw, "Critical Reflections," 1348.

29. Horn, "Third World Coalition Renews Support," 3.

30. See Phillip, "Race Sparked HLS Tension."

31. Bell, *Confronting Authority,* 42.

32. This was in contrast to the likely inferences drawn from blue-collar jobs where similar claims were subject to disparate impact review. See Elizabeth Bartholet, "Application of Title VII to Jobs in High Places," *Harvard Law Review* 95 (1982): 945, 979–80.

33. The University of Texas, for example, was prominently featured in the battles over the desegregation of higher education.

34. For the five years before the boycott, Harvard Law School's full-time enrollment was made up of roughly 13–14 percent students of color and on average enrolled a higher percentage of minorities during this period than did other Ivy League and top law schools.

35. Harvard's relatively aggressive recruitment of minority students was not matched by a similar commitment to recruit faculty, leading student protesters to note that if the U.S. Supreme Court ruling in *Regents of University of California v. Bakke* (1978) justified using race as a factor in admissions, then surely Harvard could consider race as a factor in employment. See, e.g., Donald Christopher Tyler and Cynthia Muldrow, letter to the editor, "Goal of a Boycott at Harvard Law," *New York Times,* Aug. 20, 1982, A26.

36. The gross maldistribution of a credential does not necessarily undermine its relevance, but at minimum it casts doubt on institutional claims of equal opportunity. See Duncan Kennedy, "A Cultural Pluralist Case for Affirmative Action in Legal Academia," *Duke Law Journal,* (1990): 705, 718 .

37. In May 1982, Dean Vorenberg informed the Third World Coalition that Julius Chambers and Jack Greenberg would be teaching a winter-term course, Racial Discrimination and Civil Rights. Letter from the Harvard Black Law Students Association to James Vorenberg, Dean of Harvard Law School, Mar. 9, 1982 (on file with author). See also Martin S. Goldman, "Behind the Harvard Boycott," *Student Law* 11 (1983): 18, 19.

38. Dave Horn, "Charges Fly over BLSA Course Boycott," *Harvard Law Record,* Sept. 10, 1982, 3.

39. Letter from the Third World Coalition to the Harvard Law School Community, May 24, 1982 (on file with author).

40. Derrick Bell, op-ed, "Harvard Law School Black Student Boycott," Aug. 3, 1982, 3 (unpublished manuscript, on file with author).

41. Kimberlé Williams Crenshaw, "Toward a Race-Conscious Pedagogy in Legal Education," *National Black Law Journal* 11 (1988): 1.

42. Steve Cowan, "Students and Faculty Pack Open Forum," *Harvard Law Record,* Mar. 11, 1983, 15.

43. Letter from Dean Vorenberg to Second- and Third-Year Students, July 21, 1982 (on file with author).

44. Ruth Marcus, "Minority Groups Assail Course at Harvard Law," *Washington Post,* July 26, 1982, A5.

45. Bayard Rustin, letter to the editor, "A Misguided Protest by Blacks at Harvard," *New York Times,* Aug. 17, 1982, A26 .

46. George Bisharat, "Third World Students Believe Harvard Law Is Symbol of Bias," *Boston Globe,* Feb. 19, 1984, A. See also Brad Hudson, "TWC Offers Alternative Spring Course," *Harvard Law Record,* Jan. 21, 1983, 1.

47. Bisharat, "Third World Students."

48. Hudson, "TWC Offers Alternative," 15.

49. Derrick Bell, *Race, Racism, and American Law,* 2nd ed. (Boston: Little, Brown, 1980).

50. Richard Delgado, "The Imperial Scholar: Reflections on a Review of Civil Rights Literature," *University of Pennsylvania Law Review* 132 (1984): 561.

51. Charles R. Lawrence III, "The Id, the Ego, and Equal Protection: Reckoning with Unconscious Racism," *Stanford Law Review* 39 (1987): 317.

52. Delgado, "Imperial Scholar," 573–74.

53. See, e.g., Carl T. Rowan, "Bad Behavior at Harvard," *Washington Post,* Aug. 20, 1982, A15.

54. Crenshaw, "Critical Reflections," 1364.

55. The coming together of this critical mass at Wisconsin was not mere happenstance. This condition of possibility was the product of the Wisconsin Law School's professional leadership in terms of both faculty integration and scholarly innovation.

56. Crenshaw, "Critical Reflections," 1359.

57. The first CRT workshop was held on July 8, 1989, in Madison, Wisconsin. See, e.g., Angela Onwuachi-Willig, "Celebrating Critical Race Theory at 20," *Iowa Law Review* 94 (2009): 1497.

58. The second CRT workshop was held on June 13, 1990, in Buffalo, New York, followed by the Wisconsin Conference on Race and Critical Theory, November 1990, organized by Linda Greene. See, e.g., Phillip, "Race Sparked HLS Tension," 1250n5.

59. The workshop served as a vehicle to carry the intellectual project forward, but CRT continued as an intellectual field beyond its confines.

60. James E. Turner, "Africana Studies and Epistemology: A Discourse in the Sociology of Knowledge," in *The Next Decade: Theoretical and Research Issues in Africana Studies—Selected Papers from the Africana Studies and Research Center's Tenth Anniversary Conference, 1980,* ed. James E. Turner (Ithaca, NY: Africana Studies and Research Center, Cornell University, 1984).

61. Among the path-breaking intellectuals who might be considered the forerunners of CRT are W. E. B. Du Bois and Oliver Cox. Both of their academic careers—already circumscribed by race—were further stunted due to their repudiation of racial orthodoxy. See Sean Hier, "Structures of Orthodoxy and the Sociological Exclusion of Oliver C. Cox," *Research in Race and Ethnic Relations* 11 (2000): 304.

62. See, e.g., David Levering Lewis, *W. E. B. Du Bois: The Fight for Equality and the American Century, 1919–1963* (New York, NY: Holt, 2000), 444–47 .

63. Turner, "Africana Studies and Epistemology."

64. Morris, "Retrospective on the Civil Rights Movement," 534–35.

65. Kimberlé Williams Crenshaw, "Foreword: Toward a Race-Conscious Pedagogy in Legal Education," *National Black Law Journal* 11 (1988): 4.

66. Early indicators that the faith in law-based deliverance was waning were evident in the split between the traditional Civil Rights Movement and the emerging younger black-power wing of the Student Nonviolent Coordinating Committee SNCC. See Herbert H. Haines, *Black Radicals and the Civil Rights Mainstream, 1954–1970* (Knoxville: University of Tennessee Press, 1995), 15–76.

67. Gary Peller, "Reason and the Mob: The Politics of Representation," *Tikkun* 2, no. 3 (1987): 28, 92.

68. Stephen Steinberg, *Race Relations: A Critique* (Stanford, CA: Stanford University Press, 2007), 68–77.

69. Roberto Mangabeira Unger, *Knowledge and Politics* (New York: Free Press, 1976), 3, 29–36. See also Crenshaw, "Toward a Race-Conscious Pedagogy," 2.

70. George Lipsitz, "Notes and Thoughts on I. Wallerstein et al., *Open the Social Sciences,*" presented at the Colorblind Disciplining of Race Conscious Research: Critical Intervention across the Academy Conference at CASBS, June 1–5, 2009.

FOUR

Masking Legitimized Racism

INDIGENEITY, COLORBLINDNESS, AND THE SOCIOLOGY OF RACE

Dwanna L. McKay

To counter colorblindness across the disciplines, we must gain awareness of what has been overlooked or not interrogated. The power of colorblindness is in the exclusion of accountability for or the invisibility of racial injustice, whether colorblind or legitimized. Covert racism does not somehow negate the fact that overt racism still occurs, and overt racism does not look or function the same for all racialized groups. Mainstream scholars and educators should become aware of how a historical racial discourse based on white supremacy has influenced their disciplines, and then reflect on their own assumptions about race and racism. Moreover, to counter colorblindness specific to the United States, Indigenous Peoples must be included in the work.

Beginning in the mid-1990s, scholarship on the ideology of colorblind racism gained acceptance within the mainstream of the sociology of race in the United States. Colorblind racism justifies "racial inequality as the outcome of nonracial dynamics."[1] Scholars contend that after the U.S. civil rights era, overtly racist acts gave way to covert racism in the maintenance of white privilege under the ideology of colorblindness.[2] Colorblindness is the idea that racism no longer impacts social mobility because it is illegal to deny housing, education, and employment based on race. With the advent of colorblindness, it was no longer socially acceptable to express blatant antagonism toward people of color; therefore, explicit bigotry of past centuries morphed into implicit discrimination—colorblind racism.[3] This shift allows

Portions of this essay were previously published: Dwanna L. Robertson, "Invisibility in the Color-Blind Era: Examining Legitimized Racism against Indigenous Peoples," *American Indian Quarterly* 39, no. 2 (2015): 113–53.

whites to escape all culpability for the current racial oppression of minorities. Indeed, colorblind racism enables whites to justify the current gaps in educational attainment, wages, health, and wealth between them and everyone else through ideologies of individualism and the placing of blame on cultural tendencies without acknowledgment of historical context. Colorblind racism positions the political and economic inequality of people of color as their own fault. Marginalized groups still experience inequality, but their suppression is "void of direct racial terminology."[4]

Yet this does not hold true for Indigenous Peoples in the United States.[5] Like other marginalized groups, Natives certainly experience the same covert mechanisms of colorblind racism that limit life opportunities. However, Natives also routinely suffer from overt racism in the form of racial epithets like "redskin," "injun," and "squaw" and horribly distorted depictions of Natives as sports mascots, reminiscent of the propaganda used against Black, Irish, and Jewish people in the nineteenth and twentieth centuries. This overt racism is not confined to hate groups but is present in everyday discourse and throughout the media. Moreover, the racial oppression of Natives also becomes invisible in the very visible mechanism often used to reproduce racial inequality—informal communication—with statements like being an "Indian-giver," sitting "Indian-style," learning to count through the "one little, two little, three little Indians" song, or getting together to "powwow" over a business idea. Even race theorists whose scholarship has provided critical insights into the process of making race and racism have failed to address contemporary overt racism against Indigenous Peoples. Whereas the understanding of colorblind racism led to some of the most influential theoretical frameworks of race in sociology, these theories still fail to account for the blatant and overt forms of what I conceptualize as *legitimized racism*. To legitimize is to make legitimate—that is, to justify, reason, or rationalize as in accordance with established or accepted patterns and standards.[6] In other words, the institutions that shape social norms—those seen as social authorities—reproduce symbolic racial violence against American Indians through legal structures, public education locations, consumer products, sports associations, and so on.

Society commonly rationalizes racial inequality as nonracial (colorblind racism), but Native Americans cope daily with overtly racist language, images, and behaviors without social recourse. This work attempts to reconcile the invisibility of legitimized (overt) racism with the ideologies of colorblind (covert) racism, guided by two questions: With such blatant racist acts, what accounts for the lack of attention by contemporary race theory to anti-Indian rhetoric and legitimized racism against Indigenous Peoples in the United States? How do Native people negotiate these persistent racist stereotypes and cultural appropriation in their daily lives? I argue that racism against American Indians has been socially legitimized, thereby rendering it invisible, even among race scholars, activists of color, other people of color, and often Natives themselves. Using an Indigenous epistemology and a qualitative approach, I examine what I conceive as the phenomenon of "legitimized racism." I analyze its impact and provide narratives of confrontations with legitimized racism through conversations with forty-five Indigenous people.

THE PHENOMENON OF LEGITIMIZED RACISM

Over five hundred years of Western dominance have shaped public perception of Indigenous Peoples. Overt racism against Indians has become legitimized through centuries of racist discourse created and perpetuated by hegemonic power structures. While minstrel shows have long been castigated as racist, American children are socialized into *playing* Indian. Playing Indian is actually an American tradition with roots in colonial times.[7] During the Boston Tea Party, when colonists rebelled against British rule by boarding English ships and throwing tea into the harbor, they dressed in blankets and feathers and had black soot and grease on their faces, pretending to be Indians. Columbus Day celebrations, Halloween costumes, and Thanksgiving reenactments stereotype Indigenous Peoples as a much-distorted, monolithic culture. Playing Indian is racist—in no way different from wearing blackface or participating in minstrel shows—because it collapses distinct cultures into one stereotypical racialized group. Even worse, because playing Indian is deemed socially acceptable (i.e., normal, legitimate), any other racial or ethnic group may now participate—*without recognizing the inherent racism in doing so.*

The contemporary consequences of legitimized racism stem from the historically racist discourse (established within the context of imperialism, white supremacy, and colonization) that perpetuates the mythical righteousness of the murder, rape, and enslavement of Indigenous Peoples.[8] Historically, Native peoples were portrayed as savages, Native women as sexually permissive, and Native culture as engendering laziness.[9] Contemporary American

Indians still live under the prevalence of Native misrepresentations in the media, archaic notions of Indianness, and the federal government's appropriation of "Indian" names and words as code for military purposes. But legitimized racism is not just about the production of racial images, attitudes, or identities. It is not between individuals. Rather, it is the foundation of power that cradles the dialectical interaction of human agency and social structure within the racial state.

My theoretical framework of legitimized racism builds on concepts of racism, systemic racism, colorblind racism, and internalized oppression.[10] I conceptualize legitimized racism with the following assumptions and provide definitions and examples for the concepts it builds upon: First, racism is present in the phenomenon of legitimized racism, of course. Racism rationalizes that all the members of a racialized group have the same inherent abilities, characteristics, morals, and qualities. For example, a common myth is that Indians cannot metabolize liquor like other races—if they drink, they will become alcoholics. This assumes inherent biological difference between racialized groups, rather than critically assessing how historical trauma and socioeconomic deprivation might affect rates of alcoholism for Indigenous Peoples. Second, systemic racism is also present. Systemic racism is an ideology that attaches common meanings, representations, and racial stories to groups, which in turn become embedded within social institutions that serve to justify the superordination of white people and the subordination of nonwhite people.[11] Indigenous Peoples were othered as "merciless Indian Savages" in the Declaration of Independence. To this day, Americans continue to justify the genocide of Indigenous Peoples as necessary because of Indians' supposed immorality as wild savages and continue to celebrate Columbus as a hero for discovering a land allegedly uninhabited by civilization.[12] Next, colorblind racism is present. Phrases like "To the victor go the spoils" may seem nonracial, but in the context of the Western invasion of North America, it positions Euro-Americans as strategic or lucky, avoiding any acknowledgment of the physical and cultural violence committed against people who were racialized as Indians.

Colorblind racism interconnects with legitimized racism through claims of innocence and justice. U.S. citizens are taught to believe that the United States was birthed in a fight against oppression, that it was founded on the tenets of freedom and justice for all. Social myths about the benevolence of colonialists and heroic efforts of settlers legitimize claims of innocence, replacing the fundamental truth that the United States was founded in the practices of white supremacy, patriarchy, slavery, and genocide. National holidays like Columbus Day, Thanksgiving, and the Fourth of July perpetuate society's belief in the moral superiority, innovative culture, and complete innocence of the United States. But Native people are Americans, too. To rationalize these claims of innocence and justice means we must deny Indigenous Peoples' histories and experiences. The intentional exclusion of contemporary Native Peoples' knowledge from the foundational knowledge of the United States functions to justify legitimized racism.

Finally, legitimized racism exists in its normalcy as part of the social character of the United States. To legitimize is to make something seem right or reasonable. Accordingly, racist actions, discourses, or institutions often seem ordinary and without malice in the service of legitimized racism. Indeed, anti-Indian terminology, imagery, and behavior have become *legitimized* to such a degree that even other marginalized people accept overt racism against Natives as nonracist and readily maintain and participate in it. Dressing up to play Indian with "war paint" for Halloween seems harmless. Sports teams with racist names and mascots are reputed to be honoring Indians. Culturally appropriating sacred objects like headdresses is meant to be all in good fun. Thus, another important characteristic of legitimized racism is the resistance to recognizing normalized, institutionalized, systemic racism as racist at all. White people deny it, and empathy is not easily forthcoming from other marginalized groups because they also participate in it. Individuals who protest are accused of being too sensitive or simply silly. Groups who protest are charged with being subversive and acting in their own interests and not for the good of society.[13]

Therefore, legitimized racism is not colorblind racism, even though the two ideologies share some of the same tenets. Both colorblind racism and legitimized racism deny that racism exists, making it difficult to name, confront, or change it. Whereas colorblind racism is built on covertness—not saying or doing things that could be perceived as racist—legitimized racism involves terminology, actions, and media depictions that would be considered overtly racist if applied to other racialized groups. This is not to say that other racial groups do not face overt acts of racism, but rather that these same acts may not be deemed as racist when deployed against Native Americans. For example, public outcry commonly occurs over the use of blackface because people from all backgrounds (with the exception of hate groups) recognize it as racist. But the common occurrences of playing Indian and the use of Indian mascots raise little concern, and any resistance to these common behaviors results in severe public backlash.

Significantly, the phenomenon of legitimized racism is not exclusive to Indigenous Peoples because it facilitates the means by which we appropriate and condense other cultures, as in the monolithic caricature of South Asian culture by way of "Bollywood" parties, dancing, and impersonations. Legitimized racism sanctions the common public discourse that undocumented Mexicans take away American jobs or that they receive copious amounts of public benefits that are paid for by "real" Americans, which is compounded by the tendency in the United States to racialize most Latinx Peoples as Mexican.[14] Lastly, the American national identity possesses a normative whiteness[15] that is accomplished through the public discourse of legitimized racism. Therefore, when discussing Americans, only nonwhite people need to be marked by racializing terms—Native American, Arab American, Mexican American, Asian American, and so on. But whereas legitimized racism can occur in relation to other racialized groups, it operates with a historic specificity against Indigenous Peoples. Federal Indian policy has systematically racialized Indians as inferior, incapable, and uncivilized.

Through the erasure of historical context and the appropriation of Indigenous culture, *legitimized racism* transforms overt racism into so-called benevolent acts of tradition and honor. Thus, other groups are able to assert racial power over Indigenous Peoples by reducing the complex understandings and representations of Indigenous identity to racist archetypes and cultural caricatures. Misconceptions about Indigenous Peoples are created, produced, and reproduced in stereotypes and racial bias.[16] Nevertheless, mainstream race scholars rarely engage with Indigenous Peoples in their writing.[17] In the following, I critique three prominent race theories—racial formation, white racial framing, and colorblind racism—and their engagement with American Indians.

CONTEMPORARY THEORIES OF RACE AND RACISM: A CRITIQUE

Numerous studies discuss the ill effects of colorblind racism on marginalized people's life opportunities.[18] White people now generally avoid using outright racial epithets toward people of other races. Publicly calling someone racially derogatory words is considered morally reprehensible, and therefore socially unacceptable.[19] Instead, people now speak in coded language, utilizing a colorblind racist frame to discriminate against people of color. *Yet this is not the case for Indigenous Peoples in the United States.*

Contemporary sociology commonly acknowledges that race is socially constructed and altered by social institutions and historical influence.[20] The racial classification of American Indians emerged out of the collective phenomena of sociohistorical forces and sociopolitical acts (e.g., the European discovery of America, the U.S. Constitution, and federal Indian policy).[21] Michael Omi and Howard Winant's foundational racial-formation theory posits race as a dynamic process that is "constantly being transformed by political struggle."[22] Therefore, race acts as an indicator for unequal access to resources. The sociopolitical results of the racialization of American Indians certainly speak to Omi and Winant's racial formation theory, though these theorists did not undertake an analysis of Indigenous Peoples. Importantly, Omi and Winant recognize the role of government in creating racial groups through ideological and political processes, discussing issues of immigration and the racial politics of Chicanos, Asian Americans, African Americans, Mexican Americans, and even the Vietnamese, at length.

Indeed, an appropriate site of study for racial formation theory is the complicated federal policy that established race-based authenticity measures for American Indians to exclude people claiming to be Indigenous, unlike the inclusionary one-drop rule for African Americans.[23] Yet Omi and Winant's 1994 study about race in the United States from 1960 to 1990 only mentions Indigenous Peoples very briefly, on two pages in the main text and in three endnotes that cite other readings. This, however, was an era of dynamic racial contestation between Indians and the federal government, with a sharp increase in the growth of American Indian/Alaska Native populations in U.S. censuses—from approximately 551,700 in 1960 to 1.96 million in 1990.

Joe Feagin finds that Omi and Winant's racial formation theory misses the persistence of systemic racism. According to Feagin, systemic racism exponentially reproduces itself in society's networks, social groups, and institutions in order to protect white privilege and power. Therefore, society operates through "a commonplace white racial frame—that is, an organized set of racialized ideas, stereotypes, emotions, and inclinations to discriminate."[24] Altogether, Feagin is more attentive to the racialization of Indigenous Peoples within his theory of the white racial frame. He reveals the historical racist framing by Europeans and Americans of Native peoples as inferior. Natives were seen as nonhumans and demons that needed to be hunted down and killed or driven away. Nevertheless, Feagin judges white racism against African Americans as more harsh than against Native Americans, stating: "While they have been the recurring targets of extreme white brutality and recurring genocide, Native Americans have not played as a central role in the *internal* socio-racial reality of the colonies or the United States as have African Americans."[25]

Feagin's reasoning is problematic for several reasons: First, Feagin echoes the sentiments of the "Black exceptionalism" argument, which posits that the Black-white paradigm rightly places Black people at the center of any analysis of race in the United States, while other groups of color play secondary roles in the construction of white supremacy in American race relations.[26] Regrettably, this argument ignores the fact that the colonies and the United States only became realities because Europeans (within the context of Western domination) first collapsed distinct regions, cultures, and languages of Indigenous Peoples into one racial classification: Indian.[27] Second, Feagin seemingly ranks slavery as the most egregious consequence of racialization because of its economic centrality and lasting legacy of systemic racism. The assumption that outcomes of racism (e.g., enslavement, rape, beating, starvation, and murder) can be weighed and measured is challenging. Classifying Natives as evil and as less than human acted to justify the brutality (i.e., physical and cultural genocide) levied against them in order to steal their land and resources in settlement of the Americas. Thus, Indigenous Peoples play both central and *foundational* roles in the economic and "*internal* socio-racial reality" of the United States. Finally, Feagin's use of phrases like "anti-Indian genocide" and "decimated Native Americans" invokes the "vanishing Indian" trope.[28] American Indians did suffer both genocide and decimation, but more than eight hundred tribal groups survived. Many tribal nations are experiencing rapid population growth and cultural revitalization. Without a balance of past and present, stereotypes about Indigenous Peoples are reified. Their experiences fade into monolithic, distorted historical accounts of racism, failing to be viewed as contemporary acts.

Bonilla-Silva also critiques racial formation theory, arguing that Omi and Winant focus too closely on how racial meanings are formed and reorganized rather than addressing how the U.S. racial structure continues to function within a white supremacy ideology. According to Bonilla-Silva, systemic racism birthed colorblind racism in the 1960s. To address this, Bonilla-Silva promotes a theory of racialized social systems that reward socially constructed race differentials—economic, political, social, and psychological—at all societal levels.[29] Therefore, social interactions between individuals occurring within racist systems operate within racist institutions to reproduce racist societies. American Indians could easily be used as an example of racialized social systems, given their systemic oppression for the last five hundred-plus years.[30]

Colorblind racism certainly applies to Natives. Their socioeconomic inequality is often blamed on a cultural tendency toward alcoholism, laziness, and rural living, rather than racial oppression. In other words, colorblind racism would suggest that Indians need to sober up, work harder, and move off the reservation.[31] Still, Indigenous Peoples' daily experiences do problematize the theoretical applicability of colorblind racism. One of its central tenets is that white people no longer rely upon name-calling to maintain white privilege because "the normative climate in the post–civil rights era has made illegitimate the public expression of racially based feelings and viewpoints."[32] The idea that publicly racist terminology is no longer used for the maintenance of white privilege proves a difficult fit for Native Americans. Natives continue to face overtly racist name-calling and stereotyping. Without this acknowledgment, not only do American Indians become invisible within dominant theories of race, but the overt racism they experience becomes invisible to everyone but them because it is not seen as racism.

METHODOLOGY

In order to understand what I term legitimized racism, I utilize a blended critical and Indigenous interpretive lens—a standpoint that emphasizes participative, emancipatory research and requires holistic, relational, decolonizing ethics as well as empathy, respect, and reciprocity. Indigenous epistemology acts to decolonize the academy's scientific practices, to disrupt Westernized ways of knowing, and to develop research approaches based on Indigenous knowledge and voice.[33] I chose a qualitative methodology because it is particularly appropriate for working with marginalized groups, giving value and voice to their lived experiences in a historically contextualized way.[34] My research sample consisted of forty-five Native people from twenty-nine distinct tribes, all over the age of eighteen. The analysis serves as a magnifying lens that clarifies and honors the narrative.[35] But the process of decolonization requires strategic concessions in the Western world of academia. Indigenous researchers often utilize mixed methods for interpretive and thematic analysis in order to prevent fragmenting or deconstructing the knowledge that stories hold.[36] I paid close attention, working respectfully with the data to present it as wholly as possible. I integrated theme coding for

particular discourses linked to cultural appropriation and anti-Indian rhetoric. I looked for the emergence of pattern-organizing themes and present my
research findings in thematic fashion. Narrative quotes are used to illustrate
the essence of the themes identified.

THEMES OF LEGITIMIZED RACISM
AGAINST INDIGENOUS PEOPLES

My conversations with participants revealed persistent legitimized racism in
four thematic bundles: (1) lazy, drunk, casino-rich Indians; (2) dirty squaw
or sexy maiden; (3) playing Indian; and (4) celebrating genocide. I include
narratives from conversations with participants, and to balance respect and
reciprocity, I add my own perspective and share my reflections. It is within
these four themes that we can recognize the pervasiveness of legitimized
racism.

Lazy, Drunk, Casino-Rich Indians

During each conversation, participants and I discussed typical stereotypes
about Natives that they encounter. One specific trio of tropes was consistently mentioned: the lazy Indian, the drunk Indian, and the casino-rich
Indian.[37] These constitute a prime example of legitimized racism: through
public discourse, these distorted images of Natives have become engrained,
accepted, and legitimized to such a degree that society maintains and reproduces them without question. Tom, a forty-year-old Penobscot man, describes
how people openly disparage Indians, even at his job with the state of Maine:

> I hear things like, "Show me an Indian, I'll show you a drunk Indian."
> "Indians are lazy." We won't get jobs because we get everything for free. They
> think we all get casino money and government entitlements. . . . But I still
> have to work, and I can't even drink a beer without people throwing stereo-
> types around. Even today, some people I work with at the state will say stuff.
> For some reason, they think it's acceptable to run down Native people. . . .
> That's something I wish would change. [They should realize] that hey, Natives
> are just like everybody else, so we should be respected just like everybody else.

Joy, a young Cherokee woman, exclaims, "They think we're all getting money
from the casinos or handouts from the government!" Gary, a middle-aged

Muscogee man who works for his tribal nation, also talks about the lazy, drunk, casino paradigm that Indians are seen to embody:

[Supposedly we all own] casinos, obviously. We're gamblers, drinkers, slackers. You know, I see that, but I see that in white, black [people]. You know, it's not prevalent just to us. I'm sure we have our share, but we have our share of people that are educated and are productive and community-driven and [care about] politics and the whole bit. But we'll still get that. We'll still get that cigar stand Indian on cement, you know. That's just what it is, but it's something you've gotta work through.

Both Tom and Gary assert that Natives are just like any other group of people, and this sentiment echoed throughout the conversations. For example, Will, a Chickasaw elder, says that society, in general, does not hold an accurate or positive view of Natives:

We are considered drunks. Lazy, dirty drunks. They look at the reservations and they see all the old cars just broke down and the shanty shacks, and a lot of people feel that the Indians get money all the time and that's why they live in poverty because they take their money and drink all the time. There's truth to it. There are a lot of people that will spend their last dime on booze. But then there are also a lot of people that have family and kids that don't. And they are trying to make it the best they can.

Bryan Brayboy explains that white supremacy provides the basis for the legitimized racism in the common discourses by non-Natives that all Indians get entitlements from the federal government (free money, houses, and college educations, etc.).[38] Contrary to popular belief, especially among non-Natives, American Indians did not simply relinquish their rights to lands, waters, and other natural resources. The federal government pledged through laws and treaties to compensate for land exchanges accomplished by the forced removal of tribal nations from their original homelands. Unfortunately, recompense is commonly expressed as "benefits," a term that implies assistance, subsidy, or even charity, rather than deserved reimbursement. Framing the obligatory and promised compensation by the U.S. government as merely "benefits" perpetuates the idea of Native dependency, rather than tribal sovereignty.

White supremacy also undergirds the common portrayal of Indians as lazy drunks who have never had to work for anything. Will admits freely that alcoholism and poverty plague Native people, but expresses exasperation that people think that the circumstances of poverty on reservations speaks for all

Indians. Indeed, Will and others exercise their agency by presenting a counterdiscourse that Indians are "just ordinary people," as opposed to the racist stereotype of drunk, dirty, and casino-rich Indians.

Dirty Squaw or Sexy Maiden

Birthed through the correspondence of Columbus and his shipmates, the racial stereotype of Indigenous women as naive or childlike but also savage and sexually deviant remains alive and well today.[39] Sixteen women participants discussed their experiences of being sexualized and exoticized by non-Native boys and men, almost all as early as the first stages of puberty. Maggie, a middle-aged Maliseet woman, describes the trauma of puberty as a Native girl:

> As I got into puberty, white boys seemed to have some kind of idea that I was "wild" and would be more willing to have sex with them. . . . Boys would grab me and say stuff and call me "Pocahontas." They didn't treat other [white] girls on their street that way.

Maggie understood early that she was considered different from the other girls by the boys in her neighborhood. She bore the stigma of the sexualized historical myth of Pocahontas (born Matoaka, the daughter of Algonquian chief Powhatan)—the idea that Indigenous women are highly sexualized, act wild, like to be held captive, and become sexually active at earlier ages than other racial groups of women. Native women who do not fit the ideal of the sexualized "Pocahontas" fall into the category of the dirty squaw.

The squaw trope is an example of what Daniel Morley Johnson describes as "savagism discourses," which perpetuate an anti-Indian rhetoric and an anti-Indian sentiment in contemporary society.[40] From its origins as an Iroquois word, *otsiskwa*, "squaw" means vagina or female sexual parts.[41] For some Native women or tribes, the term might imply a dirty woman; for others, a whore; and for yet others, both.[42] As a child and teenager, Eva remembers experiencing extreme prejudice numerous times:

> My dad grew up on a reservation in [the Northwest]. And we would visit every summer. When I was little I remember that there was a lot of racism around there. . . . I remember being pushed in the pool before, called squaw or dirty squaw. But I also remember [hanging out] with a close friend of mine and her friend, once, and because I was darker skinned I was accused of being dirty.

Cornel D. Pewewardy argues that children "develop racial awareness at an early age, perhaps as early as three or four years old," and non-Indian children perpetuate negative stereotypes and derogatory images toward Indian children.[43] These children have been prevented from developing authentic, healthy attitudes about Indians. In this case, Eva experienced being stereotyped as a "dirty" squaw by way of being female. Pewewardy warns that Native children exposed to constant stereotyping and belittling of their cultures "grow into adults who feel and act inferior to other people."[44] Consequently, the common use of the word "squaw" results in low self-esteem and vulnerability to symbolic and physical violence against Native women.[45]

Playing Indian

In addition to denigrating stereotypes, legitimized racism masks the demeaning and harmful savage discourses and acts of playing Indian. Every participant I spoke with indicated that they recognize the prevalent savage discourse in today's society. Some participants purposely ignore distorted media representations of Indigeneity in order to watch the same entertainment as the rest of society, but not all Native (or non-Native) people are consciously aware of the prevalence of bias against Indigenous Peoples.[46] Sadly, playing Indian is still as popular as ever in marketing imagery and popular culture.[47] We see this in the surge of "cowboy and Indian" costume parties on college campuses. Playing Indian is also fashionable, with actors, models, musicians, and other entertainers donning headdresses or other Native costumes without consequence to their careers.[48] Natalie, a thirty-year-old Otoe woman, finds the pervasiveness of cultural appropriation despicable, telling me:

> I see this all the time on campus. Groups of girls with hipster fashion, you know, with fringe on skirts and boots and braids in their hair. It sexualizes Native women so much, like we just dress provocatively on purpose. We have to sit back and watch them make fun of us. It's shameful. It's hurtful. I'm disgusted. I almost want this craze to be over, this trend of Indian designs. It sounds mean, but I wish they'd go pick on another culture.

Natalie believes that society is inherently anti-Indian, but expresses real hope, saying, "Social media is helping out. It's getting the word out that it's not right. It's also helped me understand what it means to be Indian and the responsibility that goes with it." Two-thirds of those I spoke with also expressed anger toward other Natives who claim to find no harm in stereotypes and playing Indian. But that is the very nature of legitimized racism: it uses its power to convince Indigenous people to believe what is said about them. By recognizing that Natives have been subjected to the same cultural ignorance of mainstream media, we can understand our internalization and resist participating in our own oppression.

Celebrating Genocide

Finally, all the participants complained that Americans would rather believe that Columbus "discovered" America, even though this historical myth has been debunked.[49] Columbus and his shipmates' atrocious record of enslavement, murder, and rape is relatively unknown, to the public and scholars alike. The United States still celebrates Columbus as a hero every October amid protests by Indigenous activists. The American Indian Movement released a press statement on October 6, 2000, that likened Columbus Day to a holiday celebrating Adolf Hitler with parades in Jewish communities:

> Columbus was the beginning of the American holocaust, ethnic cleansing characterized by murder, torture, raping, pillaging, robbery, slavery, kidnapping, and forced removals of Indian people from their homelands. . . . We say that to celebrate the legacy of this murderer is an affront to all Indian peoples, and others who truly understand this history.[50]

It was striking that participants complained repeatedly that Americans do not want to know the truth about Columbus. Doris, an Abinake woman, reflects on her frustration with America's obsession with Columbus:

> [Columbus Day] is just another opportunity to remind Natives that their homelands have been basically, um, destroyed, really. I understand that people were taught lies in school, but now we know better, so why can't we teach better? Why are the grade school kids still learning lies? . . . Columbus Day is especially hard for me because it's kind of the point of origin for genocide, you know? Columbus stands for all the colonizers that followed. All the brutality that followed. I think about my family and how we've maintained our culture, but barely. Honestly, though, that day is just one in a long list of reminders about what happened to us.

Doris, like most other participants, recognized that holidays like Columbus Day are emotional triggers for Natives. Maria Yellow Brave Heart and Lemyra DuBruyn argue that American Indians suffer from historical trauma and disenfranchised grief because of the massive, recurring trauma of

Western colonialism, especially since, "for American Indians, the United States is the perpetrator of our holocaust."[51] An unwillingness to assess critically the legitimized racism of Columbus Day reproduces the trauma generation after generation.

CONCLUSION

Within this chapter, I ask what accounts for the lack of attention by contemporary race theory to anti-Indian rhetoric and overt racism against Indigenous Peoples in the United States. This study shows that Natives experience legitimized racism through national holidays, racist names and mascots for sports teams, the pervasiveness of playing Indian, and ultimately, a lack of academic or social awareness of this continuing social injustice. Legitimized racism becomes invisible in its deployment against Indigenous Peoples. To be sure, legitimized racism is not just about the production or maintenance of racial images, attitudes, or identities. It is not between individuals or individuals and groups. Rather, legitimized racism is the foundation of power that holds the dialectical interaction of human agency and social structure. That is, when multilayered, intersectional, and dynamic racism becomes legitimized (normalized, institutionalized, internalized, and systemic), it becomes simultaneously overt and invisible within social norms and social institutions.

We should all care deeply about the contemporary dehumanizing effects of legitimized racism on Natives' lives, as evidenced by our disproportionately high rates of substance abuse, violence, and incarceration. Stereotypes, racist terminology, and denigrating imagery are also associated with high suicide rates among Native youth.[52] Native youth experience racism simply by turning on the television to watch a sports channel, shopping for groceries, or attending school.[53] The impact of covert and overt racism becomes even more apparent in the disproportionately high rates of poverty, chronic illness, and victimization among Indigenous communities. After surviving imposed racialization, determined extermination, forced acculturation, and coerced impoverishment, Native peoples should not be invisible within the sociology of race.

My conversations with the participants in this study reveal contemporary consequences for historical racist discourse in the form of legitimized racism. Therefore, I inquired how we as Native people negotiate such persistent racist stereotypes and cultural appropriation in our daily lives. I find that we navigate such prevalent racist regimes by deploying the counterdiscourse that positions Indigenous people as ordinary humans in opposition to taken-for-granted racist stereotypes. We realize that decolonization is an emancipatory process—something that comes with an awakened consciousness. Recognizing the role of power within social interaction, we disrupt oppressive language by speaking out. We work to debunk historical myths with critical counternarratives that expose the brutality of colonialism while simultaneously celebrating our cultural pride in the survival, strength, and honor of Native Peoples.

Legitimized racism also explains the minimal attention non-Native mainstream race scholars have paid to the racialized discourses utilized over the last five hundred–plus years against Indigenous Peoples in the United States. Historical narratives of race in America that exclude the voices of the Indigenous Peoples of the continent currently known as North America are, at best, incomplete, and at worst, invalid. The failure to acknowledge and study the phenomenon of legitimized racism obstructs our understanding of the reproduction of racialized injustice, theoretically and empirically. Clearly, Omi and Winant, Bonilla-Silva, Feagin, and other race scholars have dedicated great time and effort to exposing the processes of racialization and the evils of systemic racism. Foundational race theories like racial formation, colorblind racism, and the white racial frame bring great insight to our understanding of racism and bigotry.

Yet this gain cannot be at the expense of Indigenous Peoples in North America. The inclusion of Indigenous Peoples only strengthens race theory and lends credence to Omi and Winant's racial formation theory, reveals the inflexibility of Feagin's white-Black frame, and disrupts the assumption of Bonilla-Silva's colorblind race theory that society no longer accepts overt racism. Inclusion advances racial formation theory with examples of how U.S. policy used race to group hundreds of sovereign Native nations. Inclusion exposes the historical racist discourses (systemic racism) that continue to reproduce a contemporary social reality of the legitimate subordination of Native Americans and the superordination of the dominant, white culture. Inclusion reveals the effects of degrading stereotypes and cultural belittling (colorblind racism), which results in harmful internalized oppression among Natives.

Legitimized racism is so embedded within American society that it has become invisible. By including Indigenous Peoples, we see that racism still operates as a violent force of injustice within American society. To counter colorblindness, we must also confront the insidiousness of overt racism within social norms, structures, and institutions. Individuals, communities, and academia struggle to see/understand/confront anti-Indian terminology, imagery, and behavior as racist. The theory of legitimized racism exposes the social, political, economic, and historical origins of race and racism, not only for us, but for other groups as well. Without this understanding, social injustice grows within the invisibility of legitimized racism.

NOTES

1. Eduardo Bonilla-Silva, *Racism without Racists: Colorblind Racism and the Persistence of Racial Inequality in the United States,* 2nd ed. (Lanham, MD: Rowman & Littlefield, 2006), 2.

2. For a comprehensive treatment, see Eduardo Bonilla-Silva, *White Supremacy and Racism in the Post–Civil Rights Era* (Boulder, CO: L. Rienner, 2001); idem, *Racism without Racists;* Joe R. Feagin, *Systemic Racism: A Theory of Oppression* (New York: Routledge, 2006); idem, *The White Racial Frame: Centuries of Racial Framing and Counter-Framing* (New York: Routledge, 2010).

3. Racist expressions by hate groups are the exception to the rule.

4. Bonilla-Silva, *White Supremacy,* 48.

5. Passionate debate persists in academia over the most useful term(s) to describe Indigenous Peoples of the United States. I use the term "American Indian" because of its usage at the U.S. Census Bureau, the term "Indian" because it is the legal term used within Federal Indian Policy, and the terms "Native" and "Indigenous," interchangeably, as my preferences.

6. *Merriam-Webster's Collegiate Dictionary* (Springfield, MA: Merriam-Webster, 2003), s.v. "legitimize."

7. Philip Joseph Deloria, *Playing Indian* (New Haven, CT: Yale University Press, 1998).

8. Bryan McKinley Jones Brayboy, "Toward a Tribal Critical Race Theory in Education," *Urban Review* 37, no. 5 (2005): 426–46.

9. See, for example, Martha Elizabeth Hodes, *Sex, Love, Race: Crossing Boundaries in North American History* (New York: NYU Press, 1999); Frederick E. Hoxie, *A Final Promise: The Campaign to Assimilate the Indians, 1880–1920* (Lincoln: University of Nebraska Press, 1984); Francis Paul Prucha, *Indian Policy in the United States: Historical Essays* (Lincoln: University of Nebraska Press, 1981).

10. See Bonilla-Silva, *Racism without Racists;* Brayboy, "Toward a Tribal Critical Race Theory"; Feagin, *Systemic Racism;* and Paulo Freire, *Pedagogy of the Oppressed,* 30th anniversary ed. (New York: Continuum International Publishing Group, 2000). According to Freire, internalized oppression results when people internalize the stereotypes and negative myths communicated about their group by the oppressive regime.

11. Bonilla-Silva, *Racism without Racists;* Feagin, *Systemic Racism.*

12. Robert F. Berkhofer, *The White Man's Indian: Images of the American Indian from Columbus to the Present* (New York: Knopf, 1978); Charles W. Mills, *The Racial Contract* (Ithaca, NY: Cornell University Press, 1997); David E. Stannard, *American Holocaust: Columbus and the Conquest of the New World* (New York: Oxford University Press, 1992); Stephen Steinberg, *Race Relations: A Critique* (Stanford: Stanford University Press, 2007).

13. Vine Deloria Jr., *We Talk, You Listen: New Tribes, New Turf* (New York: Macmillan, 1970).

14. In a CNN report about a recent Brown University study, the authors highlight a Honduran restaurant manager's frustration about people labeling his food as Mexican; see Michael Martinez and Mariana Castillo, "Study Highlights Diversity of Latinos," March 20, 2013, http://inamerica.blogs.cnn.com/2013/03/20/study-hispanics-show-increasing-cultural-economic-and-social-diversity. The Brown study can be found at https://s4.ad.brown.edu/Projects/Diversity/Data/Report/report03202013.pdf.

15. Paul Spickard, *Almost All Aliens: Immigration, Race, and Colonialism in American History and Identity* (New York: Routledge, 2007), 27.

16. Michael K. Green, "Images of Native Americans in Advertising: Some Moral Issues," *Journal of Business Ethics* 12, no. 4 (1993): 323–30; Laurence M. Hauptman, *Tribes and Tribulations: Misconceptions about American Indians and Their Histories* (Albuquerque: University of New Mexico Press, 1995); Michael Yellow Bird, "Cowboys and Indians: Toys of Genocide, Icons of American Colonialism," *Wicazo Sa Review* 19, no. 2 (2004): 33–48.

17. This is not to say that American Indians have not been studied by sociologists. Extensive demographic information about Natives in the United States has been provided by C. Matthew Snipp, *On the Costs of Being American Indian: Ethnic Identity and Economic Opportunity* (Los Angeles: UCLA Institute for Social Science Research, 1988); idem, *American Indians: The First of This Land* (New York: Russell Sage Foundation, 1989); idem, "Sociological Perspectives on American Indians," *Annual Review of Sociology* 18 (1992): 351–71. Political resurgence of American Indians as a panethnic group has been studied in depth by Stephen E. Cornell, *The Return of the Native: American Indian Political Resurgence* (New York: Oxford University Press, 1988). Identity politics has also been researched by Eva Garroutte, *Real Indians: Identity and the Survival of Native America* (Berkeley: University of California Press, 2003); Carolyn A. Liebler, "Homelands and Indigenous Identities in a Multiracial Era," *Social Science Research* 39, no. 4 (2010): 596–609; and Dwanna L. Robertson, "A Necessary Evil: Framing an American Indian Legal Identity," *American Indian Culture and Research Journal* 37, no. 4 (2013): 115–40.

18. See Feagin, *White Racial Frame* and *Systemic Racism;* Eduardo Bonilla-Silva, Amanda Lewis, and David Embrick, "'I did Not Get That Job because of a Black Man': The Story Lines and Testimonies of Colorblind Racism," *Sociological Forum* 19, no. 4 (2004): 555–81; Bonilla-Silva, *Racism without Racists.*

19. Eduardo Bonilla-Silva, Carla Goar, and David Embrick, "When Whites Flock Together: The Social Psychology of White Habitus," *Critical Sociology* 32, no. 2/3 (2006): 229–53.

20. Race, though socially constructed, has a social reality. That is, there are real effects for those who are racialized and for those who do the racializing.

21. Indigenous Peoples are not a race, of course. They belong to distinct, sovereign Native nations. However, this study is about how non-Natives see Natives—the racialization of Indigenous Peoples as Indians and the consequences of legitimized racism. I utilize pan-Indian descriptors in that spirit.

22. Michael Omi and Howard Winant, *Racial Formation in the United States: From the 1960s to the 1990s* (New York: Routledge, 1994).

23. Robertson, "A Necessary Evil."

24. Feagin, *Systemic Racism,* 25.

25. Ibid., 227.

26. Leslie Espinoza and Angela P. Harris, "Afterword: Embracing the Tar-Baby—LatCrit Theory and the Sticky Mess of Race," *California Law Review* 85, no. 5 (1997): 1603.

27. The racialization of Indians began with the first correspondence of European explorers in 1492, almost a decade before enslaved Africans were brought to Santo Domingo (now the capital of the Dominican Republic) in 1501, and it was 1619 before Britain's colonies brought African slaves to Jamestown, Virginia. Furthermore, Indians were racialized institutionally in the U.S. Constitution, Article II, 1789. I do not say this to rank one evil before the other, but to inform the historical narrative.

28. The "vanishing Indian" trope has its origins in the "vanishing frontier" trope.

29. Bonilla-Silva, *Rethinking Racism, White Supremacy and Racism,* and *Racism without Racists.*

30. Bonilla-Silva briefly mentions the racial construction of "Indians" as the establishment of white supremacy by European colonialists in *White Supremacy,* and racially based policies against Native Americans in the development of the United States in *Racism without Racists,* but does not analyze these in either work through his contemporary racial ideology, colorblind racism.

31. According to Census Bureau data released in 2013, seven out of ten American Indians or Alaska Natives live in metropolitan settings.

32. Bonilla-Silva, *Racism without Racists,* 11, 41–44.

33. Margaret Kovach, *Indigenous Methodologies: Characteristics, Conversations, and Contexts* (Toronto: University of Toronto Press, 2009), 48.

34. Catherine Marshall and Gretchen B. Rossman, *Designing Qualitative Research* (Thousand Oaks, CA: Sage, 2006).

35. D. Soyini Madison, "Narrative Poetics and Performative Interventions," in *Handbook of Critical and Indigenous Methodologies,* ed. Norman K. Denzin, Yvonna S. Lincoln, and Linda Tuhiwai Smith (Thousand Oaks, CA: Sage, 2008), 395.

36. Kovach, *Indigenous Methodologies,* 131.

37. Dwanna L. Robertson, "The Myth of Indian Casino Riches," *Indian Country Today Media Network,* June 23, 2012, https://newsmaven.io/indiancountrytoday /archive/the-myth-of-indian-casino-riches-LwEnYOxhAE-iX8buIA2jxA.

38. Brayboy, "Toward a Tribal Critical Race Theory," 432.

39. Michele de Cuneo, Columbus's aristocratic shipmate, writes of his kidnapping, subsequent rape, and sexual slavery of a Carib Indian woman. This is especially disturbing when considering the current propensity for physical violence and sexual assault against Native women—more than 80 percent of rapes on Indian Homelands are committed by non-Native men. Indigenous women are victims of violent crime at 3.5 times the national average, and one in three Native women will be raped in her lifetime.

40. Daniel Morley Johnson, "From the Tomahawk Chop to the Road Block: Discourses of Savagism in Whitestream Media," *American Indian Quarterly* 35, no. 1 (2011): 104–34.

41. Tom Porter, *And Grandma Said: Iroquois Teachings as Passed Down through the Oral Tradition,* ed. Lesley Forrester (Philadelphia: Xlibris Corp., 2008), 137–39.

42. Debra Merskin, "The S-Word: Discourse, Stereotypes, and the American Indian Woman," *Howard Journal of Communications* 21, no. 4 (2010): 345–66.

43. Cornel D. Pewewardy, "Playing Indian at Halftime: The Controversy over American Indian Mascots, Logos, and Nicknames in School-Related Events," *Clearing House* 77, no. 5 (2004): 180–85.

44. Ibid., 182.

45. Merskin, "S-Word."

46. Lisa M. Poupart, "The Familiar Face of Genocide: Internalized Oppression among American Indians," *Hypatia* 18, no. 2 (2003): 86–100.

47. Deloria, *Playing Indian;* Victoria E. Sanchez, *Buying into Racism: American Indian Product Icons in the American Marketplace* (Norman: University of Oklahoma Press, 2012), 153–68.

48. Type the words "celebrity in Native headdress" or "cowboy and Indian party" into any search engine for thousands of images.

49. John Noble Wilford, *The Mysterious History of Columbus: An Exploration of the Man, the Myth, the Legacy* (New York: Random House, 1991); Timothy Kubal, *Cultural Movements and Collective Memory: Christopher Columbus and the Rewriting of the National Origin Myth* (New York: Palgrave Macmillan, 2008).

50. "RE: Indigenous People's Opposition to Celebration and Glorification of Colonial Pirate Christopher Columbus," www.aimovement.org/moipr/columbus-octoo.html.

51. Maria Yellow Horse Brave Heart and Lemyra M. DeBruyn, "The American Indian Holocaust: Healing Historical Unresolved Grief," *American Indian and Alaska Native Mental Health Research* 8, no. 2 (January 1998): 61.

52. The Surgeon General estimates 14 to 27 percent of all American Indian adolescents have attempted suicide.

53. Deloria, *Playing Indian.*

FIVE

On the Transportability, Malleability, and Longevity of Colorblindness

REPRODUCING WHITE SUPREMACY IN BRAZIL AND SOUTH AFRICA

Marzia Milazzo

On Sunday, November 29, 2015, Wilton Domingos Júnior, Roberto Penha, Wesley Rodrigues, Carlos de Souza, and Cleiton de Souza, inseparable friends since childhood, were driving around northern Rio de Janeiro to celebrate sixteen-year-old Penha's first paycheck when police officers fired more than fifty bullets into their car and then tampered with evidence to make the killing appear as self-defense. The murder was not an exceptional occurrence in Brazil, where in 2015 police killed at least 645 people in the state of Rio de Janeiro alone. The overwhelming majority of the victims of police killings in the country—79 percent—are Black boys and men like Penha and his friends, the eldest of whom was only twenty-five years old. Even in the face of undeniable evidence, former Rio state governor Luiz Pezão nevertheless insisted that the murder of the five unarmed Black youngsters "não é racismo" (is not racism).[1]

Though conspicuous in Brazil, white supremacy is clearly not a national or local peculiarity. In South Africa, conjuring the specter of the 1960 Sharpeville massacre, police in 2012 killed thirty-four and injured at least seventy-eight Black miners who were demanding living wages at the Lonmin Platinum Mine in Marikana. In the United States, meanwhile, the killing of innocent Black people by white police and vigilantes has put the international media spotlight back on institutional racism. Whereas it has shattering consequences for people of color, institutional racism also continues to provide tangible material benefits for those of us who are white. White

Brazilians earn 57 percent more than Black Brazilians. In South Africa, the average annual income for white households in 2011 was ZAR 365,134, and for Black households ZAR 60,613. Comparably, the median white household in the United States had $111,146 in wealth holdings in 2011, while the median Black household only had $7,113.[2]

Despite the material and mortal consequences of white supremacy, in Brazil, South Africa, the United States, and elsewhere in former European settler colonies and in Europe, many white people, and some people of color, depict racism as exceptional rather than structural, minimize its effects, or, like Pezão and other Rio state officials, deny its existence altogether. In doing so, they reproduce a powerful dominant racial discourse—in U.S. scholarship commonly termed *colorblindness,* in South Africa *nonracialism,* in Brazil *racial democracy,* and in Europe *new racism*—that aims to render institutional racism permanent.[3] But far from being a "new racism," a product of our time, colorblindness, as I have shown elsewhere, has a long and global history grounded in what I call an epistemology of disavowal.[4] At the core of color-blindness is an obfuscation of hierarchies of power, insistence on a politics of sameness, and disavowal of structural racism and white people's collective responsibility for colonialism and ongoing neocolonial conditions. Other contributions to this volume examine how colorblindness impacts the law, disciplinary formations, and antiracist pedagogies in the United States. This chapter expands that scope by showing that the deployment of colorblindness transcends national, historical, disciplinary, linguistic, and genre boundaries, even as it is modulated through the specific extant national logics of race.

If the killing of Black people is a structural feature of Brazilian society, then, so is the disavowal of white supremacy. In negating racism, Pezão reproduced the same hegemonic discourse that informs what is said and left unsaid about racism in the Brazilian public sphere and the media, which are controlled by a white and conservative elite. Brazil's most prominent newspaper and television network, *O Globo* and Rede Globo respectively, actively pushed for the impeachment of Brazil's democratically elected president Dilma Rousseff, leader of the leftist Partido dos Trabalhadores (Workers' Party). Following Rousseff's impeachment in May 2016, president Michel Temer tellingly unveiled an all-white-male cabinet and eliminated the Ministry of Women, Racial Equality, and Human Rights. As Rousseff has not been found guilty of any crime, the impeachment de facto represents a coup, an attempt by the white conservative elite to regain full control of the government and cut back on social programs for poor Brazilians, who are mainly Black.[5]

Journalist and sociologist Ali Kamel, executive director of journalism for the Globo media network, published a book in 2006 that exemplifies the white silencing of racism propagated in all spheres of Brazilian society, *Não Somos Racistas: Uma Reação Aos Que Querem Nos Transformar Numa Nação Bicolor* (We Are Not Racist: A Reaction to Those Who Want to Transform Us into a Two-Color Nation),[6] consisting of articles that first appeared in *O Globo*. As the title reveals, Kamel argues that Brazil is not a racist society. But Kamel also has a more specific goal: halting the implementation of racial quotas for Afro-Brazilians. To this end, he employs a litany of arguments that resemble those used by authors who demonize policies designed to remedy centuries of institutional racism elsewhere. At the same time, the ideology of *mestiçagem* (racial mixture) that underlies Brazil's racial democracy myth provides Kamel with colorblind strategies that are not available to South African and U.S. authors to the same extent. And yet, as we shall see, writers in these countries also invoke ideologies of hybridity in ways that obscure the workings of white supremacy.

The popular Brazilian news magazine *Veja* listed *Não Somos Racistas* among the ten most important books of 2006, and in 2008 the science and culture magazine *Superinteressante* selected it as one of 122 books that are "essential for understanding the world." In 2009, the news magazine *Época* named Kamel and anthropologist Yvonne Maggie, who authored the preface of *Não Somos Racistas,* among Brazil's one hundred most influential people. As a prominent journalist and director of the largest commercial television network in South America, Kamel has the power to shape public opinion and policy both within and outside Brazil. Still, *Não Somos Racistas* does not warrant critical attention simply because of Kamel's personal influence. Not only is it representative of a larger phenomenon, rather than the exceptional product of an isolated individual, but the book is relevant within the scope of this volume also because it illustrates the migration of colorblindness between journalism and academia. To corroborate his arguments, in fact, Kamel invokes an array of Brazilian scholars who also demonize affirmative action in their work. Academics in turn have provided Kamel with additional platforms on which to spread his anti–affirmative action propaganda; for example, Kamel was invited to speak alongside rector Aloísio Teixeira and other academics at a debate on university reform held in the Institute of Philosophy and Social Sciences at the Federal University of Rio de Janeiro (UFRJ) in 2004. Even as Black students remain severely underrepresented in Brazilian universities, Kamel devoted his talk to attacking university admission quotas for Afro-Brazilians.[7]

The complicity of many white academics in reinscribing racial power, as it turns out, is also a global reality. This becomes apparent if we consider the central location that colorblindness plays within a substantial body of South African scholarship on race produced mainly by white scholars since the 1994 democratic dispensation. This scholarship demonizes the employment of racial categories, vilifies policies that attempt to redress racial inequality, and minimizes or fully disavows white privilege. Disciplines with a significant impact on public policy, such as sociology, education, and economics, have become leading venues for the propagation of colorblind doctrines in South African academia. Yet no traditional discipline is immune to the phenomenon, for colorblindness impacts the logics, arguments, and findings of much post-apartheid scholarship on race produced in both the social sciences and the humanities.[8]

Sociologist Gerhard Maré's most recent book, *Declassified: Moving beyond the Dead-End of Race in South Africa* (2014), is emblematic of the widespread currency that colorblindness enjoys among many white South African academics.[9] An emeritus professor at the University of KwaZulu-Natal, Maré in 2017 was a fellow at the Institute for Advanced Study at Stellenbosch University (STIAS) and project leader of the STIAS Effects of Race project, which aims "to inform social change through challenging and undermining existing notions of racial difference," according to the project's website. The former director of the Centre for Critical Research on Race and Identity, which describes its mission as "facilitating the study of race thinking," Maré ironically argues in *Declassified* that it is high time South Africans moved beyond "race thinking and race classification."[10] Maré is one of several white South African scholars who, rather than making structural racism visible, critique abstract notions of "race thinking" and the practice of racial classification per se, as the title *Declassified* already suggests. The research emphasis on racial categories rather than structural racism that characterizes much post-apartheid scholarship on race, especially in the social sciences, is not accidental but is the consequence of an active desire to maintain white domination.

With the goal of illustrating the transportability, malleability, and longevity of colorblind discourse, this chapter examines key rhetorical strategies that Kamel and Maré employ to demonize affirmative action policies, silence structural racism, and ultimately uphold white supremacy, while placing these works alongside other texts produced in Brazil, South Africa, and the United States as well as Panama. It is striking that *Não Somos Racistas* and *Declassified,* albeit arising in different contexts, avail themselves of a shared rhetorical repository in their parallel efforts to reinscribe white domination by halting measures that aim to redress racial inequality. Close attention to Kamel's popular booklet, Maré's sociological study, and other texts that support white supremacy across borders reveals the global popularity of colorblindness among white people. The reproduction of colorblind rhetorics that is at work in the texts examined herein, I argue, is the product neither of accident nor of ignorance, but of an active interest in maintaining the racist status quo.

In *The Racial Contract,* Charles Mills remedies the colorblindness that has informed Marxist and hegemonic feminist standpoint theories by placing white epistemology at the center of philosophical analysis. Mills argues that, on matters relative to race and racism, white people usually display an "inverted epistemology, an epistemology of ignorance."[11] Mills views this epistemology, which he calls *white ignorance,* as a ubiquitous but undertheorized kind of ignorance produced directly through racial domination. In the process, Mills contends, citing sociologist Woody Doane, that white people "exhibit a general inability to perceive the persistence of discrimination and the effects of more subtle forms of institutional discrimination."[12] This is problematic as it presumes that white people are generally ignorant about racial injustice and therefore innocent.

The theory of white ignorance has gained much traction in philosophical scholarship and beyond. However it is insufficient to explain the systematic reproduction of colorblindness across disciplines, discourses, time, and national contexts.[13] In attempting to understand white people's extensive commitment to colorblind discourse, it is productive to shift the conceptual lens from ignorance to disavowal. As Kimberlé Crenshaw reminds us, "Race consciousness is central not only to the domination of blacks but also to whites' acceptance of the legitimacy of hierarchy and their identity with elite interests. Exposing the centrality of race consciousness is crucial to identifying and delegitimating beliefs that present hierarchy as inevitable and fair."[14] Centering disavowal makes visible some of the workings of race consciousness in the making of racialized meaning. It is useful to distinguish between actual ignorance and the *performance of ignorance* that serves to conceal white people's knowledge of, and investment in, white supremacy. While historically people of color have strategically feigned ignorance as a means of survival, white people strategically simulate ignorance as a mechanism of domination.

Considered to embody three archetypal racial systems, the United States (Jim Crow), South Africa (apartheid), and Brazil ("racial democracy") have long been privileged locations for the comparative study of white supremacy in history and the social sciences.[15] However, no studies have paid attention to the specific rhetorical strategies that structure white supremacist discourse in all these contexts. Understanding the workings of colorblind discourse on a global scale nevertheless is an urgent task. Critical race scholars have shown that the power of colorblind arguments does not rest on their brilliance, originality, or reliance on hard facts, but on their rhetorical ability to portray as progressive what is in fact regressive, as discriminatory what is meant to challenge discrimination, and to package colorblind logics under the disguise of common sense.[16]

Kamel and Maré implicitly try to mark their national contexts as existing beyond the allegedly anachronistic logics of race: in Kamel's argument, Brazil has "overcome" racism thanks to widespread miscegenation, while in Maré's view, South Africa has succeeded in freeing itself from the racial inequality of the apartheid era. Yet, even as they insist that we should stop talking about race, neither Kamel nor Maré manages to leave race behind. These authors' inability to transcend race is not exceptional but typical of writings that reinscribe colorblindness. In societies where racial inequality is rampant, suppressing race as a category of analysis *always* creates textual contradictions that show that enforcing colorblindness is an act of epistemic violence. They signal that the deployment of colorblind rhetoric is the product of white people's knowledge of and active investment in white supremacy rather than ignorance thereof. The insistence in silencing race within writings that are chiefly about race, I aim to show in the following pages, is itself about race: it is a manifestation of white racial consciousness and a desire to reinscribe the racist status quo.

READING RACIAL POWER

A popular idiom says that all Brazilians have *um pé na cozinha* (a foot in the kitchen), implying that everybody has African ancestors. Just as in the common description of the Afrikaans language as "kitchen Dutch" in South Africa, the kitchen here evokes servitude and domestic labor, specifically the unpaid labor of enslaved Black people. Racial and cultural mixture (*mestiçagem*) is certainly present in Brazil, yet those at the top of the social ladder remain overwhelmingly white,[17] while most Black Brazilians continue to climb only the strenuous steps that lead to many *favelas* in cities like Rio de Janeiro, where the entanglement between race and place is everywhere noticeable. The idealization of contemporary race relations in Brazil finds its predecessor in ahistorical literary representations of Brazilian slavery as an allegedly humane process punctuated by romantic encounters between Portuguese colonizers and enslaved people of African descent.[18] Although Brazil imported nearly five million slaves and was the last country to abolish slavery, in 1888, white Brazilian intellectuals have a long tradition of enforcing colorblindness by portraying slavery as a mild form of servitude while extolling racial mixture as alleged evidence of the absence of racism in Brazilian society.

The mystification of Brazil as a benevolent civilization, termed Luso-Tropicalism, is associated in particular with anthropologist Gilberto Freyre's *Casa-grande e Senzala: Formação da Família Brasileira sob o Regime de Economia Patriarcal* (1933; translated as *The Masters and the Slaves: A Study in the Development of Brazilian Civilization*). In this work, Freyre constructed an influential discourse of Brazilian exceptionalism founded on the ideology of *mestiçagem* and on comparisons with the United States and other former British colonies. The Portuguese, according to Freyre, is "o colonizador europeu que melhor confraternizou com as raças chamadas inferiores" (the European colonizer who best fraternized with the so-called inferior races) and "o menos cruel" (the least cruel) because he "sempre pendeu . . . para o cruzamento e miscegenação" (was always inclined . . . toward mixture and miscegenation).[19] Freyre presents racial mixture as alleged proof that racial discrimination against Afro-Brazilians is nonexistent. However, in his attempt to demonstrate that both Portuguese and Brazilians are "colorblind," Freyre's own racism becomes immediately apparent. As colorblindness necessarily relies on dehistoricization and decontextualization, Freyre omits the historical context that explains the relatively high incidence of miscegenation in Brazil, such as the fact that most Portuguese colonizers arriving in Brazil were young men unaccompanied by white women, and silences the fact that racial mixture in Brazil has largely been the historical product of white men raping Black women rather than the consequence of consent or intermarriage.[20]

Black Brazilian intellectuals and activists have challenged discourses such as those that Freyre propagates in his work. The late Abdias Nascimento writes in a book aptly titled *Brazil: Mixture or Massacre?* that there was nothing mild about slavery in Brazil:

The truth is that the Portuguese colonial aristocracy in Brazil was utterly racist, cruel and inhuman in its treatment of Africans as any other white slave-holding elite of the Americas. Slaves were continually and systematically tortured, murdered, abused and maltreated. Since trade routes to Africa from Brazil and back were shorter and more direct, prices were lower than in North America. Slaves were so cheap in Brazil that it was more economical to buy new replacements than to care for them—especially old or sick people, children, or the many who were deformed or crippled from torture and overwork.[21]

The myth that Nascimento deconstructs in the quote above reverberates beyond the Brazilian context, and so does the disavowal of racism at the heart of Freyre's *Casa-grande e Senzala*. Illustrating the long history of colorblindness across national borders, this disavowal is replicated in other texts that precede the World War II era. For example, in *El peligro antillano en la América Central: La defensa de la raza* (The Antillean Danger in Central America: The Defense of Race, 1925), Panamanian-Ecuadoran writer and military cadet Olmedo Alfaro argues that West Indian immigrants (whom he calls Antilleans) pose a problem for Central America, and specifically a problem for white people. Yet Alfaro denies that white supremacy motivates his agenda and mobilizes an array of colorblind tools to persuade the reader that his battle to "defend" white Panamanians from the "Antillean problem" has nothing to do with racism and everything to do with the alleged insurmountable *cultural* differences that exist between Panamanian nationals and West Indian immigrants. Alfaro, just like Freyre, would like his readers to believe that he is *"colorblind"*.[22] He writes: "No existe en nuestros pueblos el ánimo de oponerse a la invasión antillana por causas puramente raciales, sabe el mundo que aquellos colonos africanos que nuestros progenitores importaron a Ibero-América, recibieron siempre el mejor trato dentro de las costumbres de la época" (In our countries a desire to oppose the Antillean invasion for purely racial reasons does not exist[;] the world knows that the African colonials that our progenitors imported to Ibero-America always received the best treatment within the customs of the time).[23] One might think that neither Alfaro nor Freyre needs to resort to colorblindness, given that overt racism was permissible in Panama and Brazil of the early twentieth century. But this belief relies on a misunderstanding of colorblindness as merely an instrument of white supremacy among many, rather than a constitutive element thereof that goes back to the colonial era. Deception and disavowal are not negligible nor recent phenomena, but governing principles of white supremacy.

Deception and disavowal have not lost currency among contemporary white intellectuals that reinscribe white supremacy. In *Não Somos Racistas,* Kamel reproduces the exceptionalist argument of Freyre's *Casa-grande e Senzala.* Brazil is different from the rest of the world, Kamel argues, because most people in the country are racially mixed (*mestiços* or *pardos*).[24] According to Kamel, this demonstrates that racial prejudice is not a feature of Brazilian society. In his own words, "[A]inda somos uma nação que acredita nas virtudes da nossa miscegenação, na convivência harmoniosa entre todas as cores" ([W]e are still a nation that believes in the virtues of our miscegenation, in the harmonious coexistence between [people of] all colors).[25] Like Freyre, Kamel silences the fact that, far from indicating racial harmony, miscegenation has largely been the consequence of white men's sexual violence against Black women.[26] For Kamel, Freyre played only one role in Brazilian society: he valorized Black people's impact on Brazil's culture and national identity. However, considering Black people as part of the nation's cultural and racial makeup, as Freyre did, is not a gesture free from racist implications. The *symbolic* acknowledgment of African elements of national culture should not be confused with concrete benefits for Black people. The valorization of cultural hybridity and miscegenation can and does comfortably coexist with a white supremacist agenda, as Freyre's work reveals. Most importantly, the invocation of cultural and racial hybridity is a colorblind strategy often invoked by white Latin American elites (and white elites elsewhere) to curtail land redistribution and halt affirmative action policies.[27]

While the dominant national ideology of *mestiçagem/mestizaje* is not equally accessible to writers in South Africa and the United States, countries that have enforced a rigid racial classification system, hegemonic notions of hybridity are also exploited to silence racism in these contexts. For example, in order to delegitimize the racial categories necessary to implement race-based redress measures, Maré argues in *Declassified* that there are "permeable boundaries" and "many crossings within, and from and into, any group." He continues: "'Impure' is what we are and what we have always been, 'entangled' in a multiplicity of ways."[28] Maré here indirectly references the work of South African literary scholar Sarah Nuttall, who in *Entanglement: Literary and Cultural Reflections on Post-apartheid* (2009) depicts entanglement and hybridity as intrinsically progressive categories, while she argues that maintaining "categories of race difference" in post-apartheid literary criticism represents a kind of "segregated theory."[29] However, neither Nuttall nor Maré is able to do away with "categories of race difference." Tellingly, the examples of "crossings within, and from and into, any group" that Maré presents are either about gender and sexuality or about Afrikaner *verraaiers* (traitors) who defied the status quo during apartheid. This is revealing because crossing and mobility are racialized privileges that are not granted to people of color. Only from the vantage point of white privilege can racial barriers be perceived as permeable.

Problematic invocations of racial mixture also appear in a body of U.S. journalism and scholarship that presents itself as concerned with racial justice while it reinforces white supremacy in practice. Let me provide but one example that illustrates the importation of the Latin American *mestizaje* ideology into recent writings produced in the United States, as this further reveals the transportability and insidiousness of colorblind discourse. Journalist Gregory Rodriguez argues in *Mongrels, Bastards, Orphans, and Vagabonds: Mexican Immigration and the Future of Race in America* (2007) that Mexican Americans are pioneers of a revolution that will completely alter U.S. race relations. He formulates his faith in the potential of Mexican immigration as follows:

> Mexican Americans are forcing the United States to reinterpret the concept of the melting pot to include racial as well as ethnic mixing. Rather than abetting the segregationist ethos of a country divided into mutually exclusive groups, Mexican Americans continually continue to blur the lines between "us" and "them." Just as the emergence of the mestizo undermined the Spanish racial system in colonial Mexico, Mexican Americans, who have always confounded the Anglo American racial system, will ultimately destroy it, too.[30]

Rodriguez argues that Mexican immigrants, since they are increasingly marrying outside their ethnic community, will add a new positive element to U.S. society: miscegenation. Rodriguez thus presumes that there has been no racial mixing in the United States, even as every slavery society in the Americas produced a mixed population.[31] Moreover, Rodriguez, like Kamel, insinuates that miscegenation produces superior human beings untainted by racist ideology, although miscegenation has not managed to halt white supremacy in Mexico, nor will it dismantle white supremacy in the United States. Rather than undermining "the Spanish racial system," as Rodriguez contends, a selected number of Mexican *mestizos* acquired the privileges of whiteness previously reserved only for European colonizers. *Mestizo* privilege in Mexico today continues to depend on the exclusion, exploitation, and invisibilization of indigenous people and Afro-Mexicans.[32] Conjectures such as those Rodriguez presents do not undermine but rather entrench white supremacy. They also show that the invocation of *mestizaje/mestiçagem* is an especially insidious colorblind tool. Hybridity maintains an aspirational appeal as ideologies of racial mixture tend to be perceived as "less racist" than doctrines of racial purity, even though they rely on ideologies of whitening[33] and on fallacious notions of race as a biological reality to the same dimension and degree as the race separation argument.

Invoking racial mixture is not the only, nor the most effective, colorblind strategy that Kamel employs in *Não Somos Racistas*. Kamel explicitly denies the existence of institutional racism, arguing that racial discrimination in Brazil "não é estrutural" (is not structural).[34] As he contends that there have been no institutional barriers against Afro-Brazilians after the abolition of slavery, Kamel silences the fact that Black people were abandoned without land, education, or any kind of support from the state after manumission, while Europeans were given free land and money to migrate to Brazil.[35] The United States, meanwhile, provides Kamel with a convenient means of comparison that he exploits to further construct Brazil as being allegedly free from racism. Kamel argues that in the United States racism is "rotineramente mais duro, mais explícito, mais direto" (routinely harder, more explicit, more direct), while in Brazil "indubitavelmente, há menos racismo" (undoubtedly, there is less racism).[36] *Não Somos Racistas* depicts racism as a feeling and a generalizable human characteristic, something that all people *have*. In this way, Kamel reproduces a depoliticized and fallacious understanding of race as being merely synonymous with skin color, what legal scholar Neil Gotanda has defined as *formal-race unconnectedness*.[37] The only racism that Kamel acknowledges as existing in Brazil is not actually racism, then, but individual prejudice.

Maré, in *Declassified*, similarly denies that racism is a structural element of South African society. He even goes one step further than Kamel, arguing that structural racism *itself* is a myth. Race and racism, Maré writes, "can all serve as the basis for discrimination—but this is not systemic as the operation of capitalism is."[38] The vast majority of Black people remain poor in South Africa, where the unemployment rate in 2014 was 40 percent for Black people, but only 8 percent for white people.[39] Maré nevertheless places racial discrimination firmly in the past and refers to Black people as "the 'previously disadvantaged'" as well as erroneously argues that in South Africa there has been a "deracialization of capitalism."[40] For Maré's arguments to be effective, of course, any empirical data on racial inequality must be omitted.

Even as he silences racism, Maré explicitly denies that he is enforcing colorblindness. He writes: "It is in the notion of non-racialism that I believe the most helpful possibility of a future beyond 'race' continues to lay. Non-racialism is not to be seen as colour-blindness—not in the least. Indeed, non-racialism relies on critical colour awareness."[41] The dichotomy between nonracialism and colorblindness that Maré postulates is false. During the anti-apartheid struggle, the nonracialism promoted by the African National Congress (ANC) represented a practical antiracist strategy intended to foster unity and collaboration across racial lines while still advancing Black people's decolonial agenda.[42] Although it is rooted in an ANC history of antiracist resistance, nonracialism no longer serves progressive purposes today. In a typical case of yesterday's solutions becoming today's problems, the terms "nonracialism" and "colorblindness" have become de facto synonymous in South Africa.[43] They also function as one and the same thing within *Declassified*. Maré explains that he uses the terms "race thinking" and "racialism" interchangeably.[44] Moving toward nonracialism for Maré thus implies moving away from "race thinking," rather than doing away with institutional racism.

Kamel and Maré also both demonize the employment of racial categories per se, a powerful colorblind strategy in the Brazilian and South African contexts, where battles over the legitimacy of racial classification in general, and the specific content of such classification, have dominated debates on affirmative action. Maré argues that "classification of fellow humans into 'races', through the power granted to the state, remains a crime against humanity, no matter what justification is offered."[45] Racial categorization, Maré adds, bears the potential for "racism and group violence."[46] Kamel comparably argues that racial categories "são em si racistas. Porque não devemos falar em negros, pardos, ou brancos, mas apenas em brasileiros" (are in themselves racist. Because we must not speak about blacks, browns, or whites, but merely about Brazilians).[47] As they displace violence away from institutional racism, these arguments also obfuscate the fact that race is both embodied and a social construct that cannot be escaped through a mere act of willpower.

In a move that demonstrates how colorblind logics not only migrate across journalism and academia but are also reciprocally validated in these realms, on the very first page of *Não Somos Racistas* Kamel names several Brazilian anthropologists, historians, and sociologists who also disparage race-based affirmative action policies in their scholarship. In *A Persistência da Raça: Ensaios Antropológicos sobre o Brasil e a África Austral* (The Persistence of Race: Anthropological Essays on Brazil and Southern Africa, 2005), anthropologist Peter Fry, whose work Kamel invokes as authoritative in *Não somos racistas,* reproduces arguments eerily similar to those that Kamel advances. Fry argues that, in relying on three main racial categories (*negros, brancos, indios*), affirmative action strengthens the "idea of race" and negates the miscegenation that characterizes the Brazilian population. Fry also denies that racism is institutionalized in Brazil, which he presents as being radically different from the United States, South Africa, or Zimbabwe. Like Kamel, who states that "acreditar que raças existem é a base de todo racismo" (believing in the existence of races is the basis of all racism),[48] Fry reiterates the familiar colorblind argument that recognizing the existence of different racial groups is itself racist. Maré does the same in *Declassified,* where he argues that "race thinking" causes "the dehumanization and mass extermination of fellow human beings."[49] These authors erroneously portray thought as something disembodied that exists outside of history and materiality, a move that allows them to deflect attention away from white people's collective role as central agents of white supremacy. They direct the reader's attention toward race as an abstract concept, rather than toward racism as an ingrained dimension of economic and political systems that allow white people to benefit handsomely from the oppression and exploitation of people of color.

Racism cannot be undone by discontinuing the collection of racial data. Kwame Ture and Charles Hamilton, who coined the term "institutional racism" in *Black Power* (1967), distinguish between overt acts of racial violence and intolerance (individual racism) and the collective, covert, and structural domination of people of color (institutional racism).[50] Institutional racism is the normalization of white supremacy in institutions, laws, policies, and practices that produce racially differential access to jobs, services, spaces, wealth, and so forth. If governments stopped collecting racial data, this would not halt structural racism, but rather would prevent the monitoring of racial inequality and the possibility of implementing race-based redress measures. Of course, governments use racial classification for a range of purposes beyond remedial policies. But it is only when racial categorization is put at the service of racial justice and redistribution that it becomes a problem for authors like Kamel and Maré. White supremacy, meanwhile, is the one "crime against humanity" that both fail to name.

The silencing of racism leads to textual paradoxes that reveal the location of white racial consciousness as being central to the deployment of colorblind rhetoric. Even as Kamel contends that racial terminology should *not* be used, he ironically argues for employing the racial category *pardo* (brown or racially mixed) to speak about all Brazilians. It is relevant to notice how comfortable Kamel is with *pardo,* so much so that this category is never questioned but remains fixed in the text, in contrast with *branco* (white) and *negro* (Black), which are disputed. Kamel's choice of *pardo* as a term seemingly able to encompass Brazil's "racial essence" is intimately tied to the reproduction of the racial democracy ideology. Kamel portrays *pardo* as a self-evident signifier rather than the reflection of an ideology, a mirror of how the white elite wants to see Brazil: as a country where neither Black nor white people exist, but everybody allegedly is racially mixed. And if everybody is mixed, nobody is white and can be held accountable for racism.

Kamel argues that employing the binary racial categories *Black* and *white* (which are used to implement racial quotas in Brazil) makes sense in the United States, where racial classification is defined by the one-drop rule, but in Brazil it is impossible to know who is white and who is Black because most people are *pardos.* To support his contention, Kamel cites former Brazilian president Fernando Henrique Cardoso, who, during the visit of then South African president Thabo Mbeki, argued that "branco no Brasil é um conceito relativo" (white is a relative concept in Brazil).[51] What neither Cardoso nor Kamel says is that there is a recognizable white caste in Brazil that is in control of the economy, the government, and the media. In arguing that the categories *Black* and *white* are U.S. importations, Kamel also silences the fact that the Movimento Negro (Black Movement) and Afro-Brazilian publications committed to social justice, such as the journal *Quilombo,* which Nascimento edited from 1948 until 1950, have long employed the term *negro* to collectively describe all Brazilians of African descent regardless of appearance.[52]

Decades of Afro-Brazilian mobilization led the Brazilian government to adopt a range of affirmative action policies in the mid-1990s and early 2000s, such as admission quotas for Black and indigenous people in Brazil's prestigious public universities.[53] Kamel nevertheless defines the employment of racial quotas for people of color in Brazil as "a importação acrítica de uma solução americana para um problema americano" (the uncritical importation of an American solution to an American problem).[54] Although Kamel argues that racism does not exist in Brazil, he defines racial quotas as "a adoção de medidas racistas para combater o racismo" (the adoption of racist measures to combat racism).[55] This way, he makes visible the paradoxical logics of colorblindness, a discourse that reveals itself as both self-contradictory and violent in its insistence on silencing racism.

Kamel misses the mark on the U.S. context as he disparages what he calls "a construção racista americana segundo a qual todo mundo que não é branco é negro" (the racist American construction according to which everyone who is not white is black).[56] The rejection of racial binarism, in fact, is a colorblind strategy also employed in the United States. Consider, for example, the U.S. Supreme Court case *Parents Involved in Community Schools v. Seattle School District No. 1,* which in 2006 struck down affirmative action programs aimed at desegregating public schools in Seattle, Washington, and Louisville, Kentucky. Employing the same colorblind rhetoric used in three previous cases that curtailed affirmative action policies in higher education, the Court held that the programs violated the equal protection clause of the Fourteenth Amendment. The concurring judges rejected the classification of students into Black and white that the Seattle School District had implemented as a means to remedy school segregation, arguing that "[c]lassifying and assigning children according to a binary conception of race is an extreme approach."[57]

Questioning the legibility of race is a colorblind strategy deployed across national contexts and genres. Just as Kamel asks, "Quem é branco no Brasil?" (Who is white in Brazil?),[58] Justice Kennedy in *Parents Involved* queries, "Who exactly is white and who is nonwhite?"[59] In *Declassified,* Maré similarly recounts the story of a teacher who was required to record the race of her pupils for the sake of monitoring. Apparently unable to do so, the teacher appealed to the Department of Education, asking: "How black is black? And when is a pupil coloured?"[60] Maré cites this example to argue that it is impossible to identify someone's race just by looking at the person and therefore race-based remedial measures cannot be implemented effectively.

What these examples teach us is that calling into question racial classification, the legibility of race, and the lived realities of discrimination and privilege that racial categories embody is a colorblind move that impacts the production of knowledge, public discourse, and the law on a transnational scale, with harmful costs for people of color and handsome benefits for white people. Maré could have argued that, for the sake of monitoring inequality, it does not matter whether the pupil that the aforementioned teacher attempted to categorize is Coloured or Black because *both* groups continue to face discrimination in South Africa. What is important is that neither

Black nor Coloured people enjoy the privileges of whiteness. In the same vein, the U.S. Supreme Court in *Parents Involved* could have recognized that "assigning children according to a binary conception of race" with the aim of desegregating the Seattle school district is a rational measure. That this did not occur has little to do with hard facts and everything to do with the desire to uphold white supremacy that motivates the deployment of colorblind rhetoric. The argument that racial classification and racial remediation policies are not *perfect* and therefore should be abandoned altogether is a white supremacist tool. Kamel and Kennedy know very well that they are white and precisely for this reason deny that white people exist.

In South Africa, aside from extending the welfare system, the main strategy adopted by the ANC government to reduce racial inequality has been the implementation of market-based affirmative action policies, such as Black Economic Empowerment (BEE), aimed at increasing the number of Black people in the middle and upper classes. While these policies have managed to partially deracialize the wealthier sectors of society, the vast majority of the South African population is as poor and exploited today as it was during apartheid.[61] Yet rather than arguing that race-based remedial policies should be expanded to further benefit the majority, Maré describes affirmative action as damaging for Black people themselves: "The consequences of appointing unqualified people to jobs are multiple: the psychological damage to individual self-worth of those who fail and are blamed for their failure, and the effect on colleagues; the confirmation of racial stereotypes, ... and the resulting failures in service delivery for exactly the poor and marginalized whom the government aims to help."[62] Maré erroneously assumes that desegregating the workplace is equivalent to giving jobs to "unqualified" people of color. While he deceptively presents himself as concerned with the welfare of Black people, Maré reproduces white supremacist arguments that equate being Black with being unskilled and generally unfit to work alongside white people.

While he disparages affirmative action, Maré directs the reader's attention toward intraracial inequality as a means to further direct attention away from the reality of white economic dominance in South Africa. He writes: "Previously, the correlation of inequality with races was there for all to see— the exceptions were few. Now, and increasingly, inequality within the races is growing fastest."[63] This emphasis on intraracial inequality (which here implies inequality among *Black* people) is a common colorblind strategy used in South African scholarship. For example, in *Class, Race, and Inequality in*

South Africa (2005), Jeremy Seekings and Nicoli Nattrass attempt to demonstrate "the steadily declining importance of interracial inequality and rising importance of intraracial inequality" in post-apartheid South Africa, arguing that "by 2000, there were about as many African people as white people in the top income quintile."[64] In this way, the authors mystify a very simple fact: white people constitute less than 9 percent, and not 50 percent, of the South African population. For Seekings and Nattrass, the fact that white people occupy circa 50 percent of the top earning quintile does not demonstrate that racial inequality remains rampant, but rather illustrates that in the post-apartheid era there has been a "shift from race to class."[65] Yet if class can autonomously explain inequality, why focus on the racialized phenomenon of intraracial inequality? Seekings and Nattrass's book reveals the operation of white racial consciousness, as it exhibits contradictions inherent in scholarship that enforces colorblindness while producing knowledge about racial inequality.

With the aim of convincing readers that economic inequality is a product of class rather than racial disparities, Maré also strategically concentrates on the upper echelons of South African society, which are increasingly multiracial, while the poor remain overwhelmingly Black. Demonstrating how the deployment of colorblindness is modulated through the local dynamics of race, Kamel does exactly the opposite. In order to prove that inequality in Brazil is allegedly not a consequence of racism but merely classism, Kamel presents statistics that aim to show that in Brazil "negros e brancos pobres se parecem" (poor Blacks and whites are similar).[66] Maré and Kamel thus take advantage of the dissimilar class and race dynamics of their respective societies and focus on different racial groups to achieve the same goal. Given that in Brazil there are also poor white people (they are a small minority compared to Black people, a fact that Kamel does not disclose), Kamel focuses on the racial composition of the lower classes in his attempt to silence racism. Although Kamel previously argued that in Brazil it is impossible to tell who is white and who is not white, he now contends that racial quotas for Black people are illegitimate because a sector of the white Brazilian population is also poor. Whites, then, do exist, but only when it is convenient for Kamel's argument. In the meantime, Kamel silences the fact that there is hardly a Black middle class in Brazil and that the upper class is virtually exclusively white. Maré, conversely, focuses on the new Black elite, whom he stigmatizes as being "filthy rich" and prone to "conspicuous consumption."[67] And yet, it is white people who continue to be "filthy rich" and own 85 percent of the

South African land and economy—white monopoly capital accumulated over centuries of slavery, colonialism, apartheid, and the ongoing exploitation of cheap Black labor—while Black people, even members of the small Black elite, do not have intergenerational wealth and continue to be burdened by the so-called "Black tax" as they financially support family members who continue to be poor. What are systemically made to disappear in these texts are white wealth, its intrinsic dependence on the theft of Black people's lives, land, and labor, and the white supremacist violence deployed to preserve it.

CONCLUSION

This chapter has shown that as colorblindness travels across time, national contexts, and genres, it is regulated through specific national logics of race, yet shares fundamental similarities that transcend borders. It is remarkable that what appear to be vastly different racial regimes and sociopolitical contexts produce strikingly similar dominant racial strategies and ideologies, to the extent that texts as heterogeneous as those examined herein rely on a shared rhetorical arsenal in their shared attempt to silence and reinscribe racism. The rhetorical convergence across three countries (and more) that this chapter has illustrated demonstrates that the white deployment of colorblind rhetoric is a deliberate strategy. It is not the product of white ignorance, but of *white knowledge.* Scholarship on colorblindness that does not account for white knowledge, agency, and active investment in whiteness risks reinscribing the colorblindness that it aims to contest. Consider how, although ignorance was structurally produced by the apartheid regime through spatial segregation, Black Consciousness leader Steve Biko importantly insisted on bringing white people's knowledge about their privilege to the forefront of analysis, rather than their alleged obliviousness about racial domination.[68]

No matter how hard one might try, this chapter has hopefully shown, silencing institutional racism in societies structured in white supremacy and antiblackness always creates contradictions at the textual level. But it also produces metadiscursive paradoxes. If race thinking is not appropriate in contemporary South Africa, for example, as Maré contends, then why think about race? If race does not exist, as Kamel argues, then why write about race? The fact that Maré and Kamel have written and published books that delegitimize affirmative action policies for people of color implies that, at least to the authors themselves, race is not simply worth thinking about, but does *matter* a great deal.

Since enforcing colorblindness is an act of epistemic violence, the authors of the works examined herein do not manage to do away with race, yet they insist that their readers should do so. In the process, they reinforce white supremacy through the deployment of colorblind rhetorics that constantly displace the cause of inequality *elsewhere:* in the past, class, racial categories themselves, "racial thinking," racial consciousness, and so forth. They argue that these realities can explain inequality independently from the white supremacy that enables the institutionalized reproduction of colorblindness in academia, law, and the media across national borders. As they display visible convergences between hegemonic racial discourse in Brazil, South Africa, the United States, and elsewhere, these works reveal the workings of white racial consciousness in the making of racialized meaning and force us to grapple with the longevity, malleability, and insidiousness of colorblindness as a global technology of white supremacy.

ACKNOWLEDGMENTS

I thank Pallavi Banerjee, Daniel HoSang, George Lipsitz, N. Michelle Murray, Tendayi Sithole, and LaTonya Trotter for their invaluable comments on earlier versions of this essay. Thank you to Elisa Larkin Nascimento for allowing me to access precious resources at the Instituto de Pesquisas e Estudos Afro Brasileiros (IPEAFRO) that have enhanced this essay and to Tatiana Lima for her guidance and assistance. I completed a draft of this essay while on academic leave from Vanderbilt University on an Andrew W. Mellon Postdoctoral Fellowship in the Department of English at Rhodes University, for which I am grateful.

NOTES

1. On the murder of the five Brazilian youngsters, see Jonathan Watts, "Rio de Janeiro Police Officers Arrested for Killing of Black and Mixed-Race Youths," *Guardian,* Dec. 1, 2015, www.theguardian.com/world/2015/dec/01/rio-de-janeiro -military-police-killings-youths. On police killings and racism in Brazil, see Amnesty International, "You Killed My Son: Homicides by Military Police in the City of Rio de Janeiro," Aug. 3, 2015, www.amnesty.org/en/documents/amr19/2068/2015/en; and Elsa Buchanan, "Brazil: Police Killed 645 People in Rio de Janeiro State in 2015," *International Business Times,* July 7, 2016, www.ibtimes.co.uk/thurs-7-july

-brazil-police-killed-645-people-rio-de-janeiro-state-2015–1569304. On Pezão's response to the killing, see Vinícius Lisboa, "Governador do Rio diz que assassinato de cinco jovens não foi racismo," *Agência Brasil,* Nov. 30, 2015, http://agenciabrasil .ebc.com.br/geral/noticia/2015-11/governador-diz-que-assassinato-de-5-jovens -nao-foi-racismo.

2. On the Marikana massacre, see, for example, Greg Marinovich, *Murder at Small Koppie: The Real Story of the Marikana Massacre* (Johannesburg: Penguin South Africa, 2016). On racial inequality in Brazil, see, for example, Elisa Larkin Nascimento, *The Sorcery of Color: Identity, Race, and Gender in Brazil* (Philadelphia: Temple University Press, 2007); and Edward Telles, *Race in Another America: The Significance of Skin Color in Brazil* (Princeton, NJ: Princeton University Press, 2004). On racial inequality in South Africa, see, for example, Alan Emery, "Class and Race Domination and Transformation in South Africa," *Critical Sociology* 34, no. 4 (2008): 409–31; and Statistics South Africa, "Census 2011," www.statssa.gov .za/publications/P03014/P030142011.pdf. On racial inequality in the United States, see, for example, George Lipsitz, *How Racism Takes Place* (Philadelphia: Temple University Press, 2011); and Laura Shin, "Why a Typical White Household Has 16 Times the Wealth of a Black One," *Forbes,* Mar. 26, 2015, www.forbes.com/sites /laurashin/2015/03/26/the-racial-wealth-gap-why-a-typical-white-household-has-16 -times-the-wealth-of-a-black-one.

3. For comparative transnational studies on colorblindness, see, for example, Amy E. Ansell, "Casting a Blind Eye: The Ironic Consequences of Color-Blindness in South Africa and the United States," *Critical Sociology* 32, nos. 1–2 (2006): 333–56; and Howard Winant, *The World Is a Ghetto: Race and Democracy since World War II* (New York: Basic Books, 2001).

4. Marzia Milazzo, "White Supremacy, White Knowledge, and Anti–West Indian Discourse in Panama: Olmedo Alfaro's *El peligro antillano en la América Central,*" *Global South* 6, no. 2 (2012): 65, 68, 80. See also Colin W. Leach, "Against the Notion of a 'New Racism,'" *Journal of Community and Applied Social Psychology* 12 (2005): 432–45; and George Lipsitz, "The Sounds of Silence: How Race Neutrality Preserves White Supremacy," in this volume.

5. On the impeachment of Dilma Rousseff and its aftermath, see Marshall Eakin, "Brazil's Right-Wing Coup: Dilma Rousseff's Impeachment Endangers More than the Nation's Democracy," *Salon,* May 28, 2016, www.salon.com /2016/05/28/brazils_right_wing_coup_partner.

6. Ali Kamel, *Não Somos Racistas: Uma Reação aos que Querem nos Transformar Numa Nação Bicolor* (Rio de Janeiro: Nova Frontera, 2006). All translations are mine.

7. On the talk, see ibid., 9.

8. I examine the reproduction of colorblindness in a body of post-1994 South African scholarship produced in economics, education, literature, philosophy, and sociology in Marzia Milazzo, "The Rhetorics of Racial Power: Enforcing Colorblindness in Post-Apartheid Scholarship on Race," *Journal of International and Intercultural Communication* 8, no. 1 (Feb. 2015): 7–26.

9. Gerhard Maré, *Declassified: Moving beyond the Dead-End of Race in South Africa* (Auckland Park, S. Afr.: Jacana, 2014).

10. Ibid., book cover.

11. Charles Mills, *The Racial Contract* (Ithaca, NY: Cornell University Press, 1997), 18.

12. Charles Mills, "White Ignorance," in *Race and Epistemologies of Ignorance,* ed. Shannon Sullivan and Nancy Tuana (Albany, NY: SUNY Press, 2007), 20.

13. Marzia Milazzo, "On White Ignorance, White Shame, and Other Pitfalls in Critical Philosophy of Race," *Journal of Applied Philosophy* 34, no. 4 (Aug. 2017): 557–72.

14. Kimberlé Crenshaw, "Race, Reform, and Retrenchment: Transformation and Legitimation in Antidiscrimination Law," in *Critical Race Theory: The Key Writings That Formed the Movement,* ed. Kimberlé Crenshaw, Neil Gotanda, Gary Peller, and Kendall Thomas (New York: New Press, 1995), 112.

15. See, for example, George Fredrickson, *White Supremacy: A Comparative Study in American and South African History* (Oxford: Oxford University Press, 1982); Charles Hamilton, ed., *Beyond Racism: Race and Inequality in Brazil, South Africa, and the United States.* (Boulder, CO: Lynne Rienner, 2001); Anthony Marx, *Making Race and Nation: A Comparison of South Africa, the United States, and Brazil* (Cambridge: Cambridge University Press, 1998); and Winant, *The World Is a Ghetto.*

16. According to Crenshaw ("Race, Reform, and Retrenchment"), colorblindness functions as a rhetorical prophylactic intended to prevent the recognition of and reckoning with white supremacy.

17. See Telles, *Race in Another America.*

18. Abdias Nascimento, *Brazil, Mixture or Massacre? Essays in the Genocide of a Black People,* trans. Elisa Larkin Nascimento, 2nd ed. (Dover, MA: Majority Press, 1989), 3.

19. Gilberto Freyre, *Casa-grande e Senzala: Formação da Família Brasileira sob o Regime de Economia Patriarcal* (Rio de Janeiro: Livraria José Olympio, 1958), 265.

20. Nascimento, *Brazil, Mixture or Massacre?,* 63.

21. Ibid., 38.

22. Milazzo, "White Supremacy, White Knowledge."

23. Olmedo Alfaro, *El peligro antillano en la América Central: La defensa de la raza,* 2nd ed. (Panama City: Imprenta Nacional, 1925), 16.

24. Kamel, *Não Somos Racistas,* 26.

25. Ibid., 40.

26. Providing important insights into this matter, Abdias Nascimento writes that "sexual abuse of African women in slavery is a form of the same rape and pillage inherent in war. . . . Mulatto populations are the logical product of this violence in any slave society, and their existence is more likely to prove racism's presence, justifying this collective form of abuse, than its absence." Nascimento, *Africans in Brazil: A Pan-African Perspective* (Trenton, NJ: Africa World Press, 1992), 110.

27. See Joshua Lund, *The Impure Imagination: Toward a Critical Hybridity in Latin American Writing* (Minneapolis: University of Minnesota Press, 2006), xv.

28. Maré, *Declassified*, 143.

29. Sarah Nuttall, *Entanglement: Literary and Cultural Reflections on Post-apartheid* (Johannesburg: Wits University Press, 2009), 31.

30. Gregory Rodriguez, *Mongrels, Bastards, Orphans, and Vagabonds: Mexican Immigration and the Future of Race in America* (New York: Vintage, 2007), xvii.

31. Nascimento, *Brazil, Mixture or Massacre?*, 64–65.

32. Christina A. Sue, *Land of the Cosmic Race: Race Mixture, Racism, and Blackness in Mexico* (Oxford: Oxford University Press, 2013), 15.

33. See Nascimento, *Sorcery of Color*, 61.

34. Kamel, *Não Somos Racistas*, 74.

35. See Nascimento, *Brazil, Mixture or Massacre?*

36. Kamel, *Não Somos Racistas*, 22, 23.

37. Neil Gotanda, "A Critique of 'Our Constitution Is Colorblind,'" in Crenshaw et al. (ed.), *Critical Race Theory*, 257–75.

38. Maré, *Declassified*, 169.

39. Statistics South Africa, "Employment, Unemployment, Skills and Economic Growth," www.statssa.gov.za/presentation/Stats SA presentation on skills and unemployment_16 September.pdf.

40. Maré, *Declassified*, 63, 35.

41. Ibid., 22.

42. On the history of the ANC, see, for example, Ben Turok, *The Historical Roots of the ANC* (Auckland Park, S. Afr.: Jacana, 2010).

43. Achille Mbembe writes, "Reactionary and conservative forces have co-opted nonracialism, which they now equate with colour-blindness. They use nonracialism as a weapon to discredit any attempt to deracialise property, institutions and structures inherited from an odious past." Mbembe, "Blind to Colour—or Just Blind?," *Mail & Guardian*, July 18, 2014, http://mg.co.za/article/2014-07-17-blind-to-colour-or-just-blind.

44. Maré, *Declassified*, 28.

45. Ibid., 126.

46. Ibid., 55.

47. Kamel, *Não Somos Racistas*, 51.

48. Ibid., 43.

49. Maré, *Declassified*, 150.

50. See Kwame Ture and Charles V. Hamilton, *Black Power: The Politics of Liberation in America* (New York: Vintage, 1967), 3.

51. Kamel, *Não Somos Racistas*, 24.

52. See Abdias Nascimento, *Quilombo: Vida, Problemas e Aspirações do Negro* (São Paulo: Editora 34, 2003).

53. See, for example, Sérgio Da Silva Martins, Carlos Alberto Medeiros, and Elisa Larkin Nascimento, "Paving Paradise: The Road from 'Racial Democracy' to Affirmative Action in Brazil," *Journal of Black Studies* 34, no. 6 (2004): 789; and Mónica Treviño González, "Opportunities and Challenges for the Afro-Brazilian

Movement," in *Brazil's New Racial Politics,* ed. Bernd Reiter and Gladys L. Mitchell (Boulder, CO: Lynne Rienner, 2010), 123.

54. Kamel, *Não Somos Racistas,* 23.

55. Ibid., 41.

56. Ibid., 23.

57. *Parents Involved in Community Schools v. Seattle School District No. 1,* 551 U.S. 701 (2007), Syllabus, 4, https://supreme.justia.com/cases/federal/us/551/701.

58. Kamel, *Não Somos Racistas,* 77.

59. *Parents Involved* (2007), Opinion of Kennedy, 17.

60. Maré, *Declassified,* 111.

61. See Kevin A. Whitehead, "Racial Categories in the Social Life of Post-apartheid South Africa" (PhD diss., University of California, Santa Barbara, 2010).

62. Maré, *Declassified,* 97.

63. Ibid., 114.

64. Jeremy Seekings and Nicoli Nattrass, *Class, Race, and Inequality in South Africa* (New Haven, CT: Yale University Press, 2005), 308, 45.

65. Ibid., 6.

66. Kamel, *Não Somos Racistas,* 79.

67. Maré, *Declassified,* 115, 104.

68. See Steve Biko, *I Write What I Like: Selected Writings* (Chicago: University of Chicago Press, 2002), 19.

SIX

How Colorblindness Flourished in the Age of Obama

Kimberlé Williams Crenshaw

Emerging in the wake of Barack Obama's monumental election, a new center of gravity took hold in American racial discourse, one that was framed as a racially pragmatic alternative to the polarizing and counterproductive contestations over race. This discursive shift bore significant consequences in the struggle against colorblind ideology. On the eve of the election, racial justice advocates were already facing increasing pressure to abandon remnants of race-conscious discourse in the face of colorblind victories in both the legal and political arenas. The emergence of postracialism only deepened the erosion of race justice discourse. Underlying postracialism's buoyant introduction to the American scene was a conservative riptide that pulled racial justice constituencies into a discourse that legitimized a morbidly unequal status quo. That postracialism's condition of possibility was a political victory that few stakeholders of racial justice thought they would ever witness is one of the great ironies of civil rights history.

POSTRACIALISM

Postracialism rode to the center of American political discourse on Barack Obama's coattails,[1] carrying along with it a long-standing conservative project of associating colorblindness with racial enlightenment and racial justice advocacy with grievance politics.[2] As one commentator explained

Portions of this article were originally published as Kimberlé Williams Crenshaw, "Twenty Years of Critical Race Theory: Looking Back to Move Forward," *Connecticut Law Review* 43, no. 5 (July 2011): 1253–352.

following the election, "America has done its part. Without a blink of an eye, we have just boldly ushered in a new, post-racial era. Once again, we have proven ourselves a nation of leaders: a representative democracy in its truest sense."[3] Obama's widely heralded avoidance of so-called racial grievance not only opened the door to "a new era of American politics";[4] it also opened up liberal and progressive civil rights constituencies to rhetorical frames that were forged in retrenchment politics.

Obama as a postracial figuration is key to the remaking of old debates into a new common sense, one that draws the masses as well as elites, whites as well as racial Others, into a familiar script about the benign nature of race and the opportunity that exists in American society. In the new postracial era, racial discourse and agitation are increasingly understood to be history's shadow. By the logic that suggests that broken glass ceilings at the top deliver trickle-down opportunities below, the assumption follows that there is no longer walled-off space for race.

Ironically, the overwhelming racial salience of the election of one African American allowed a conservative ideology that had been mobilized to reverse countless civil rights victories to become repackaged as a celebratory expression of a new American cosmopolitanism. Colorblind ideology had fueled a host of right-wing projects throughout the 1990s and the early twenty-first century, including African American businessman Ward Connerly's assault on both affirmative action and the collection of racial data which were a driving force in California's and Michigan's restrictions on affirmative action policies,[5] and efforts by organized interests to attack the Voting Rights Act and Title VII. Given its disingenuous deployment as a battering ram for civil rights rollbacks, colorblindness had never been fully embraced by moderates and liberals, even though they often affirmed its ultimate goals and purportedly race-neutral baselines. Having failed to achieve the broad-scale endorsement of civil rights organizations and mainstream media, colorblindness might be characterized as a reasonably popular act that played well to specialized audiences, but one that never enjoyed the bandwidth of a truly crossover phenomenon. Postracialism brought rock star marketability to colorblindness's legitimizing project, rebranding it with an internationally recognized symbol attached to its conservative rhetorical content. While the celebratory dimension of the "Obama phenomenon" pulled countless people into its orbit, the colorblind rhetoric of racial denial stripped ongoing efforts to name and contest racial power of both legitimacy and audience.

The rise of postracialism as a new sensibility triggered by the Big Event was itself a familiar dynamic in the narrative of racial progress. The postreform trajectory of civil rights discourse has long revealed that modest victories are inevitably appropriated as ammunition by those seeking to limit the scope of racial reform.[6] Often with such advancements comes rhetoric that celebrates the inherent egalitarianism of American society while repudiating the long-term struggle and sacrifice that made the breakthrough possible. Indeed, when viewed from this vantage point, such victories point not to the efficacy of race-conscious advocacy but to the exceptionalist myth that America inevitably rights its historic wrongs. Rather than celebrating the courageous acts of millions of ordinary citizens who rose against racial subordination, colorblind adherents critique the mobilization that made breakthroughs possible as not only unnecessary but actually counterproductive.

Particularly perverse is the way those who risked censure, social discipline, and even death to fight for racial change have been bludgeoned by the symbolic victories that their vision and activism helped make possible.[7] The desire among apologists of the social order to be "liberated" at last from civil rights advocacy was visible throughout the campaign and in its immediate aftermath. Even among Obama's opponents, the silver lining that many of them saw in his possible victory would be that leading civil rights advocates would be put out of business. This phenomenon was readily apparent the night of the election as pundits tallying up the night's big losers fingered Jesse Jackson, Al Sharpton, and by extension, other racial justice advocates. Presumably, all had just become unemployed if only Americans would take Obama's election as an opportunity to turn away from racial grievance.[8] Indeed, as one columnist argued, "racial progress has reduced the need of African-Americans for racial-grievance leaders like Jackson and Sharpton, but America has not progressed enough to put these types of leaders out of business."[9]

Beyond mere punditry, the denigration and outright persecution of critics of the racial order has historically involved public and private repression. During the early nineteenth century, abolitionists were cast as dissidents with a "wicked plan of exciting the Negroes to . . . massacre."[10] This sentiment was reflected in laws passed by a number of southern states that banned the mailing of abolitionist materials and imposed criminal penalties on subscribers to abolitionist newsletters.[11] During the twentieth century, Student Nonviolent Coordinating Committee organizers and Freedom Riders were called "outside agitators" and incarcerated in state penitentiaries primarily for their advocacy against the racial order.[12] COINTELPRO, the FBI's covert program, went further, utilizing law enforcement to destabilize, disrupt, and neutralize racial justice movements and their leaders.

Thus, the "Mission Accomplished" theme echoed by those who proclaimed that the great attraction of Barack Obama was that he eschewed racial complaint reflected a troubling irony. That the courageous leaders and advocates who made Obama's breakthrough possible could be so effortlessly reduced to historical deadweight underscores the frustrating paradox of racial reform. As a harbinger of what was to come, the monumental victory was taken to affirm the claim that race didn't matter, a claim that could only be bolstered by using Obama's race as evidence to sustain the claim. Indeed, contrary to the thrust of colorblind proscriptions against noticing race, Obama's Blackness was harnessed to prove that the remaining markers of racial subordination were no longer indicators of unjustified exclusion. Obama's election instead pointed to an alternate reality, one of unlimited opportunity that too many low-achieving African Americans were simply disinclined to grasp. The dialectic of transformation and legitimation that had taken years to play out in the context of formal equality became instantly apparent in the aftermath of Obama's victory. Broad segments of the population seemed to believe that with Barack Obama now in the White House, the chapter on race could at last be closed.[13]

This overinvestment in the symbolic significance of the Obama victory obscures the ongoing operation of racial power in much the same way that formal equality sanitized patterns of institutional exclusion in the formative years of Critical Race Theory. In the same way that elite law schools congratulated themselves for being institutions in which merit flourished, many commentators upheld the election of Barack Obama as evidence that the competition over political power is indeed colorblind.[14] In both instances, the assertions rested on efforts to associate any semblance of race neutrality with the absence of racial power. Yet in the same way that the mere assertion of colorblind merit did not exhaust the operation of race in American law schools, Obama's victory proved little about the value of colorblindness either as a tactic for gaining power or as a frame for how it is exercised.

Some critics of postracialism may agree that Obama's victory represented a foundational element of the postracial era, yet they frame his contributions to the rise of postracialism as merely accidental or structurally imposed. Obama's capacity to resist the postracial expectations, it may be surmised, were quickly tamed by the punitive outcry prompted by his comment that the arrest of distinguished Harvard professor Henry Louis Gates in his own home was ill-advised. Some saw the president's subsequent reticence to engage racial matters as a survivalist shift toward racial inscrutability. However, throughout his campaign and presidency, Obama proved to be far more than a political Sphinx to which postracialism became attached. Obama's campaign and subsequent presidency reflected an acute awareness about racial performance. His navigation through and around existing racial scripts came to signify postracialism by virtue of what he affirmed and what he omitted, what he drew attention to and what he obscured.

Despite the common refrain that President Barack Obama was the brightest example of the limitless potential of postracial politics, the Obama campaign reflected the continuing significance of race consciousness among the electorate, pundits, and candidates. Obama's measured performance of racial avoidance along with his selective staging of racially salient messaging revealed that the candidate was uniquely adept in maneuvering the complex terrain of race. Yet however remarkable this particular accomplishment was, it served as meager evidence that the sociopolitical terrain is itself colorblind. Barack Obama's unique victory stands neither as a pathway that can be readily replicated across American society nor as a shining example of what colorblind social practice can deliver. Indeed, the public image of Obama's "race neutrality" masked an intense race-conscious campaign to counter his racial deficit where necessary and to bolster his racial capital where advantageous. This was anything but an avoidance of race; it was, instead, a deft encounter with it.

While race might have been downplayed in the candidate's public posture, strategists were well aware that ignoring the racial reservations of white voters would have been politically disastrous. Race was a factor to be managed, not only in Obama's public appearances but also in the all-out ground campaign for votes in the key battleground states.[15] This imperative to disarm the racial reservations among white voters required Obama's white supporters to engage in an intraracial conversation with other whites. Although barely reported in the mainstream press, this direct engagement sidestepped, if not wholly reversed, the prevailing expert-based communications strategies that advised racial avoidance. In key swing states such as Pennsylvania and Ohio, whites were mobilized to talk with other whites in a ground campaign focused on neutralizing Obama's racial disadvantage.[16] This is a far cry from the myth that Obama won by running a nonracial campaign. To the contrary, race was definitively and repeatedly engaged. Thus, postracialism, when defined in terms of the Obama campaign, cannot be taken to mean "beyond race" or even colorblind; instead, it symbolized a particular kind of approach toward dominant racial sensibilities.

Even the celebration of Obama's public performance as "race-neutral" was not a concession to the colorblind values of the electorate but rather an accommodation to the color-conscious prisms through which Obama's embodiment would be interpreted. Obama's racial performance was being read by voters of all races in a complex effort to assess what kind of Black president Obama was likely to be.[17] Such dynamics were captured in the repeated (and often disdainful) references to the intraracial conversations among African Americans that portrayed these debates under the misleading frame of "whether Obama was Black enough."

An equally pointed conversation was taking place in public among whites about the quantum of Obama's Blackness that would be acceptable to white voters, but this was less frequently identified as an intraracial discourse about whiteness and more often packaged as a factual inquiry into Obama's inroads or deficits among white voters. Many commentators, pundits, voters, and observers later labeled Obama's racial maneuvering as postracial, but what was crystallized was a flavor of Blackness made palatable to "the mainstream" by its disassociation with racial complaint.[18] While packaged as racial transcendence, it is legible against a backdrop saturated with racial meaning, portrayed through a growing repertoire of dissociative gestures, and always, it seems, subject to disciplinary revocation.[19] Neither this frame nor the debate that it sought to capture was an expression of colorblindness on the part of the candidate or the electorate. As Devon Carbado and Mitu Gulati might put it, Obama "worked" his identity in ways that would communicate his desired message to audiences looking for different racial codes.[20]

"A MORE PERFECT UNION" AND IDEOLOGIES OF RACIAL SYMMETRY

Far more significant, however, in defining the space that postracialism came to occupy was the rhetorical posture that Obama enacted in his framing of racial power. Obama's stately Philadelphia speech during the 2008 campaign, "A More Perfect Union," demonstrated the candidate's abilities to appeal to constituencies from across the racial terrain. But the speech also provided more sobering glimpses of racial frames that had been actively deployed by the Supreme Court and by other legal institutions to limit the remedial scope of antidiscrimination law and the very perception of racial injury. That it was barely noticed suggests how the postracial gloss of a charismatic Black-identified candidate could effectively repackage a colorblind framework into a galvanizing performance that left spectators from across the spectrum in awe.

Interestingly, for a campaign that was framed and received as a transcendence of racial divides, the speech largely engaged only the animus and tension between African Americans and whites. This in part reflected the terms on which the controversy that prompted the speech was framed. After tapes of Obama's Chicago pastor Rev. Jeremiah Wright surfaced that contained damning critiques of American society, the campaign was nearly derailed. The unanswered question of whether the obvious anger that his pastor expressed would be read onto Obama potentially compromised his provisional acceptance among whites as a nonangry Black man. This burden remains a racially specific obstacle for almost any Black candidate whose electoral aspirations rely to some extent on white voters.

The surfacing of Wright's sermon—a profoundly telling marker of this challenge—couldn't have come at a worse time. At the same time, another thorny issue that was repeatedly presented by the media was the question of how other nonwhites would "line up" in this epic moment. Thus, Obama's speech aimed to bring what was widely framed as two warring sides to the table, and to avoid the vexed question of which "side" other nonwhites were poised to take.[21]

In stepping through the racial minefield created by the surfacing of the Wright's fiery sermon, Obama courageously confronted the contemporary legacy of racism.[22] Seeking to contextualize Wright's volatile rhetoric in an older generation's debilitating encounter with the country's racial past, Obama insisted that "the anger is real; it is powerful; and to simply wish it away, to condemn it without understanding its roots, only serves to widen the chasm of misunderstanding that exists between the races."[23] Yet the upshot of this "misunderstanding" was an appeal that seemed to be taken directly from the classic "race relations" approach.[24] Key moments in the candidate's address framed racial conflict as a misunderstanding between social equals rather than a matter of exclusion and power. In perhaps the most memorable passage of the speech, Obama drew out a parallel between his white grandmother and his Black pastor, and by extension, between whites and African Americans, that effectively framed both sides as warring factions whose pain was both legitimate and misunderstood by the other.

While balance and symmetry were the admirable and in some sense beguiling features of Obama's oratory, underneath this statesmanlike intervention was an asymmetrical analysis that distributed responsibilities and obligations differently between African Americans and whites. Obama's efforts to frame the grievances that reflected centuries of discrimination as on par with white anger over affirmative action convincingly mixed material inequalities with white anxieties, continuing exclusions with underenforced remedies, and minority rights with majority power.[25] To bridge the divides that proved so divisive, candidate Obama's prescriptions included a full complement of actions for African Americans that were both public (admonishing them to "bind your grievances to ... the larger aspirations of all Americans") and private (urging African Americans to "read to your children" and to be good fathers).

For their part, white Americans were asked to understand that the anger was real even if its roots were buried in the past, and that the consequences of the past continued into the current milieu. Beyond that, however, whites were prescribed no parallel responsibility in the home (one could imagine, for example, encouraging white Americans to "read to your children about this history I have just set forth" or "watch *Roots*"). Neither were they encouraged to rethink their underinvestment in the civil rights vision built on the idea of "We the People." Universal messages of equality and dignity were the hallmarks of civil rights visionaries such as Martin Luther King Jr., yet in admonishing Black Americans to bind their grievances to the plight of their fellows, Obama subtly reinforced a damaging distortion of the Civil Rights Movement as an expression of special interest politics. Completely missing was the recognition not only that movement activists bound their aspirations to a more inclusive vision of community from the beginning, but that the interventions they sparked set the terms on which advances for women, other people of color, workers, and other disenfranchised groups could gain traction. Considering this history, a truly balanced prescription might have included an invitation to white Americans to reckon with the habits of thought and privilege that may have undermined their ability to invest in the vision of equal belonging that was repeatedly expressed throughout civil rights history. Yet in Obama's framing, the failure of white Americans to see racial justice through a racially inclusive reboot of "We the People" became the responsibility of civil rights leadership.

This message was subtle and largely overlooked in the masterful way that Obama spoke into the moment. In its deft circumvention of the contours of white dominance, the performance was a tour de force that has, at the same time, come to define a sensibility that is at odds with more critical accounts of race. Packed into the speech were embodiments of the very ideologies of racial symmetry and purported moral equivalencies between segregation and affirmative action that have grounded the rollback of civil rights remediation. "A More Perfect Union" rehearses critical moves in the colorblind arsenal such as the parallel between the indignities wrought by segregation in the past and the resentments of some white Americans toward their "diminished overrepresentation" today. Having thus reduced the contemporary significance of racism to the enduring echoes of the past, what remains of race itself is a symmetrical concept of racial identity. Everybody has one racial identity, so equality can be realized by colorblind treatment of everyone. Embodied in universalist impulses like "a rising tide lifts all boats," this logic ignores not only the asymmetrical dimensions of race but also the yawning inequalities that are reproduced when racially dissimilarly situated people are treated as though they are the same.[26]

Like the Supreme Court, Obama's focus on past discrimination locates the source of contemporary disparities in the past. The consequences of past discrimination may be contemporaneously material, but the solutions require nothing but patience among whites and bootstrapism among Blacks. This echoes the Supreme Court's acknowledgment that societal discrimination may well exist, but relieves institutions of any requirement to acknowledge or remedy it. The responsibility for eliminating so-called societal discrimination rests on behavioral uplift, universal policies, and, presumably, the mere passage of time.[27] Locating the future of race equity in universal rather than targeted programs also replicates the Court's repudiation of institutional or structural justifications for remedial action.[28]

Obama's spectacular gloss on these concepts provided a soothing voice-over to a set of ideas that has fueled a rightward drift in civil rights for decades. Although each element represented a conceptual pillar of colorblind ideology, the unique performative dimensions of Obama's rhetoric facilitated its postracial branding. The postracial stance embodied the acknowledgement of continuing racial injuries packaged with a repeal of any lingering societal indictment for them, optimistically delivered by an exceptional African American destined for the White House.

Postracialism thus emerged as a rhetoric that was both grounded in and an extension of colorblindness. Both its original articulation and its modern rebrand advanced the notion that the intergenerational residue of white supremacy in the United States is fairly superficial, time-bound, and ultimately transparent. This view of racial power as an aftereffect of the past has been undergirded by the formalist conception of equality embraced by the post–civil rights judiciary.[29] Colorblindness as doctrine undermined litigation strategies that rely on race-conscious remediation, and soothed social anxiety about whether deeper levels of social criticism, remediation, and reconstruction might be warranted.

While colorblindness declared racism to be a closed chapter in our history, postracialism provided reassurance to those who weren't fully convinced that this history had ceased to cast its long shadow over contemporary affairs. Postracialism's gentler escape was routed through the possibility that racial power could be sidestepped, finessed, and ultimately overcome by individual initiative and bias-free consumers. Racial dominance was merely circumstance that could be navigated along the continuing path of social progress.[30] As an ideological rebrand that accompanied a symbolically monumental event, postracialism was more than colorblindness with a different name. As embodied by a walking symbol of hard work, family values, and nonconfrontation, postracialism became an instructive guide for racial Others—particularly African Americans. Like the Philadelphia speech, the president's messages to African Americans rehashed self-help strategies and promoted rising-tide solutions to widening inequalities. Yet even these racially targeted messages were destined to be inadequate responses in the face of tragic events that reflected the country's very real struggles with racial injustice. When the president was confronted with a racial tragedy that could not be ignored, his response was a race-targeted initiative that underscored the nuances and political utility of postracialism.

POSTRACIALISM AND MBK

Nothing represented the presidential embodiment of postracialism more than the president's signature racial justice initiative: My Brother's Keeper (MBK). With this initiative, conceived in the aftermath of the public outcry over the killing of Trayvon Martin, President Obama made good on a promise to use his bully pulpit to address the crisis facing African American boys.[31] He entered the packed East Room of the White House backed by a phalanx of young boys of color, mostly African American. Joining Obama was a bipartisan assemblage of notable figures representing a wide political spectrum, including civil rights advocate Al Sharpton, conservative talk show host Bill O'Reilly, and New York City mayor Michael Bloomberg. These handpicked representatives of the political establishment joined a room filled with corporate executives, sports stars, government officials, philanthropic leaders, service providers, and advocates.[32]

After introducing the boys as participants in Chicago mayor Rahm Emanuel's "Becoming a Man" program, the president recalled how he'd met the boys during an after-school gathering and how, during their exchange, he'd told them about the personal frustrations and anger that sparked a series of bad choices when he was their age.[33] What connected Obama's youthful errors in judgment with the obstacles facing the boys in the "Becoming a Man" program was a simple shared fact of family life: fatherlessness. It was only because better life influences and role models happened to intervene, Obama recounted, that he was able to take advantage of the second chances denied to less fortunate boys.[34] The president then recounted the sobering statistics on Black and Latino children, following each data point with an emphatic comment about its consequences for the later maturation of boys. The moral was impossible to miss: the Black community needed, still and always, to reckon with its own plague of fatherlessness and its adverse influence on boys. "If you're African American, there's about a one in two chance you grow up without a father in your house—one in two. If you're Latino, you have about a one in four chance. We know that boys who grow up without a father are more likely to be poor, more likely to underperform in school." Such statistics contribute to the "cycles of hopelessness [that] breed violence and mistrust,"[35] Obama explained. Then, gesturing to Trayvon Martin's parents and to the parents of Jordan Davis, another young Black teenager killed by a white civilian, in this case in an altercation over loud music,[36] the president unveiled My Brother's Keeper, an initiative that promised a "more focused effort on boys and young men of color who are having a particularly tough time."[37] Obama officials clearly framed the program's mission in such a way as to sidestep a bruising fight over federal government involvement in a race-targeted program. The $200 million initiative would draw on private resources—commitments from foundations, corporations, and other private sources—thereby ensuring that program administrators wouldn't have to face down congressional and political resistance to a new government entitlement.[38]

The animating rationale for MBK was also custom-built to fit within the available ideological space for a racially targeted initiative. First and perhaps most importantly, it singled out no governmental, institutional, or historical conditions that may have helped create the "particularly tough time" that boys of color were facing. While the program's founding brief detailed the many senses in which Black boys found themselves at risk, it didn't appear that racism, discrimination, prejudice, or economic and political disempowerment numbered among the relevant causes. Nor, amazingly, did the criminal justice system and its protocols of racial profiling warrant dishonorable mention—an especially conspicuous omission given the draconian practices of the police departments overseen by the initiative's notable endorsers Michael Bloomberg and Rahm Emanuel. In fact, at the very moment Bloomberg was joining forces with the president to save boys of color, his police department was locked in a struggle with Black and Latino plaintiffs alleging racial discrimination, harassment, and intimidation.[39] Emanuel, for his part, would suffer the grievous political fallout from the release, a year later, of a video showing a Chicago cop brutally gunning down a mentally incapacitated African American.[40]

To any reasonable observer, the notion that Emanuel and Bloomberg could pass as serious interlocutors in the struggles facing Black boys should have raised eyebrows. After all, the guiding rationale behind the acquittal of George Zimmerman for gunning down Trayvon Martin was virtually identical to the justifications offered by defenders of policing practices that accounted for the disproportionate surveillance and killing of Black people.[41] But the popular Black revolt against police violence prompted by the killings of Michael Brown and Eric Garner was months away. Since My Brother's Keeper was silent on matters of policing and racial stereotyping, the presence of neither the mayors of New York and Chicago, nor of the Fox News pundit Bill O'Reilly, occasioned no comment—beyond the laudatory observation that their attendance meant that MBK enjoyed bipartisan approval.

This was far from the only sign, however, that the culture-first agenda of MBK would studiously bypass the structural and institutional forces behind the plight of Black boys and men. The president's colloquy included no mention of the decades-long defunding of many public institutions, schools, and youth development programs that contributed to the boys' particularly hard time, nor did he allude to the devastating decline of American industry or the many ills associated with it, such as job insecurity, falling wages, and the increasing wealth gap. Likewise, Obama glided by racial discrimination in the employment market, the crucial role of residential segregation in limiting access to information networks and to well-paying jobs, and the school-to-prison pipeline that remorselessly truncates the life chances of young Black men.

In the place of analysis, President Obama offered reminiscences about how he'd acted out in his own teen years as a response to his coming of age with an absent dad. Yet even as he expressed gratitude for the more "forgiving" circumstances that rescued him, he neglected to suggest that any such circumstances were racially inflected. Instead, crediting his own loving family for helping him through perilous times, he failed to observe that their solidly white middle-class makeup made it far more likely that he'd be spared the many obstacles embedded within the highly segregated and economically distressed communities that the boys standing behind him had to face. In this airbrushed portrait of boys at risk, the narrative of endangerment boiled down to their entrapment within families that were ill-equipped to protect and nurture them.

The implementation phase of MBK, not surprisingly, followed the same depoliticized playbook. With a private funding structure, MBK proffered no interventions that implicated federal resources. The president did not call on Congress to authorize any new expenditures, to pass any laws, or to reverse any part of the civil rights infrastructure that was unraveling under the Roberts Court.

With the operational budget for My Brother's Keeper thus secured without messy confrontations in the public sector, the challenge of articulating the initiative's public rationale fell to the presidential memorandum creating a "My Brother's Keeper Task Force."[42] The memorandum sought to establish a national effort to significantly improve the expected life outcomes for boys and young men of color (including African Americans, Hispanic Americans, and Native Americans). It instructed more than a dozen federal agencies to develop indicators for measuring the well-being of boys until the age of twenty-five. And it gave the task force ninety days to issue a preliminary report on evidence-based interventions and issues facing boys and young men of color.

In time, the private funding commitments would swell to more than $1.6 billion in combined grants and low-interest financing, with partnerships with the NBA, UBS America, JPMorgan Chase, and other corporations pledging to provide mentorships and summer jobs for boys of color.[43] It was widely publicized as a model for similar governmental initiatives at the local level. Cities across the country were called to join the "My Brother's Keeper Challenge" and, in coordinating charitable donations, to promote more positive future life outcomes for boys of color. Tellingly, Ferguson, Missouri, became one such city, holding a town hall in the midst of the crisis surrounding the killing of Michael Brown.[44] Yet true to form, neither Brown's death nor the broader issue of police violence surfaced as a concern during the MBK town hall in Ferguson.

After its launch, MBK received substantial media coverage, most of it quite positive, from across the political spectrum.[45] Interestingly, conservative organizations and public interest law firms that had been dedicated critics of traditional affirmative action programs were muted in their responses. A few complained that race-targeted initiatives like MBK encouraged victimhood discourse and that they unfairly excluded at-risk white boys. But these comments were quite tame compared to the cries of reverse discrimination that typically accompanied race-targeted measures. Fox TV's Bill O'Reilly—usually a dependable voice to denounce race-conscious remedial programs—enthusiastically embraced the initiative's objectives.

BLACK MALE ENDANGERMENT AS PREDICATE
FOR A VICTIM-BLAMING RACIAL POLITIC

My Brother's Keeper may have seemed to casual observers like a trademark innovation of the postracial Obama presidency. In reality, it marked the scaling up of an entire industry of racially targeted interventions that give very little attention to the structural and institutional features of racial hierarchy. Central to this industry was the revival of gender disrepair as the focal point of dysfunction in the Black community.

Tellingly, the narrative of failed families as the principle site of racial inequality commands such widespread assent in the citadels of elite opinion and federal power that no participant or pundit seemed to notice the bizarre disconnect at the heart of MBK's reason for being. This was, after all, an initiative that President Obama explicitly linked to the vigilante-style slaying of Trayvon Martin and Jordan Davis in Florida. Yet both Martin and Davis had Black fathers who were active in their lives. What Obama took to be the most pressing problem for troubled and at-risk Black boys in America was quite literally a nonproblem for the victims of the tragic shootings that furnished MBK with its rhetorical reason for being.

For such a glaring and foundational misalignment to escape serious notice, a countervailing ideological accord had to have taken root within the mainstream media and the civil rights establishment. Under the terms of this accord, the condition of fatherlessness was scripted as the primary cause behind the societal endangerment of all Black males[46]—a transclass vulnerability that Black males share irrespective of the actual level of their fathers' involvement in their lives. Yet the unspoken factor that took Trayvon Martin's and Jordan Davis's lives was in fact racism—a fact made abundantly clear in the racist justifications proffered by both boys' killers. Commentators defending the killers' actions likewise referred to the racist image of young Black men as unhinged superpredators.[47]

But the conventions within a postracial polity militated against any frontal indictment of a manifestly racist discourse. So, as the gatekeepers of polite public discourse duly sidestepped the racist rationales for their deaths, Martin and Davis became stand-ins for a discourse on Black male endangerment that elided racism altogether. In its place was a focus on the attitudes, habits, and sociocultural environment of Black boys themselves. The implicit message of MBK seemed to be that threats to the bodily security of Black males can be averted by enhancing the reputational capital of a feared group of men.

For the many racial justice allies who lent their support to this framing, the exclusive focus on Black male suffering was simply a matter of common sense. But it was no more "common sense" to link Martin's and Davis' deaths to fatherlessness than it would have been to link the murder of Emmett Till to his father's absence or the family structure of other Black boys in the 1950s. This particular endangerment narrative in fact rested on a body of linkages, inferences, and silences that only count as "common sense" within postracialism's predetermined confines of ideologically permissible engagement. In this sense, MBK was seeded in an ideological sweet spot within postracialism's narrow parameters, a point of convergence between those who worry about Black males and those who fear them.

This convergence has proved powerful and destructive. It provided a crack within postracialism's antigrievance commitments from which a race-targeted intervention could break through. At the same time, however, it has permitted those who oversee institutions that kill and imprison Black males to find common cause with those who are left to grieve them. And in the process, it permitted colorblind neoconservatives such as Bill O'Reilly to join forces with race adversaries like Al Sharpton in an agenda they could all endorse.

CONTEMPORARY POSTRACIALISM, TRUMP, AND THE LEGACY OF THE OBAMA ADMINISTRATION

As postracialism became the vehicle for a colorblind agenda, the material consequences of racial exploitation and social violence—including the persistence of educational inequity, the disproportionate racial patterns of criminalization and incarceration, and the deepening patterns of economic stratification—slid further into obscurity. Under the thrall of postracialism, these stubborn conditions posed little challenge to interpreting the historical election of one politician as the end of racism. Obama's election gave credence and authority to this process. It also naturalized the assumption that the remaining vestiges of racial discrimination were essentially moments of individual prejudice rather than the persistent and organized effects of institutions and structures. Even when the Obama administration announced a program that was racially targeted, such as the "My Brother's Keeper Challenge," it was never framed in terms of racial power, institutions, or structures that were in need of repair. The postracial approach foregrounded interventions that were premised on the assumption that what needed to be corrected was at the individual, cultural, and familial level, presuming, for example, that gender disrepair was the cause of problems and crisis in the Black community.

Contemporary postracialism thus reflects the deradicalization of the racial justice movement through a symbol of racial transcendence mobilized to demonstrate the inherent colorblindness of American democracy. To be candid, what racial justice advocates wound up with was not eight years in power but rather eight years without the power to name, eight years without the power to fully mobilize, eight years without the power to demand accountability or to agitate our highest elected officials to renew the stalled project of racial transformation. Instead, we faced an interruption in the possibility to forcefully express such demands against the repeated claim that for all important intents and purposes, that battle was largely over.

The racial backlash that followed the postracial presidency might tempt students of racial history to view postracialism as a curious but ultimately short-lived ideological moment. In the midst of white nationalism's resurgence, nostalgia for postracialism is not incomprehensible. Yet hindsight may suggest that among the conditions of Trump's possibility are the debilitating politics of colorblindness and its rearticulation through postracialism. In their defense of meritocracy and their willingness to abandon structural discourses in favor of behavioral interventions to address racial inequality, postracialists effectively conceded that racial disparities have nothing to do with collective, structural, or historical harms. Once the notion of collective responsibility is erased and the assumptions of a naturalized racial hierarchy are no longer robustly contested in public discourse, the political exploitation of white racial grievance cannot be surprising. The crucial dimensions that unite Trump's base are tied to expectations that they have been unfairly taxed, unfairly deprived, and unfairly indicted for the failings of others.

To be sure, a part of Trump's rise can be understood as backlash to Obama's tenure. But the depth of the backlash as well as the tepid responses to it have been made possible by postracialism's failure to maintain and advance a strong analysis of the ways in which race and racism still operate through our institutions, structures, and culture. This is the ground that was left exposed. It is now a foundation on which a virulent nationalism thrives.

This trajectory of race discourse—from colorblindness to the rise of postracialism and currently the re-legitimation of white nationalism—raises anew the vexed relationship between liberal and critical conceptions of knowledge and power. Liberal ambivalence expressed through colorblindness in the 1980s and through postracialism during the Obama years presents similar dynamics. In both periods, racial constituencies confronted doctrinal and political retreats that severely limited the scope of civil rights advocacy. In both periods, liberal visions of race reform and radical critiques of class hierarchy failed in different ways to address the institutional, structural, and ideological reproduction of racial hierarchy. In both periods, the collapse of racial barriers convinced many advocates and laypersons alike that fundamental transformation was at hand. And in both periods, racial progress was associated with an accommodationist (individualized) orientation to the terms of racial power rather than a sustained collective contestation of it.

These continuities would be sobering in the absence of Trumpism, and are even more vexing for critics of the status quo and the concessions to colorblindness that preceded its rise. Yet other dynamics exist today that suggest possibilities remain to reconstitute a robust critical race project that builds on the insights of the past. Today, as before, critical masses of thinkers continue to attend to the contemporary operation of race, producing literature that links specific institutional dynamics through which race is produced to the broader structures of racial power that continue to rationalize them. In much the same way that students and young scholars came to understand more fully the discursive terrain of race in the context of specific institutional struggles over integrating the faculty and curriculum in elite institutions, the struggles today to expose and critique the racial continuities between white supremacy in the past and the waves of retrenchment discourses echoing across campuses today present an important opportunity for critical race scholars across the disciplines.

CONCLUSION

The call to critical race scholars in all disciplines is not only to reveal how disciplinary conventions themselves constitute racial power, but also to provide an inventory of the critical tools that can be deployed to weaken and potentially dismantle its capacity to self-replicate. The stakes are high, yet the capacity to understand and see how liberalism's concessions fortified the grounding upon which retrenchment discourses have been scaffolded points to important contemporary struggles unfolding both within and outside the academy today. Contesting the erosion of ideas and frameworks that animated movements and strategies that have remade, albeit partially, the material and symbolic workings of our society are battles worth waging. Foregrounding the historic struggles to right the wrongs that grounded the Republic's ignoble beginnings, unearthing the courageous acts of resistance against both state power and its epistemic foundations that created the very possibility to sustain critical thought are key dimensions of the Countering Colorblindness project. The centrality of this project to the continuing struggles to dismantle illegitimate racial power ensures that these ideas will continue to be scrutinized and disciplined.

The fact that constituents of social justice are in a struggle is thus a given. Not only is forward momentum not guaranteed, but history has shown that retrenchment can radically alter the lives and social status of generations of racially aggrieved people. Yet heightened challenges merely elevate the need to strengthen a counternarrative against colorblindness. The counternarrative must be capable of reversing the premature societal settlement on racial injustice that has unleashed the virulent cycle of racial retrenchment that we are experiencing today. To meet this challenge, we need to make and remake praxis that is critical, interdisciplinary, and intersectional.

NOTES

1. Juan Williams, "Obama's Color Line," *New York Times,* Nov. 30, 2007, A23.

2. See, e.g., Shelby Steele, "Obama's Post-Racial Promise," *Los Angeles Times,* Nov. 5, 2008, www.latimes.com/opinion/opinion-la/la-oe-steele5–2008novo5 -story.html; also *The Situation Room,* CNN.com, Jan. 11, 2008; and an interview with Bill Moyers, www.pbs.org/moyers/journal/01112008/transcript2.html.

3. Phillip Morris, "America Begins its Journey into a Post-Racial Era," *Cleveland Plain Dealer,* Nov. 6, 2008, A1, www.cleveland.com/morris/index.ssf/2008/11 /phillip_morris_america_begins.html.

4. This sentiment—that Obama ushered in a new, postracial era in American politics—was widely echoed within the national press. See, e.g., Matt Bai, "Post-Race," *New York Times,* Aug. 10, 2008, MM34; and Robert S. Boynton, "Demographics and Destiny," *New York Times,* book review, Jan. 16, 2009, www .nytimes.com/2009/01/18/books/review/Boynton-t.html. Despite the postracial celebration underwriting this coverage, the majority of white Americans did not vote for Obama. See Timothy Noah, "What We Didn't Overcome: Obama Won a Majority of Votes. He Didn't Win a Majority of White Votes," Nov. 10, 2008, www .slate.com/id/2204251.

5. Ward Connerly, "It Is Time to End Race-Based 'Affirmative Action,'" *University of St. Thomas Journal of Law and Public Policy* 1 (2007): 56, 62.

6. Typical of those who took the opportunity to advance their preexisting agendas was Ward Connerly, who latched onto Obama's victory to argue that "liberation from the debilitating paradigm" associated with affirmative action was "now possible." Of course, had Obama lost, it is unlikely that Connerly would have asserted the opposite, namely, that the failure of the first viable Black candidate suggested that now was not the time to eliminate affirmative action. See Ward Connerly, "A Triumph of Principle over Color," *Sacramento Bee,* Nov. 16, 2008.

7. See, generally, Kimberlé Williams Crenshaw, "Race, Reform, and Retrenchment: Transformation and Legitimation in Antidiscrimination Law," *Harvard Law Review* 101, no. 7 (1988): 1335.

8. This line reemerged as a caption to explain Reverend Jackson's tears on election night. See Kevin Leininger, "Obama Win Takes Race off the Table," *Fort Wayne [TX] News-Sentinel,* Nov. 6, 2008. This and other comments implicitly dismissed the likelihood that Rev. Jackson was emotionally moved by the historic significance of the moment, as were millions of other Americans. That even opponents of Obama could profess pride without being subject to critique while Jackson was

ridiculed suggests that underlying the critique was a firm belief that much if not all of racial justice advocacy was mere opportunism. While some in the racial justice community share such views of Jackson and Sharpton, the critiques launched by conservative pundit George Will and others seem to apply to the entire body of racial justice advocacy.

9. Clarence Page, "Al Sharpton Weighs His Next Big Loss," *Chicago Tribune,* Aug. 22, 2001, N23.

10. Letter from Postmaster General Kendall to Pres. Andrew Jackson, Aug. 7, 1835, in *The Correspondence of Andrew Jackson,* ed. John Spencer Bassett (Washington, DC: Carnegie Institution of Washington, 1931), 5:361.

11. E.g., *Acts of the General Assembly of the Commonwealth of Virginia, 1835–36* (Richmond, 1836), chap. 66, sec. 3.

12. See Raymond Arsenault, *Freedom Riders: 1961 and the Struggle for Racial Justice* (New York: Oxford University Press, 2006), 214–46; and Bruce D'Arcus, "Dissent, Public Space, and the Politics of Citizenship: Riots and the 'Outside Agitator,'" *Space and Polity* 8 (2004): 355, 365.

13. While pundits and commentators throughout Obama's 2008 campaign had tentatively explored this theme, a wide range of media figures confidently embraced it after his election. See, e.g., John O'Sullivan, "The Conservative Interest," *National Review,* Feb. 21, 2008, www.nationalreview.com/2008/02/conservative-interest -john-osullivan.

14. E.g., Clarence Page, "Jackson's Eloquent Tears," *Chicago Tribune,* Nov. 9, 2008, C40.

15. Howard Winant describes his experience as a soldier in this ground campaign in "Just Do It: Notes on Politics and Race at the Dawn of the Obama Presidency," *Du Bois Review* 6 (2009): 49.

16. Don Gonyea, "Union Leader Confronts Race Issue in Campaign," *Morning Edition,* Oct. 10, 2008, www.npr.org/templates/story/story.php?storyId=95591135. See also "Act Three: Union Halls," *This American Life,* Oct. 24, 2008, www .thisamericanlife.org/radio-archives/episode/367/ground-game; and Avi Zenilman and Ben Smith, "Labor Confronts Race Issue," *Politico,* Nov. 2, 2008, www.politico .com/ news/stories/1108/15176.html.

17. See Debra J. Dickerson, "Colorblind," *Salon,* Jan. 22, 2007, www.salon .com/2007/01/22/obama_161; also Stanley Crouch, "What Obama Isn't: Black Like Me on Race," *Daily News,* Nov. 2, 2006, www.nydailynews.com/archives/opinions /obama-isn-black-race-article-1.585922.

18. In one sense, there is nothing particularly new about the aggregate preferences of white Americans for racial performances that are regarded as "race neutral" or "colorblind." Part of the shock and spectacle generated around O. J. Simpson was that the inference of "safety" that seemed to go along with Simpson's muted Blackness was violently disrupted when he was indicted for murder. Simpson's re-racialized image on the cover of *Newsweek* was a flashpoint in this drama. What is potentially new in this moment is the migration of this well-rehearsed presentation from popular culture to politics and, along with it, its repackaging as a blanket

prescription about how to be successful while Black. "Black" is specifically marked here because the messages of safety and palatability are currently tied to threatening and vengeful characterizations of Black grievance. Parallel demands on other non-whites are likely to find expression in contexts where their "otherness" is specifically marked and rationalized as a justification for differential treatment. The specific contours of postracial performance are thus likely to differ depending on the context and relevant stereotypes that are salient for each nonwhite group.

19. One study reportedly describes Obama as "the type of black political leader who has been historically most popular among whites—one who was not part of the civil rights movement, who accommodates rather than confronts, and who maintains close personal and political ties to whites." See Paul Bedard, "Obama Is Changing America's View of Blacks," *Washington Whispers* blog, Mar. 28, 2011, www.usnews.com/news/blogs/washington-whispers/2011/03/28/obama-is-changing-americas-view-of-blacks. That this acceptance is conditional is suggested by the very limited leeway the candidate and then president had to hint at, much less directly critique, racism.

20. Devon Carbado and Mitu Gulati, "Working Identity," *Cornell Law Review* 85 (1999): 1259, 1262.

21. Despite Obama's efforts to sidestep it, the news media extensively covered this question of what "sides" other minority groups were taking. See, e.g., Jeff Chang, "Why Latinos and Asian Americans Went for Hillary," *Huffington Post,* Feb. 6, 2008, www.huffingtonpost.com/jeff- chang/why-latinos-and-asian-ame_b_85359. html; and Angie Chuang, "Racial Rifts: Obama's Candidacy a Rorschach Test for Nation's Minorities," *Seattle Times,* July 16, 2008.

22. "But we do need to remind ourselves that so many of the disparities that exist between the African-American community and the larger American community today can be traced directly to inequalities passed on from an earlier generation that suffered under the brutal legacy of slavery and Jim Crow. Segregated schools were, and are, inferior schools; we still haven't fixed them, fifty years after *Brown v. Board of Education*. And the inferior education they provided, then and now, helps explain the pervasive achievement gap between today's black and white students." Barack Obama, "A More Perfect Union," Mar. 18, 2008, www.nytimes.com/2008/03/18/us/politics /18text-obama.html; a video of the speech can be seen at www.washingtonpost.com /graphics/national/obama-legacy/jeremiah-wright-2008-philadelphia-race-speech .html.

23. Obama, "A More Perfect Union."

24. For a critical history of the race relations school of sociology, and the argument that the race relations school represented by the Chicago School of Sociology suppressed structural accounts of racial power to create a relatively benign portrait of race relations, see Stephen Steinberg, *Race Relations: A Critique* (Stanford, CA: Stanford University Press, 2007). Steinberg recounts how Du Bois, Oliver Cox, and Carter J. Woodson, among others, wrote against the prevailing sensibilities in sociology and history and were discredited in some quarters as advocates rather than scholars (50).

25. Obama's "symmetry" might well be seen as conceding too much to "racial grievance" in light of the sensibility among some whites that empathetic intervention to equalize inequalities constitutes a loss for whites. For a recent contribution to this literature, see, e.g., Michael I. Norton and Samuel R. Summers, "Whites See Racism as a Zero-Sum Game That They Are Now Losing," *Perspectives on Psychological Science* 6 (May 2011): 215–18.

26. *Adarand Constructors, Inc. v. Peña,* 515 U.S. 200, 240 (1995). Justice Thomas, concurring in part, argued that there is a moral equivalence between segregation and affirmative action, in contrast with Justice Stevens, who argued that there is a difference between a welcome mat and a no trespass sign.

27. See *City of Richmond v. J. A. Croson Co.,* 488 U.S. 469 (1989). The decision by Justice O'Connor argued that the failure to identify specific acts of past discrimination upon which to predicate affirmative action leaves only societal discrimination for which there is no constitutional remedy.

28. See, e.g., ibid., 486.

29. I have discussed aspects of this process and its import for race-conscious advocacy previously. See Crenshaw, "Race, Reform, and Retrenchment," 1346.

30. In the talking-point gloss on how to move a racial justice agenda without engaging in the dreaded discourse of complaint, one of the common refrains is, "Martin Luther King didn't say he had a complaint; he said he had a dream!" Of course, the dream made little sense without the complaint, which he brilliantly and evocatively set forth in the first three-quarters of his riveting speech.

31. Trayvon Martin was a seventeen-year-old African American who was shot to death by a man named George Zimmerman when he was walking home while wearing a hoodie. Zimmerman became suspicious of Martin, pursued him, and ultimately killed him, claiming self-defense, but many have suspected racism was a major factor in the altercation. See Lizette Alvarez and Cara Buckley, "Zimmerman Is Acquitted in Trayvon Martin Killing," *New York Times,* July 13, 2013, www .nytimes.com/2013/07/14/us/george-zimmerman-verdict-trayvon-martin.html.

32. Barack Obama, "Remarks by the President on 'My Brother's Keeper' Initiative," Feb. 27, 2014, https://obamawhitehouse.archives.gov/the-press-office /2014/02/27/remarks-president-my-brothers-keeper-initiative (hereafter referred to as Obama, MBK Initiative). See also Valerie Jarrett, "My Brother's Keeper: A New White House Initiative to Empower Boys and Young Men of Color," *Huffington Post,* Feb. 27, 2014, www.huffingtonpost.com/valerie-jarrett/my-brothers-keeper-a -new_b_4868528.html.

33. Dana Ford, "Obama Unveils 'My Brother's Keeper,' Opens Up about His Dad, Drugs, and Race," CNN, Feb. 27, 2014, http://politicalticker.blogs.cnn .com/2014/02/27/obama-announces-my-brothers-keeper; Michael D. Shear, "Obama Starts Initiative for Young Black Men, Noting His Own Experience," *New York Times,* Feb. 27, 2014, www.nytimes.com/2014/02/28/us/politics/obama-will -announce-initiative-to-empower-young-black-men.html.

34. "I didn't have a dad in the house. And I was angry about it, even though I didn't necessarily realize it at the time. I made bad choices. I got high without

always thinking about the harm that it could do. I didn't always take school as seriously as I should have. I made excuses. Sometimes I sold myself short." Obama, MBK Initiative.

35. Ibid.

36. Davis was murdered after a violent encounter over loud rap music coming from his car. See Kristal Brent Zook, "The Lessons of Jordan Davis's Murder, Revisited," *Nation,* Nov. 23, 2015, www.thenation.com/article/the-lessons-of-jordan-daviss-murder-revisited.

37. Obama, MBK Initiative.

38. See Executives' Alliance to Expand Opportunities for Boys and Men of Color, *Investments for Change: Year in Review* 2–3 (2015).

39. See *Floyd v. City of New York,* 959 F. Supp. 2d 540 (S.D.N.Y. 2013), https://casetext.com/case/floyd-v-city-of-ny-2.

40. See Department of Justice, Civil Rights Division, *Investigation of the Chicago Police Department* (2017); Julie Bosman and Mitch Smith, "Chicago Police Routinely Trampled on Civil Rights, Justice Dept. Says," *New York Times,* Jan. 13, 2017, www.nytimes.com/2017/01/13/us/chicago-police-justice-department-report.html.

41. See Devon W. Carbado, Cheryl I. Harris, and Kimberlé Williams Crenshaw, "Racial Profiling Lives On," *New York Times,* Aug. 14, 2013, www.nytimes.com/2013/08/15/opinion/racial-profiling-lives-on.html.

42. Barack Obama, "Presidential Memorandum—Creating and Expanding Ladders of Opportunity for Boys and Young Men of Color," Feb. 27, 2014, https://obamawhitehouse.archives.gov/the-press-office/2014/02/27/presidential-memorandum-creating-and-expanding-ladders-opportunity-boys-.

43. See My Brother's Keeper Task Force, *My Brother's Keeper 2016 Progress Report 4* (2016), 16–17, https://obamawhitehouse.archives.gov/sites/whitehouse.gov/files/images/mbk-2016-progress-report.pdf.

44. Ibid. See, e.g., Jay Rey, "Partnership of Buffalo Schools, Brooklyn College Aims to Help Boys of Color," *Buffalo News,* Aug. 24, 2016, https://buffalonews.com/2016/08/24/partnership-buffalo-schools-brooklyn-college-aims-help-boys-color; New York State Department of Education, "$7 Million in Grants Now Available for My Brother's Keeper Challenge," Aug. 11, 2016, www.nysed.gov/news/2016/7-million-grants-now-available-my-brothers-keeper-challenge.

45. Barack Obama, "Remarks by the President at Launch of the My Brother's Keeper Alliance," May 4, 2015, https://obamawhitehouse.archives.gov/the-press-office/2015/05/04/remarks-president-launch-my-brothers-keeper-alliance.

46. See, e.g., Joyce Kelly, "Father Absence 'Decimates' Black Community in U.S.," Reuters, June 14, 2007, www.reuters.com/article/us-usa-fathers-idUSN0419185720070614.

47. See Eric Wemple, "Fox News's Bill O'Reilly Blames Trayvon Martin's Death on Hoodie," *Washington Post,* Sept. 16, 2013, www.washingtonpost.com/blogs/erik-wemple/wp/2013/09/16/fox-newss-bill-oreilly-blames-trayvon-martins-death-on-hoodie; Dana Ford, "George Zimmerman Was 'Justified' in Shooting Trayvon

Martin, Juror Says, CNN, July 17, 2013, www.cnn.com/2013/07/16/us/zimmerman-juror; Nicole Flatlow, "Juror: Some on Panel Thought the Killing of Unarmed Teen Jordan Davis Was 'Justified,'" *Think Progress,* Feb. 20, 2014, https://thinkprogress.org/juror-some-on-panel-thought-the-killing-of-unarmed-teen-jordan-davis-was-justified-33df7991e1f3. Flatlow highlights comments from the Martin and Davis cases where jurors explained the actions in both incidents were justified.

———

PART TWO

Moves

The essays in this section explore the distinct moves made within academic disciplines—especially research designs, theories, and methods—that facilitate colorblind constructions of objectivity, knowledge production, and disciplinary authority. The contributors demonstrate the ways that colorblind constructions mobilized in academic disciplines come to influence and circulate within other fields, including legal arguments, public policy, and social movements. In that recent Supreme Court decisions indicate that colorblindness may soon constitute a firm constitutional limitation on the extent to which racial inequality may be directly addressed through law and policy, the imperative to make such connections has never been stronger. The essays also identify strategies designed to counter colorblindness in disciplinary settings, including new research frameworks, collaborations, and public policy interventions.

One of the central "moves" utilized within colorblind research paradigms concerns the ways they putatively incorporate, rather than entirely exclude, race-related topics. As the contributors reveal, the terms of this incorporation demand critical analysis.

The first three essays in the section can be read together to understand how this process operates across different scholarly fields. First, Loren Kajikawa investigates the elevation of classical music to the center of the curriculum within most schools of music, understanding this move not simply as a disciplinary anomaly, but as part of a distribution of resources and rewards that valorizes whiteness and diminishes its alternatives. Kajikawa shows that race is also produced sonically—we are taught to hear the sound of race across a range of musical genres—a dynamic often neglected by musicologists.

Next, Barbara Tomlinson explicates a particular mode of textual interpretation within recent feminist scholarship that serves to place white women and white women's experiences as the locus of feminist authority. At "the scene of argument," she demonstrates, white feminists appropriate the utility and status of intersectionality for their own ends, muting its antiracist core and diminishing scholarship by Black women as rationally and ontologically deficient. Tomlinson's essay also reveals how interdisciplinary fields like women's and gender studies can still reproduce colorblind logics.

Tomlinson's arguments articulate productively to the chapter by Devon Carbado on "colorblind intersectionality." Carbado challenges the prevailing interpretations of intersectionality, examining how formal equality frameworks in law and civil rights advocacy produce and entrench racialized modes of gender normativity. He introduces the concept of colorblind intersectionality to describe instances in which whiteness helps to produce and is part of a cognizable social category but is invisible or unarticulated as an intersectional subject position.

Generative connections can also be discerned in the section's final two essays. Historian Leah Gordon's contribution details the history of scholarship on racial disparities within K–12 education. Gordon explains that this research has long drawn on phobic fantasies about the cultures, families, and values of people of color as reasons for school failure. Instead of reckoning with the ways in which the unequal distribution of resources and opportunities have failed students of color, this research has served to naturalize their abandonment by the state and to blame and shame them for it.

The patterns documented by Gordon are essential to understanding the connection between affirmative action discourse and policy formation. Political scientist and legal scholar Luke Harris and philosopher Uma Narayan analyze the ways in which "preferential treatment" circulates as a moral narrative in critiques of affirmative action in ways that disavow and naturalize pervasive and continued forms of racial discrimination. Both Gordon's and Harris and Narayan's essays demonstrate the keen insights produced when scholars bring together methods and theoretical frameworks from multiple disciplines to trace the workings of colorblindness in the legal arena. Indeed, it is within the affirmative action debate that we can understand the ways that colorblindness has become the most common and acceptable baseline from which legal actors and policy advocates debate racial inequality—a baseline that holds constant the belief that this contestable theory is the bedrock principle on which all current discourses about race should be built. At the same time, this baseline treats the manifestly unjust racial distribution of opportunities and life chances in this society as a norm that cannot be questioned or disturbed.

SEVEN

The Possessive Investment in Classical Music

CONFRONTING LEGACIES OF WHITE SUPREMACY IN U.S. SCHOOLS AND DEPARTMENTS OF MUSIC

Loren Kajikawa

> In the interrelationships of its musics, the Music Building parallels only imperfectly the twentieth-century world of musics. But in its juxtaposition of the central classical repertory to satellite styles deemed less significant, it reflects the modern world more explicitly in the sociocultural sense—the relationship of a dominant culture to its satellites or of a major power to third-world colonies.
>
> **BRUNO NETTL** [1]

Three music school anecdotes:

A young rap artist is a student at ———— College. She has been writing songs and recording in her bedroom studio since middle school. Although she is beginning to attract the attention of other artists and fans across the country, she is majoring in journalism and doesn't see any reason to be involved with the music department.

A recent PhD in ethnomusicology is hired by the School of Music at ———— University as an adjunct instructor. His job is to teach courses in popular and world music that enroll well and bring much-needed tuition dollars to the school. Although his work is essential to the school, he remains on a year-to-year contract while professors teaching about classical music receive tenure and make twice his salary.

The gospel choir is one of the most popular ensembles in the Department of Music at ———— College. The director of the group, an African American, appears alongside her students in brochures touting the vitality of the institution. However, the gospel choir does not actually count toward ensemble requirements for the music degree, and most of the students in the choir are nonmajors. In fact, professors in the music department warn their students not to sing with the choir because they might pick up bad habits.

In the past few decades, music departments in U.S. colleges and universities have attempted to become more diverse and inclusive through initiatives designed to broaden their curricula and attract underrepresented students to campus. Faculty members and administrators have implemented strategies designed to increase ethnic and racial minority representation, but they have largely left untouched the institutional structures that privilege the music of white European and American males. This privilege is disguised by race-neutral celebrations of musical excellence that make colorblindness (or colordeafness) the default mode of daily interaction. In most schools, improving representation through token gestures that celebrate diversity is the only imaginable response to the United States' long history of racial inequality.

This chapter explores how U.S. music schools share a "possessive investment" in classical music that perpetuates, or is at least complicit with, white supremacy.[2] To be gainfully employed in most, if not all, schools and departments of music means coming to terms with systemic racial inequality. Although colorful brochures portray music departments as centers of musical activity on campus, the overwhelming majority of music that is taught and performed within their walls remains—for lack of a better term—classical. Although "classical music" can refer to a period in music history (roughly 1730 to 1820), it is more often used in common parlance as an umbrella for the entire span of Western art music. In this chapter, I intend this latter meaning as a way to signify the idealization of an unbroken tradition that stretches from our fragmentary understanding of music in ancient Greece to the most recent works by contemporary composers. In other words, I agree with Robert Walser that classical music is a social fiction intended to tie disparate practices and historical contexts together into a category representing the most prestigious music in the world.[3] This exalted status provides justification for schools to devote the majority of their resources to maintaining a racially exclusive status quo. As such, the study of performance in schools and departments of music is not a colorblind commitment to great music (great music, after all, being a matter of perspective). It is a system that privileges the music of white European and American male composers and tends to exclude the music of almost everyone else.

The consequences of this bias go beyond the kind of music taught in classrooms. The fetishization of classical performance standards also impedes an institution's ability to recognize the full humanity and artistry of the world beyond its doors. The conventions of music instruction, which focus primarily on reproducing past works, prevent imagining alternative ways of coming together as musicians and as people. In addition, the legacy of white supremacy plays a role in restricting access to colleges and universities by determining who is qualified to be there, both as students and as teachers. In this way, specialization in classical music weds schools to the service of elite interests and limits its potential to serve an antiracist agenda.

To be sure, there are important differences among music departments. Not only are there differences in size, areas of strength, and student and faculty demographics, but some schools have done more than others to challenge racism in their respective institutions. There are no one-size-fits-all solutions to the challenges of inclusivity. Nor is the purpose of this essay to condemn the ongoing study and performance of Beethoven and Mozart as inherently racist. As I hope to make clear, however, the kind of music being taught and performed on college campuses is one facet of a discipline whose racialized legacy impedes our collective ability to imagine a more just and equitable future. By exploring the intertwined histories of music and race in U.S. music departments, this chapter seeks to shed light on present institutional imbalances and to encourage creative and transformative thinking about the future of the discipline.

THE POLITICS OF EXCLUSION

As ethnomusicologist Bruno Nettl once observed, although institutions are officially named "School of Music" or "Department of Music," they are clearly not devoted to the study, advocacy, and performance of all music: "They are, it has been clear all along, schools of Western European art music."[4] Nettl uses the word "clear" to convey the overwhelming commitment to the classical repertoire within U.S. music schools. Accepted as normal by most instructors and students, this status quo permeates daily routines and habits of thought—so much so that most college brochures and websites simply advertise that prospective students can major in "music"

without any qualifying adjectives. The institution's near-exclusive commitment to white European and American male composers is taken for granted.
Through the use of colorblind language, classical music, like whiteness, manages to avoid becoming an object of scrutiny. Its privileged status is built into
the very foundation of the school.[5] Rarely are students encouraged to ask
how music departments got this way.

Just as most colleges were not designed initially to serve nonwhite students, university music schools were never intended to teach anything other
than classical music. They were, in fact, built on a culture of exclusion. Most
U.S. music departments were founded in the late nineteenth and early twentieth centuries, and they reflected the standards and tastes of white, Anglo-
Saxon elites who believed that European art music possessed qualities separating it from the music of darker-skinned, lower-class Americans. The
founding of music schools on college campuses coincided with a period of
mass immigration and internal migration that threatened to remake the
cultural landscape of U.S. metropolitan areas. As cultural elites worried
openly about the racial integrity of the United States, classical music was
swept into a process of cultural gerrymandering that sought to maintain
Anglo-Saxon hegemony.[6] As historian Lawrence Levine explains in his landmark study of cultural hierarchy in the United States, Anglo-Saxon elites
troubled by the influx of immigrants from eastern and southern Europe
sought to maintain order and control by imposing their values on public
spaces, such as art museums, parks, and concert halls. Levine demonstrates
in great detail how modern cultural institutions were founded in the image
of Euro-American upper classes and used as a disciplining force against putatively undesirable elements in the American populace.[7]

As the works of European composers were enshrined as the epitome of civilization, American classical music emerged as one pillar of a "high art" culture
that defined itself against popular entertainment of the day (e.g., jazz, dance
music, movies). Not surprisingly, the aesthetic qualities prized in symphonic
music—melodic and harmonic development—were found to be missing in the
music of more "primitive" peoples.[8] The adjectives used to distinguish classical
music from other forms of music derived from contemporary racial science.
The term "highbrow" (in opposition to "lowbrow"), for example, comes from
the phrenologist's lexicon and describes the superior cranial shape of northern
Europeans.[9] In this way, classical music and whiteness were co-productive,
meaning that they defined and reinforced one another through a shared opposition to undesirable racial, ethnic, and class groups.

A 1918 editorial published in New Orleans's *Times-Picayune,* for example, warned readers of the harmful influence of jazz, using a metaphor, "the house of the muses," to make its point. The author explained this great house as having an "assembly hall of melody" and even more refined "inner sanctuaries of harmony." But jazz, as it happens, was confined to "the basement hall of rhythm," where one can hear "the hum of the Indian dance, the throb of the Oriental tambourines and kettledrums, the clatter of the clogs, the click of Slavic heels, the thumpty-tumpty of the negro banjo, and, in fact, the native dances of the world."[10] This hierarchical picture of music mirrored a hierarchy of human types with racialized bodies at the bottom and white people on top.

In some cases, American classical music was bound up even more closely with the political project of white supremacy. Virginia-born composer and legislator John Powell, for example, used music to promote virulently racist ideas about the nature of blacks. As musicologist Lester Feder delineates, Powell sought to illustrate the incompatibility of white and black cultures as well as the dangers to civilization posed by black contamination (i.e., miscegenation). His main purpose both as a composer and as a legislator was to clearly define whiteness and protect it from black influence.

Powell's 1918 composition *Rhapsodie Nègre* was a symphonic piece that titillated audiences with its depictions of "primal sensuality." Describing the work as his attempt to portray black characteristics ("Negro" in his terms), he explained that his composition reflected the Negro's fundamental lack of impulse control. In his words, "Beneath pretenses to culture, no matter how thoroughly they are put on, the Negro remains a genuine primitive."[11]

As the main architect of Virginia's Racial Integrity Act of 1924, which legally confined white identity to those persons free from the contamination of "any blood other than Caucasian," Powell sought to enshrine white privilege in all facets of American life. White people, according to him, singularly possessed the intellectual capacity and self-control necessary for true civilization, which was in turn represented by the creation of musical masterworks. Deeply invested in racial purity, Powell used his music to sound out what he believed to be the essential differences between white and black people. Symphonic structure, he explained, is "big, complex, and heroic"; it is "self-generating, produced entirely from the internal resources of its themes"; and it is "transcendent," capable of communicating an "immediate musical experience to all people across time and space." Black music, however, lacks this will to power and is subject to the instinctive, animal whims of the body.

Negroes were, according to Powell, "the child among peoples," and therefore his music "depicts bodily rhythm overpowering willed civilization, returning to savagery."[12]

Powell's ideas about music and race were not exceptional for his time or his station. Established by white elites in the late nineteenth and early twentieth centuries, U.S. music schools helped to reinforce the supremacy of Euro-American culture by maintaining a strict separation between classical music and other genres considered to be less cultivated. The fears about racial contamination that John Powell voiced through his compositions have been echoed in each moral panic that has greeted new forms of popular music, from jazz to rock to hip hop. Although throughout the twentieth century the African American influence on U.S. popular music has been impossible to deny (and, for most people, impossible to resist), I have heard from both students and colleagues about teachers, past and present, who warn their students about the dangers of popular music and the damage that might occur to their bodies or instruments by performing the wrong way. As bastions of high culture that depend on drawing a line between classical music and other modes of musical expression, music departments practice a thinly veiled form of segregation.

Even if many musicians, composers, and scholars today believe that racial segregation is unjust and acknowledge the value of diverse musical forms from the United States and around the world, they continue to participate in a system that privileges the work of white composers and treats as secondary in importance the contributions of people of color. The University of Oregon, my employer at the time of this writing, advertises that its core values are "grounded in the strength of the traditional canon," a phrase that serves as a euphemism for music written by white European male composers.[13] Although I have affection for the music taught in our building and others like it across the country, I hear appeals to the traditional canon or other laudatory terms (e.g., "masterworks") as racially exclusionary statements of value.

What is more, reminders of the racist attitudes embedded within classical music culture continue to surface at regular intervals. In May 2016, Michael Butera, head of the National Association of Music Education, representing over sixty thousand music teachers nationwide, explained the lack of diversity in his profession by stating that "blacks and Latinos lack the keyboard skills needed for this field" and suggesting that music theory was too difficult a subject for minorities.[14] In addition to such public statements, which hark back to John Powell's prejudiced ideas about black deficiencies in musical aptitude, numerous mundane examples of musical racism permeate music schools. For example, a friend at another institution recently forwarded me a meme that colleagues had circulated among themselves for fun. The Photoshopped image featured an upright piano whose keyboard had been narrowed from eighty eight to just five keys. The caption, which read "Announcing Kawai's all new keyboard for composing rap arrangements," mockingly implied that hip hop music is so melodically and harmonically simplistic that five notes are all one needs to create it. Posted to a Facebook page called "Classical Music Humor," the image generated over eight hundred comments and nearly forty thousand shares. Although many replies to the post called out the downright racism of the joke, more than half of the comments doubled down with statements such as, "I didn't know rap music had any notes in it" or "[I] Don't know why people find this so offensive. Most of rap music is just trash."[15] Many of the comments, even those that refrained from directly attacking rap, took for granted that there is no way contemporary rap or pop music could possibly live up to works by Beethoven and other classical composers. Such outright dismissals of rap and other forms of popular music echo the *Times-Picayune* editorial from a century ago denouncing jazz as the expression of primitives.

I do not have space to respond in full to the misguided claim that rap music is simple just because it lacks the same melodic and harmonic range found in nineteenth-century symphonic music. As numerous scholars have documented, hip hop producers have their own aesthetic values and ideas about complexity that exist independent of such irrelevant criteria.[16] What is striking about this Facebook post and its thread of comments is that those who dismiss rap as unmusical and crude never explicitly mention race, confirming George Lipsitz's observation that "colorblindness does not do away with color, but rather reinforces whiteness as the unmarked norm against which difference is measured."[17]

In fact, the race-neutral language of these negative comments mirrors the race-neutral terminology of music education, in which certain standards of excellence are simply taken for granted. Departments of music teach courses named "keyboard skills," "aural skills," "musicianship," and "music theory," implying a universal approach to musical cultivation. Although music curricula avoid mentioning race explicitly, they tend to prioritize certain approaches to hearing, performing, and understanding music that reinforce the cultural superiority of classical music. In this way, music—a core component of the liberal arts—supplies the means for a disavowing enactment of race.

THE POSSESSIVE INVESTMENT IN CLASSICAL MUSIC

The great irony of the privilege afforded to the traditional canon in music departments is that the audience for classical music continues to shrink, even among the most affluent and educated members of society. Classical recordings, for example, represent less than 1 percent of the market in music sales.[18] Symphony orchestras across the country struggle to make ends meet, and most of those that have survived get more of their operating budget from charitable donations than ticket sales.[19] It appears that we are witnessing, as musicologist Robert Fink once put it, the "twilight of the canon," a time when the cultural authority once vested in classical music no longer holds sway.[20]

What has undermined the supremacy of the canon is nothing less than a panoply of genres either rooted in or deeply influenced by Afro-Diasporic traditions. Most popular music, from the most obscure indie rock and underground hip hop recordings to the most wide-reaching mainstream Top 40 hits, have assimilated performance practices derived from the same black music traditions that white cultural guardians once decried as dangerously inferior. But these changes have not meant an end to cultural hierarchy or debates about musical value. Instead, the landscape has shifted in ways that make classical music increasingly irrelevant to a majority of musicians and music consumers. Styles derived from blues and jazz, such as rock and hip hop, have canons of their own. Listeners passionately debate the merits of MF Doom, Beyoncé, David Bowie, and countless others, and often look down at other pop artists and songs that they consider to be of lesser quality. In other words, questions of beauty, nuance, and value have not vanished; they have simply shifted away from classical music. Although it would pain the cultural crusaders of the late nineteenth and early twentieth centuries, millions of middle- and upper-class people in the United States today consider themselves cultured without feeling the need to familiarize themselves with Bach, Beethoven, or Brahms.

These developments create an ironic predicament for music departments now situated on university campuses where diversity and inclusivity have become buzzwords: in the era of Black Lives Matter, music schools remain committed to a curriculum that often implies black music does not. Certainly, a large part of the blame lies with colorblind ideology. As previously discussed, music departments present themselves and the subjects they teach in race-neutral language, obscuring the extent to which their institutions rest on racially exclusive foundations. But this answer alone is not fully satisfactory. In my experience, students, professors, and administrators are often painfully aware of the relatively narrow scope of their curriculum and its overwhelming focus on the music of white men. Yet they do very little to make substantive change, suggesting that the problem is more than an inability to recognize race.

An important piece of this puzzle can be found by understanding classical music as a kind of property. In her landmark essay "Whiteness as Property," Cheryl Harris argues that there exists in U.S. legal practice a "property interest" in whiteness, meaning that whiteness and property have been mutually dependent concepts from the nation's founding. The possession of whiteness enabled whites to own land and to own slaves (and to be free from enslavement). In Harris's words, "Slavery linked the privilege of whites to the subordination of Blacks through a legal regime that attempted the conversion of Blacks into objects of property. Similarly, the settlement and seizure of Native American land supported white privilege through a system of property rights in land in which the 'race' of the Native Americans rendered their possession rights invisible and justified conquest."[21] The implication here is that the very concept of possession (i.e., the full rights of ownership) was extended initially only to whites. As such, whiteness itself became a form of property: *an ownership of the ability to own.* Thus, the possession of whiteness had significant material benefits and social advantages.

Throughout U.S. history, it is not difficult to see how possessing whiteness, which Harris terms a form of "status property," has opened up greater access to material resources. From the period stretching from emancipation to the signing of the 1964 Civil Rights Act, 1965 Voting Rights Act, and 1968 Fair Housing Act, a variety of explicit and legalized forms of racial discrimination allowed whites greater access to employment, political representation, and housing opportunities. The possession of whiteness thus allowed for the accumulation of both cultural and material capital.

The full importance of Harris's argument, however, rests in the way she pinpoints how whiteness as property continues to have value long after the outlawing of legal discrimination. In post–civil rights America, she explains, "relative white privilege" is taken as "a legitimate and natural baseline" for all matters concerning ownership and access to resources.[22] In other words, by simply outlawing future racial discrimination but doing nothing affirmative to address past injustice, the legal system enshrined the ill-gotten gains of legalized white supremacy into the very foundation of modern property rights: "property is assumed to be no more than the right to prohibit infringement on settled expectations, ignoring countervailing equitable claims that are predicated on a right to inclusion."[23]

To own whiteness today is to be empowered to ignore the legacy of racial discrimination. It is the right of white people (or others who have acquired a stake in their privilege) to do as they please without any acknowledgment of the racist practices that contributed to the resources they enjoy. This freedom to stand blameless and independent of history allows for continued unequal access to resources and further perpetuates inequality. In this way, whiteness—like a house in a "good" neighborhood or a portfolio of stocks and bonds—can be passed down through the generations as inherited wealth. As Harris summarizes, whiteness as property is, in its most direct form, "the legal legitimation of expectations of power and control that enshrine the status quo as a neutral baseline, while masking the maintenance of white privilege and domination."[24]

There are numerous ways that whiteness and classical music can be considered related forms of property. For centuries, classical music was explicitly regarded as the music of white elites, an expression of their superior European heritage. To have access to classical music—to effectively possess it as a performer or patron—meant having access to other forms of property that were reserved for whites, such as expensive musical instruments, music lessons, and concert subscriptions. This codependency of whiteness and classical music was a main reason why black participation in classical music was restricted by whites and simultaneously sought after by African Americans seeking upward mobility. To "own" classical music is to display a form of cultural capital that reinforces white belonging and privilege. This legacy lives on in the students proficient enough to gain admission to the music major and in the difficulty that schools often have recruiting qualified minority applicants. In an age where public school music education has been slashed or eliminated altogether, college music programs often serve elite students whose families have the resources (cultural and material) to prepare them for college-level music studies.

In another way, the exclusionary practices of music departments represent ongoing investments in both whiteness and classical music. For decades, classical music's status as the only music worthy of being studied went unchallenged. In this time, music departments accumulated resources, such as expensive instruments, buildings and concert halls, and faculty members specializing in performance and ensemble instruction. In addition, a body of teaching literature, historical texts, and cultural practices cohere around the classical tradition. Although there have been efforts to ensure the teaching and performance of different types of music, the settled expectation that classical music must remain the central focus of instruction usually goes unquestioned. In fact, this expectation of power and control is so pervasive that it allows administrators to resist demands for other kinds of music instruction and to continue leveraging classical music's prestige for institutional resources.

THE POLITICS OF INCLUSION

As a contemporary example of the possessive investment in classical music, consider the way that schools have incorporated popular music—rock, hip hop, and other genres—into their curricula. In the past few decades, thanks in large part to the work of ethnomusicologists, U.S. music schools have added courses and created new programs exploring a variety of previously marginalized traditions. There are numerous reasons for these changes, ranging from pressure placed on schools by outside forces, such as accrediting bodies, to the impassioned work of individual students, faculty members, administrators, and staff who believe in the importance and beauty of music outside the Western classical tradition.

These changes, though positive in some respects, have not yet stimulated a widespread reevaluation of institutional priorities and commitments. Although most campuses now offer courses exploring the history and cultural dynamics of diverse musical forms around the world, including American popular music, such coursework tends to be considered elective or geared toward fulfilling the general education requirements of nonmajors. In other words, music departments have been slow to change their core curricula, the parts that form the foundation of the study of performance, history, theory, and ensemble work.

What is more, the "vestiges of systemic racialized privilege" that continue to prioritize classical music are now maintained in part by widespread student interest in learning about *other* types of music.[25] Especially at public research schools where market-based ideologies play an increasingly large role in setting institutional priorities, academic units are pitted against one another in competition for tuition dollars, which are distributed proportionally to units based on how many students they teach and how many majors they graduate. This competition for student credit hours has compelled deans and department chairs—like good administrators at any corporation—to diversify their offerings, adding new courses on popular topics. Under financial pressure to pay for the small class sizes and one-on-one instruction demanded by conservatory-style instruction, many schools have found it advantageous to turn to music once considered untouchable. At many institutions across the country, large lecture classes on the history of rock and roll, hip hop, and the blues now subsidize intimate studio lessons in classical music performance. In this way, even curricular changes that appear to redress past exclusions can find themselves co-opted to preserve the status quo.

All is not as unchanging as it might seem, however. In the popular imagination, the phrase "classical music" might evoke a fixed canon centered around Mozart and Beethoven.[26] But in actual practice, what counts as legitimate and worthy of support in music departments has varied significantly over time. Classical music is neither as static nor as impermeable as some might assume. Like whiteness, it is a relatively recent fiction, and it has adapted to changing historical circumstances to preserve its place within the university.

Just as a number of European ethnic groups were initially regarded as inferior and unassimilable but eventually worked their way into the American mainstream, an assemblage of composers and unruly musical styles have become accepted as legitimate in music schools. Over the years, classical music has absorbed a number of foreign elements, such as the twelve-tone music of Arnold Schoenberg and the antiestablishment provocations of John Cage, all the while maintaining a strict boundary separating serious art music from allegedly nonserious forms. Although this expanded canon is made up of works that are not performed equally as often or seen as absolutely essential to the knowledge of music majors, the classical music tradition as it is represented in history textbooks, syllabi, and performance schedules now encompasses a historically and stylistically broad field, ranging from the earliest notated liturgical chants of the ninth century to the most recent computer-generated sound pieces of electronic music composers. It might seem counterintuitive for all of this music to be part of a singular tradition, but in the music building they are united and share in the prestige of the Western tradition.[27]

To secure a place and resources within music departments often means identifying with the Western tradition and its accumulated prestige. Defining particular composers and their work as extensions of the classical legacy or claiming that other forms of music represent serious art on par with great masterworks invests them with cultural capital. Key to this status is a distancing from folk and popular music, which are regarded as less complex, as mere entertainment, or as expressions of traditional and presumably less cultivated peoples.

With few exceptions, the music of black Americans has been lumped into the nonserious category, and popular music, which throughout much of the twentieth century has been influenced directly or indirectly by the musical contributions of African Americans, is the main "other" against which classical music defines itself.[28] Among African American music traditions, jazz has had the most success crossing this musical color line and finding a home in music departments. What began as something dismissed by cultural elites in the early twentieth century has now been promoted by many cultural institutions as America's Classical Music, and access to campus resources have followed. But even jazz has been included on the condition that yet other forms of black music be kept at arm's length.

THE POLITICS OF RESISTANCE

Whiteness and classical music represent two social categories whose histories are deeply intertwined and mutually constitutive. The line between classical music and its others, like that between white and black racial groups, is fundamental to understanding how power circulates through (and beyond) music institutions. I have dwelled on the possessive investment in classical music not because I want schools and departments of music to fail or to be replaced by schools of rock. Rather, because these institutions have played a role in helping to define whiteness and white privilege (and have in turn benefited from their association with both), music departments can have a role to play in remedying past injustices and creating a more just and equitable future.

The current volume is an attempt to think through the ways that academic disciplines and disciplinary boundaries enable racial inequality to persist without being challenged. Confronting the legacy of white supremacy in U.S. schools and departments of music will necessitate rethinking how things are done both within existing paradigms and beyond them. Many departments already have made attempts to diversify their curricula, but they have allowed their core requirements to remain wedded to relatively narrow ideas of music proficiency. Not only does this status quo stifle forms of creativity that might emerge from our schools, but it also sends the wrong message to students about the kind of music, culture, and, by extension, people that really count. As George Lipsitz points out, white supremacy often hinges on a "*refusal to see* the humanity of people of color."[29] By pressing for more inclusive notions of musical beauty and excellence, music departments can challenge this harmful legacy. Indeed, recent calls from within the discipline to transform music instruction have recommended that coursework and degree requirements move away from reproducing music of the past and instead focus more on the "three pillars" of creativity, diversity, and integration.[30] Such changes could remake the racial composition of U.S. music departments.

At the same time, however, playing music well will not undo racial inequity. We cannot pretend that a commitment to music alone is inherently beneficial. Music schools have long justified their existence by appealing to the aesthetic grandeur and prestige of the music that they teach, but these are highly problematic ways of articulating music's importance.[31] As an alternative, musicologist William Cheng provocatively wonders if empathy (i.e., listening well) might actually be understood as a kind of musicality. If so, might schools envision their roles as fostering musical activity that is not only about competing for greater acclaim and higher status, but also about "reaching out" and "reaching back," lending help to those in need and seeking opportunities for "care and repair."[32] As Cheng puts it, too often we treat music as just vibrations (mere), at times to the detriment of agendas that might support *just* vibrations (fair, good, conscionable).[33]

One of Cheng's goals is to stimulate new ways of appreciating music that are not limited to formal attributes or technical skill. Although it is important for students to improve at their instruments, to understand different musical forms, and to appreciate the achievements of various composers and musicians, music courses rarely ask students to reflect on the ethical and social implications of their work. This oversight is significant because music is fundamentally about community. As Christopher Small and others have emphasized, music gives people a way of expressing both their individuality and their collectivity, negotiating and rehearsing roles that they play in society. The communities that schools and departments of music foster tend to be built on selectivity and competitiveness (prestige).[34] Teachers attempt to give their students the tools to do well, to gain access to power and resources, both of which are certainly significant. The challenge is how to balance excellence and inclusivity.

Graduates of U.S. music schools have confronted this problem in various ways. Some have helped to organize ensembles, such as the Women's Philharmonic in San Francisco (now the Community Women's Orchestra in Oakland) and the Rainbow City Band in Seattle, that seek to build community and highlight the work of women and minority composers.[35] Others, such as those involved in The Crossroads Project, the ensemble Newspeak, and The Dream Unfinished: A Symphonic Benefit for Civil Rights, have made political consciousness and activism an explicit goal for their work.[36] And others still, such as Seattle-based violinist Quentin Morris and Los Angeles–based violinist Vijay Gupta, have committed themselves to education and outreach activities that bring new musical opportunities to underserved communities.[37]

One way to understand these musicians and their work is to say that they value community as much as if not more than they aspire to aesthetic perfection. Rather than direct their energies to the most prestigious and elite venues and audiences, they embrace the marginalized and embattled. The work of these and other individuals and organizations suggests that there are other ways of appreciating the beauty of music that go beyond the technical dimensions of sound. By following such socially engaged models, schools of music might undertake new initiatives that not only promote a more just academic environment, but also reinvigorate their buildings and concert halls by expanding their sense of community.

As long as musical standards remain tied to traditional notions of excellence, however, music schools will continue to model forms of exclusion that mirror and reinforce social inequality. When the goals for diversity and inclusion are limited to attracting ethnic and racial minority students to campus, music schools' near-exclusive focus on performing works by white European and American males becomes naturalized and reinscribed into our institutions. For these reasons, thinking beyond traditional disciplinary lines is essential to the reparative work that music schools might do. Current disciplinary boundaries marginalize music and trivialize its importance relative to other disciplines where issues of race and inequality are routinely addressed. The very idea of "music" and "musical excellence" has reified into a construct that not only favors the privileged but also cuts music off from the world at large. This separation is troubling because the history of racial inequality in the United States—as the life of composer John Powell illustrates well—is an interdisciplinary one. Racial inequality cuts across social, economic, and cultural spheres. Why then should the way we redress this history be bound by discipline? Why, ultimately, should music be kept separated from political science, history, or critical race studies?

The work necessary to push academic institutions to do more to counter social inequality is invariably interdisciplinary, open to collaboration, and resistant toward traditional hierarchies of taste and authority. In Music, Race, and Politics, a class co-designed and co-taught with my former Ethnic Studies colleague Daniel Martinez HoSang, we consider music as a world-making practice with inseparable ties to political and social dynamics. Rather than base the class around a particular period or genre, which tends to steer a course toward formal analysis and "great man" versions of history, we consider the cultural work that music does and the way musical activity shapes how people interact with one another. We study the origins and history of the disco scene in San Francisco, which helped give birth to the modern gay liberation movement. And we invite musicians and activists to class, such as the Los Angeles–based group Quetzal, to discuss the way they bring songwriting and community organizing together in their work.

This way of thinking and teaching about music is more than just diversifying our curriculum. It cuts to the heart of what music means and how it can be used. Music is often portrayed as a kind of frivolous pleasure. Great music, we are encouraged to believe, lives in a world beyond politics, history, and culture. When we enter the concert hall, classroom, or studio space, we are supposed to leave all of that at the door and escape into "the music itself."[38] But music is so much more than a temporary reprieve from the social world. As George Lipsitz, Robin D. G. Kelley, Josh Kun, Gaye Theresa Johnson, and numerous other scholars have helped us to understand, music allows people to imagine new worlds and to rehearse identities not yet possible in the realm of formal politics.[39] The musical imagination, therefore, has an important role to play in confronting the most pressing challenges of the twenty-first century, including the ongoing legacy of racism and racial inequality in the United States.

Giving our students the tools they need to succeed as musicians and scholars should include a curriculum that dares them to dream and search for what is good. We can no longer tolerate a discipline that prioritizes aesthetic objects over the people who create, perform, and listen to them. As a discipline, music needs not only to become more diverse and inclusive but also to come out into the world and help to create spaces for everyone to play.

NOTES

1. Bruno Nettl, *Heartland Excursions: Ethnomusicological Reflections on Schools of Music* (Urbana: University of Illinois Press, 1995), 110.

2. I have adopted this phrase from George Lipsitz's *Possessive Investment in Whiteness: How White People Profit from Identity Politics* (Philadelphia: Temple University Press, 1998).

3. See Robert Walser, "Eruptions: Heavy Metal Appropriations of Classical Virtuosity," *Popular Music* 11, no. 3 (1992): 265.

4. Nettl, *Heartland Excursions,* 82.

5. The process by which whiteness avoids being named and, thus, protects itself from scrutiny is called "exnomination." See John Fiske, *Media Matters: Everyday Culture and Political Change* (Minneapolis: University of Minnesota Press, 1994), 42.

6. At the University of Oregon, where I taught at the time of this writing, the first Department of Music was founded in 1886 and then replaced by the School of Music in 1900. Even Harvard, an institution whose history stretches back to the seventeenth century, did not appoint its first professor of music until 1875.

7. Lawrence Levine, *Highbrow/Lowbrow: The Emergence of Cultural Hierarchy in America* (Cambridge, MA: Harvard University Press, 1988), 171–242.

8. Proponents of classical music understood melodic and harmonic development as the cornerstone of refined music. An overdeveloped and unchecked sense of rhythm, however, was associated with racial otherness and the body, becoming a metonym for blackness. See Susan McClary and Robert Walser, "Theorizing the Black Body in African American Music," *Black Music Research Journal* 14, no. 1 (1994): 75–76; and Ronald Radano, *Lying Up a Nation: Race and Black Music* (Chicago: University of Chicago Press, 2003).

9. Levine, *Highbrow/Lowbrow,* 221–23.

10. "Jass and Jassism," *Times-Picayune* [New Orleans], June 20, 1918, as reproduced in *Keeping Time: Readings in Jazz History,* ed. Robert Walser (New York: Oxford University Press, 1999), 6.

11. "Programme notes to the *Rhapsodie Nègre,*" as quoted in J. Lester Feder, "Unequal Temperment: The Somatic Acoustics of Racial Difference in the Symphonic Music of John Powell," *Black Music Research Journal* 28, no. 1 (Spring 2008): 32–33.

12. Feder, "Unequal Temperment," 38–43.

13. University of Oregon School of Music and Dance website, "About Us: Culture and Values," http://music.uoregon.edu/about/our-values-and-culture.

14. Associated Press, "Music-Education CEO Says Minorities Lack 'Keyboard Skills,' Loses Job," *Billboard,* May 13, 2016, www.billboard.com/articles/business /7370409/michael-butera-music-education-advocacy-fired.

15. "Classical Music Humor," Facebook page, www.facebook.com/classical musichumor/photos/a.207042772650787.61098.207019572653107/999143260107397.

16. Saying that rap music is simple because it lacks harmonic and melodic development is as irrelevant as saying that classical music is simple because it lacks the rhythmic layering or the diversity of timbre found in sample-based hip hop. For more information on hip hop aesthetics and musical production, see Tricia Rose, *Black Noise: Rap Music and Black Culture in Contemporary America* (Hanover, NH: Wesleyan University Press, 1994); Robert Walser, "Rhythm, Rhyme, and Rhetoric in the Music of Public Enemy," *Ethnomusicology* 39, no. 2 (1995): 193–217; Joseph Schloss, *Making Beats: The Art of Sample-Based Hip Hop* (Middletown, CT: Wesleyan University Press, 2004).

17. George Lipsitz, "The Sounds of Silence: How Race Neutrality Preserves White Supremacy," in this volume.

18. During one week in June 2016, not a single recording of classical music sold more than one hundred copies in the United States. Norman Lebrecht, "The Worst Ever U.S. Classical Sales Chart," *Slipped Disc,* June 27, 2016, http://slippedisc .com/2016/06/worst-ever-us-classical-sales-chart.

19. Michael Cooper, "It's Official: Many Orchestras Are Now Charities," *New York Times,* Nov. 15, 2016, C1.

20. Robert Fink, "Elvis Everywhere: Musicology and Popular Music Studies at the Twilight of the Canon," *American Music* 16, no. 2 (1998): 135–79.

21. Cheryl Harris, "Whiteness as Property," *Harvard Law Review* 106, no. 8 (June 1993): 1721.

22. Ibid., 1714.

23. Ibid., 1791.

24. Ibid., 1715.

25. Ibid., 1791.

26. There is some truth to this image of the classical repertoire, which began to coalesce in the late nineteenth century as performances of great works by dead composers overtook those of the living. For more on this development, see Lydia Goehr, *The Imaginary Museum of Musical Works: An Essay in the Philosophy of Music* (Oxford: Clarendon Press, 1992); and William Weber, *The Rise of Musical Classics: A Study in Canon, Ritual, and Ideology* (New York: Oxford University Press, 1992).

27. Although there has been some inclusion of recent repertoire (jazz, EDM, rock, etc.), we should not forget that the lack of apparent diversity in pre-twentieth-century Western music history stems from a legacy of exclusion not an absence of nonwhite or women musicians. A recent panel at the American Musicological Society took aim at this problem by calling for a new approach to music history that places the Western tradition in a global context. Gabriel Solis and Olivia Bloechl,

co-organizers, "Toward a Critical World History of Music: Developing Theory for an Emergent Field," American Musicological Society, annual meeting, Vancouver, November 5, 2016.

28. As George Lewis argues, the status of "serious" composer for John Cage and other white midcentury American composers depended, in part, on the way they distanced themselves from the music of Charlie Parker, Dizzy Gillespie, and other black American jazz innovators. George Lewis, "Improvised Music after 1950: Afrological and Eurological Perspectives," *Black Music Research Journal* 16, no. 1 (Spring 1996): 91–122.

29. Lipsitz, "Sounds of Silence"

30. Ed Sarath et al., *Transforming Music Study from Its Foundations: A Manifesto for Progressive Change in the Undergraduate Preparation of Music Majors* (College Music Society, Nov. 2014), www.mtosmt.org/issues/mto.16.22.1 /manifesto.pdf.

31. The idea that the beauty of music on its own represents some kind of social good rings hollow after Hitler, one of the twentieth century's greatest lovers and patrons of classical music.

32. William Cheng, *Just Vibrations: The Purpose of Sounding Good* (Ann Arbor: University of Michigan Press, 2016), 10.

33. Ibid., 15.

34. For more on the cultural dynamics of U.S. music schools, see Henry Kingsbury, *Music, Talent, and Performance: A Conservatory Cultural System* (Philadelphia: Temple University Press, 2001).

35. www.communitywomensorchestra.org and http://rainbowcityband.com. Other examples include the many gay men's choruses around the country, the Minnesota Philharmonic Orchestra (www.mnphil.org), New York's Queer Urban Orchestra (www.queerurbanorchestra.org), and Chicago's Noise Bias (www .noisebias.org).

36. The Crossroads Project (www.thecrossroadsproject.org) brings music, science, and visual art together to create an immersive experience where audience members can learn and reflect on climate change. The ensemble Newspeak's 2013 program *Coming Together/Attica* (https://newspeakmusic.org/2013/06/coming-together-attica-2) explored incarceration, isolation, and the important pursuit of human rights within the American prison system, using texts written by Sam Melville and Richard X. Clark, both inmates at Attica prison during the 1971 uprising. New York City's The Dream Unfinished: A Symphonic Benefit for Civil Rights (http://thedreamunfinished.org) performs classical music to raise money for a number of social justice organizations. Other examples include Julliard graduates Kate Rigg and Lyris Hung of Slanty-Eyed Mama (www.slantyeyedmama.com), an Asian American duo who use their classical training as a foundation for their outrageous, genre-bending performance art, and Los Angeles–based Street Symphony (http://streetsymphony.org), which raises money for organizations working on homelessness and mass incarceration issues.

37. See www.quintonmorris.org and http://vijayviolin.com.

38. For critiques of "the music itself" as ideology, see Susan McClary, *Feminine Endings: Music, Gender, and Sexuality* (Minneapolis: University of Minnesota Press, 1991) and *Conventional Wisdom: The Content of Musical Form* (Berkeley: University of California Press, 2000).

39. See, for example, George Lipsitz, *Dangerous Crossroads: Popular Music, Postmodernism, and the Politics of Place* (New York: Verso Books, 1997); Robin D. G. Kelley, *Freedom Dreams: The Black Radical Imagination* (Boston: Beacon Press, 2003); Josh Kun, *Audiotopia: Music, Race, and America* (Berkeley: University of California Press, 2005); and Gaye Theresa Johnson, *Spaces of Conflict, Sounds of Solidarity: Music, Race, and Spatial Entitlement in Los Angeles* (Berkeley: University of California Press, 2013).

ACKNOWLEDGMENTS

This essay grew out of numerous conversations with students, colleagues, and administrators at the University of Oregon and at other institutions, and I'm grateful for all of the input, both formal and informal. I also want to express my gratitude to Tamara Levitz, whose paper "In the Shadow of the Zoot Suit Riots: Racial Exclusion and the Foundations of Music History," presented at the 2014 meeting of the American Musicological Society in Milwaukee, Wisconsin, served as an inspiration. I also thank Lydia Van Dreel for answering my questions about progressive politics in contemporary classical music and Will Cheng for reading an early draft of this chapter.

EIGHT

Powerblind Intersectionality

FEMINIST REVANCHISM AND INCLUSION
AS A ONE-WAY STREET

Barbara Tomlinson

At the scene of argument, the conventions of disciplinary research and writing teach people to pursue and propose colorblind solutions to colorbound problems. Colorblindness is often taken to be a legitimate position exactly because it serves to suppress the contemporary presence of racial hierarchies. Colorblindness is not a social theory, a moral imperative, or a route to racial equality but rather a way to hide, excuse, justify, and protect the unfair gains and unjust enrichments of centuries of expressly racist practices and policies. Colorblindness proceeds from an uninterrogated baseline norm that imagines a world where racism does not exist until an isolated and aberrant event or individual injects it into social life. As a result, colorblindness is inevitably and constitutively infused with unacknowledged structures of power.

People who see themselves as colorblind in a society suffused with racist oppression and exploitation are not so much evading color as evading acknowledgment of power. The discursive frame of colorblindness functions to place off-limits and beyond the pale of legitimate discussion a crucial axis of identity and power, encouraging "powerblind" discursive practices that reinforce racial hierarchies. Powerblindness is even more insidious than colorblindness in that it is not even articulated as an ideological commitment, yet serves to structure social relations.

I argue in this chapter that colorblindness and powerblindness pervade white feminist critiques of the concept of intersectionality, a concept developed by women of color. These critiques use powerblind strategies in repeated

Portions of this article were originally published in Barbara Tomlinson, *Undermining Intersectionality: The Perils of Powerblind Feminism* (Philadelphia, PN: Temple University Press, 2018).

attempts to wrest intersectionality from its origins in, and its continuing commitment to struggle against, racist suppression and subordination. Such moves need not be based in racial aversion or animus; they emanate as well from an unstated but deeply rooted commitment to a willed blindness to power that pervades neoliberal culture and politics. It is not simply that the critics neglect intersectionality's antiracist origins and intentions but that they advance arguments that seek to make intersectionality safe for power. The reward structures of neoliberal institutions cultivate experts who are unwilling or unable to identify power or to challenge it. Deeply political problems are translated into matters in need of greater technical or administrative expertise. Collective public problems become rendered as private and personal concerns. Pretending that asymmetrical power does not exist constitutes the core condition of bourgeois respectability within the neoliberal framework. Inside the audit cultures of academic institutions, inside the economy of prestige and attention online and in print, and inside competitions for fellowships and grants from philanthropic institutions rewards flow freely to power-aversive formulations.

The academic disciplines that emerged in the eras of conquest and colonization to help rationalize and legitimize European world dominance are saturated with racist presumptions and assumptions. Their *either/or* rather than *both/and* perspectives have long served to legitimate the domination of men over women, rich over poor, white over nonwhite, straight over not straight. Training in the disciplines instructs people *not to see* the social subordinations that they can witness every day with their own eyes, if those eyes are open. This state of affairs is to be expected. In Cedric Robinson's deft formulation, social systems deploy race as justification for relations of power that "are unrelentingly hostile to their exhibition." Claims of naturalism and inevitability are mere contrivances grounded in specific interests, histories, and "mechanisms of assembly." As "unstable truth systems," Robinson argues, racial regimes are always in a process of modification, amendment, emendation, revision, and reorganization.[1] Colorblind and powerblind discourses are part of this system of continuing modification.

Many chapters in this volume look at texts or situations that purport to be colorblind, and demonstrate that they are not. This chapter analyzes feminist texts that do not directly evoke colorblind discourses but deploy colorblindness and powerblindness as part of a textual structuring of racial dominance that demonstrates a more hidden allegiance not just to colorblindness, but to what Eduardo Bonilla-Silva and Tukufu Zuberi call "white logic and white methods."[2] I examine here two texts concerned with intersectional theorizing. Both texts appropriate intersectional theorizing by devaluing the intellectual labor of women of color, enveloping that labor in an unmarked "feminism." Both texts are examples of what I call "neoliberal asset-stripping," attempts to delegitimate the intersectional thinking of women of color in order to appropriate the valuable conceptions of intersectionality for management by an unmarked—but white—feminism. They are blind not only to the social and historical workings of racist power but also to the racialized power that scholars wield in the tactics they deploy at the scene of argument. These tactics contain uninterrogated ideological allegiances. As Jochen Walter and Jan Helmig explain, "Discourses do not simply depict or reproduce the world, but instead *constitute* and *construct* reality in a selective and contingent manner. They have a *productive character* which means that discourses are practices which are systematically *producing* the very objects that they apparently describe."[3]

The chapter examines colorblind and powerblind discourses in two critiques of intersectionality written by white feminists: "The Complexity of Intersectionality" by Leslie McCall and "Doing Difference" by Candace West and Sarah Fenstermaker.[4] Both texts appropriate intersectionality by gestures enveloping women of color in an unmarked "feminism." One text reframes the racial politics of intersectionality's emergence as the production of a racially unified feminism. The other text frames the thinking of intersectional scholars of color as deficient in order to claim the simultaneity of social categories long posited by intersectionality as their own contribution—a new discovery of a racially unmarked but implicitly white feminism.[5] The pervasive nature of such powerblind critiques in white feminist critiques of intersectionality is significant. One key purpose of intersectional thinking is to discern in any given social and historical situation *which differences make a difference.* By evading racism, marginalizing it, or relegating it to the historical past, white feminists are not just embracing colorblindness; they are associating themselves with a powerblindness that is fundamentally fatal to feminism's entire project.

THE MANAGERIAL LOGIC OF THE COLONIAL MATRIX

Before turning to analyze examples of colorblind and powerblind white feminist discourses, I want to situate them in the arguments about coloniality developed by Walter D. Mignolo. In *The Darker Side of Western*

Modernity, Mignolo argues that Western knowledge is necessarily and constitutively a *colonial matrix* of power and knowledge.[6] This matrix was established by Europe treating its dominant particulars as universals, as the baseline norm that defines the fully human. Europe framed its culture and modernity as dynamic and progressive, as the zero point of observation. Other parts of the world were seen as not yet fully developed, but rather embedded in nature and tradition, inert and fixed, defined by the terms of colonial difference.[7] In consequence, those considered fully human—as *humanitas*—are charged with managing knowledge production and establishing the categories of thought. Those classified as not fully human, as more connected to nature than to history, as *anthropos,* are deemed rationally and ontologically deficient. Mignolo argues that, historically,

> rational classification meant racial classification. And rational classifications do not derive from "natural reason," but from "human concepts" of natural reason. Who establishes criteria of reason and who classifies? . . . And who are classified without participating in the classification? People who inhabit the *exteriority* (the outside invented in the process of defining the inside) created from the perspective of the zero point of observation (*anthropos*).[8]

The racialized power produced and perpetuated by this process does not stem from the conscious intentions and actions of culpable individual scholars, but rather emerges as part and parcel of a framework for managing all of Western civilization and its institutions of knowledge production. Its managerial logic does not exclude *anthropos*—for our purposes, all racialized, gendered, sexualized others—from academic knowledge production. But it controls the unequal terms by which *anthropos* can be admitted and participate. Everyone is included, but not everyone has the right to include. As Mignolo emphasizes,

> Inclusion is a one-way street and not a reciprocal right. In a world governed by the colonial matrix of power, he who includes and she who is welcomed to be included stand in codified power relations. The locus of enunciation from which inclusion is established is always a locus holding the control of knowledge and the power of decision across gender and racial lines, across political orientations and economic regulations.[9]

In these settings, then, whites not only manage the categories of thought and the terms of debate; they also manage the conditions by which people of color are permitted to participate in systems of knowledge production.

According to Mignolo, the logic of the colonial matrix is not a vestigial remnant of history but continues to shape all the knowledge practices of Western civilization. Adopting its precepts is not voluntary or conscious; rather, "It is a managerial logic that by now has gone beyond the actors who have created it and managed it—and in a sense, it is the colonial matrix that has managed the actors and all of us."[10] Because feminist studies presents itself as concerned with social justice and attracts scholars who think of themselves as progressive, one might expect not to find there scholarly logics based on the colonial matrix, logics claiming colorblind "neutrality." But at the level of argumentation, research design, and execution, retentions of disciplinary frameworks and interdisciplinary inventions are replete with masks, moves, and mechanisms steeped in colorblind logics. There is a tendency to make the "interdisciplinary evasion"—that is, assuming that declaring feminist studies interdisciplinary means that the problems of the disciplines go away. But because disciplinary allegiances and perspectives remain, scholars may badly mishandle arguments and strategies characterizing other disciplines.

Even academic disciplines that claim to produce knowledge explicitly for transformative social change, such as feminist studies, can be seen to use strategies of disciplinary authority to limit and control the terms of inclusion of racialized subjects. In *Why Stories Matter: The Political Grammar of Feminist Theory*, Clare Hemmings argues that feminist studies' reframing of its own past is not innocent, but structured in dominance, reinforcing racial, sexual, and even gendered power. Hemmings provides strong evidence that narratives of feminist history are constructed in repeated and patterned ways motivated by the positions scholars occupy or wish to occupy.[11] The result is the creation of a closed feminist past that incessantly frames new achievements as transcending and eradicating old problems. Black women and lesbians are included not for their influence on feminist scholarship and histories, but as marginal figures, emerging and disappearing to fit the dominant story of white feminist history. Hemmings argues that "problematic configurations of race and sexuality are key rather than tangential to how feminist progress narratives operate . . . erasure of a complex past is a necessary condition of their positivity."[12] Such narratives position the critiques provided by Black feminists and other women of color, lesbians, and poststructuralists as having performed an important service—but *in the past*. In these histories, concepts of difference are seen as serving as *catalysts* for feminist discussion that quickly became unnecessary once feminism presented itself as "incorporating" difference. Dominant white feminists stand in "codified power relations" to the racialized feminists and others they welcomed—not as cognitive equals, but as evidence of the capaciousness of feminist studies.

Feminist studies declares itself an interdisciplinary field of inquiry, but it is composed of subgroups of scholars who also share allegiance to the disciplines of their training and practice—in the case of the white scholars I analyze here, forms of sociology. Sociology has been a managerial discipline from its inception in race relations theory, which chose to focus on "race relations" rather than racial subordination.[13] It is also what Foucault might call a "hegemony-seeking" discipline. According to Linda Martín Alcoff, Foucault contrasted "subjugated knowledges"—here, the intersectional thinking of women of color—with "hegemony-seeking knowledges," arguing that "subjugated or local knowledges always tend to do less violence to the local particulars and are also less likely to impose hierarchical structures of credibility based on universal claims about the proper procedures of justification that foreclose the contributions of many unconventional or lower-status knowers."[14]

Exactly because they see themselves as on the side of social justice, feminists may fail to see how their own practices of reading and writing serve as discursive technologies of power, framed in terms of the colonial matrix of knowledge and allegiances to hegemony-seeking disciplines. Under such circumstances, specific rhetorical strategies can serve as potent tools of dominance, infusing the reading situation with strategies of racial subordination that go unremarked because they are authorized by tradition and convention.

BLIND TO (SOME) COLOR, BLIND TO (SOME) POWER

Since its inception in the nineteenth century, the intersectional thinking of women of color was frequently ignored.[15] In the 1970s and 1980s, Black feminists and other feminist scholars of color vigorously argued that categories such as gender, race, and class are not stable and discrete but, rather, variable and changing constellations that are *interrelated, co-constitutive,* and *simultaneous.*[16] By the 1980s and 1990s their arguments insisting on the heterogeneity of social difference created a dramatically successful intervention in feminist studies.

This moment provoked a shock and sense of loss for many white feminists: they were forced to abandon illusions of the wholeness and homogeneity of the category "woman," its primacy as a social category, and the centrality of white women as representatives of feminism. I argue that significant traces of this moment of loss remain, that this intervention is still being resisted at the scene of argument through the specific claims and rhetorics of scholarly texts. Feminist critiques of intersectionality are replete with arguments and citations seeking to discredit and delegitimate the intersectional thinking of scholars of color in order to appropriate intersectionality for a general, unmarked, "colorblind" white feminism.[17]

While it includes arguments about and by racialized subjects, as in many other disciplines, feminist studies systematically forecloses inquiries into the nature of its *own* historical reliance on deployments of racial power and hierarchy, of privileging colorblind solutions to colorbound problems. Colorblind tactics pretend to overlook, and thereby make invisible, white racial dominance. If one is blind to color, one is also blind to power. One of the privileges of racial colorblindness is to pose as blind to power when speaking as *humanitas,* as the one who classifies, who benefits from strategies of colorblindness that rely on, yet disavow, the presumed superiority of *humanitas* over the racialized position of *anthropos,* those who have been classified and are to be managed.

The construction of *humanitas* and *anthropos* was a thoroughly gendered enterprise: it was European male elites who developed systems of classification to justify the subordination of others through various categories— geographical, racial, gendered. In this historical tradition, European women were not positioned as *humanitas.* Given this history of power in social relations, the position of contemporary professional white women who are dominant in feminist studies appears anomalous. They are no doubt subject to subordination, but not to the degree or in the ways that colonized and racialized people continue to be. In the discipline of feminist studies, they are in the position to welcome racialized others, yet still hold "the control of knowledge and the power of decision across gender and racial lines."[18] To hold the "control of knowledge" authorizes dominant white feminists to decide the nature and value of any intellectual contributions by racialized subjects. This process comes into sharp relief through the history of intersectional and multidimensional analysis: the intellectual production of women of color, intersectional thinking, has successfully challenged and altered disciplinary thinking, making it a central site for examining the problems of colorblind discourses in feminist studies. When they adopt a "colorblind" stance, dominant white feminists assume they can transmogrify theoretical and conceptual history and appropriate this intellectual production. The rhetoric to accomplish this both deploys and denies white racial power. As a result, the subject position of the white feminist tends to be unmarked within its own discourse, but all too visible to those it seeks to manage.

"Colorblinding" rhetorics erase racial specificity, encourage authors and readers to feel that they are not white but neutral and "colorblind," appropriate intersectionality for the subject position of the "unmarked" white woman, and hide the stripping of intellectual assets from women of color. I argue that such colorblinding rhetoric appears at the scene of argument in the introduction to Leslie McCall's "The Complexity of Intersectionality," one of the most widely cited feminist articles on intersectionality,[19] providing an illustrative example of a broader process. The article begins:

> Since critics first alleged that feminism claimed to speak universally for all women, feminist researchers have been acutely aware of the limitations of gender as a single analytical category. In fact, feminists are perhaps alone in the academy in the extent to which they have embraced intersectionality— the relationships among multiple dimensions and modalities of social relations and subject formations—as itself a central category of analysis. *One could even say that intersectionality is the most important theoretical contribution that women's studies, in conjunction with related fields, has made so far.*[20]

Despite intersectionality being a result of the theorizing of women of color, *race does not appear here.* In praising intersectionality in her introduction, McCall erases the racial specificity of the scholars who developed intersectional theorizing. Rather, in a remarkable move of appropriation, she declares intersectionality a product of "women's studies" ("in conjunction with related fields"). The passage alludes to disciplinary differences, while treating racial difference as invisible. This "colorblinding" rhetoric is a move of neoliberal "asset-stripping," transferring the intellectual assets of intersectionality to an apparently raceless "colorblind" feminism.

In a footnote, McCall credits several intersectional scholars, noting:

> As for the origins of the term itself, it was probably first highlighted by Kimberlé Crenshaw (1989, 1991). Many other key texts introduced the conceptual framework and offered similar terms: see [A.] Davis 1981; Moraga 1983; [B.] Smith 1983a; hooks 1984; Moraga and Anzaldúa 1984; Glenn 1985; Anzaldúa 1987, 1990; King 1988; Mohanty 1988; Spelman 1988; Sandoval 1991.[21]

With this note, McCall simply erases the racial specificity of the cited "feminist researchers." Nothing in the passage signals to readers that nearly all of the scholars cited identify as women of color: five as Black, three as Latina, and one each as Japanese American and South Asian, with only one of the ten identifying as white. McCall's "colorblindness" is not innocent in the argument of the text. The passage elides racial difference in order to claim the knowledge production of women of color as a legacy of *feminism* and creates *feminism* as a singular site for intersectionality by eliding the intersectional work of ethnic, queer, racial, and American studies. The result is to claim intersectionality to speak only through gender—to historicize intersectionality "nonintersectionally."

"Colorblinding" rhetorical strategies appear in both the passage and the footnote, congruent with what Hemmings argues to be systematic treatment of women of color in feminist histories.[22] I note five strategies that serve to devalue the theoretical and analytical arguments of women of color and to relegate them to the historical past. First, the sources cited in the footnote, for an article published in 2005, are limited to the decade 1981–1991.[23] With the exception of Evelyn Nakano Glenn, the text ignores all further work done by the intersectional scholars it lists. The intellectual production of these scholars of color is thus encapsulated in the past.

Second, the text itself begins with a tendentious "colorblinding" feminist origin story: "Since critics *first alleged* that feminism claimed to speak universally for all women, *feminist researchers* have been acutely aware of the limitations of gender as a single analytical category" (emphasis added). This narrative implies that the response of "feminist researchers" to "critics" was immediate, erasing conflicts of race and power from a contentious disciplinary history: as Judith Butler points out, in the 1980s "the feminist 'we' rightly came under attack by women of color who claimed that the 'we' was invariably white, and that the 'we' that was meant to solidify the movement was the very source of a painful factionalization."[24] Nothing in the passage signals to readers that those relegated to the footnote were prominent among the critics objecting to the suppression of racial difference in feminism.

Third, while a "range of disciplines" is mentioned, the specific training of the cited scholars is not, as if scholars trained in law, philosophy, or political science were simply contributing a basis for the development of sociological theory.

Fourth, the footnote deprecates the intellectual labor of these scholars of color, reducing their theorizing and analysis to the apparently lucky identification of one or more catchy "terms," rather than the sustained development of an analytic strategy.

Fifth, in erasing the racial identities of the scholars it cites, the footnote also erases the influence of the politics of *racism* in the development of intersectional thinking—its role as a tool for analyzing and countering subordination. The women on McCall's list are not just feminists who incidentally are also primarily women of color. They are all feminists who see gender justice as inextricably linked to racial justice. The scholarly work of most if not all those cited emerged from experience with organized social action groups and social movements countering racism. Examples include Angela Davis's continuing commitment to organized efforts for social justice,[25] Barbara Smith's participation in the Combahee River Collective,[26] and Kimberlé Crenshaw's involvement in organized action at Harvard Law School leading to the development of Critical Race Theory.[27] Chela Sandoval notes that the form of "oppositional consciousness" she advocates "was enacted during the 1968–90 period by a particular and eccentric cohort of U.S. feminists of color who were active across diverse social movements."[28] The result of suppressing the significance of the cited scholars' race and training is a "colorblinding" rhetoric that systematically diminishes and trivializes the conceptual labor of women of color, in the process of appropriating their intellectual assets according to the "hegemony-seeking" logics characterizing the discipline of sociology. These rhetorical strategies at the scene of argument display a hidden allegiance to colorblindness: they rewrite the history of a traumatic historical moment by folding intersectional critics into a feminism "writ large," eliminating the motivating force of racism in the development of intersectional thinking. They also make visible a revanchist desire to regain territory, to restore white racial centrality in the discipline of feminist studies.

THE SOCIAL CONSTRUCTION OF STRAW BODIES

Discussions of racial difference, such as critiques of intersectionality, tend to reinscribe *whiteness* as if it were *"colorblindness."* Structurally, commentary on and critiques of intersectionality are inevitably racializing discourses: the originating intersectionality is a production of women of color, yet critiques are generally written by white women who rely on the subject position of the "neutral" or "unmarked" white woman. This "unmarked" subject position of the white woman treats herself as "colorblind" to the interdisciplinary and disciplinary expertise about race of those whose positions she critiques, often while presenting implausible echoes of the arguments of women of color.

Given the historically sedimented logic of the colonial matrix, it is not surprising to find that "colorblind" critiques may frame the concepts proposed by women of color to be fixed and inert, cognitively deficient, embedded in tradition and in nature.

In such circumstances, texts may represent themselves as colorblind /powerblind through the use of the *representation* form of the *straw person fallacy:*[29] Robert Talisse and Scott F. Aikin, in their analysis of the straw person fallacy, note that in the representation form, critics (1) misattribute and misrepresent the arguments of their target and (2) suppress and ignore their target's relevant arguments. Critics may quote their target's words out of context, for example, misrepresenting the target's actual claim, or oversimplify the claims, then attack the oversimplification. The critics covertly replace the target's precise argument with false but superficially similar claims that they discredit. This discrediting is "knocking down a straw person." To be persuasive, a straw person argument requires an audience that is ignorant or uninformed about the original argument. This tends to be precisely the case when white-dominated audiences interested in gender encounter multidimensional analyses of gender and race. An illustrative example of the representation form of the straw person argument is found in the widely cited article "Doing Difference" by Candace West and Sarah Fenstermaker in *Gender and Society*.[30] The example I examine here purports to critique an argument made by Patricia Hill Collins.

In *Black Feminist Thought,* Patricia Hill Collins makes a series of detailed and sensitive arguments countering notions of biological determinism and developing conceptions of social construction. She argues that "while expressions of gender and race are both socially constructed, they are not constructed in the same way," so the struggles of different groups "to articulate self-defined standpoints represent similar yet distinct processes." Collins maintains: "While race and gender are both socially constructed categories, constructions of gender rest on clearer biological criteria than do constructions of race. Classifying African-Americans into specious racial categories is considerably more difficult than noting the clear biological differences distinguishing females from males."[31] Collins is not claiming that gender is based on biology, but that processes for articulating self-defined standpoints in groups differ because socially constructed methods of gender classification rely on notions of a clear biological binary—a binary continually reinscribed, for instance by requiring the parents of children born hermaphroditic to choose whether the child should be "classified" male or female.[32] Collins cites Harvard sociologist Orlando Patterson's *Slavery and Social Death* to clarify the point she is making about variation in socially constructed methods of identifying gender and race. Patterson argues that slavery is characterized by a *generalized condition of dishonor* conveyed by visible marks of servitude, but in the Americas it was not color but rather hair type that served as the badge of slavery. This was the case because skin color in both whites and Blacks varied more widely than most assume, in part because of geographical origin and also because of miscegenation. According to Patterson, "Hair type rapidly became the real symbolic badge of slavery, although like many powerful symbols it was disguised, in this case by the linguistic device of using the term 'black.'"[33] Collins draws on Patterson's arguments about the role of hair texture and skin color in creating and legitimating social death for Afro-diasporic people to illustrate how the myth of biological difference as destiny in relation to gender has been even easier to sustain than the parallel myth about race.

West and Fenstermaker ignore both the proximate and larger context of Collins's comment to allege that by mentioning the widely shared social perception that women are marked by biological difference, Collins herself is embracing biological essentialism. Their zeal to catch a woman of color making what they allege to be an error that feminists have long critiqued about out-of-date theories of "sex differences" and "sex roles"—and thus to render her rationally and ontologically deficient—leads them to make a claim that directly contradicts Collins's careful arguments about social construction. West and Fenstermaker demonstrate her "mistake" by adding emphasis to Collins's own words:

> While race and gender are both socially constructed categories, constructions of gender *rest on clearer biological criteria* than do constructions of race. Classifying African-Americans into specious racial categories is considerably more difficult than noting the *clear biological differences* distinguishing females from males. . . . Women do share common experiences, but the experiences are not generally the same type as those affecting racial and ethnic groups.[34]

They go on to argue:

> Of course Collins is correct in her claim that women differ considerably from one another. . . . The problem, however, is that what unites them as women are the "clear biological criteria distinguishing females from males." Here, Collins reverts to treating gender as a matter of sex differences (i.e., as ulti-

mately traceable to factors inherent to each sex), in spite of her contention that it is socially constructed. Gender becomes conflated with sex, as race might speciously be made equivalent to color.[35]

West and Fenstermaker treat Collins's echo of socially constructed notions of biological binaries as if it were a theory proposed by Collins about the nature of gender. But Collins is not reporting what she theorizes about the nature of gender; she is discussing how gender and race are constructed in society. This kind of misreading is not uncommon among students and scholars first encountering discussions of social construction.

Part of the powerblind strategy is to ignore sentences on the same and next page that would demonstrate to their readers that the critics' interpretation of Collins is false. Collins indicates that "expressions of gender and race are both socially constructed" and notes that "women do share common experiences." "Expressions" and "experiences" are not biological criteria inherent to each sex. Focused on denigrating Collins's claims about gender, however, West and Fenstermaker neglect her claims about race, failing to mention Collins's citation of Patterson or to explain Patterson's argument, which would clarify the contrast Collins is making. The critics are being casual about something important. While discrediting Collins for allegedly making a feminist error, they miss the moral and political challenge offered by scholarship that contends with the afterlife of slavery and social death.

West and Fenstermaker's use of the representation form of the straw man fallacy is embedded in sedimented social constructions of race that link Black women to bodies and biology and that judge their thinking as "behind the times" and self-contradictory. The critics' rhetoric reaffirms racial hierarchy.

VENTRILOQUIZING STRAW WOMEN OF COLOR

White privilege entails the ability and the propensity to criticize the intellectual production of women of color without acknowledging one's own racial identity and one's own role in structures of racial subordination. White privilege allows commonplaces about concerns with race to accompany rhetorical devices that reinforce racial hierarchy. White privilege authorizes freedom to choose whether one points to the racial identities of scholars of color or whether one ignores them. White privilege assumes that in the segregated academies and journals where we do our work the preponderance of readers will be white and will know little about scholarship on race, so that "authoritative" claims about what racialized scholars say and think will appear plausible to these readers.

Deploying revanchist moves to regain white centrality in feminism while addressing audiences unfamiliar with the scholarship of women of color makes the second form of the straw person fallacy particularly significant in analyzing colorblind/powerblind discourses. Talisse and Aikin term this the *selection* form of the fallacy (as opposed to the representation form).[36] In the selection form, critics misrepresent a "generic" position by "selecting" or posing a fictitious, imprecise, naive, uninformed, or inept formulation of the view they wish to be seen as refuting, while implying that they are taking up and successfully refuting the best arguments.

I turn again to West and Fenstermaker's "Doing Difference," which provides many examples of the selection form of the straw person fallacy. The article as a whole promotes ethnomethodology to redress the perceived lack of unity and quality of various metaphors and methods for multidimensional theorizing that appear in an introductory survey anthology.[37] The vast number of citations to their article indicates that apparently West and Fenstermaker have been successful in conveying the impression to audiences unfamiliar with racial studies that they have effectively refuted the best arguments about intersectionality and created a significantly more sophisticated notion of multidimensionality. Although arguments about the simultaneous experiencing of gender, race, and class had been commonplace in scholarship by women of color for several decades, "Doing Difference" ultimately presents itself as discovering this simultaneity and has been widely cited in that regard.[38] The ability of the article to achieve this rewriting of history rests to a substantial degree on the misrepresentation and denigration of the thinking of intersectional scholars of color, achieved through the selection form of the straw person fallacy.

For example, West and Fenstermaker use rhetorical strategies that "ventriloquize" arguments of racialized others that they falsely present as "typical" generic positions. In colorblind and powerblind discourses, the act of false refutation may well be less significant than the rhetorical device of broadcasting weak arguments *as if they were the best arguments*—that is disseminating caricatures of what Black scholars think or what women of color would say. Selecting weak arguments for refutation—including arguments already refuted by the very texts of intersectional scholars cited in their own article—gives the impression that arguments by and about race and intersectional thinking by women of color are generally unintelligent and can be easily quashed and surpassed by white scholars.

Talisse and Aikin argue that the selection form of the straw person fallacy both *depends on* and *perpetuates* the ignorance of its audience. Like the representation form, the selection form succeeds when audiences are unfamiliar with the specific arguments of racialized scholars and fail to explore them further. Audiences have no reason not to be satisfied with the information they receive from "authoritative" sources whose articles appear in peer-reviewed edited scholarly journals. Audiences assume that critics are vetted to make sure that they counter the strongest arguments available. When only weak arguments are presented, audiences unfamiliar with scholarship on race assume that there are no stronger arguments available. Talisse and Aikin argue that the selection form of the fallacy "is vicious because it is posited on a misrepresentation of the variety and relative quality of one's opposition. . . . When it succeeds, it convinces one's audience not only of the correctness of one's view, but also of the absence of reasoned and intelligent opposition to it."[39] According to Talisse and Aikin, correcting the selection form of the fallacy requires audiences to come to understand the larger discourses that critics purport to be accounting for and representing accurately. Particularly when critics use rhetorical devices to appear to be "even-handed" or "friendly" to these positions, the selection form of the straw person fallacy can serve to reestablish in a new and especially strong context the notion that women of color are cognitively inferior.

I focus here on a series of questions posed in "Doing Difference" that West and Fenstermaker present as revealing troubling "theoretical implications" of intersectionality, implications that require or lead to a desire to count, hierarchize, or calculate relationships among intersecting features. The line of argument engages with the anthology introduction of Margaret L. Andersen and Patricia Hill Collins. West and Fenstermaker's questions are embedded in the rhetoric of the first-person plural ("we"), presenting a false scene of "collaborative thinking" that serves to camouflage the degree to which the critics' argument relies on both representation and selection forms of the straw person fallacy. Deployed in this way, the first-person plural—used previously to fold together white feminists and women of color—establishes as plausible a jointly held *false* position, held *neither* by the critics *nor* by the intersectional scholars they cite.

Two important argumentative problems are entwined in the passages pertaining to this argument: one involving the accurate attribution of claims, the other involving the correct definition of "theoretical implications." The form of misattribution in "Doing Difference" silently replaces the best scholarly arguments about intersectional analysis with general political positions of the type found in political commentary and blogs. The shortcut of substituting general positions for the specific positions of individual scholars presents "what women of color must be thinking" as less flexible, less farseeing, and less complex than what the white scholars are thinking; evidence that would refute such a position—such as passages in the critics' primary source texts on intersectionality (such as Collins, and Andersen and Collins)[40] that demonstrate more careful argument and complex thinking than shown by the critics themselves—are interpreted simplistically or simply not acknowledged. In consequence, theoretical development of scholarly ideas in feminist studies is truncated because critics are refuting "straw positions" rather than the actual positions of those they criticize, reinforcing the notion that white critics can easily dismiss the limited thinking of scholars of color.

In "Doing Difference," two general questions are presented without grounding as if they revealed "theoretical implications" specific to the theorizing through the metaphor of the "intersection": (1) Will people "count" and "rank" number and "quantity" of oppressions? (2) Will people assume that groups will "bond" if both have the same number of categories of oppression? First, these are *questions,* not "implications." Second, they are *not* "implications" of the metaphor of "intersection."[41] They are not suggested, tied to, or implied by the term "intersection." They do not demonstrate a possible *result* or *consequence* or *entailment* or *implication* of thinking *intersectionally.* They are, rather, simply made-up political and intellectual questions that might emerge in *any* discussion of multiple oppressions. In fact, thinking "intersectionally"—in terms of both/and rather than either/or—as intersectional women of color feminists have done, works precisely to loosen the traction of such questions.

The critics advance their claims through a pattern of specific moves. They gesture toward a comment or quotation apparently by a racialized scholar, pose a question as if it emerged from the comment or in consequence of it, provide a naive or unsophisticated answer to that question as if the answer represents the commonly held position of these racialized scholars, and then finally reveal as *faulty* the fictitious unsophisticated answer they have supplied to the fictitious unsophisticated question they have fabricated. The critics then "solidify" their correction of the fictitious argument by pulling the words of another racialized scholar out of context to imply that she is supporting their criticism.

For example, in one case, West and Fenstermaker ask:

What conclusions shall we draw from comparisons between persons who are said to suffer oppression "at the intersection" of all three systems and those who suffer in the nexus of only two? *Presumably, we will conclude* that the latter are "less oppressed" than the former (assuming that each categorical identity set *amasses a specific quantity of oppression*). Moraga warns, however, that "the danger lies in ranking the oppressions. *The danger lies in failing to acknowledge the specificity of the oppression.*"[42]

The first-person plural ("Presumably, *we* will conclude . . . ") falsely presents a position held neither by the critics nor by the intersectional scholars they cite. However, the conventions of argument would lead uninformed readers to assume that the position is either of the intersectional scholars of color cited by West and Fenstermaker or other ("generic") women of color. West and Fenstermaker do not claim *for themselves* what "presumably, we will conclude," because they cite as authoritative a counterargument against this presumption. The implication is that the word "intersection" or the compulsion of intersectional scholars or the "generic" woman of color *demands* counting the "specific quantity of oppression" in a category, *demands* comparisons and the ranking of oppressions. *None of this is the case.* Such a position is explicitly countered in Collins's *Black Feminist Thought*—also cited in "Doing Difference"—which provides much more complex refutations of such arguments than do West and Fenstermaker and their selection-form straw persons.[43] If the intersectional scholars they cite did not make these arguments, who did? Why is that position voiced as if it might be found in contemporary arguments by intersectional scholars? In fact, why is it presented as a contemporary position needing refutation when such positions have long been criticized. In fact, the critics demonstrate that they know the long history refuting such positions when they cite the authority of decades-old articles by racialized scholars.

For example, when considering the question of "calculation of oppressions," West and Fenstermaker rebut the naive position implied to be that of Andersen and Collins or some "generic" woman of color, by turning to the words of Cherríe Moraga. They argue: "Moraga warns, however, that 'the danger lies in ranking the oppressions. *The danger lies in failing to acknowledge the specificity of the oppression.*'"[44]

The critics here display the familiar diorama wherein dominant whites present people of color as disciplining one another for the benefit of whites, here "staged" for ill-informed white readers. Andersen and Collins are fully aware of Moraga's argument: her 1981 article was reprinted in the first section of their anthology, a few pages after the preface that West and Fenstermaker quote.[45] Furthermore, Moraga made the point about facets of her own identity in a specific context; the claim cannot and should not be taken out of that context and presented as a universal rule closing down future argumentative options. The critics deploy the decontextualized "rule" that they attribute to Moraga to foreclose future political and analytic choices. Such rhetorical foreclosures serve as attempts to delegitimize the question of *which differences make a difference,* a question of great significance at the intersections of race and gender.

The rhetorical structure framing the other "troubling theoretical implication" of "intersection" is almost identical. The opening questions echo a phrase of Andersen and Collins's about "simultaneous and intersecting *systems of relationship and meaning*" that West and Fenstermaker quoted previously.[46] Thinking through the metaphor of "intersection," the critics speculate, has a "theoretical implication" that might lead to concluding that disparate groups with different but the *same number* of oppressions are eager to "bond." West and Fenstermaker ask:

> What conclusions shall we draw from potential comparisons between persons who experience oppression on the basis of their race and class (e.g., working-class men of color) and those who are oppressed on the basis of their gender and class (e.g., white working-class women)? Would the "intersection of two systems of meaning in each case be sufficient to predict common bonds among them?" Clearly not, says June Jordan: "When these factors of race, class and gender absolutely collapse is whenever you try to use them as *automatic concepts of connection.*"[47]

This point-counterpoint is a fascinating construction. It presents two rather inept questions of limited theoretical and political interest, rather than the strongest positions of intersectional scholars (for example, positions found in the critics' cited sources).[48] West and Fenstermaker provide no argument explaining why they should treat as their original contribution a refutation that appears in much more sophisticated form in the very texts they cite. The first question about quantity of oppression is not attributed; it would appear to be naive and distant from the concerns of most intersectional scholars. The second question—"Would the 'intersections of two systems of meaning in each case be sufficient to predict common bonds among them?'"—is structured with quotation marks, but no source is cited; an online search finds it only in "Doing Difference" and its reprints. The question appears to be a fictional ventriloquized construction designed to implicate Andersen and Collins by repeating some of their words previously quoted ("intersecting," "systems of meaning"). As fictional constructs, the questions reinscribe the polarities of *humanitas* and *anthropos*.

Having insinuated that the compulsion to calculate implicates the "generic" woman of color and intersectional scholars such as Andersen and Collins, West and Fenstermaker provide correction not in their own voice, but *once again* in the voice of a woman of color. The passage manages this move by treating June Jordan as if she were involved in the same conversation, when she is not. The text frames Jordan's comment as a refutation of the question vaguely attributed to Andersen and Collins or some generic woman of color by inserting a connecting phrase, "Clearly not, says June Jordan"—as if Jordan is responding specifically to the question posed. At the scene of argument, juxtaposing the fictional "quoted" question, the fictional connecting phrase that implies Jordan is responding to that question, and the quotation from Jordan all work to frame Jordan as the critics' Black woman ally. But Jordan was never asked this question, and she is not answering it. Jordan's essay is a sustained meditation on the complexity of local and global relations among people of the same and different classes, races, and genders. In fact, Andersen and Collins are fully aware of Jordan's argument: Jordan's 1985 essay was reprinted in the first section of their 1992 anthology,[49] a few pages after the preface that the critics quote.[50] Producing Jordan to counter fictional simplistic propositions treats her as a puppet being ventriloquized. The rhetorical structure of "false quotation" and "false rebuttal" serves to present as relevant not intersectional scholars' strongest arguments, but arguments already refuted in the texts cited by the critics.

Like the European colonial administrators in Africa who ceded limited power to traditional leaders to rule over others, and like the settler colonialist troops in the U.S. west who recruited unassimilated but nonhostile Native Americans to work as "friendlies," the feminist critics seek to secure their dominance yet hide their racial privilege by using the words of women of color—taken out of context—to undermine the legitimacy of other women of color. Yet unlike the European colonial administrators in Africa or the settler colonialist troops in the U.S. west, the critics do not even interact with the people they use as proxies. Instead, they conjure them into existence as imaginary friends of white feminism whose words are used to delegitimate positions of other women of color, positions with which those being quoted actually agree.

CONCLUSION

As I have demonstrated, colorblind and powerblind rhetorics are used in feminist studies to erase racial specificity, make authors and readers feel that they are colorblind, hide the stripping of intellectual assets from women of color, proclaim white innocence, devalue the research of women of color, and hoard academic resources—honors, awards, and recognition—for white scholars who purport to supersede the work of women of color. Strategies include incorporation, appropriation, erasure, ventriloquizing, arguing with straw persons, and adopting imaginary allies. These ways of positioning intersectional scholars appear plausible because they are congruent with dominant notions that racialized people are unsophisticated and simple thinkers—that "we" have theories suitable for them but "they" do not have theories adequate for us.[51] These argumentative problems do not stem from feminist scholars' *intentions,* but from their use of conventional rhetorics and arguments, imbued with uninterrogated white racial privilege. Further, white privilege infuses and authorizes the metadiscursive regimes framing how feminist scholars approve these critiques—vetted, edited, published, anthologized, and cited as authoritative—according to what they perceive to be the shared, "colorblind" standards of feminist scholarship. Interrogating feminist metadiscursive regimes would encourage resisting the resort to straw man fallacies and easy misrepresentations that often seem plausible because they align with histories and epistemological structures of racial dominance. Walter Mignolo shows that these moves are grounded in modernity's long-standing distinction between *humanitas* and *anthropos,* between the definers and the defined, between the subjects of knowledge and its objects.[52] The "colorblind" standards that permeate feminist scholarship suggest that dominant white knowledge about gendered racial arguments is sufficient for mounting critiques of intersectionality. It is not.

NOTES

1. Cedric Robinson, *Forgeries of Memory and Meaning: Blacks and Regimes of Race in American Theater and Film before World War II* (Chapel Hill: University of North Carolina Press, 2007), xii.
2. Eduardo Bonilla-Silva and Tukufu Zuberi, "Toward a Definition of White Logic and White Methods," in *White Logic, White Methods: Racism and*

Methodology, ed. Eduardo Bonilla-Silva and Tukufu Zuberi (Lanham, MD: Rowman & Littlefield, 2008), 3–27.

3. Jochen Walter and Jan Helmig, "Discursive Metaphor Analysis: (De) Construction(s) of Europe," in *Political Language and Metaphor: Interpreting and Changing the World,* ed. Terrell Carver and Jernej Pikalo (New York: Routledge, 2008), 119–31, citing Michel Foucault, *The Archaeology of Knowledge* (New York: Pantheon Books, 1972); emphasis in the original.

4. Leslie McCall, "The Complexity of Intersectionality," *Signs* 30 no. 3 (2005): 1771–800; Candace West and Sarah Fenstermaker, "Doing Difference," *Gender and Society* 9, no. 1 (1995): 8–37.

5. See Barbara Tomlinson, *Undermining Intersectionality: The Perils of Powerblind Feminism* (Philadelphia: Temple University Press, 2018), chap. 5.

6. Walter D. Mignolo, *The Darker Side of Western Modernity: Global Futures, Decolonial Options* (Durham, NC: Duke University Press, 2011).

7. Ibid., 173.

8. Ibid., 83.

9. Ibid., xv.

10. Ibid., 16.

11. Clare Hemmings, *Why Stories Matter: The Political Grammar of Feminist Theory* (Durham, NC: Duke University Press, 2011), 13.

12. Ibid., 57.

13. Stephen Steinberg, *Race Relations: A Critique* (Stanford, CA: Stanford University Press, 2007).

14. Linda Martín Alcoff, "Mignolo's Epistemology of Coloniality," *CR: The New Centennial Review* 7, no. 3 (2007): 80.

15. See Vivian M. May, *Pursuing Intersectionality: Unsettling Dominant Imaginaries* (New York: Routledge, 2015); Toni Cade Bambara, ed., *The Black Woman: An Anthology* (New York: Signet, 1970); Paula Giddings, *When and Where I Enter: The Impact of Black Women on Race and Sex in America* (New York: William Morrow, 1984); and Beverly Guy-Sheftall, ed., *Words of Fire: An Anthology of African-American Feminist Thought* (New York: New Press, 1995).

16. See, for example, Bambara (ed.), *The Black Woman;* Hazel V. Carby, "White Women Listen! Black Feminism and the Boundaries of Sisterhood," in *The Empire Strikes Back: Race and Racism in Seventies Britain,* ed. Centre for Contemporary Cultural Studies (London: Hutchinson, 1982), 212–35; Patricia Hill Collins, "Learning from the Outsider Within: The Sociological Significance of Black Feminist Thought," *Social Problems* 33, no. 6 (1986): 514–32; idem, *Black Feminist Thought: Knowledge, Consciousness and the Politics of Empowerment* (New York: Routledge, 1991); Combahee River Collective, "Combahee River Collective Statement," in *Home Girls: A Black Feminist Anthology,* ed. Barbara Smith (New York: Kitchen Table/Women of Color Press, 1983), 264–74; Kimberlé Williams Crenshaw, "Demarginalizing the Intersection of Race and Sex: A Black Feminist Critique of Antidiscrimination Doctrine, Feminist Theory, and Antiracist Politics,"

University of Chicago Legal Forum 16, no. 1 (1989): 139–67; idem, "Mapping the Margins: Intersectionality, Identity, and Violence against Women of Color," *Stanford Law Review* 43 (1991): 1241–99; Angela Y. Davis, *Women, Race, and Class* (New York: Vintage, 1981); Bonnie Thornton Dill, "Our Mothers' Grief: Racial Ethnic Women and the Maintenance of Families," *Journal of Family History* 13 (1988): 415–31; Giddings, *When and Where I Enter;* Evelyn Nakano Glenn, "Racial Ethnic Women's Labor: The Intersection of Race, Gender, and Class Oppression," *Review of Radical Political Economics* 17, no. 3 (1985): 86–108; Elizabeth Higginbotham, "Laid Bare by the System: Work and Survival for Black and Hispanic Women," in *Class, Race, and Sex: The Dynamics of Control,* ed. Amy Swerdlow and Helen Lessinger (Boston: G. K. Hall, 1983), 200–215; idem, "Race and Class Barriers to Black Women's College Attendance," *Journal of Ethnic Studies* 13 (1985): 89–107; bell hooks, *Ain't I a Woman: Black Women and Feminism* (Boston: South End Press, 1981); Aída Hurtado, "Relating to Privilege: Seduction and Rejection in the Subordination of White Women and Women of Color," *Signs: Journal of Women in Culture and Society* 14 (1989): 833–55; Leith Mullings, "Uneven Development: Class, Race, and Gender in the United States before 1900," in *Women's Work: Development and the Division of Labor by Gender,* ed. Eleanor Leacock and Helen Icken Safa (South Hadley, MA: Bergin & Garvey, 1986), 41–57.

17. See Sirma Bilge, "Intersectionality Undone: Saving Intersectionality from Feminist Intersectionality Studies," *Du Bois Review* 10, no. 2 (2013): 405–24; idem, "Whitening Intersectionality: Evanescence of Race in Current Intersectionality Scholarship," in *Racism and Sociology,* ed. Wulf D. Hund and Alana Lentin (Berlin: LIT Routledge Verlag, 2014), 175–205; Barbara Tomlinson, "Colonizing Intersectionality: Replicating Racial Hierarchy in Feminist Academic Argument," *Social Identities: Journal for the Study of Race, Nation, and Culture* 19, no. 2 (2013): 254–72; idem, "To Tell the Truth and Not Get Trapped: Desire, Distance, and Intersectionality at the Scene of Argument," *Signs: A Journal of Women in Culture and Society* 38, no. 4 (Summer 2013): 993–1017; and idem, *Undermining Intersectionality.*

18. Mignolo, *Darker Side of Western Modernity,* xv.

19. As of May 10, 2018, the article in question had nearly 4,500 citations in Google Scholar.

20. McCall, "The Complexity of Intersectionality," 1771.

21. Ibid., 1771n1. Texts cited include Crenshaw "Demarginalizing"; idem, "Mapping the Margins"; Davis, *Women, Race, and Class;* Cherríe Moraga, *Loving in the War Years* (Cambridge, MA: South End Press, 1983); Smith (ed.), *Home Girls: A Black Feminist Anthology;* bell hooks, *Feminist Theory: From Margin to Center* (Boston: South End Press, 1984); Cherríe Moraga and Gloria Anzaldúa, eds., *This Bridge Called My Back: Writings by Radical Women of Color,* 2nd ed. (New York: Kitchen Table Press, 1984); Glenn, "Racial Ethnic Women's Labor"; Gloria Anzaldúa, *Borderlands/La Frontera: The New Mestiza* (San Francisco: Spinsters/ Aunt Lute, 1987); idem, ed., *Haciendo Caras: Making Face, Making Soul; Creative and Critical Perspectives by Feminists of Color* (San Francisco: Aunt Lute Books,

1990); Deborah K. King, "Multiple Jeopardy, Multiple Consciousness: The Context of a Black Feminist Ideology," *Signs: A Journal of Women in Culture and Society* 14 (1988): 42–72; Chandra Talpade Mohanty, "Under Western Eyes: Feminist Scholarship and Colonial Discourses," *Feminist Review* 30 (1988): 61–88; Elizabeth V. Spelman, *Inessential Woman: Problems of Exclusion in Feminist Thought* (Boston: Beacon Press, 1988); Chela Sandoval, "U.S. Third World Feminism: The Theory and Method of Oppositional Consciousness in the Postmodern World," *Genders* 10 (1991): 1–24.

22. Hemmings, *Why Stories Matter.*

23. The note fails to mention prominent sociologists of color working on multidimensionality during that period, particularly the foundational work of Patricia Hill Collins ("Learning from the Outsider Within" and *Black Feminist Thought*), president of the American Sociological Association in 2009. Although McCall overlooks Collins in the list of founding scholars, she later cites a more recent book chapter: "It's All in the Family: Intersections of Gender, Race, and Nation," in *Decentering the Center: Philosophy for a Multicultural, Postcolonial, and Feminist World,* ed. Uma Narayan and Sandra Harding (Bloomington: Indiana University Press, 2000), 156–76.

24. Judith Butler, "Contingent Foundations: Feminism and the Question of 'Postmodernism,'" in Seyla Benhabib, Judith Butler, Drucilla Cornell, and Nancy Fraser, *Feminist Contentions: A Philosophical Exchange* (New York: Routledge, 1995), 49.

25. Angela Y. Davis, *Abolition Democracy: Beyond Empire, Prisons, and Torture* (New York: Seven Stories Press, 2005).

26. Combahee River Collective, "Statement."

27. Kimberlé Crenshaw, Neil Gotanda, Gary Peller, and Kendall Thomas, "Introduction," in *Critical Race Theory: The Key Writings That Formed the Movement,* ed. Crenshaw, Gotanda, Peller, and Thomas (New York: New Press, 1995), xiii–xxxii; Kimberlé Williams Crenshaw, "Twenty Years of Critical Race Theory: Looking Back to Move Forward," *Connecticut Law Review* 43, no. 5 (July 2011): 1253–352.

28. Chela Sandoval, *Methodology of the Oppressed* (Minneapolis: University of Minneapolis Press, 2000), 44.

29. Robert Talisse and Scott F. Aikin. "Two Forms of the Straw Man," *Argumentation* 20 (2006): 345–52.

30. Candace West and Sarah Fenstermaker, "Doing Difference," *Gender and Society* 9, no. 1 (1995): 8–37. As of May 10, 2018, there were nearly 2,000 citations in Google Scholar to this article, and some 870 to its reprints.

31. Collins, *Black Feminist Thought,* 28, 27, citing Orlando Patterson, *Slavery and Social Death: A Comparative Study* (Cambridge, MA: Harvard University Press, 1982.

32. Alice Dreger, "'Ambiguous Sex'—or Ambivalent Medicine? Ethical Issues in the Treatment of Intersexuality," *Hastings Center Report* 28, no. 3 (1998): 24–36.

33. Patterson, *Slavery and Social Death,* 61.

34. West and Fenstermaker, "Doing Difference," 16, quoting Collins, *Black Feminist Thought,* 27; emphasis added.

35. West and Fenstermaker, "Doing Difference," 16, quoting Collins, *Black Feminist Thought,* 28.

36. Talisse and Aikin, "Two Forms of the Straw Man."

37. Margaret L. Andersen and Patricia Hill Collins, eds., *Race, Class, and Gender* (Belmont, CA: Wadsworth, 1992).

38. Tomlinson, *Undermining Intersectionality,* chap. 5.

39. Talisse and Aikin, "Two Forms of the Straw Man," 347, 351.

40. Andersen and Collins (eds.), *Race, Class, and Gender;* and Collins, *Black Feminist Thought.*

41. West and Fenstermaker do not explain why a general comment about ranking oppressions should be tied to the word "intersect." The metaphor of "intersection" does not entail calculable, countable, measurable, or quantitative "amassing [of] a specific quantity of oppression"; nor does it assume one should rank the number of oppressive acts to determine the "amount" of oppression. In fact, such assumptions are *countered* by thinking intersectionally.

42. West and Fenstermaker, "Doing Difference," 13, quoting Cherríe Moraga, "The Güera," in *This Bridge Called My Back: Radical Writing by Women of Color,* ed. Cherríe Moraga and Gloria Anzaldúa (New York: Kitchen Table Press, 1981), 29; emphasis added to West and Fenstermaker, in original of Moraga.

43. In *Black Feminist Thought,* for example, Collins argues that "adhering to a both/and conceptual stance does not mean that race, class, and gender oppression are interchangeable" (226); the compulsion to count that West and Fenstermaker are refuting assumes interchangeability. Collins criticizes standpoint and additive approaches that quantify and rank oppressions in ways characteristic of positivism and define privilege in relation to its other: "Additive models of oppression are firmly rooted in the either/or dichotomous thinking of Eurocentric, masculinist thought. . . . This emphasis on quantification and categorization occurs in conjunction with the belief that either/or categories must be ranked. The search for certainty of this sort requires that one side of a dichotomy be privileged while its other is denigrated. Privilege becomes defined in relation to its other" (205–7, 225). She points out that depending "on the context, an individual may be an oppressor, a member of an oppressed group, or simultaneously oppressor and oppressed. . . . Each individual derives varying amounts of penalty and privilege from the multiple systems of oppression which frame everyone's lives" (225, 229). Collins argues that attention should focus on how variables *interconnect,* each system needing the others in order to function, "part of one overarching structure of domination. . . . Embracing a both/and conceptual stance moves us from additive, separate systems approaches to oppression and toward what I now see as the more fundamental issue of the social relations of domination" (222, 226). "By embracing a paradigm of race, class, and gender as interlocking systems of oppression," Collins says, "Black feminist thought reconceptualizes the social relations of domination and resistance. . . . Assuming

that each system needs the others in order to function creates a distinct theoretical stance that stimulates the rethinking of basic social science concepts" (222).

44. West and Fenstermaker, "Doing Difference," 13, quoting Moraga, "The Güera," 29; emphasis in original of Moraga.

45. The critics cite *This Bridge Called My Back* as the source of their quotation of Moraga; they do not cite its appearance in the essay collection by Andersen and Collins, *Race, Class, and Gender,* that they say impelled their critique.

46. Andersen and Collins (eds.), *Race, Class, and Gender,* xiii, quoted in West and Fenstermaker, "Doing Difference," 12; emphasis added.

47. West and Fenstermaker, "Doing Difference," 12–13, quoting June Jordan, "Report from the Bahamas," in *On Call: Political Essays* (Boston, MA: South End Press, 1985), 46; emphasis added.

48. These include Andersen and Collins (eds.), *Race, Class, and Gender;* and Collins, *Black Feminist Thought.*

49. June Jordan, "Report from the Bahamas," in Andersen and Collins (eds.), *Race, Class, and Gender,* 28–37.

50. West and Fenstermaker cite *On Call: Political Essays* as the source of their quotation of Jordan; they do not cite its appearance in the compilation of essays by Andersen and Collins that they say impelled their critique.

51. See María C. Lugones and Elizabeth V. Spelman, "Have We Got a Theory for You! Feminist Theory, Cultural Imperialism, and the Demand for 'The Women's Voice,'" *Women's Studies International Forum* 6, no. 6 (1983): 573–81.

52. Mignolo, *Darker Side of Western Modernity.*

NINE

Colorblind Intersectionality

Devon W. Carbado

In 1989, Kimberlé Crenshaw published "Demarginalizing the Intersection of Race and Sex: A Black Feminist Critique of Antidiscrimination Doctrine, Feminist Theory, and Antiracist Politics."[1] Drawing explicitly on black feminist criticism, Crenshaw introduced what would become an enormously influential theory: intersectionality. Since the publication of "Demarginalizing," intersectionality has traveled to and built bridges across a significant number of disciplines. Moreover, scholars across the globe regularly invoke and draw upon intersectionality, as do human rights activists, community organizers, political figures, and lawyers.

Yet despite intersectionality's travels, its interface at "home"—specifically within Critical Race Theory—has been remarkably undertheorized. In particular, scholars have not expressly linked the Critical Race Theory critique of colorblindness to intersectional critiques of social formations. As a result, the Critical Race Theory literature on colorblindness and the intersectionality literatures generally are not in conversation with each other. To disrupt this disaggregation, this essay "moves" intersectionality back to its initial articulation and then "moves" it forward to new sites and concerns. Setting intersectionality on this journey is crucial against the backdrop of several critiques of the theory that artificially constrain its generative, normative, and analytical capacity. Recovering the critical dimensions of intersectionality is key to unlocking its obscured but crucial interrogation of colorblindness.

Portions of this article were originally published in Devon W. Carbado, "Colorblind Intersectionality," *Signs: Journal of Women in Culture and Society* 38, no. 4 (Summer 2013): 811–45.

To highlight intersectionality's interrogation of colorblindness, I locate my analysis in the context of specific civil rights disputes and contestations and engage social categories that are ostensibly beyond the theoretical reach and normative concern of intersectionality: men, masculinity, and sexual orientation.[2] My aim is to show how colorblindness is implicated in the juridical and civil rights production of normative gender identities. To do so, I introduce the concept of "colorblind intersectionality," by which I mean instances in which whiteness constitutes but is unarticulated and racially invisible as an intersectional social formation.[3] My hope is that my deployment of colorblind intersectionality initiates a broader effort to relocate intersectionality as both a product and a representation of Critical Race Theory.

My starting point is a discussion of interpretations of intersectionality that my subsequent articulation of colorblind intersectionality interrupts. I perform this theoretical brush-clearing to create space for my explication of two "case studies," one from legal doctrine and the other from civil rights advocacy.[4] As you will see, both case studies are useful illustrations of colorblind intersectionality at work.

The first case study involves a lawsuit in which a casino fired one of its white female bartenders because she refused to comply with the casino's grooming and makeup policy. Here, I show how the court's resolution of the case mobilized colorblind intersectionality in ways that rendered white heterosexual women the essential subjects of sex discrimination law. The second case study focuses on gay rights advocacy against "Don't Ask, Don't Tell." Here, I show how gay rights proponents mobilized colorblind intersectionality in ways that rendered white gay men the essential subjects of challenges to the "Don't Ask, Don't Tell" policy. While "Don't Ask, Don't Tell" is now a dead letter, the colorblind intersectionality that shaped the campaign against the policy persists in more recent gay rights interventions, including gay rights advocacy for marriage equality.

As a prelude to engaging the case studies, I briefly describe and respond to various critiques of intersectionality. I do so because those critiques increasingly stand in the way of or elide the possibility for precisely the kind of exposure and contestation of colorblindness this essay performs.

THEORETICAL PRELUDE: CRITIQUING THE CRITIQUES

Intersectionality provides a productive but widely underutilized framework for interrogating colorblindness. But a range of criticisms of the theory stand in the way of that very possibility. Indeed, notwithstanding the grounding of intersectionality in a theoretical enterprise (Critical Race Theory) that challenges key colorblind tropes such as essentialist notions of identity, static rather than dynamic representations of power, and Aristotelian egalitarianism rooted in sameness and difference, intersectionality has been interpreted by various readers to embrace precisely the terms that it contests. To grasp intersectionality as a critical move in the repertoire of arguments against colorblindness, a brief response to some of the misfired critiques of the theory is warranted. A rough articulation of those critiques looks something like this:

1. Intersectionality is only or largely about black women and/or race and gender;

2. Intersectionality is an identitarian framework;

3. Intersectionality is a static theory that does not capture the dynamic and contingent processes of identity formation;

4. Intersectionality is overly invested in subjects;

5. Intersectionality has traveled as far as it can go; there is nothing more the theory can teach us; and

6. Intersectionality should be replaced by or at least applied in conjunction with [fill in the blank with an alternative framework].

As to the first criticism concerning the scope of intersectionality, the simple response is that intersectionality does not necessarily and inherently privilege any social category. Race and gender and black women specifically figure prominently in "Demarginalizing" because of the particular juridical and political sites in which Crenshaw sought to intervene. These sites directly targeted black women for condemnation, erasure, and marginalization. Crenshaw's articulation of these dynamics should not lead one to conclude that there is an already mapped terrain over which intersectionality must and can only travel. Ironically, the claim that intersectionality is just about black women reproduces a version of the representational problem Crenshaw interrogated. Crenshaw's aim in "Demarginalizing" was not simply to mark the unwillingness of courts to recognize black women's discrimination claims based on race and sex (here, courts were essentially saying that black women's experiences were the same as white women's—with respect to sex—and black men's—with respect to race; therefore, there was no juridical need to recognize black women as a distinct social group). Crenshaw also sought to highlight the refusal of courts to permit black women to represent a class of plaintiffs that included white women or black men (here, courts were essentially saying that black women were too different to represent either white women or black men as a group). The problem, then, was not simply that courts were prohibiting black women from representing themselves; the problem was also that courts were prohibiting black women from representing gender or race per se. Too similar to be different and too different to be the same, black women were "impossible subjects" of antidiscrimination law.[5] They had very limited representational currency. The critique that intersectionality is necessarily and only about black women reflects a similar representational problem: black women cannot specifically name themselves in a theory (they are too similar to be different); nor can they function as the backdrop for the genesis and articulation of a generalizable framework about power and marginalization (they are too different to be the same).

None of this is to deny that many of the articles on intersectionality focus on black women and/or race and gender. Surely, however, that is not, in itself, a problem. It is becoming increasing unspeakable (theoretically backwards/monopolistic/identitarian/categorically hegemonic) to frame theoretical and political interventions around black women. That is an unfortunate development in which far too many progressive scholars have acquiesced or actively participated. But even assuming that one thinks that it is problematic for intersectional analyses to focus on black women and/or race and gender, establishing that the theory is focused in this way does not answer the question of whether intersectionality lacks the capacity to travel to and mark the production of other social processes and locations. This more limited reading of intersectionality is not only theoretically unnecessary, it is descriptively inaccurate and easily falsifiable. Scholars have mobilized intersectionality to engage multiple axes of "difference"—"class," "sexual orientation," "nation," "citizen," "immigrant," "disability," "terrorist" (and not "just race" and "gender"); and they have employed the theory to analyze a range of complex social processes—"classism," "homophobia," "islamophobia," "xenophobia," "nativism," "ageism," "ableism" (and not "just antiblack racism and sexism"). Seemingly, the genesis of intersectionality in black feminist theory limits the ability of some scholars both to imagine the potential domains to which intersectionality might travel and to see the theory in places in which it is already doing work.

The next three criticisms of intersectionality (that the theory is identitarian, static, and invested in subjects) are curious given the theory's genesis in law and Critical Race Theory. Intersectionality reflects a precommitment to neither subjects nor identities per se but to marking and mapping the production and contingency of both. Part of what Crenshaw sought to do in "Demarginalizing" was to illustrate the constitutive and ideologically contingent role that law plays in creating legible and illegible juridical subjects and identities. Her effort in this respect is part of a broader intellectual tradition in Critical Race Theory to demonstrate how the law constructs (and does not simply describe) social categories. How and why this gets redescribed as an investment in fixed and static identities and subjects is puzzling.

With respect to the fifth criticism of intersectionality—namely, that the theory has traveled as far as it can go—the claim is more of a normatively contingent roadblock to the theory rather than an on-the-theoretical-ground limitation. My hope is that this essay will bear that out. This brings me to the final criticism, which is not a criticism at all but rather a suggestion (against the backdrop of the preceding criticisms) that scholars should replace intersectionality with, or at least apply the theory alongside, some alternative framework. Among the candidates advocates of this view have marshaled to perform this work are "cosynthesis,"[6] "interconnectivity,"[7] "multidimensionality,"[8] and most recently, "assemblages."[9] Proponents of these theories implicitly and sometimes explicitly suggest that each has the *inherent* ability to do something—discursively and substantively—that intersectionality *inherently* cannot do or does considerably less well.

There is a false necessity to this claim both discursively and with respect to legal intervention, political mobilization, and knowledge production.[10] As to the discursive, all of the foregoing theories—from cosynthesis to assemblages—seem to imagine the synthesis or interaction of things that are otherwise apart. In other words, at the level of appellation, they are no more dynamic than intersectionality. This deficiency reflects a more general problem—to wit, that there are discursive limitations to our ability to capture the complex and reiterative processes of social categorization. The very articulation of the idea that race and gender are coconstitutive, for example, discursively fragments those categories—into race and gender—to make that point. The strictures of language require us to invoke race, gender, sexual orientation, and so on, one discursive moment at a time.

With respect to legal intervention, political mobilization, and knowledge production, there is no "analytic reason" to read intersectionality as more limiting than cosynthesis, multidimensionality, interconnectivity, or assemblages.[11] Scholars who do so constitute the very thing they purport only to describe—intersectionality. This is the sense is which Barbara Tomlinson in this volume speaks of feminist discourses as "technologies of power" and invites feminist scholars to interrogate their reading practices. This interrogation would enable them to see that they are mapping the margins of intersectionality, constructing its fields of relevance, even as they claim merely to be describing a theory whose borders are always already "just here," somewhere other than "there," the place where intersectionality "really" should be but has neither the commitment nor the capacity to go.

The remainder of this essay takes intersectionality precisely to those domains in which the theory is perceived to have little or no purchase. In the context of doing so, I will elaborate on what I mean by colorblind intersectionality. My goal is to illustrate some of the specific ways in which civil rights activists, scholars, lawyers, and policymakers can deploy intersectionality to both expose and contest various iterations of *colorblind* intersectionality. I begin with a discussion of an antidiscrimination case that, though not formally about race, implicates both whiteness and colorblindness in ways that shore up white heterosexual women as essential subjects of sex discrimination law.

ESSENTIALLY FEMALE:
OR FEMALE LIKE A WHITE HETEROSEXUAL WOMAN

In August 2000, Darlene Jespersen, a successful and well-liked bartender who had worked at Harrah's Casino in Reno for over two decades, found herself out of a job. Harrah's fired Jespersen because she refused to comply with the company's grooming policy. Instituted in February 2000 as a part of Harrah's Beverage Department Image Transformation Program, the policy mandated that Harrah's female employees wear makeup. Jespersen refused to do so. Harrah's then terminated her employment, and Jespersen responded with a sex discrimination lawsuit.[12]

Jespersen rested part of her legal argument on a case that was decided some twenty years earlier, *Price Waterhouse v. Hopkins*.[13] In that case, the accounting firm Price Waterhouse denied Ann Hopkins, a white woman, partnership. The record revealed that one partner explicitly informed Hopkins that she was too "masculine," and another told her that, to improve her chances the following year, she should "walk more femininely, talk more femininely, dress more femininely, wear make-up, have her hair styled, and wear jewelry."[14] The Court found in Hopkins's favor based on an antistereotyping and gender nonconformity theory: employers cannot require females to be feminine and males to be masculine.

Jespersen argued that *Price Waterhouse* applied to her case. Her claim, in effect, was that via its grooming policy, Harrah's Casino was asking Jespersen to "dress more feminine, wear makeup [and] have her hair styled."[15] Harrah's was forcing her to align her sex (female) with a normative gender alignment (femininity). The court rejected this argument, and Jespersen lost her case. The Ninth Circuit, the highest court to hear the case, adopted a formal equality approach that reflected both gender normativity and colorblind intersectionality.

To appreciate the court's formal equality approach, one has to understand the legal doctrine the court employed to adjudicate the case: the "equal burdens" framework. Under this framework, a company's grooming policy constitutes sex discrimination if it burdens one sex more than the other. The court's application of this standard was overly formalistic. In concluding that Harrah's grooming policy equally burdened men and women, the court reasoned that the policy regulated men's and women's hairstyles, men's and women's clothing, men's and women's shoes, men's and women's fingernails, and men's and women's faces. This formal equality approach obscured the fact that the grooming policy was quite literally producing normative masculinity and femininity and instantiating impermissible sex stereotyping. The policy ensured that men looked and acted like men (masculine) and women looked and acted like women (feminine). Women must wear makeup ("face powder, blush, and mascara" and "lip color must be worn at all times"). Men are prohibited from doing so. Women may wear colored nail polish. "No colored polish is allowed" for men. Men are not permitted to have ponytails. Women's hair must be "teased, curled, or styled." Men's hair "must not extend below top of shirt collar."[16]

The foregoing differential grooming standards align with our normative assumptions about how men and women should make themselves up. Conventionally, we expect women to wear makeup, not men. Conventionally, we expect men to have short hair, not women. Conventionally, we expect women to wear colored nail polish, not men. These conventions about self-presentation align with a normative gender imperative that women are and should be feminine and that men are and should be masculine. Harrah's grooming policy was preventing Jespersen from being female and masculine.

That Harrah's might have been concerned about female masculinities—and specifically with respect to Jespersen—is a reasonable conclusion in light of how Jespersen embodied her gender. Harrah's insistence that Jespersen in particular abide by the grooming policy has to be considered against the backdrop of this image. Harrah's might have concluded that its grooming policy was not going to overly feminize Jespersen; it was simply going to render her makeup—her overall embodiment—more like a woman. Nothing in the policy required her to wear body-revealing clothing. Indeed, her uniform, particularly in the context of Vegas, where cocktail waitresses are typically scantily dressed, was somewhat gender-bending. At the very least, Harrah's managers might have thought, Jespersen had to be intelligible as a woman. Its makeup and grooming requirements could help to accomplish exactly that. This suggests that, had Jespersen been more conventionally feminine, her refusal to wear makeup might not have triggered litigation. The problem was her "Ask Pat" appearance, against which Harrah's grooming policy was a corrective. Whether thinking along the foregoing lines actually motivated Harrah's decision-making is unclear. Nevertheless, it is not unreasonable to think that Jespersen's particular self-presentation—her particular female masculinity—was a subtext in the case, and not just for Harrah's but for the court as well.

And indeed, the court's reasoning does hint that the particularities of Jespersen's self-presentation informed the decision. One reason the court found the grooming policy to be permissible was that it did not render Jespersen vulnerable to sexual harassment. From the court's perspective, it mattered that Harrah's was not overly effeminizing Jespersen as a sex object.

Another way to think about how Jespersen's female masculinity worked as a subtext in the case is to imagine a scenario in which the partners at a major law firm fired Brian, a male litigator, for showing up to court obviously made up—mascara, nail polish, red lipstick. Assume that this litigator brings a case against his partners alleging sex discrimination. Would he win? Probably not, notwithstanding that this case more squarely approximates *Price Waterhouse* in the sense that, unlike *Jespersen,* it does not involve a formal grooming policy.

Judge Richard Posner, a well-known and influential appellate judge, has pretty much said that plaintiffs in such a case would lose. According to Posner, antidiscrimination law does not create a right for "male workers to wear nail polish and dresses and speak in falsetto and mince about in high heels."[17] Note how explicitly Posner trades on normative masculinity. Posner, among many other judges, would not be persuaded by the claim that Brian was the victim of impermissible sex stereotyping. He would insist that the law firm properly fired Brian because he failed to abide by the most basic norms of professional self-presentation. Brian, he might add, does not have a right to make himself up (like a woman). That Brian would likely lose his case, at least under Posner's analysis, helps to explain why Jespersen lost hers.

That the *Jespersen* court did not apply a gender-nonconformity or anti–sex stereotyping theory does not mean that Harrah's victory was secured. As suggested earlier, the court could have applied the "equal burdens" test less formalistically to find in Jespersen's favor. More particularly, the court could have drawn upon the gendered history of makeup to conclude that the makeup requirements were rooted in a sex-gender system that disadvantages women.[18] By the mid-twentieth century, makeup had become a necessary part of being a woman, a social technology for gender conformity. At the same time, this technology helped to legitimize especially white women's entrance into the workplace, particularly during World War II. As white women increasingly participated in formerly male spheres—politics, economic activities, and the labor market—makeup served to appease an anxiety concerning this intrusion and integration. Makeup signified that the gender integration of white women would not mean the disruption of gender hierarchy. While some employers were troubled by the use of makeup on the job (for both safety and cultural reasons), others welcomed it.[19]

The grooming policy in *Jespersen* is best understood in light of the history of makeup. The "*un*equal burden" of makeup is less about the monetary or preparation costs (though neither is trivial), and more about the hierarchical gender roles makeup historically effectuated and maintained. Whether women who "freely" choose to wear makeup reinscribe that hierarchy is open to debate. But when a company mandates that women wear makeup, and prohibits men from doing so, it is enforcing normative gender roles whose symbolic and distributional consequences have been decidedly unequal. To put all of this slightly differently, while Harrah's grooming policy imposed impermissible sex-stereotyping burdens on both women and men—quite literally making up the former as feminine and the latter as masculine—the history of makeup as a kind of gender palliative suggests that the policy *un*equally burdens women by reinforcing gender hierarchy. In legitimizing this hierarchy as an equal burden, the Ninth Circuit left Harrah's free to make Jespersen female like a heterosexual *white* woman.[20]

And it is important to explicitly mark the operation of whiteness here. One way to do so is to explore how the case would have been litigated had Darlene Jespersen been black. While one cannot answer this question with absolute certitude, engaging it helps to highlight how race is implicated in the formal equality analysis the *Jespersen* court employs, how whiteness operates in the case as an unarticulated racial default, and how blackness can function as social axis through which both female identity and sexism are refused.

Consider first the point about race and formal equality. Recall again the equal burdens test. This test becomes even more problematic when black women are imagined as litigants. Black women spend more than 7.5 billion dollars on cosmetics annually,[21] more than three times the amount that white women spend. Precisely because black women have historically been masculinized, they have had to expend more energy and resources quite literally making themselves up as women. Whether we should conceptualize this effort as a form of mimicry (in the sense of acquiescence or resistance or both) I do not presume to decide.[22] The point is that, historically, an "Ain't I a woman" imperative has structured black women's political interventions (include us in feminist agendas because we are women) and their self-representational practices (include us in your conception of womanhood because we have performed the role).

There are other ways in which repositioning Darlene Jespersen as black broadens our understanding of the *Jespersen* court's formalism. At no point does the *Jespersen* court explicitly engage race. Implicit in the court's analysis is a formalistic understanding of women as women, racially unmodified. Facilitating this gender essentialism, at least in part, is the fact that Darlene Jespersen is white. Her whiteness is not a particularity of gender, but gender itself. In this respect, as a legal figure, Jespersen does not have an explicit racial marker. At no point does she have to worry about being "only" a white women over and against some more generalizable female subjectivity. She can, and indeed in the context of the litigation does, stand in for gender per se. Her whiteness—both juridically unmarked and juridically incorporated—facilitates this representational authority. Because in the case whiteness operates invisibly as the default around which the court adjudicates Jespersen's sex discrimination claim, the *racial* dimension of Jespersen's gender identity is both erased (in that whiteness is not formally expressed in the court's opinion) and incorporated (in that whiteness anchors the court's gender analysis). In this sense, one might say that the *Jespersen* litigation reflects colorblind intersectionality: whiteness is doing racially constitutive work in the case but is unarticulated and racially invisible as an intersectional subject position.[23]

One consequence of colorblind intersectionality is that white women can simultaneously be "just women" and stand in for all women; white men can be "just men" and stand in for all men; and white gays and lesbians can be "just gays and lesbians" and stand in for all gays and lesbians. The fact that whiteness is intersectionally unmarked across each of the preceding (and other) social positions shores up whiteness as the default and normative racial category through and on which gender, sexuality, class, and so on are expressed. At the same time, colorblind intersectionality instantiates non-whiteness as *the* racial modifier of gender, sexuality, class, and so on. In this respect, there is a relationship between the notion of women of color as "different" and the unarticulated racial intersectionality of Jespersen's white identity.

Naming the elision of Jespersen's race as an intersectional activity is crucial not only to articulating how colorblindness can function as a racial preference for whites (here white women) but also to highlighting how gender can function as a repository for the expression of that preference. This suggests that we should avoid framing the intersection of race and gender to mean the intersection of nonwhiteness and gender. That dominant way of theorizing intersectionality erases the racial intersectionality of white people and makes it easier for whiteness to operate as the "natural" and unmarked racial backdrop for other social positions, rather than as a particular and "different" representation of them. Moreover, framing whiteness outside of intersectionality legitimizes a broader epistemic universe in which the racial difference and racial consciousness of whiteness travels undisturbed as a race-neutral phenomenon over and against the racial difference, racial consciousness, and racial particularity of people of color.[24] The *Jespersen* case is a part of this universe. Throughout the litigation, whiteness anchors the intelligibility of Jespersen as a woman and the intelligibility of her claim as an alleged instance of sex discrimination. This is the sense in which her gender is intersectionally but invisibly constituted as white.

The erasure and incorporation of whiteness in the litigation ensured that, at least to some extent, Jespersen's intersectional subjectivity as a white woman was not doctrinally fragmented. Jespersen did not have to choose between being white and being a woman. Unlike the doctrinal position in which black women sometimes found themselves, where courts refused to recognize their discrimination claims based on race and sex,[25] Jespersen did not have to quarantine her race to represent her gender. Her whiteness did not corrupt her standing as a woman. On the contrary, colorblind intersectionality drew on that whiteness to keep her sex discrimination claim juridically "pure."

Nor, unlike black women, did Jespersen have to worry about whether she could represent gender per se. Her whiteness did not call into question her capacity to stand in for all women. She occupied the category "woman" without racial specificity. That is virtually impossible for a black woman to do so. Her race is always already particularizing her gender, thus diminishing her gender's representational capacity. Against the backdrop of whiteness as a racial default, blackness renders a black woman's gender and her sex discrimination claim at least implicitly racially "impure" and thus juridically quasi-suspect.

While Jespersen did not have to worry about the representative role her whiteness would perform in the litigation, she did have to worry about her sexual orientation. Jespersen did not identify herself as a lesbian in the case. That disclosure would have undermined her claim. In part this is because federal antidiscrimination law does not prohibit employers from discriminating on the basis of sexual orientation. Thus, had Jespersen highlighted her sexual orientation, Harrah's might have articulated a sexual orientation defense—namely, that the company terminated Jespersen because she was a lesbian (likely, the company would not have argued that its grooming policy was necessary to prevent Jespersen from *looking like a lesbian,* though one gets the sense that, in part, that is precisely what was at stake). Because federal sex discrimination law almost always presupposes heterosexuality, Jespersen had to judicially closet her lesbian identity and doctrinally pass as a heterosexual. Had Jespersen been black, the incentive for her to cover in this way likely would have been even stronger. This is because the historical masculinization of black women would have made the lesbian subtext in the case even more salient.

There is another way in which we might we broaden our understanding of *Jespersen* by switching Jespersen's identity from white to black. Consider, again, Harrah's grooming policy: "Face powder, blush, and mascara" and "lip color must be worn at all times." Moreover, women's hair must be "teased, curled, or styled."[26] Would dreaded or braided hair constitute hair that is "teased, curled, or styled"? Assume that Harrah's answered that question in the negative and prohibited Jespersen, who we are now imagining is black, from wearing her hair in braids. Would that constitute sex discrimination?

The question is not academic. This is precisely the issue *Rogers v. American Airlines* engages, a case in which American Airlines prohibited its employees from wearing all-braided hairstyles.[27] Renee Rogers, a black female employee, challenged the policy, asserting that it discriminated against her based on race and gender.

The court disagreed. It reasoned that the grooming policy did not reflect sex discrimination because it applied to both women and men. The court further noted that because the policy restricted braided hair, irrespective of racial identity, the policy was race neutral. In reaching this conclusion the court invoked Bo Derek's braided hairstyle in the movie *10*. The court credited American Airlines' argument that Renee Rogers "first appeared at work in the all-braided hairstyle on or about September 25, 1980, soon after the style had been popularized by a white actress in the film '10,'" and rejected Rogers's claim that braided hair "has been, historically, a fashion and style adopted by Black American women, reflective of cultural, historical essence of Black women in American society."[28] For the court, from an antidiscrimination perspective, braided hair had no significance.[29] Failing to consider the ways in which hair is racially constitutive,[30] the court concluded that American Airlines' prohibition on braided hairstyles had "at most a negligible effect on employment opportunity."[31]

Reading the *Rogers* case in conjunction with *Jespersen* produces at least three additional intersectional insights. The first is that Harrah's grooming policy is not only gendered, it is raced. Black women and white women are likely to be differently situated with respect to (a) whether they can "tease" their hair (assuming an objective standard as to what that means), (b) whether they would have to chemically treat their hair to satisfy Harrah's policy, (c) whether Harrah's would perceive their hairstyles to be "teased, curled, or styled" (a grooming standard that is intended to produce a professionalized feminine look, one for which black women would not be the "natural" exemplars), and (d) whether the express prohibition of certain hairstyles (such as braids) would have a disparate impact on black women.

A second intersectional insight that reading *Rogers* and *Jespersen* together produces pertains to litigation. Assume that in our hypothetical case Harrah's concluded that dreaded or braided hair does not constitute hair that is "teased, curled, or styled" and terminated Jespersen. Would she have a cause of action? In light of *Rogers,* the answer is no. The fact that the prohibition of braids formally would apply to women irrespective of race would defeat a claim that the prohibition constitutes sex discrimination.

Third, and more generally, once we unpack and articulate how whiteness colors and is embedded in the *Jespersen* case, it raises a question about one aspect of the intersectionality problem Crenshaw identified in "Demarginalizing": whether expressly invoking blackness in a sex discrimination case, against an unarticulated baseline of whiteness, renders such claims less viable in the sense of appearing less authentically about gender per se.

None of this is to say that Jespersen herself was trading on her whiteness. The point, instead, is a structural one—namely, that her whiteness was not marked as an intersectional subject position in the way that an African American woman's blackness would have been. Engaging the *Jespersen* case along these intersectional lines provides a clear window on at least one of the ways in which colorblind intersectionality works: to produce an unarticulated intersectional imperative for Darlene Jespersen to be female like a white heterosexual woman.

ESSENTIALLY GAY:
OR GAY LIKE A WHITE HETEROSEXUAL MAN

While Harrah's grooming policy required Darlene Jespersen to be female like a heterosexual white woman, gay rights advocates have historically required their gay civil rights icons to be gay like a white heterosexual man, or more colloquially, "straight acting." This white *hetero*normative investment created a white *homo*normative strategy, one that shaped gay rights opposition to, among other homophobic policies, the "Don't Ask, Don't Tell" policy.

Criticism of the strategy of analogizing race to sexual orientation, as well as its particular deployment in the context of "Don't Ask, Don't Tell," is by now a familiar mode of contestation.[32] Yet revisiting this chapter in the rhetorical framing of gay rights advocacy provides another vantage point from which to observe colorblind intersectionality at work.

To challenge "Don't Ask, Don't Tell," some gay rights proponents analogized the rhetoric the military deployed to exclude (out) gays and lesbians from military service to the rhetoric it deployed to exclude African Americans. They reasoned that because most people have repudiated the latter, we as a society should also repudiate the former. This analogizing of rhetoric was the predicate for a formal equality analogy about discrimination—namely, the exclusion of African Americans from the military is like the exclusion of (out) gays and lesbians. The analogy sets up an equivalency between race-based and sexual orientation–based military exclusion. Buttressed by colorblind intersectionality, the analogy obscured important civil rights history, elided the existence of black gays and lesbians, normalized whiteness as the natural but unarticulated racial default for the expression of gay identity, and produced a civil rights discourse that traded on white normative masculinity.[33]

According to David Smith, the spokesperson for the gay and lesbian coalition group Campaign for Military Service, the language the military employed to exclude blacks from military service is like the language the military employed to exclude gays and lesbians. Smith's argument has additional force if we examine two texts: a Department of Defense Directive (Defense Directive) justifying the military's discrimination against gays and lesbians, and a 1942 statement from the Secretary of the Navy (Navy Statement) supporting racial segregation in the armed forces. The Defense Directive reads, in part:

> The presence in the military environment of persons who engage in homosexual conduct or who, by their statements, demonstrate a propensity to engage in homosexual conduct, seriously impairs the accomplishment of military mission. The presence of such members adversely affects the ability of the armed forces to maintain discipline, good order and morale; to foster mutual trust and confidence among service members; to insure the integrity of the system of rank and command; to facilitate assignment and worldwide deployment of service members who frequently must live and work in close conditions affording minimal privacy; to recruit and retain members of the armed forces; to maintain the public acceptability of military service."[34]

Now consider the Navy Statement, which in relevant part reads:

> Men on board ships live in particularly close association; in their messes, one man sits beside another; their hammocks or bunks are close together; in their tasks such as those of gun crew, they form a closely knit, highly coordinated team. How many white men would choose, of their own accord, that their closest associates in sleeping quarters, at mess, and in gun crews should be of another race?[35]

These texts suggest that at different historical moments in America the armed forces have employed military necessity arguments to justify both racial segregation in and the exclusion of (out) gays and lesbians from the military. Blackness and homosexuality threaten military discipline, organization, morale, and readiness. Fair enough? Maybe. But this discursive analogy then became the basis for a comparison about discrimination: Gay exclusion from the military is like black exclusion from the military. Part of the problem here is that this formal *in*equality claim obscures the history of Jim Crow and the ways in which that history was sexualized. Rather than employing the politics of Jim Crow to discuss how racial regimes regulate sexuality (and how sexuality is often a technology for policing racial boundaries), gay rights proponents imposed a "gay gaze"—or sexual orientation qua sexual orientation frame—onto the racial exclusion of blacks from the military. As George Chauncey puts in a related context, "Claiming the two experiences have been the same does no justice to history and no service to the gay cause."[36]

Yet it would be inaccurate to say that gay rights proponents completely ignored black civil rights history. In fact, they traded on the moral authority of the civil rights movement. But they did so without actually engaging the racial conditions under which African Americans were fighting for reform. The gay rights advocacy against "Don't Ask, Don't Tell" selectively incorporated African American history—and African Americans—to compare sexual orientation per se (read: presumptively white gays and lesbians of today) with race per se (read: presumptively black heterosexuals of the Jim Crow era). Underwriting the advocacy was the notion that, in a historical sense, gays are like African Americans; in a contemporary sense, gays are "just like everybody else" (the white normative heterosexuals in contemporary society).

This strategy should disturb us. It exploits and displaces black civil rights history, trades on white privilege, and renders whiteness an invisible particularity of gay identity. Like the *Jespersen* litigation, gay rights advocacy against "Don't Ask, Don't Tell" reflected colorblind intersectionality. Throughout the gay rights campaign against "Don't Ask, Don't Tell," gay identity was (almost entirely) intersectionally constituted as white. Naming this as an intersectional activity is crucial not only to articulating colorblindness as a racial preference for whites but also to highlighting gay identity as a repository for the expression of that preference. In the context of the gay rights challenges to "Don't Ask, Don't Tell," whiteness anchors our intelligibility of gay identity (and blackness is heterosexualized as a social category whose disadvantages and civil rights aspirations reside in the domain of history).

The colorblind intersectionality of the gay rights advocacy helps to explain why black gay rights advocates focused on the white, and not black, casualties of "Don't Ask, Don't Tell," despite the fact that African Americans were disproportionately affected by the policy.[37] Too masculine to be gay and too feminine to be men, black gay men cannot be gay like a white heterosexual man. Thus, while Perry Watkins, a black army sergeant, established an important milestone when he became the first openly gay serviceman to successfully challenge "Don't Ask, Don't Tell,"[38] gay rights advocates largely marginalized him in their campaign. As Tom Stoddard, the important gay activist lawyer who directed the Campaign for Military Service, said, "There was a public relations problem with Perry Watkins."[39] Watkins often performed in drag at recreational centers, social clubs, and other official and unofficial military gatherings. Notwithstanding that the military sometimes specifically requested these performances, they were at odds with the boy-next-door representative gay man around whom gay rights proponents sought to structure their advocacy.

Watkins was very aware that this representative gay man was racialized. In his view, gay right proponents preferred "poster children," many of whom had "lied" about their sexual orientation, over "a black man who had to live the struggle nearly every day of his life."[40] From Watkins's perspective, much of the public gay rights advocacy against "Don't Ask, Don't Tell" rendered him invisibly out.

Enter Keith Meinhold. A white navy petty officer who revealed that he was gay on *ABC World News Tonight,* Meinhold became the "poster child" for the gay rights campaign. He appeared on the cover of *Newsweek* magazine, in full navy uniform, performing the role of the all-American boy.

The subhead accompanying his image asks, "How far will Clinton go?"[41] On the one hand, one could say that this cover invites the reader to conclude that Clinton would have to go very far. On the other hand, one could argue that after reading Meinhold's story, the American public would come to see him as an ordinary man, "but for" his sexual orientation, and conclude that Clinton would not be going too far if he admitted men like Meinhold—men who were "gay like white heterosexual men"—into the military.

Joseph Steffan, a former midshipman who was expelled from the Naval Academy a few weeks before graduation, made a similar public appearance. Consider the following account:

The host is interviewing Joseph Steffan. . . . Raised in the Midwest, Catholic, a choir boy in his local church, Steffan was the kid next door. Clean-cut, an excellent student, exceptional in track, he took as his date for the senior prom the high school's homecoming queen. From his small town in Minnesota, Joe Steffan entered Annapolis. At the Academy he was ranked in the top ten in his class, became battalion commander his senior year, and received the

Newsweek

February 1, 1993 : $2.95

GAYS
AND THE
MILITARY

How Far Will Clinton Go?

Petty Officer
Keith
Meinhold

unique honor of twice singing, solo, the national anthem at the Army-Navy game.

The TV monitor shifts to a film of Joe Steffan, standing on a platform as the Army-Navy game is about to begin, bearing erect, singing the anthem against the red, white, and blue backdrop of the American flag waving in the stadium breeze. The television studio camera again trains its lens on Joe Steffan's face, his sincere gaze, his serious eyes. . . . Joseph Steffan . . . is now "out" to the USA.[42]

Significantly, it is not just Steffan who is "out" here. For in this context, Steffan, like Meinhold, functions as a representative gay man. He is respectable. He is accomplished. He is an athlete. He is American. He is white. He is normatively masculine. *And* he is also gay. I employ "and" and not "but" here because the theater invites us to conceptualize Steffan's gay identity as incidental or beside the point with respect to his military manhood. Steffan's normative masculinity, which his whiteness helped to intersectionally constitute, rendered him gay like a white heterosexual man.

To the extent that "Don't Ask, Don't Tell' is now a dead letter, one can query whether it makes sense to interrogate how gay rights contestations of this policy managed questions of race. Why should we care about that now? Surely gay rights advocacy today is more intersectionally nuanced? With respect to gay rights advocacy for marriage equality, the answer is "no."[43] An emerging slogan in the marriage equality discourse is that "Gay is the New Black."[44] This slogan relegates racial inequality to the domain of history, stages a gay civil rights agenda that treats race as largely irrelevant, obscures the existence of black LGBT communities, and conceptualizes racial equality in formalistic terms. The advocacy marks African Americans as a group whose civil rights aspirations have already been fulfilled. Like the "Don't Ask, Don't Tell" advocacy, the "Gay is the New Black" frame reproduced colorblind intersectionality. Here, too, whiteness is an unarticulated intersectional subject position; and here, too, the representation currency of whiteness overdetermines the content of gay identity.

One might think of the "Gay is the New Black" frame as yet another expression of and commitment to formal equality. Because blacks no longer experience de jure racial discrimination as a matter of law, the slogan renders black subordination and disadvantage a thing of the past. This reasoning acquiesces in and helps to fuel a broader colorblind ideological machinery that has either stopped the civil rights clock for African Americans or is causing it to tick counterclockwise. Under the "Gay is the New Black" slogan, there is no African American social subject around whom to structure a civil rights intervention. To put it the way Chandan Reddy might, African Americans become part of a historical "remembering" to mark a society that once was racially regressive—"an early and primitive moment of national development"—but is now regressive in terms of sexual orientation.[45] Under the "Gay is the New Black" frame, the subordination of African American blackness is not only being rearticulated; it is being disappeared to history. The implication of the slogan is that African Americans, with the full panoply of formal rights, including the right to marry, are effectively the new whites. Consistent with one of the dominant logics of colorblindness, African Americans are black only in terms of the color of their skin. In terms of structural subordination, "Gay is the New Black."

The "Gay is the New Black" refrain is the most recent manifestation of the heteronormative aspirations of mainstream gay rights organizing. This investment raises a question about whether, instead of conceptualizing gay as the new black, we might profitably think of gay—or, more specifically, middle-class gay men—as the new straight. Doing so would not be to deny the real vulnerability—to both discrimination and violence—that white gay men have. The argument here would simply mirror claims about race and whiteness.[46] Just as scholars of race have explored, for example, how the Irish and the Jew became white,[47] one might begin a conversation about whether certain expressions of gay identity are becoming the new straight. In exploring this question, one need not treat heterosexuality and straight identity as precisely the same thing. One might, instead, understand straight to denote the manifestation of normatively appropriate ways of being, including, but not limited to, expressions of masculinity.

Alternatively, but along similar lines, one might conceptualize white middle-class gay identity as a kind of ethnic whiteness: the more white middle-class gay men assimilate their identities to white heteronormative standards, the more they move from the periphery of white privilege to its core. Under this view, white gay men in particular are becoming the "new white." This conceptualization of gay identity trades on an understanding of whiteness as a zone within which people are differentially positioned as a result of both their willingness and perceived capacity to assimilate. Under this framework, masculinity is one axis along which middle-class gay men can shore up, express, and naturalize their whiteness. To put the point slightly differently, the homonormativity of the gay rights marriage equality campaign instantiates a naturalization process through which white gay men are incorporated into a white mainstream identity. This incorporation moves them from a kind of "first-class white-citizens-in-waiting" status to first-class white citizens proper. Understood in this way, the colorblind intersectionality of the "Gay is the New Black" frame effectively is structured around a white racial and normatively masculine prerequisite. People who do not satisfy these intersectional standards are not naturalized as gay within mainstream gay rights advocacy, a naturalized status that is itself a prerequisite for incorporation into the mainstream body of the United States.

Significantly, I am not making a strong claim that we should conceptualize gay identity as either the new straight or the new white. I simply mean to mark how (paradoxically?) the "Gay is the New Black" slogan reflects a *white* racial and *hetero*normative orientation. The "Gay is the New Black" frame and the colorblind intersectionality that underwrites it help to produce gay male subjects who, like Meinhold and Steffan, are gay like a white heterosexual man.

This brings me back to the introduction. There I suggested that it is erroneous to conceptualize intersectionality as a theory whose exclusive focus is the intersection of race (read: nonwhite) and gender (read: female identity). Moreover, there are significant costs to doing so. Framing intersectionality as just about women of color gives masculinity, whiteness, and maleness an intersectional pass. That, in turn, leaves colorblind intersectionality unnamed and uninterrogated, further naturalizing white, male heterosexuality as the normative baseline against which the rest of us are intersectionally differentiated.

NOTES

1. Kimberlé Williams Crenshaw, "Demarginalizing the Intersection of Race and Sex: A Black Feminist Critique of Antidiscrimination Doctrine, Feminist Theory, and Antiracist Politics," *University of Chicago Legal Forum* 1989, no. 1 (1989): 139–68.
2. Indeed, two important and ambitious anthologies on masculinities are explicitly framed in terms of multidimensionality (over and against intersectionality): Frank Rudy Cooper and Ann C. McGinley, eds., *Masculinities and Law: A Multidimensional Approach* (New York: New York University Press, 2012); and Athena D. Mutua, *Progressive Black Masculinities* (New York: Routledge, 2006). For an approach that frames the issue expressly in intersectional terms, see the introduction to Devon W. Carbado, ed., *Black Men on Race, Gender, and Sexuality: A Critical Reader* (New York: New York University Press, 1999).

3. There are other "blind" forms of intersectionality that we should similarly interrogate. "Genderblind intersectionality," "classblind intersectionality," and "religionblind intersectionality" come readily to mind.

4. I am employing "case studies" loosely to mean contextual examples.

5. Mae Ngai, *Impossible Subjects: Illegal Aliens and the Making of Modern America* (Princeton, NJ: Princeton University Press, 2004).

6. Peter Kwan, "Jeffrey Dahmer and the Cosynthesis of Categories," *Hastings Law Journal* 48, no. 6 (1997): 1257–92.

7. Francisco Valdes, "Beyond Sexual Orientation in Queer Legal Theory: Majoritarianism, Multidimensionality, and Responsibility in Social Justice Scholarship, or Legal Scholars as Cultural Warriors," *Denver Law Review* 75, no. 4 (1998): 1409–64.

8. Athena Mutua, "The Rise, Development, and Future Directions of Critical Race Theory and Related Scholarship," *Denver University Law Review* 84, no. 2 (2006): 329–94; Darren Hutchinson, "Ignoring the Sexualization of Race: Heteronormativity, Critical Race Theory, and Anti-Racist Politics," *Buffalo Law Review* 47, no. 1 (1999): 1–116; Valdes, "Beyond Sexual Orientation in Queer Legal Theory."

9. Jasbir K. Puar, *Terrorist Assemblages: Homonationalism in Queer Times* (Durham, NC: Duke University Press, 2007).

10. I want to be clear that I am not suggesting that the foregoing works are unimportant. On the contrary, they perform critical interventions that bring to the fore important social justice questions that progressive scholars often marginalize. My critique, then, is a very specific one—namely, that in taking up the topics they explore, proponents of alternative frameworks to intersectionality often artificially limit (explicitly or implicitly) the work that intersectionality can perform.

11. Sumi Cho, "Post-Intersectionality," *Du Bois Review: Social Science Research on Race* 10, no. 2 (2014): 385–404.

12. Devon Carbado, Mitu Gulati, and Gowri Ramachandran, "The Jespersen Story: Makeup and Women at Work," in *Employment Discrimination Stories,* ed. Joel Wm. Friedman (New York: Foundation Press, 2006), 105–52; Tracey E. George, Mitu Gulati, and Ann C. McGinley, "The New Old Legal Realism," *Northwestern University Law Review* 105, no. 2 (2011): 689–736.

13. *Price Waterhouse v. Hopkins,* 490 U.S. 228 (1989), https://supreme.justia.com/cases/federal/us/490/228.

14. Ibid., 235.

15. *Jespersen v. Harrah's Operating Co., Inc.,* 392 F. 3d 1076 (9th Cir. 2004), https://finduslaw.com/jespersen-v-harrahs-operating-company-inc-392-f3d-1076-9th-cir-2004.

16. Ibid.

17. *Hamm v. Weyauwega Milk Products, Inc.,* 332 F. 3d 1058, 1067 (7th Cir. 2003), https://casetext.com/case/hamm-v-weyauwega-milk-products-inc.

18. Carbado, Gulati, and Ramachandran, "Jesperson Story."

19. Paula Black, *The Beauty Industry: Gender, Culture, Pleasure* (London: Routledge, 2004).

20. For a more extended analysis of this case, see Devon Carbado and Mitu Gulati, *"Acting Like a White Woman," in Acting White? Re-thinking Race in Post-racial America* (Oxford: Oxford University Press, 2013).

21. Stephanie D. Smith, "Beauty Beat: Essence Panel Explores Beauty Purchasing," *Women's Wear Daily,* May 19, 2009.

22. Homi K. Bhabha, "Of Mimicry and Man: The Ambivalance of Colonial Discourse," in *Locations of Culture* (London: Routledge, 2004), 121–31.

23. Note that this is precisely what Crenshaw is problematizing in "Demarginalizing." Although she does not frame her analysis in terms of color-blindness, she is clear that "a white woman claiming discrimination against females may be in no better position to represent all women than a Black woman who claims discrimination as a Black female and wants to represent all females. The court's preferred articulation 'against females' is not necessarily more inclusive—it just appears so because *the racial contours of the claim are not specified. The court's preference for 'against females' rather than 'against Black females' reveals the implicit grounding of white female experiences in the doctrinal conceptualization of sex discrimination.*" Crenshaw, "Demarginalizing," 144; emphasis added.

24. Part of the problem with colorblindness is that we do not conceptualize it as a racial ideology. For a conceptual model of how we might do so, see Devon W. Carbado and Cheryl Harris, "The New Racial Preferences," *California Law Review* 96, no. 5 (2008): 1139–214.

25. Crenshaw, "Demarginalizing."

26. *Jespersen v. Harrah.*

27. *Rogers v. American Airlines, Inc.,* 527 F. Supp. 229 (S.D.N.Y. 1981), https://law.justia.com/cases/federal/district-courts/FSupp/527/229/2369655.

28. Ibid., 231–32.

29. Paulette Caldwell, "A Hair Piece: Perspectives on the Intersection of Race and Gender," *Duke Law Journal* 1991 (1991): 365–96; idem, "Intersectional Bias and the Courts: The Story of *Rogers v. American Airlines,*" in *Race Law Stories,* ed. Rachel F. Moran and Devon W. Carbado (New York: Foundation Press, 2008), 571–600.

30. Angela Onwuachi-Willig, "Another Hair Piece: Exploring New Strands of Analysis under Title VII," *Georgetown Law Journal* 98, no. (2010): 1079–132.

31. *Rogers v. American Airlines,* 231.

32. Devon W. Carbado, "Critical What What?" *Connecticut Law Review* 43, no. 5 (2011): 1593–645.

33. This white normative masculinity excluded not only black men but also black women. Because I am interested in interrogating maleness and masculinity as inter-sectional subjectivities, my focus is on the former.

34. Quoted in Randy Shilts, *Conduct Unbecoming: Lesbians and Gays in the U.S. Military—Vietnam to the Persian Gulf* (New York: St. Martin's Press, 1993), 378–79.

35. Quoted in John Sibley Butler, "Homosexuals and the Military Establishment," *Society* 31, no. 1 (1993): 16–17.

36. George Chauncey, *Why Marriage? The History Shaping Today's Debate over Gay Equality* (New York: Basic Books, 2005), 161.

37. Josh Rosenthal and Christopher Contreras, "Piling One Prejudice onto Another" (Center for American Progress, Feb. 23, [2010]), www.americanprogress.org/issues/2010/02/prejudice_another.html.

38. *Watkins v. U.S. Army,* 875 F. 2d 699 (9th Cir. 1989), https://law.justia.com/cases/federal/appellate-courts/F2/875/699/179345.

39. Quoted in Keith Boykin, *One More River to Cross: Black and Gay in America* (New York: Anchor Books, 1996), 218.

40. Ibid., 219–20.

41. *Newsweek,* Feb. 1, 1993, cover.

42. Mary Fainsod Katzenstein, "The Spectacle of Life and Death: Feminist and Lesbian/Gay Politics in the Military," in *Gay Rights, Military Wrongs: Political Perspective on Lesbians and Gays in the Military,* ed. Craig A. Rimmerman (New York: Routledge, 1996), 233–34.

43. For an indication of how marriage equality proponents have mobilized race in the context of litigation, see Russell Robinson, "Marriage Equality and Postracialism," *UCLA Law Review* 67 (2014): 1010–81. For a critique of how gay rights proponents have employed *Loving v. Virginia,* the case that rendered antimiscegenation laws unconstitutional, in their advocacy, see Chandan Reddy, "Time for Rights? Loving, Gay Marriage, and the Limits of Legal Justice," *Fordham Law Review* 76, no. 6 (2008): 2849–72 . Significantly, and as I have argued elsewhere, I am not arguing that race/sexual orientation analogies should never be employed; see Devon W. Carbado, "Black Rights, Gay Rights, Civil Rights," *UCLA Law Review* 47, no. 6 (2000): 1467–520. Robin Lenhardt's work, for example, provides a sense of how one might engage in this kind of comparative project; see R. A. Lenhardt, "Forgotten Lessons on Race, Law, and Marriage: The Story of *Perez v. Sharp,*" in *Race Law Stories,* ed. Rachel F. Moran and Devon W. Carbado (New York: Foundation Press, 2007), 343–80; idem, "Beyond Analogy: *Perez v. Sharp,* Antimiscegenation Law, and the Fight for Same-Sex Marriage," *California Law Review* 96, no. 4 (2008): 839–900.

44. This slogan appeared on the December 2008 cover of the *Advocate* magazine and has circulated more broadly in gay rights discourses about marriage equality. For an indication of the extent to which this is so, see Robinson, "Marriage Equality and Postracialism."

45. Reddy, "Time for Rights," 2862.

46. Cheryl I. Harris, "Whiteness as Property," *Harvard Law Review* 106, no. 8 (1993): 1707–91; George Lipsitz, "'Constituted by a Series of Contestations': Critical Race Theory as a Social Movement," *Connecticut Law Review* 43, no. 5 (2011): 1458–78.

47. Noel Ignatiev, *How the Irish Became White* (New York: Routledge, 1995); Karen Brodkin, *How Jews Became White Folks and What That Says about Race in America* (New Brunswick, NJ: Rutgers University Press, 1998).

TEN

Causality, Context, and Colorblindness

EQUAL EDUCATIONAL OPPORTUNITY AND
THE POLITICS OF RACIST DISAVOWAL

Leah N. Gordon

When Chief Justice John Roberts argued in the 2007 *Parents Involved in Community Schools v. Seattle School District No. 1* decision that "the way to stop discrimination on the basis of race is to stop discriminating on the basis of race," he linked the concept of equality of educational opportunity to the colorblind politics of racial disavowal, reinterpreting racial equality to obscure histories and ongoing patterns of racial oppression, discrimination, and disparity.[1] Arguing that the "racial classifications" under consideration, a Seattle school desegregation plan that considered race to promote racial balance, violated *Brown v. Board of Education*'s (1954) promise of equality of educational opportunity, Roberts exemplified how colorblind racial logics could work hand in hand with other ostensibly race-neutral concepts—in this case equality of opportunity—to perpetuate racial inequality. Many liberal scholars, civil rights activists, and policymakers had for years relied on notions of equal educational opportunity when promoting the redistribution of resources to minority students, school integration, and policies that held school systems accountable for achievement gaps.[2] Early twenty-first-century colorblind conservatives employed the same language, however, to legitimize retreats from affirmative action and school desegregation.

This seeming contradiction has a long history; it is rooted in the ways in which the capacious concept of equality of educational opportunity has been used for both purposes that are emancipatory and those that reinforce racial hierarchy. Today's colorblind contradictions have antecedents, as this chapter will show, in academic debates over the causes of educational inequality in the 1960s and 1970s, years when opportunity-based egalitarianism was largely the language of the antiracist left. Situating the current politics of colorblindness in this longer historical trajectory illuminates the agenda setting capacities of social knowledge. It shows how visions of race, justice, and equality forged in the disciplines can frame social policy and law, making some approaches to contesting racial hierarchy—and not others—seem actionable. Conservative repurposing of liberal scientific egalitarianism, moreover, exemplifies how disciplinary knowledge can not only travel beyond its original construction sites, but also be used for purposes its producers never intended.[3]

The chameleonlike character of the concepts "equal opportunity" and "equal educational opportunity" is not a recent development. A basic tenet of American liberalism and an objective embraced by both conservative proponents of colorblindness and their progressive opponents, equality of opportunity is among the most enduring political ideals in the twentieth-century United States.[4] While the "protean" character of American liberalism has long perplexed historians, many describe liberalism, which prioritizes individual liberty, civil rights, political equality, and fair opportunity while accepting competitive markets as just tools for distributing social and economic goods, as the nation's dominant political philosophy.[5] Despite Lyndon Johnson's famous 1965 call for "not just equality as a right and a theory but equality as a fact and equality as a result," versions of opportunity-based egalitarianism typically infused mid-twentieth-century racial liberalism (the civil rights agenda that prioritized attacks on legal segregation, discrimination, and white prejudice) and Great Society liberalism.[6] Defined as a right of citizenship in *Brown v. Board,* equality of educational opportunity motivated campaigns to implement school desegregation across the country in the post-*Brown* decades, undergirded federal efforts to increase educational resources for low-income students during the War on Poverty, and provided a language deployed by activists on all sides of debates over compensatory education, community control, bilingualism, fiscal neutrality (the fair distribution of educational resources between school districts), busing, standards, and accountability.[7]

At the same time, opportunity-based egalitarianism's conservative potential has been evident throughout the twentieth century. Black Power theorists Stokely Carmichael (Kwame Ture) and Charles Hamilton described equal opportunity as part of the ideological system rationalizing white supremacy. Others argued that equal educational opportunity was a myth that legitimized unequal educational results and an ideology that convinced Americans to fight poverty through schooling rather than through potentially more effective jobs or welfare policies.[8] In fact, as descriptions of the social order and normative ideals, notions of equal educational opportunity have been among the "rearticulated elements of traditional liberalism" that racial conservatives employed for "racially illiberal goals" in the late twentieth century.[9] Opportunity-based egalitarianism and its educational varieties are among the ideas that, as Eduardo Bonilla-Silva puts it, helped depict "contemporary racial inequality as the outcome of nonracial dynamics," "exculpate" whites "from any responsibility for the status of people of color," and "rationalize minorities' contemporary status as the product of market dynamics, naturally occurring phenomena, and blacks' imputed cultural limitations."[10]

This chapter investigates debate that circulated around three prominent texts on education, opportunity, and inequality: James S. Coleman's *Equality of Educational Opportunity* (1966); Kenneth Clark's *Dark Ghetto* (1965); and Whitney Young's *To Be Equal* (1964). Since each volume interpreted social science for an audience of educators, policymakers, and concerned citizens, their histories illuminate the agenda-setting power of social research, including how often unacknowledged colorblind assumptions in social science could legitimize social and educational policies that "blamed the victim" or rationalized an unequal status quo. This debate occurred between 1964 and 1974, years when arguments over the utility of integration to the African American freedom struggle, the appropriateness of colonial metaphors for describing domestic race relations, the sources of the increasingly visible "urban crisis," deficiency paradigms, and Great Society liberalism's promise and pitfalls often divided antiracist liberals and radicals.[11] This intellectual history reveals how notions of equality of educational opportunity, which Coleman employed in ways that obscured systematic racial harm while Young and Clark used them to expose racial power, functioned at the dawn of the era of formal equality.

The first part of the chapter focuses on Coleman's government-sponsored report, *Equality of Educational Opportunity,* among the most authoritative and widely cited surveys of educational inequality of the Civil Rights Act era. The Coleman Report revealed how the measurement of racial inequality, especially when linked to notions of objectivity associated with scientism (social scientific reliance on investigative norms of the natural sciences), could complicate the description of racist causality.[12] Despite highlighting racial disparities in educational inputs and outputs, Coleman's analysis of the factors blocking equality of educational opportunity obscured systemic and institutionalized racial discrimination, isolated educational inequality from white supremacist contexts, legitimized reduced investments in the schooling of poor and minority students, and resulted in victim blaming. Others, however, effectively used the language of equality of educational opportunity to further antiracist political agendas. The second half of the chapter shows that Kenneth Clark, Whitney Young, and many on the African American social scientific left used notions of equal educational opportunity to expose the causal importance of systemic discrimination and to highlight educational inequality's inseparability from the broader political and economic context, one marked by histories and ongoing patterns of white supremacy.

COLEMAN, DEFICIENCY PARADIGMS, AND CAUSAL AMBIGUITY

Commissioned under the 1964 Civil Rights Act for the Office of Education, James S. Coleman's *Equality of Educational Opportunity* was an emblem of Great Society liberalism's alliance with quantitative social science, a textual expression of the midcentury liberal faith that scientific objectivity—especially large-scale statistical analysis—was essential to informing effective social policy. Surpassed perhaps only by Daniel Patrick Moynihan's report on the African American family in its familiarity to those outside the social sciences,[13] the Coleman Report generated symposia, edited volumes, and both academic and popular debate.[14] Coleman, who spent his career at the University of Chicago and Johns Hopkins University (1959–73), and by his death in 1995 had been elected to the National Academy of Sciences, awarded ten honorary degrees, and served as president of the American Sociological Association, was one the nation's leading sociologists of social organization. Trained by Paul Lazarsfeld, Robert Merton, and Seymour Martin Lipset at Columbia, Coleman contributed to mathematical sociology, network analysis, theories of social capital, and the study of human behavior.[15] The Coleman Report, which launched a line of research on the "achievement gap" that flourishes still today, was requested by President Lyndon Johnson as he launched the War on Poverty. It was published a year after the 1965 Elementary and Secondary Education Act substantially expanded federal involvement in the education of poor children.[16] Coleman applied the latest statistical techniques and one of the largest data sets thus far available for educational researchers to a burning policy question: whether school desegregation or compensatory educational funding could more effectively equalize educational opportunity. Since segregationist stalling tactics ensured that progress toward statistical school desegregation remained slow before 1968, it is little surprise that this question persisted ten years after *Brown v. Board of Education*.[17]

If one defines color consciousness in terms of willingness to measure racial inequality, the Coleman Report certainly qualified. The report highlighted correlations between student racial characteristics, school-level educational inputs (per-pupil spending, quality of facility, curricular and extracurricular options, teacher preparation, levels of segregation, the demographics of a student's peers, etc.) and educational outputs (student performance on standardized tests). The nation's schools were profoundly segregated by race and socioeconomic status, the sociologist found, while also making clear that segregation went hand in hand with resource inequality. His data on test scores also revealed that while minority children (especially African American and Puerto Rican) lagged behind whites in their "verbal and nonverbal skills" when they began school, these differences in achievement (which later scholars would term "achievement gaps") increased with years in the classroom.[18]

At the same time, the Coleman Report epitomized how a study of racial inequality could contribute to the politics of racist disavowal. The vision of racial injustice underlying the report was liberal in political leaning, methodologically individualistic, and compatible with deficiency paradigms on the rise in the era of the Moynihan Report. The centrality of "opportunity" to the project's conceptual framing naturalized a competitive ethos that treated inequality in economic or social status among adults as inevitable. If all citizens entered the competitive ring with ambiguously defined "equal educational opportunities," then presumably inequality in social and economic status among adults was fair. In addition, despite Coleman's interests in social organization, the report's methodological orientation paralleled the astructural social survey tradition of the 1940s and 1950s, which critics accused of atomism for isolating individuals from social or political economic context.[19] It also shared premises with psychologically inflected deficiency paradigms, which rooted "social dislocations" in family life, cultural norms, and what Coleman's colleague Daniel Patrick Moynihan (drawing on terminology originated by Kenneth Clark) described as an intergenerational "tangle of pathology."[20] The Coleman Report's atomism stood at odds with earlier sociological traditions, including the social structural analyses of the interwar Chicago School of sociology and political economic approaches associated with the Depression-era interracial left, that treated racial conflict and harm as a consequence of broad social, political, and economic structures: capitalism, colonialism, and white supremacy. Associated with liberal and radical thinkers like Oliver Cromwell Cox, W. E. B. Du Bois, E. Franklin Frazier, Charles S. Johnson, and Ralph Bunche in the 1930s and 1940s, theories that situated racial inequality in the intersections of social structure and political economy, that theorized oppression and exploitation, and that treated race and class harms as closely linked resurfaced in the Black Power era. These frameworks remained beyond Coleman's purview, however.

Like the status attainment school of educational sociology with which it is often associated, the Coleman Report largely described racial inequality in education without theorizing its mechanisms; it thus obscured what might be called racist causality.[21] Although the report measured teacher morale, student "sense of control" over environment, and whether students attended schools with tracking, it proved ambiguous on questions of causality, especially on the role school-based discrimination played in generating achievement gaps.[22] Coleman largely downplayed, or overlooked, the discriminatory tracking and guidance programs, classroom and disciplinary practices, curricula, and teacher assignment policies that African American communities had resisted throughout the twentieth century, that a generation of African American sociologists exposed in the 1920s, 1930s, and 1940s, and that many African American autobiographers of the 1960s and 1970s detailed.[23]

In addition, the Coleman Report elided racial power by separating educational inequality from the larger political, economic, spatial, and sociological contexts in which schools and students were situated. Coleman acknowledged how "racial housing concentration" and white flight shaped school segregation, but treated these processes as natural, presumably inevitable background factors, rather than as a spatial landscape built through the intersection of private and public policy.[24] He thus removed educational inequality from the history of systematic, institutionalized, often state-sanctioned or state-initiated patterns of discrimination in housing markets, real estate lending, zoning, and employment.[25] In doing so, he treated as beyond his analytic purview social scientific research on the twentieth-century "race problem" (much by African American authors) as well as emerging scholarship on the "urban crisis," such as appeared in Kenneth Clark and Talcott Parsons's *The Negro American* in 1965 and would shape the Kerner Commission's 1968 analysis of a nation "moving toward two societies, one black, one white—separate and unequal."[26]

By downplaying discrimination within schools and the mechanisms generating segregation and racial inequality outside them, Coleman opened the door for blaming the victim, even as he developed a powerful defense of school desegregation. His work revealed how deficiency paradigms could function, much as they would a half century later, hand in hand with the assumption that a colorblind social, political, and economic order had emerged, to legitimize inaction against systemic and institutionalized racial injustice. Coleman suggested that the resources schools provided students could not make up for the disadvantages minority children faced in nonschool contexts, but he emphasized not the political economic context—discriminatory housing, employment, and lending policies that locked African American families into overcrowded segregated neighborhoods and low-status jobs—but instead contexts typically invoked in deficiency paradigms. He blamed poor test scores either on "poverty, community attitudes, and low educational level of parents" or, in an implicit though perhaps unintentional attack on community control efforts, on the educational deficiencies of teachers who had themselves been educated in segregated, minority communities.[27]

In addition, Coleman found that a child's academic performance was substantially affected by the class status (and in a society where minority students were disproportionately poor, the racial composition) of her or his classmates. Concentrating minority students in the same schools, he thus suggested, harmed them academically. While integrationists found this conclusion useful, advocates of community-controlled schooling argued that it reinforced the notion that African American educational spaces were inherently inferior and that black children needed white children to learn.[28] In fact, the report's most surprising finding was that although most minority students attended schools where they had less access to resources that seemed related to academic success (such as science labs, libraries, or high-quality curricula), this lack of resources appeared responsible for relatively little variation in achievement when one controlled for socioeconomic status.[29] While Coleman used this evidence to push for school desegregation, the data worried many advocates of compensatory education and community control who feared it would legitimize reduced investment in poor and minority students.[30] Both Coleman's analysis and more recent colorblind discourse, then, depicted racial inequalities as attributes of the communities affected, rather than consequences of the nation's social, political, or economic institutions and structures. It is worth noting, however, that in the current moment, the links between colorblindness and deficiency paradigms are often implicit, while colorblind social theories are tied to the rejection, not the promotion, of school desegregation.

It is difficult to know why Coleman downplayed the causal importance of discrimination and the political and economic contexts in which achievement gaps were situated, but the silver lining (albeit a dangerous one, when viewed with late-twentieth-century colorblindness in mind) is that researchers could use the Coleman Report to support a range of diverse educational policies. In all likelihood a sense of what constituted rigorous quantitative method, what data were at hand, and what the Johnson administration had asked of him shaped Coleman's unwillingness to clarify causality. Coleman expressed concern about the ways his statistical methods could distort and simplify, since, as he noted, while a child was affected by the totality of her educational environment, surveys that reduced "the various aspects of the environment to quantitative measures must inherently miss many elements, both tangible and more subtle, that are relevant to the child." At the same time, he believed that the benefits of "a systematic statistical comparison" were "a lesser evil than the possible observer bias introduced by impressionistic and qualitative studies of school environments."[31] Whatever the cause of his orientation to causality, many scholars used the Coleman Report's ambiguously presented data to promote the egalitarian educational reforms they had already been pursuing. Some joined Coleman in using the report to advocate large-scale integration programs by race and class, using busing if possible. Others ignored the questions Coleman's research raised about community control or compensatory education and cited the report when advocating those approaches. In fact, while historians highlight tensions between advocates of compensatory education (in segregated contexts) and school integration, many who responded to the Coleman Report in places like the *Journal of Negro Education* took a by-any-means-possible approach to securing educational resources for minority youth, calling for both integration and compensatory funding.[32]

CAUSALITY AND CONTEXT IN CRITIQUES OF AND ALTERNATIVES TO THE COLEMAN REPORT

How the Coleman Report functioned to obscure racial power is especially evident when one views this text alongside theories of educational inequality published in the same period by prominent voices on the African American social scientific left. These scholars stand in a long tradition of what we might today call countering colorblindness, since their work centered on the systemic character of racial discrimination and its intersections with racial and socioeconomic oppression. Drawing on the interwar and wartime scholarship of W. E. B. Du Bois, Oliver Cromwell Cox, and the African American Chicago School (including Charles S. Johnson, E. Franklin Frazier, St. Clair Drake, and Horace Cayton) and in tune with 1960s-era African American liberal integrationist, as well as more radical, thinkers, a number of Coleman's scholarly contemporaries theorized educational inequality in ways that exposed the nature, mechanisms, and critical causal importance of systemic and institutionalized racism. Charles H. Thompson, dean of Howard University's School of Education, and Whitney Young, executive director of the Urban League, remained liberal integrationists who focused on expanding antidiscrimination legislation, desegregating schools, and establishing necessary social welfare and economic redevelopment programs for the nation's urban cores. By 1965, psychologist Kenneth Clark, best known for the famous doll studies employed in *Brown v. Board of Education,* increasingly embraced theories of internal colonialism and advocated alternatives to the public schools for African Americans.[33] All three thinkers, nonetheless, found the concept of equality of educational opportunity useful for advocating the version of racial justice they promoted. In contrast to Coleman, however, these scholars called for equality of educational opportunity in ways that emphasized the causal significance of systemic and institutional racism, within and beyond schools.

While recognizing the ambiguity of the term "equality of educational opportunity," Thompson, Young, and Clark embraced the concept and used it to advocate compensatory approaches to racial justice. In his 1968 response to the Coleman Report, Thompson best articulated the difficulty of defining the concept when he asked,

> What does equality of educational opportunity mean? Does it mean the *same* opportunity to get an education? Or does it mean an opportunity to get the *same* education? Or opportunity to be educated up to the level of one's capabilities and future occupational prospects? Or opportunity to learn whatever one needs to develop one's own peculiar potentialities? . . . Does equal educational opportunity mean compensatory education? Is only racially integrated education equal, irrespective of whether lack of integration is intentional or accidental?[34]

Young, in a volume whose title *To Be Equal* also questioned the term's meanings, used the analogy of a track meet where one participant was barefoot and ran on sand to argue that equality of opportunity required more than equality before the law. Since "the scales of justice have been heavily weighted against the Negro for over three hundred years," Young held, they "will not suddenly in 1964 balance themselves by applying equal weights." Shifting metaphors, he further emphasized the need for a compensatory approach to racial equality. Since African Americans were "educationally and economically malnourished and anemic," he held, it was "not 'preferential treatment' but simple decency to provide [them] for a brief period with special vitamins, additional, food, and blood transfusions."[35] Kenneth Clark's *Dark Ghetto,* which emerged from research conducted through Harlem's Youth Opportunities Unlimited (HARYOU), an organization that sought to improve educational and employment opportunities for, and to politically mobilize, Harlem's youth, also emphasized blocked opportunity. Part social science, part reflection on a policy experiment, and part an "anguished cry of the author," Clark's book aimed "to describe and interpret what happens to human beings who are confined to depressed areas and whose access to the normal channels of economic mobility and opportunity is blocked."[36]

While acknowledging that schools seemed to make academic achievement gaps worse the longer students attended them, Clark and Young provided answers to why this was the case that were anything but causally ambiguous. The factors that built segregated cities and schools in the first place—housing, lending, and employment discrimination; white flight; and African American powerlessness to secure needed resources for segregated schools—were the root of the problem. But discrimination within school systems, they argued unequivocally, made these problems much worse.[37]

According to Clark, school-based discrimination was a chief cause of achievement gaps. Of course, African American communities had been protesting biased testing, tracking, disciplinary, and guidance systems; low teacher expectations; curricula that ignored or distorted African American history; and ineffective vocational and remedial programs throughout the twentieth century. These issues were especially pressing in New York City in the mid-1960s, where segregated schools under white leadership generated movements for community control of schooling by African American and Latino parents and educators.[38] Arguing that "the schools are presently damaging the children they exist to help," Clark made clear that segregated school systems where low-status children received a different type of education from those of higher status; where testing, tracking, and low teacher expectations

were the norm; and where racist assumptions were typical generated disparities in academic achievement.[39]

Clark emphasized that a series of racist assumptions—that "there is no
point in 'their' [African American students] having high academic aspirations since 'their' lives will be restricted to menial jobs"; that "Negro children
are inherently inferior in intelligence and therefore cannot be expected to
learn as much or as readily as white children"; and that "all one would do, if
one tried to teach them as if they could learn, would be to develop in them
serious emotional disturbances, frustrations, and anxieties"—rationalized an
inferior type of schooling for poor and minority students. Especially when
institutionalized, these views, which Clark described as "an alibi for educational neglect," were a primary cause of achievement gaps. While Clark did
not avoid damage imagery, he remained clear about causality. "Once one
organizes an educational system where children are placed in tracks or where
certain judgments about their ability determine what is done for them or
how much they are taught or not taught," the psychologist argued, "the horror is that the results seem to justify the assumptions." Still, it was not African
American families or communities, but school systems that "induce and
perpetuate the very pathology which they claim to remedy." In much the
same way that an arm that is bound for a long time would atrophy, Clark put
it chillingly, "children who are treated as if they are uneducable almost invariably become uneducable."[40]

The other way Thompson, Clark, and Young analyzed equality of educational opportunity while exposing racial harm was by situating educational
segregation and inequality in a nuanced and careful analysis of the political,
economic, social, and spatial contexts that produced it. In doing so, they built
on a long tradition in African American political thought of treating the race
issue as a war to be pursued "on many fronts."[41] In contrast to Coleman,
Clark, Young, and Thompson made clear that racist schools were one part of
a multifaceted, interlocking, and complex racial system. Clark situated his
analysis of educational injustice in a robust theory of internal colonialism,
arguing: "The dark ghettos are social, political, educational, and—above
all—economic colonies" whose "inhabitants are subject peoples, victims of
the greed, cruelty, insensitivity, guilt, and fear of their masters."[42] Thompson
emphasized that "the attempt . . . to secure equality of *educational* opportunity by Negroes" could not be separated "from their efforts to obtain equal
opportunity for employment, equal access to decent housing of their choice
. . . equal opportunity to enjoy public accommodations . . . equal opportunity

to participate in the body politic ... [and] equal opportunity to obtain impartial administration of justice."[43] In fact, thinkers who, like Young, turned to questions of educational inequality from a vantage point outside the schools were especially well suited to integrating educational reform into multidimensional plans for racial progress without falling into a trap of educationalization (asking schools to generate social transformations they could not possibly accomplish alone).[44] "Educational and social gaps" were inextricably intertwined, Young maintained, since African Americans, especially in large cities, were "consigned" to insufficient employment, education, health care, and welfare facilities at the same time that they were "confined" to segregated "urban ghettos" with overpriced and "substandard" housing.[45] In *To Be Equal,* Young showed the constructed nature of many of the political and economic patterns that appeared as simple background factors in Coleman's analysis. Young's chapter on housing segregation, for example, carefully chronicled the private, state, and federal policies and practices— restrictive covenants, redlining, blockbusting, and racist violence—that built the landscape of residential segregation that the Coleman Report acknowledged simply in passing.[46]

Young also challenged tendencies toward educationalization by highlighting the dangers of "unilateral or monolithic" solutions to the race problem. One problem was that individuals frequently shifted the blame to others: "The real estate man or the builder says the problem is economic; business, or the employer, says the problem is education; and the educators say that the problem is a matter of housing."[47] And yet, believing firmly that "none of these so-called causes is guilty alone," Young called for a domestic Marshall Plan to address not just segregation but also unemployment, insufficient housing, poor schools, social welfare and health care needs, and the concentration of poverty in the nation's African American central cities concurrently. Exhibiting the capaciousness of opportunity-based egalitarianism, Young presented redistributive policies directed at African American communities as necessary for fair competition. An emergency situation, he suggested, required a "special effort program" to "bring the majority of American Negroes to the point at which they can compete on an equal basis."[48] While he included an impressive set of recommendations for educational reform—which centered on programs to bring the best teachers to segregated urban schools immediately while pressing for desegregation in the long term—Young made clear that "closing the intolerable economic, social, and educational gap that separates the vast majority of us Negro citizens from other Americans" was a multifaceted process that educators could not accomplish alone.[49]

Coleman's statistical study, Clark's "anguished cry" from an "involved observer," and Young's synthesis of available data for an audience of policy-makers and a concerned public all aspired to different types of scientific objectivity. It is difficult to know what array of factors shaped these thinkers' scholarly choices.[50] What is clear, however, is that Clark worried that certain types of scientific research risked simplifying "complex realities" and "subordinating the difficult and multifaceted realities to the constraints of the methods."[51] Clark noted that a friend had once described him, in jest, as a person who "would not permit 'the facts to interfere with the truth,'" and over the years he had appreciated the "profound significance" of this statement. While *Dark Ghetto* included quantitative measures of racial inequality and segregation, the volume also aimed "to move . . . beyond . . . facts that are quantifiable and are computable, and that distort the actual lives of individual human beings into rigid statistics," but missed emotional and experiential truths.[52] Although he was less explicit about how the distinction between "fact" and "truth" related to questions of causality, Clark's careful attention to the perspectives of Harlem's residents, combined with his recognition that all scientific analysis was in some ways interpretive, helps to explain why he was willing to make causal claims about educational racism that Coleman's methods and notions of objectivity led him to avoid.[53]

Ultimately, Clark, Young, and Thompson examined the obstacles advocates of equal educational opportunity faced in ways that avoided victim blaming. Each took on questions of causality directly, suggesting that systemic and institutionalized racial discrimination shaped inequality in educational performance. They also situated educational inequality in wider political, economic, and spatial (not only familial, community, or cultural) contexts. By delineating the racist attitudes and policies generating the educational disparity that Coleman's data chronicled, and by pointing to the inseparability of educational racism and the political economy of metropolitan racial inequality, these scholars used opportunity-based egalitarianism to expose white supremacy in the era of formal equality and to demand racially targeted, distinctly substantive, often redistributive social and educational policies.

Of course, some scholars concerned with racial inequality in education between 1964 and 1974 rejected opportunity-based egalitarianism as a political ideal outright. Some associated with the largely white New Left, including Christopher Jencks, Samuel Bowles, and Herbert Gintis, questioned the centrality of education to notions of equal opportunity by suggesting that education was the wrong lever if one's goal was a social and economic order with less social and economic disparity.[54] Thinkers associated with Black Power movements also critiqued the ideological work of notions of equal educational opportunity. For example, Black Panther leader Huey P. Newton treated the idea as a myth that the reality of exploitative schooling (which he believed directed him and his poor African American peers to "the trash heap of society, where we would have to work long hours for low wages") belied.[55] While less focused on education, Kwame Ture and Charles Hamilton treated the concept of equal opportunity as part of the American ideological system that rationalized white supremacy.[56] In contrast to thinkers like Clark, Young, and Thompson, then, some further left suggested that in a capitalist, white supremacist social order, opportunity-based egalitarianism's primary function was ideological—to rationalize an unequal status quo.

CONCLUSION

The many ways equality of educational opportunity could be interpreted and deployed were evident in years when opportunity-based egalitarianism had not been taken up by advocates of colorblindness but was squarely the language of the antiracist left. Between 1964 and 1974, as scholarship on unequal educational opportunities gained national attention, some research on the topic obscured the causes and contexts of racial oppression, while other work illuminated them. Coleman's *Equality of Educational Opportunity* exposed correlations between inequality in educational resources and student achievement but did not point to the causal importance of systemic or institutionalized discrimination. Despite the volume's utility to advocates of school desegregation, Coleman's rigorous compilation of "the facts" of racial disparity obscured some of "the truth" of racist causality. In contrast, in part because he approached postwar scientism with some skepticism, Clark made clear that racism—pervasive and institutionalized—and not any failure in minority students or communities, caused the inequality in educational opportunity whose consequences Coleman recorded. The other way studies of equal educational opportunity could obscure racial harm was by decontextualizing. The Coleman Report removed educational inequality from the political, economic, and spatial contexts that shaped it. In so doing, the volume helped to naturalize systematic and state-sanctioned discrimination in housing, employment, and the provision of public services, patterns that built the landscape of metropolitan inequality the students Coleman measured navigated every day. In contrast, Clark, Thompson, Young, and many across the African American left situated analyses of educational inequality within the political, economic, social, and spatial contexts generating racial inequality, following a long tradition of civil rights activists in suggesting that the fight against educational injustice must be conceived of as a war "on many fronts."

Later in the century, racial conservatives would divorce calls for equality of educational opportunity from theories of systemic discrimination, attention to white supremacist contexts, *and* integrationist politics. In 1964 Young had worried about this possibility, noting the "great danger that people will quickly and easily read into the establishment of new civil rights laws and into the removal of signs and symbols that so disturb them the confusion that the problem is solved and all is well."[57] Of course, the educational inequalities that Coleman, Clark, Young, and Thompson agreed required urgent action in the mid-1960s continued to fester in the 1990s, as Jonathan Kozol's *Savage Inequalities* (1991), and work on the dismantling of desegregation, made clear.[58] What was new, however, was that by the end of the twentieth century and the beginning of the twenty-first, many writing under the aegis of conservative think tanks like the Heritage Foundation, Hoover Institute, and American Enterprise Institute rationalized retreats from affirmative action and school desegregation using a language of equal educational opportunity that was blind to history, power, and racism.[59] As became clear in the *Parents Involved* decision and in attacks on affirmative action in universities, calls for equal educational opportunity could easily be used to oppose school desegregation or race-conscious college admissions policies.[60] Late-twentieth- and early-twenty-first-century advocates of school choice and vouchers, as well as opponents of teacher tenure, moreover, frequently used the rhetoric of equal educational opportunity to promote conservative reforms, including choice programs that benefited a handful of poor children while making conditions worse for those left behind.[61] Despite the antiracist left's long pursuit of equality of educational opportunity, the concept's basic ambiguity enabled twenty-first-century racial conservatives to devise colorblind interpretations of this ideal, views that convinced many that racial injustice had been "solved and all is well" in just the ways Young feared.

NOTES

1. *Parents Involved in Community Schools v. Seattle School Dist. No. 1,* No. 05–908, 426 F. 3d 1162, and No. 05–915, 416 F. 3d 513 (2017), www.law.cornell .edu/supct/html/05–908.ZO.html.

2. Prudence L. Carter and Kevin G. Welner, eds., *Closing the Opportunity Gap* (New York: Oxford University Press, 2013). For examples from the Brookings Institute and the Progressive Policy Institute, see Linda Darling-Hammond, "Unequal Opportunity: Race and Education," March 1, 1998, www.brookings.edu /research/articles/1998/03/spring-education-darling-hammond; and "The New Progressive Declaration: A Political Philosophy for the Information Age," July 10, 1996, http://web.archive.org/web/20020619202816/http://www.ppionline.org /ppi_ci.cfm?knlgAreaID=128&subsecID=174&contentID=839.

3. This approach to the history of unintended consequences of "equal educational opportunity" is inspired by Alice O'Connor, *Poverty Knowledge: Social Science, Social Policy, and the Poor in Twentieth-Century U.S. History* (Princeton, NJ: Princeton University Press, 2001).

4. For philosophical and historical work on the competing interpretations of equality of educational opportunity see Debra Satz, "Equality, Adequacy, and Education for Citizenship," *Ethics* 117, no. 4 (2007): 626; and Christopher Jencks, "Whom Must We Treat Equally for Educational Opportunity to Be Equal?" *Ethics* 98, no. 3 (1988): 518–33. On equal opportunity more broadly, see J. R. Pole, *The Pursuit of Equality in American History* (Berkeley: University of California Press, 1978); and Frank Dobbin, *Inventing Equal Opportunity* (Princeton, NJ: Princeton University Press, 2009).

5. Gary Gerstle, "The Protean Character of American Liberalism," *American Historical Review* 99, no. 4 (1994): 1043–73; John David Skrentny, *The Ironies of Affirmative Action: Politics, Culture, and Justice in America* (Chicago: University of Chicago Press, 1996), 23; Gareth Davies, *From Opportunity to Entitlement: The Transformation and Decline of Great Society Liberalism* (Lawrence: University Press of Kansas, 1996), 2; Alan Brinkley, *The End of Reform: New Deal Liberalism in Recession and War* (New York: Vintage Books, 1995).

6. Lyndon B. Johnson, "Commencement Address at Howard University: To Fulfill These Rights," June 4, 1965, http://teachingamericanhistory.org/library /document/commencement-address-at-howard-university-to-fulfill-these-rights. On racial liberalism, see Lani Guinier, "From Racial Liberalism to Racial Literacy: *Brown v. Board of Education* and the Interest-Divergence Dilemma," *Journal of American History* 91, no. 1 (2004): 92–118; and Walter A. Jackson, *Gunnar Myrdal and America's Conscience: Social Engineering and Racial Liberalism, 1938–1987* (Chapel Hill: University of North Carolina Press, 1990).

7. On *Brown v. Board,* see John D. Skrentny, *The Minority Rights Revolution* (Cambridge, MA: Harvard University Press, 2002); Martha Minow, *In Brown's Wake: Legacies of America's Educational Landmark* (New York: Oxford University Press, 2010); and Risa L. Goluboff, *The Lost Promise of Civil Rights* (Cambridge,

MA: Harvard University Press, 2007). On the War on Poverty and standards movements, see Michael B. Katz, *The Undeserving Poor: America's Enduring Confrontation with Poverty* (New York: Oxford University Press, 2013), chap. 3; and Harvey Kantor and Robert Lowe, "From New Deal to No Deal: No Child Left Behind and the Devolution of Responsibility for Equal Opportunity," *Harvard Educational Review* 76, no. 4 (2006): 474–502. On busing, compensatory education, community control, and fiscal neutrality, see Jack Dougherty, *More Than One Struggle: The Evolution of Black School Reform in Milwaukee* (Chapel Hill: University of North Carolina Press, 2004); Adam R. Nelson, *The Elusive Ideal: Equal Educational Opportunity and the Federal Role in Boston's Public Schools, 1950–1985* (Chicago: University of Chiago Press, 2005); and James Ryan, *Five Miles Away, a World Apart: One City, Two Schools, and the Story of Educational Opportunity in Modern America* (New York: Oxford University Press, 2010).

8. Kwame Ture and Charles V. Hamilton, *Black Power: The Politics of Liberation*, Kindle ed. (1967; New York: Vintage Books, 1992), chap. 1, para. 38; Michael B. Katz, *Class, Bureaucracy, and Schools: The Illusion of Educational Change in America* (New York: Praeger, 1975) 109, xxii; David Labaree, "The Winning Ways of a Losing Strategy: Educationalizing Social Problems in the U.S.," *Educational Theory* 58, no.4 (2008): 447–60; Kantor and Lowe, "From New Deal to No Deal."

9. Eduardo Bonilla-Silva, *Racism without Racists: Color-Blind Racism and Racial Inequality in Contemporary America* (Lanham, MD: Rowman & Littlefield, 2010), 7; Kimberlé Williams Crenshaw, "Color Blindness, History, and the Law," in *The House That Race Built: Black Americans, U.S. Terrain*, ed. Wahneema H. Lubiano (New York: Pantheon Books, 1997), 285.

10. Bonilla-Silva, *Racism without Racists*, 2, 3.

11. U.S. Department of Labor, Office of Policy, Planning, and Research, *The Negro Family: The Case for National Action* (Washington, DC: U.S. Government Printing Office, 1965) (this document was known as the Moynihan Report, in reference to its principal author, Assistant Secretary of Labor Daniel Patrick Moynihan); James T. Patterson, *Freedom Is Not Enough: The Moynihan Report and America's Struggle over Black Family Life—from LBJ to Obama* (New York: Basic Books, 2010); Katz, *Undeserving Poor*, chaps. 2 and 3; O'Connor, *Poverty Knowledge*, chaps. 8 and 9; and Daryl Michael Scott, *Contempt and Pity: Social Policy and the Image of the Damaged Black Psyche, 1880–1996* (Chapel Hill: University of North Carolina Press, 1997).

12. On scientism, see Mark Solovey, "Riding Natural Scientists' Coattails onto the Endless Frontier: The SSRC and the Quest for Scientific Legitimacy," *Journal of the History of the Behavioral Sciences* 40, no. 4 (2004): 400; Dorothy Ross, *The Origins of American Social Science* (Cambridge: Cambridge University Press, 1991); Sarah E. Igo, *The Averaged America: Surveys, Citizens, and the Making of a Mass Public* (Cambridge, MA: Harvard University Press, 2007), 28; and O'Connor, *Poverty Knowledge*, chap. 1. On quantification, see Theodore M. Porter, *Trust in Numbers: The Pursuit of Objectivity in Science and Public Life* (Princeton, NJ: Princeton University Press, 1995); and Ian Hacking, "Biopower and the Avalanche of Printed Numbers," *Humanities in Society* 5 (1982): 279–95.

13. U.S. Department of Labor, Office of Policy, Planning, and Research, *The Negro Family*.

14. The *Harvard Educational Review* and the *Journal of Negro Education* issued special issues in response to the Coleman Report in 1968. A number of compilation volumes emerged as well, including Harvard Educational Review, ed., *Equal Educational Opportunity* (Cambridge, MA: Harvard University Press, 1969); Frederick Mosteller and Daniel P. Moynihan, eds., *On Equality of Educational Opportunity: Papers Deriving from the Harvard University Faculty Seminar on the Coleman Report* (New York: Random House, 1972).

15. Peter V. Marsden, "The Sociology of James S. Coleman," *Annual Review of Sociology* 31 (2005): 2–3; Sally B. Kilgore, "The Life and Times of James S. Coleman," *Education Next* 16, no. 2 (Spring 2016), http://educationnext.org/life-times-james-s-coleman-school-policy-research.

16. On the expanding federal role in education policy in the 1960s, see Carl Kaestle and Allyssa E. Lodewick, eds., *To Educate a Nation: Federal and National Strategies of School Reform* (Topeka: University Press of Kansas, 2007).

17. Joseph F. Kett, *Merit: The History of a Founding Ideal from the American Revolution to the 21st Century* (Ithaca, NY: Cornell University Press, 2013), 240; James S. Coleman et al., *Equality of Educational Opportunity* (1966; New York: Arno Press, 1979). On the War on Poverty's educational efforts, see Kantor and Lowe, "New Deal to No Deal"; and Katz, *Undeserving Poor,* chap. 3. On stalled progress toward school desegregation before 1968, see Gary Orfield, Susan Eaton, and the Harvard Project on School Desegregation, *Dismantling Desegregation: The Quiet Reversal of Brown v. Board of Education* (New York: New Press, 1996), xiv, 7–8.

18. Coleman et al., *Equality of Educational Opportunity,* 8–9, 3, 21 (quote); James Coleman, "The Concept of Equality of Educational Opportunity," *Harvard Educational Review* 38, no. 1 (1968): 7–22. For an important contemporary critique of the racial, and antidemocratic, implications of using test scores to measure academic achievement, see Lani Guinier, *The Tyranny of the Meritocracy: Democratizing Higher Education in America* (Boston: Beacon Press, 2015).

19. Leah N. Gordon, *From Power to Prejudice: The Rise of Racial Individualism in Midcentury America* (Chicago: University of Chicago Press, 2015), 8–10, 14–15, 66–72; Jean Converse, *Survey Research in the United States: Roots and Emergence, 1890–1960* (Berkeley: University of California Press, 1987).

20. U.S. Department of Labor, Office of Policy, Planning, and Research, *The Negro Family,* 29. On deficiency paradigms in twentieth-century psychology and sociology, see Ellen Herman, *The Romance of American Psychology* (Berkeley: University of California Press, 1995), chaps. 7 and 8; Scott, *Contempt and Pity;* O'Connor, *Poverty Knowledge;* Patterson, *Freedom Is Not Enough.*

21. Walter R. Allen, Susan A. Suh, Gloria Gonzalez, and Joshua Yang, "Qui Bono? Explaining—or Defending—Winners and Losers in the Competition for Educational Achievement," in *White Logic, White Methods: Racism and Methodology,* ed. Tukufu Zuberi and Eduardo Bonilla-Silva (Lanham, MD: Rowman & Littlefield,

2008), 222–23. On the complexities of racial causality, see Paul W. Holland, "Causation and Race," in Zuberi and Bonilla-Silva (eds.), *White Logic, White Methods*, 93–109; and Tukufu Zuberi, *Thicker Than Blood: How Racial Statistics Lie* (Minneapolis: University of Minnesota Press, 2001).

22. Coleman et al., *Equality of Educational Opportunity*, 163, 288–89, 23.

23. Coleman and his colleagues did find some isolated evidence of discrimination in guidance counseling but did not theorize educational discrimination as a chief cause of achievement gaps or inequalities in educational inputs (ibid., 529–32). On African American resistance to educational discrimination, see James Anderson, *The Education of Blacks in the South, 1860–1935* (Chapel Hill: University of North Carolina Press, 1988); and Davidson Douglas, *Jim Crow Moves North: The Battle over Northern School Segregation, 1865–1954* (New York: Cambridge University Press, 2005). For an example of this social scientific tradition, see the Mayor's Commission on Conditions in Harlem (MCCH), *The Negro in Harlem: A Report on Social and Economic Conditions Responsible for the Outbreak of March 19, 1935* (New York: Municipal Archives and Records Center, 1935), chap. 6. For a few (of many) examples from African American autobiographies of the 1960s and 1970s that chronicle systematic discrimination within austensibly integrated, often northern and western, schools, see Huey P. Newton, *Revolutionary Suicide* (1973; New York: Penguin Books, 2009), 50; Lewis Green Robinson, *The Making of a Man: An Autobiography* (Cleveland: Green & Sons, 1970); William Lorenzo Patterson, *The Man Who Cried Genocide: An Autobiography* (New York: International, 1971); and Mwlina Imiri Abubadika, *The Education of Sonny Carson* (New York: Norton, 1972).

24. Coleman et al., *Equality of Educational Opportunity*, 31–32, 36.

25. Thomas Sugrue, *The Origins of the Urban Crisis: Race and Inequality in Postwar Detroit* (Princeton, NJ: Princeton University Press, 1996); George Lipsitz, *How Racism Takes Place* (Philadelphia: Temple University Press, 2011); idem, *The Possessive Investment in Whiteness* (Philadelphia: Temple University Press, 2006).

26. On research on the production of housing segregation from the 1940s and 1950s see Robert Weaver, *The Negro Ghetto* (New York: Russell & Russell, 1948); and St. Clair Drake and Horace Cayton, *Black Metropolis: A Study of Negro Life in a Northern City* (1945; New York: Harper & Row, 1962). On the "urban crisis," see Kenneth Clark and Talcott Parsons, *The Negro American* (Boston: Beacon Press, 1965); and National Advisory Commission on Civil Disorders, *Report of the National Advisory Commission on Civil Disorders* (New York: Bantam Books, 1968), 203, 1.

27. Coleman et al., *Equality of Educational Opportunity*, 21. For a discussion of deficiency paradigms in the status attainment school, see Allen et al., "Qui Bono?" 222–23. On deficiency paradigms, see Bonilla-Silva, *Racism without Racists*. On families, see Coleman, "The Concept of Equality of Educational Opportunity," 22. On teachers, see Coleman, et al. *Equality of Educational Opportunity*, 8. For example, Coleman wrote: "Having a teacher without a college degree indicates an element of disadvantage, but in the concrete situation, a child may be taught by a teacher who

is not only without a degree but who has grown up and received his schooling in the local community, who has never been out of the State, who has a 10th-grade vocabulary, and who shares the local community's attitudes" (ibid.).

28. Coleman et al., *Equality of Educational Opportunity*, 22. On integrationist support for Coleman's peer effects argument, see Charles H. Thompson, "Race and Equality of Educational Opportunity: Defining the Problem," *Journal of Negro Education* 37, no. 3 (1968): 197–98; and Alan B. Wilson, "Social Class and Equal Educational Opportunity," in Harvard Educational Review (ed.), *Equal Educational Opportunity*, 84. On resistance to the negative portrayal of black educational spaces, see Noel Day, "The Case for All-Black Schools," 205–12, and Charles Hamilton, "Race and Education: A Search for Legitimacy," 187–202, in Harvard Educational Review (ed.), *Equal Educational Opportunity*.

29. Coleman et al., *Equality of Educational Opportunity*, 9–10, 21–22.

30. U.S. Commission on Civil Rights, *Racial Isolation in the Public Schools: Summary of a Report* (Washington, DC: Commission on Civil Rights Publications, 1967); Kett, *Merit*, 241. On Pan African and liberation schools in the 1960s and 1970s, see Russell John Rickford, *We Are an African People: Independent Education, Black Power, and the Radical Imagination* (New York: Oxford University Press, 2016). On struggles over community control, see Wendell E. Pritchett, *Brownsville, Brooklyn: Blacks, Jews, and the Changing Face of the Ghetto* (Chicago: University of Chicago Press, 2002); Dougherty, *More Than One Struggle*.

31. Coleman et al., *Equality of Educational Opportunity*, 37.

32. For examples of calls for integration *and* compensatory education, see articles by Charles Thompson, Robert Carter, John H. Fischer, and Edmund W. Gordon and Adelaide Jablonsky, all in the roundtable on the Coleman Report published in the *Journal of Negro Education* 37, no. 3 (1968). On integrationist uses of the Coleman Report, see Thomas W. Mahan, "The Busing of Students for Equal Opportunities," *Journal of Negro Education* 37, no. 3 (1968): 292; "Integrated Schools," *New York Amsterdam News,* Mar. 14, 1970; "Policy Statement," *New York Amsterdam News,* Apr. 4, 1970; "School Desegregation Critics Hit by 24 Social Scientists," *Atlanta Daily World,* Sept. 29, 1978; Bayard Rustin, "The President vs. Desegregation," *New York Amsterdam News,* Apr. 4, 1970. For those who used the Coleman moment to emphasize the need for community control and additional resources for minority schools, see Day, "The Case for All-Black Schools", Hamilton, "Race and Education"; and Kenneth Clark, "Alternative Public School Systems," in Harvard Educational Review (ed.), *Equal Educational Opportunity*.

33. Kenneth B. Clark, *Dark Ghetto: Dilemmas of Social Power* (New York: Harper & Row, 1965) 11; idem, "Alternative Public School Systems," *Harvard Educational Review* 38, no. 1 (1968): 100–113.

34. Thompson, "Race and Equality of Educational Opportunity," 194.

35. Whitney Young, *To Be Equal* (New York: McGraw-Hill, 1964), 23. On the importance of the concept of opportunity in the history of the Urban League, see Touré Reed, *Not Alms but Opportunity: The Urban League and the Politics of Racial Uplift* (Chapel Hill: University of North Carolina Press, 2008).

36. Clark, *Dark Ghetto,* xxii.

37. Ibid., 111–25; Young, *To Be Equal,* chaps. 3 and 5.

38. Douglas, *Jim Crow Moves North,* 163–66, 178–79; Kathryn M. Neckerman, *Schools Betrayed: Roots of Failure in Inner-City Education* (Chicago: University of Chicago Press, 2007); John L. Rury and Shirley A. Hill, *African American Struggle for Secondary Schooling, 1940–1980: Closing the Graduation Gap* (New York: Teachers College Press, 2012), 104–8; Thomas J. Sugrue, *Sweet Land of Liberty: The Forgotten Struggle for Civil Rights in the North* (New York: Random House, 2008), chaps. 6 and 13; Young, *To Be Equal,* 123; Rickford, *We Are an African People;* Pritchett, *Brownsville, Brooklyn.*

39. Clark, *Dark Ghetto,* 124.

40. Ibid., 127–28. This paragraph and the next expand on points I have made in Leah N. Gordon, "If Opportunity Is Not Enough: Coleman and His Critics in the Era of Equality of Results," *History of Education Quarterly* 57, no. 4 (2017): 601–15.

41. For an example of the language of "a war on many fronts" from the 1940s, see Martin D. Jenkins, "Editorial Comment: Education for Racial Understanding," *Journal of Negro Education* 13, no. 3 (1944): 266–67. For examples from the long tradition of social scientific work on "the race problem," see Gordon, *From Power to Prejudice,* chaps. 4 and 5, as well as W. E. B. Du Bois, *The Philadelphia Negro* (1899; New York: Cosmo Classics, 2007); Charles S. Johnson, *The Negro in American Civilization* (New York: Henry Holt, 1930); Gunnar Myrdal, *An American Dilemma* (New York: Harper, 1944); and E. Franklin Frazier, *The Negro in the United States* (New York: Macmillan, 1957).

42. Clark, *Dark Ghetto,* 11.

43. Thompson, "Race and Equality of Educational Opportunity," 191.

44. On educationalization, see Labaree, "Winning Ways"; Kantor and Lowe, "New Deal to No Deal."

45. Young, *To Be Equal,* 10.

46. Ibid., chap. 5.

47. Ibid., 18.

48. Ibid., 26.

49. Ibid., 27. This analysis expands on my discussion of Young's *To Be Equal* in Gordon, "If Opportuity Is Not Enough," 611–12.

50. On Clark's stance as an "involved observer," see Clark, *Dark Ghetto,* xv.

51. Ibid., xix.

52. Ibid., xxiii, xix.

53. Ibid., xxiv.

54. Christopher Jencks, *Inequality: A Reassessment of the Effect of Family and Schooling in America* (New York: Harper & Row, 1972); Samuel Bowles, "Towards Equality," *Harvard Educational Review* 38, no. 1 (1968): 89–99; Samuel Bowles and Herbert Gintis, *Schooling in Capitalist America* (New York: Basic Books, 1976).

55. Newton, *Revolutionary Suicide,* 50. For other examples of African American autobiographers' critiques of opportunity-based egalitarianism (especially in school

curricula), see Robinson, *Making of a Man*, 28–29; Patterson, *Man Who Cried Genocide*, 151, 25, 8; and Abubadika, *Education of Sonny Carson*, 12–13.

56. Ture and Hamilton, *Black Power*.

57. Young, *To Be Equal*, 15.

58. Jonathan Kozol, *Savage Inequalities: Children in America's Schools* (New York: Crown, 1991); Orfield, Eaton, and Harvard Project on School Desegregation, *Dismantling Desegregation*.

59. For a few examples of opportunity-based egalitarianism employed in efforts to defeat affirmative action, see Allan P. Sindler, "Equal Opportunity: On the Policy and Politics of Compensatory Minority Preferences," American Enterprise Institute, 1983, www.aei.org/publication/equal-opportunity-on-the-policy-and-politics-of-compensatory-racial-preferences; Clint Bolick and Mark B. Liedl, "Fulfilling America's Promise: A Civil Rights Strategy for the 1990s," The Heritage Foundation, June 7, 1990, www.heritage.org/research/reports/1990/06/fulfilling-americas-promise-a-civil-rights-strategy-for-the-1990s; Charles T. Canady, "America's Struggle for Racial Equality," Hoover Institution, *Policy Review,* Jan. 1, 1998, www.hoover.org/research/americas-struggle-racial-equality.

60. For an example of the language of equal opportunity being used to oppose affirmative action in college admissions, see D. W. Miller, "Opportunity without Preference," Hoover Institution, *Policy Review,* Nov. 1, 1998, www.hoover.org/research/opportunity-without-preference.

61. For examples of equal opportunity being used to defend vouchers and school choice, see Ken Ardon and Cara Stillings Candal, "Vouchers Offer Equal Opportunity," *Boston Globe,* Aug. 12, 2015, www.educationviews.org/vouchers-offer-equal-opportunity; and Joseph P. Viteritti, "Stacking the Deck for the Poor: The New Politics of School Choice," Brookings Institute, June 1, 1996, www.brookings.edu/articles/stacking-the-deck-for-the-poor-the-new-politics-of-school-choice. On attacks on teacher tenure, see *Vergara v. California* (2014), http://studentsmatter.org/case/vergara/equal-opportunity.

ELEVEN

————

Affirmative Action as Equalizing Opportunity

CHALLENGING THE MYTH OF "PREFERENTIAL TREATMENT"

Luke Charles Harris and Uma Narayan

Editors' Note. We are reprinting this classic essay by Luke Charles Harris and Uma Narayan, which appeared in 1994 at a time of growing critiques that race-based affirmative action programs constituted an unwarranted "preferential treatment" for Black applicants. Harris and Narayan argue that such critiques obscure the vast array of forces that privilege and subsidize white applicants. The deployment of "preferential treatment" in this context demonstrates the ways that colorblind logics have become weaponized in the struggle to sustain the boundaries of U.S. apartheid and racial hierarchy. Indeed, an exhaustive body of contemporary research demonstrates that racialized disparities in education, wealth, income, and employment have changed little in the twenty-five years since this article was first published.

INTRODUCTION

Affirmative action is an issue on which there has been considerable public debate. We think, however, that it is a policy that has often been misunderstood and mischaracterized, not only by those opposed to it, but even by its defenders. In this essay, we intend to describe these misconceptions, to explain why we consider them misconceptions, and to offer a much stronger defense of affirmative action policies than is usually offered. In the first section, we examine and challenge prevalent misrepresentations of the scope of

Originally published as Luke Charles Harris and Uma Narayan, "Affirmative Action and the Myth of Preferential Treatment: A Transformative Critique of the Terms of the Affirmative Action Debate," *Harvard Black Letter Law Journal* 11, no. 1 (1994) 1–36.

affirmative action policies, misconceptions about the groups of people these policies are designed to benefit, and about the benefits they are intended to achieve. In the second section, we address misunderstandings about the rationale for affirmative action policies, and take issue with those who regard affirmative action as bestowing "preferential treatment" on its beneficiaries. We argue that affirmative action policies should be understood as attempts to equalize opportunity for groups of people who confront ongoing forms of institutional discrimination and a lack of equal opportunity. In the third and fourth sections respectively, we take issue with those who defend affirmative action on the grounds that it is a form of compensation, and with those who defend it on the grounds that it promotes diversity and a range of other long-term goals. We argue that such rationales mischaracterize affirmative action as providing justifiable "preferences" to its beneficiaries. In the final section, we argue that the "stigma argument" against affirmative action dissolves if affirmative action is understood as equalizing opportunities, and not as bestowing preferences.

CLARIFYING THE SCOPE
OF AFFIRMATIVE ACTION POLICIES

The debate on affirmative action often misrepresents the scope of these policies in several important ways. The most perturbing of these misrepresentations is the widespread tendency to construe these policies as race-based policies alone, and further, to talk about African Americans as the only racial group they are intended to benefit. This picture of affirmative action policies is, to put it bluntly, false. Even when these policies were first initiated, they were designed to benefit members of other disadvantaged racial minorities besides African Americans. For example, almost two-thirds of the students admitted under the affirmative action program of the Davis Medical School that was challenged in the landmark *Bakke* case in 1978 were Latino or Asian American.[1] Nonetheless, almost the entire public debate surrounding the case discussed it in terms of Blacks and whites only. Even more oddly, the opinions of the Justices of the Supreme Court who considered this case, the majority opinions as well as the dissenting opinions, discussed affirmative action only as benefiting African Americans. In the context of the racial politics of the United States, we believe such a misrepresentation of the scope of these policies is not only false but also dangerous, since it is easier to negatively stereotype these policies when African Americans are viewed as their only beneficiaries.

Thus, even at their inception, when affirmative action policies were predominantly race-based, they were designed to remedy the institutional exclusion of a number of racially disadvantaged groups. In many institutional contexts, they have long since expanded to cover other grounds on which groups of people face discrimination and unequal opportunity. A great many educational institutions, professions, and trades have opened their doors to women as a result of affirmative action, promoting the entry of women into a range of formerly male domains, from law schools to corporations to police departments. This has benefited not only women of color, but many middle-class white women as well. Affirmative action policies in some institutions such as professional schools have also promoted the entry of working-class applicants, including working-class white men, a fact that is seldom discussed and little known. Derrick Bell points out that "special admissions criteria have been expanded to encompass disadvantaged but promising white applicants" and that, for example, the open admissions program of New York's City University system, which was initiated by minority pressure, has benefited even greater numbers of lower-middle-class and working-class whites than Blacks.[2]

We need to remember that the world in which affirmative action policies were initiated was a world where a great many prestigious institutions and professions were almost exclusively enclaves of upper-class white men, and where many of the blue-collar trades were predominantly the preserve of white working-class men. Affirmative action has been crucial in opening up the former to women, to members of racial minorities, and to working-class whites, and in opening up the latter to women and members of racial minorities. We are not arguing that each and every instance of affirmative action does or should consider each category of class, race, and gender. Which factors should be considered depends on the patterns of exclusion within a particular occupation and institution. For instance, affirmative action policies in the blue-collar trades and police and fire departments need to affirmatively promote the entry of women of all races and of minority men, since they were the groups who faced obstacles to entry, not white working-class men. On the other hand, student admissions policies at institutions that used to be women's colleges attended predominantly by white upper-class women, such as our institution, Vassar College, should seek to affirmatively recruit students of color and students from working-class backgrounds, including white working-class men. What we are arguing is that, taken as a whole, affirmative action policies in many contexts have long operated on multiple criteria of inclusion, even though they continue to be portrayed as policies that either only benefit or principally benefit African Americans.

The prevalent failure to consider the range of people that affirmative action policies have benefited breeds a number of misplaced objections to these policies. For instance, many people argue that affirmative action policies should be class-based instead of race-based, since they believe that middle-class African Americans do not need or "deserve" affirmative action.[3] This view is problematic in a number of ways. First, many proponents of this view pose the issue as a choice between race and class, ignoring the fact that affirmative action policies have been both class-based and race-based. Second, proponents of this view believe that middle-class Blacks do not suffer from the effects of discrimination despite substantial evidence to the contrary.

In 1985, independent studies by the Grier Partnership and the Urban League revealed striking disparities in the employment levels of Blacks and whites in Washington, DC, an area that constitutes one of the "best markets" for Blacks.[4] Both studies cite racial discrimination as the major factor that accounts for this difference. A 1991 study by the Urban Institute examined employment practices in the Chicago and Washington, DC, areas by sending equally qualified and identically dressed white and Black applicants to newspaper-advertised positions. The testers were also matched for speech patterns, age, work experience, physical build, and personal characteristics. The study found repeated discrimination that increased with the level of the advertised position, and revealed that whites received job offers three times more often than equally qualified Blacks.[5]

The limitation of the view that middle-class Blacks do not suffer racial discrimination becomes clear when we attend to gender-based affirmative action policies. No one has seriously suggested that the sexism and gender-based discrimination women face in a variety of institutions is merely a product of their class status, or that middle-class status shields white women from these effects. Just as affirmative action policies that attend only to class disadvantages are unlikely to remedy the institutional exclusions faced by women, they would surely fail to remedy race-based exclusions faced by members of several racial minority groups. In short, the effects of gender and race bias would be only partially curtailed by purely class-based policies. Indeed, purely class-based policies would mostly benefit working-class white men, whose race and gender are not the sources of invidious discrimination. As some recent feminist works teach us, we must, therefore, pay particular attention to the interconnected ways in which factors such as class, race, gender, and sexual orientation work together to sustain disparities between different groups of Americans in a variety of institutional and social contexts.

There is, then, no need to pit class against race (or against gender) as the only valid basis for affirmative action. An array of factors that contribute to institutional discrimination, such as class, race, gender, and disability, should be taken into account. When several factors intersect and jointly contribute to a process of discrimination, as in the case of a working-class Black woman, each factor should be considered. When only one aspect of a person's identity adversely affects his or her opportunities in a given setting—for instance, class status in the case of working-class white men, or race in the case of middle-class Black men—then only those factors should be taken into account.

Another prevalent objection to affirmative action policies that seems connected to misunderstanding its actual scope is the objection that truly disadvantaged poor Blacks have not benefited from these policies. The impression that affirmative action benefits only the Black middle class and that few working-class or poor Blacks benefit from these programs is mistaken. The vast majority of Blacks were working class prior to the Civil Rights Era and the promulgation of civil rights laws and affirmative action initiatives. These efforts have combined to play a major role in the creation of the Black middle class that exists today. Sociologist Robert Blauner points out that due to occupational mobility that is in part a product of affirmative action, nearly 25 percent of Black families had incomes of more than $25,000 (in constant dollars) in 1982, compared with 8.7 percent in 1960. Moreover, the proportion of employed Blacks who held middle-class jobs rose from 13.4 percent in 1960 to 37.8 percent in 1981. The number of Black college students rose from 340,000 in 1966 to more than one million in 1982.[6] From sanitation departments to university departments, from the construction industry to corporate America, these programs have helped to open doors once tightly sealed. An empirically accurate assessment of affirmative action policies shows that they have benefited not only poor and working-class Blacks, but poor and working-class people of all races, including some white working-class men and women. White working-class opposition to these policies based on the belief that they are the "victims" of such programs is based on a mistake, a mistake facilitated by discussions of these policies that portray them as only benefiting Blacks.

Lastly, some people also argue against affirmative action on the grounds that it has not solved a host of problems pertaining to poverty in the inner city and the "underclass."[7] It is entirely true that affirmative action has not solved these problems. Neither has it solved problems such as rape, domestic violence, and sexual harassment. However, we do not think these are legitimate objections, since they more obviously overinflate the scope of what these policies were intended to accomplish. Affirmative action policies cannot be, and were not intended to be, a magic solution to all our social problems. Indeed, no single policy can solve every social problem we confront. Their purpose is a limited though important one, to partially counter the ways in which factors such as class, race, gender, and disabilities function in our society to impede equal access and opportunity, thereby promoting greater inclusion of diverse Americans in a range of institutions and occupations. They have clearly succeeded in this goal, and should not be condemned for failing to solve problems they were not intended to solve.

REENVISIONING THE RATIONALE FOR AFFIRMATIVE ACTION: FROM "PREFERENTIAL TREATMENT" TO "EQUAL OPPORTUNITY"

We believe that many mistaken views about affirmative action result from misunderstandings about the justification or rationale for such policies. Unfortunately, the debate on affirmative action has largely been a dialogue between two broadly characterizable positions. On the one hand, its critics describe it as a form of "reverse discrimination" that bestows "undeserved preferences" on its beneficiaries. On the other hand, its defenders continue to characterize the policy as "preferential treatment" but argue that these preferences are justified, either as "compensation" or on grounds of "social utility." Few question the assumption that affirmative action involves the "bestowal of preferences" or challenge the premise that it marks a sudden deviation from a system that, until its advent, operated strictly and clearly on the basis of merit. Setting out a view of affirmative action that rejects these ideas is our central task here.

In our view, affirmative action is not a matter of affording "preferential treatment" to its beneficiaries. Our position is that affirmative action is best understood as an attempt to promote equality of opportunity in a social context marked by pervasive inequalities, one in which many institutional criteria and practices work to impede a fair assessment of the capabilities of those who are working class, women, or people of color. Thus, affirmative action is an attempt to equalize opportunity for people who continue to face institutional obstacles to equal consideration and equal treatment. These obstacles include not only continuing forms of blatant discrimination, but, more importantly, a variety of subtle institutional criteria and practices that unwarrantedly circumscribe mobility in contemporary America. These criteria and practices are often not deliberately designed to discriminate and exclude. The fact remains, however, that they nevertheless function to do so, as our subsequent examples demonstrate. Thus, in countering such forms of discrimination, affirmative action policies attempt only to "level the playing field." They do not "bestow preferences" on their beneficiaries. Rather, they attempt to undo the effects of institutional practices and criteria that, however unintentionally, amount in effect to "preferential treatment" for whites.

Those who believe that affirmative action constitutes "preferential treatment" assume (a) that the criteria and procedures generally used for admissions and hiring are neutral indicators of "merit," unaffected by factors such as class, race, or gender, and (b) that such criteria are fairly and impartially applied to all individuals at each of the stages of the selection process. In the rest of this section, we will try to show why those two assumptions are seriously open to question.

Although test scores on standardized tests are often "taken as absolute by both the public and the institutions that use the scores in decision-making," there is ample evidence that they do not predict equally well for men and women. A study of three college admissions tests (the SAT, the PSAT/NMSQT, and the ACT) reveals that although women consistently earn better high school and college grades, they receive lower scores on all three tests. Phyllis Rosser argues that "if the SAT predicted equally well for both sexes, girls would score about 20 points higher than the boys, not 61 points lower."[8] Standardized test scores adversely affect women's chances for admission to colleges and universities, their chances for scholarships, and entry into "gifted" programs, as well as their academic self-perceptions. Similarly, James Crouse and Dale Trusheim argue, on the basis of statistical evidence, that the scores are not very useful indicators for helping to "admit black applicants who would succeed and reject applicants who would fail."[9]

The literature on such standardized tests demonstrates that they are often inaccurate indicators even with respect to their limited stated objective of predicting students' first-year grades in college and professional school. Yet they are often used as if they measured a person's overall intelligence and foretold long-term success in educational institutions and professional life. As a result of these unsupported beliefs, affirmative action policies that depart from strict considerations of these test scores are often taken to constitute the strongest evidence for institutional deviation from standards of merit, and constitutive elements of the "preference" thought to be awarded to women and minority applicants.

There are also many other examples of established rules, practices, and policies of institutions that, no matter how benign their intention, have the effect of discriminating against the members of relatively marginalized groups. For instance, word-of-mouth recruitment where the existing labor pool is predominantly white male reduces the chances of women or people of color applying for the jobs in question, as do unions that influence or control in hiring for well-paid jobs in the construction, transportation, and printing industries when they recruit through personal contacts. A 1990 study reports that over 80 percent of executives find their jobs through networking, and that about 86 percent of available jobs do not appear in the classifieds.[10] "Last hired, first fired" rules make more recently hired women and minorities more susceptible to layoffs. The "old boy network" that results from years of social and business contacts among white men, as well as racially or sexually segregated country clubs or social organizations, often paid for by employers, also have discriminatory impacts on women and minorities. Furthermore, stereotyped beliefs about women and minorities often justify hiring them for low-level, low-paying jobs, regardless of their qualifications for higher-level jobs.[11]

Indeed, some empirical studies show that many Black candidates for jobs are rated more negatively than white candidates with identical credentials. Other studies demonstrate that the same resume with a woman's name on it receives a significantly lower rating than when it has a man's name on it, showing that gender bias operates even when there is no direct contact with the persons evaluated. Still other problematic practices include evaluations where subjective assessments of factors such as "fitting in," "personality," and "self-confidence" serve class, race, and gender prejudice.

Personal interviews, job evaluations, and recommendations all have an inescapable subjective element that often works in the favor of better-off white men. As Lawrence A. Blum writes:

> Persons can fail to be judged purely on ability because they have not gone to
> certain colleges or professional schools, because they do not know the right

people, because they do not present themselves in a certain way. And, again, sometimes this sort of discrimination takes place without either those doing the discriminating or those being discriminated against realizing it.[12]

Often these denials of equal opportunity have a lot to do with class background, as well as race or sex, or with a combination of these.

Interview processes that precede being selected or hired are often not as "neutral" as assumed. A two-step experiment done at Princeton University began with white undergraduates interviewing both white and Black job applicants. Unknown to the interviewers, the applicants in the first stage of the experiment were all confederates of the experimenters and were trained to behave consistently from interview to interview. This study reported that interviewers spent less time with Black applicants and were less friendly and outgoing than with the white applicants. In the second stage of the experiment, confederates of the experimenters were trained to approximate the two styles of interviewing observed during the first stage of the study when they interviewed two groups of white applicants. A panel of judges who reviewed tapes of these interviews reported that white applicants subjected to the style previously accorded Blacks performed noticeably worse in the interviews than other white applicants. In this respect, there is also substantial evidence that women are asked inappropriate questions and subjected to discrimination in interviews.

None of the discriminatory institutional structures and practices we have detailed above necessarily involve conscious antipathy toward women and minorities or the operation of conscious sexist or racist stereotypes. Some discriminatory structures and practices involve unconscious stereotypes at work, from which women and people of color are hardly immune in their evaluations of other women and minorities. Many of the examples we discuss involve practices central to hiring and promotion that work to disadvantage many marginalized Americans even when all persons involved sincerely believe themselves to be fair and impartial. Because the processes of getting through an educational program, or being hired, retained, and promoted in a job, involve the possibility, for example, of women and minority applicants being subject to a variety of such practices, it seems likely that few, if any, women or people of color are apt to escape the cumulative adverse effects of these practices. In the context of these structures and practices that systematically disadvantage some Americans, it would be naive, at best, to believe that our society is a well-functioning meritocracy.

The problem is far more complicated than what is captured by the common perspective that working-class people, women, and minorities have generally not had equal advantages and opportunities to acquire qualifications that are on par with those of their better-off, white male counterparts, and so we should compensate them by awarding them preferences even though they are less well-qualified. Their qualifications, in fact, tend to be undervalued and underappraised in many institutional contexts. Moreover, many of the criteria that are unquestioningly taken to be important impartial indicators of people's competencies, merit, and potential, such as test scores, not only fail to be precise measurements of these qualities, but systematically stigmatize these individuals within institutions in which these tests function as important criteria of admission.

We do not, however, wish to deny that factors such as class, race, and gender often impede persons from acquiring qualifications. Numerous studies, for instance, have shown that Black school districts received less funding and inferior educational resources compared with similar white districts, often as a result of decision-making by whites.[13] There is also increasing evidence of disadvantaging practices in the precollege advising offered to minority students. Evidence suggests that teachers often interpret linguistic and cultural differences as indications of low potential or a lack of academic interests on the part of minority students; and guidance counselors often steer female and minority students away from "hard" subjects, such as mathematics and science, which are often paths to high-paying jobs.

In such contexts, even if the criteria used to determine admission and hiring were otherwise unproblematic, it is not at all clear that taking them simply "at face value" would fairly or accurately gauge the talents and potential of disparate individuals. When some candidates have to overcome severe educational and social obstacles that others do not, similarity of credentials may well amount to a significant difference in talent and potential. Thus, treating identical credentials as signs of identical capabilities and effort may, under prevailing conditions of inequality, significantly devalue the worth of credentials obtained in the teeth of such obstacles. We would argue that individuals who obtained their credentials in the face of considerable obstacles are likely to do better than those who have similar or even somewhat better credentials obtained without coping with such obstacles, especially over a period of years, where they have opportunities to remedy their burdens. Affirmative action policies with respect to admissions and hiring recruit individuals for positions where "success" depends on the nature of one's performance over several years. Such recruitment should rightly concern itself with a person's evidenced potential for success rather than simply assess what their capabilities appear to be, based on the comparison of credentials acquired by individuals under distinctly different circumstances.

We are not arguing, however, that affirmative action policies are, or can be, magical formulas that help us determine with perfect precision in every case the exact weights that must be accorded a person's class background, gender, and minority status so as to afford him or her perfect equality of opportunity. Particular institutions must use practical wisdom and good-faith efforts to determine the exact measures that they will undertake to promote equality within their frameworks, as well as monitor and periodically reassess the parameters and scope of their institutional policies. Nor do we wish to deny that some persons recruited as a result of affirmative action policies might turn out to be incompetent or demonstrate significant limitations in their ability to meet requirements. After all, the same incompetencies and limitations are manifested by some who are recruited by "regular" channels. No recruitment policies are immune to these problems. What we do argue is that in contexts where, for example, class, race, and gender operate to impede equality of opportunity, affirmative action policies have enabled many talented and promising individuals to have their talent and promise more fairly evaluated by the institutions in question than would otherwise have been the case.

THE LIMITATIONS OF THE COMPENSATION RATIONALE FOR AFFIRMATIVE ACTION

Affirmative action has frequently been defended on the grounds that it provides preferential treatment to members of marginalized groups as reparation or compensation for injustices they have suffered. The term "compensation" draws heavily on the model of recompense or payment of damages that is found in tort law. In the context of tort remedies, the particular agent who is responsible for injuring another compensates the specific person injured by paying what is judged to be an appropriate sum of money for the actual extent of the injury he or she has caused. This rationale tends to raise a number of questions precisely at those points where affirmative action policies seem to differ from the practice of tort-based compensation. Some argue that those who are "paying the price" for affirmative action have no direct responsibility for any harms or injuries suffered by any of its beneficiaries. Others raise the question of why the specific form of payment involved, construed as preferences for jobs or preferential entry to educational institutions, is the appropriate form of compensation, rather than monetary awards. Such critics reinforce these arguments by pointing out that affirmative action policies do not seem to be the most equitable form of compensation because those who have been most injured are probably not the ones receiving the compensation, since their injuries have resulted in their not having "the qualifications even to be considered."

There have been attempts to defend the compensation rationale against these objections.[14] However, we believe that it remains an inadequate and problematic rationale for affirmative action. In suggesting that affirmative action compensates individuals for damage done by phenomena such as racism or sexism, this rationale implies that the problem is one of "damaged individuals" rather than a problem due to structures, practices, and institutional criteria within our institutions that continue to impede a fair assessment of the capabilities of some Americans. We have argued in the previous section that there is ample evidence to show that many prevalent criteria and procedures do not fairly gauge the capabilities of members of marginalized groups. The compensation model, however, does not question the normative criteria used by our institutions or encourage critical reflection about the processes of assessment used to determine these "qualifications"; as a result, it fails to question the view that affirmative action involves "preferential treatment." We consider this a serious weakness, since it does not challenge the view that affirmative action policies promote the entry of "less qualified" individuals. Instead, it merely insists that "preferences" bestowed on less qualified individuals are justified as a form of compensation.

The compensation literature also conflates the rationale for race- and gender-based affirmative action policies with that for policies that promote institutional access for veterans. Policies based on veteran status may indeed be understood as compensation for their risks, efforts, and injuries sustained in the service of the nation, which may also have impeded or detracted from their employment or educational goals. However, it does not necessarily follow that a rationale that works best to explain one type of special assistance program works equally well to explain all others. In this respect, not only is a person's veteran status usually less visible than their race or gender, but veteran status per se does not very often render persons targets of prejudice and institutional discrimination.

THE LIMITATIONS OF THE SOCIAL UTILITY RATIONALES FOR AFFIRMATIVE ACTION

We believe that our rationale for affirmative action is stronger than the "social utility" arguments that have been proffered in its defense. To illuminate our perspective, we will focus on one of the best known of such defenses, that offered by Ronald Dworkin.[15] Dworkin understands affirmative action to involve "preferential treatment" and discusses affirmative action policies only as pertaining to Blacks. His argument can be summarized as follows. First, he argues that affirmative action policies that "give preferences" to minority candidates do not violate the "right to equal treatment" or the "right to equal consideration and respect" of white male applicants. Dworkin argues that these rights would be violated if a white male suffers disadvantage when competing with Blacks because his race is "the object of prejudice or contempt," but that this is not the case with affirmative action policies. Second, Dworkin argues that the "costs" that white male applicants suffer as a result of affirmative action policies are justified because such policies promote several beneficial social ends, the most important of which is their long-term impact in making us a less race-conscious society. Other beneficial social ends that Dworkin argues are served by affirmative action include providing role models for Blacks, providing more professionals such as doctors and lawyers willing to serve the Black community, reducing the sense of frustration and injustice in the Black community, and alleviating social tensions along racial lines. Whereas Dworkin focuses on the negative claim that affirmative action policies do not violate the right to treatment as an equal, or the right to equal consideration and respect for the interests of white men, we make the positive and much stronger claim that affirmative action policies are justified because they are necessary to ensure the right to treatment as an equal for the members of marginalized groups, in a social context where a variety of social structures and institutional practices conspire to deny their interests equal consideration and respect. While we have no quarrel with Dworkin's claims about the social benefits of affirmative action, we do not rest our case for affirmative action on such consequentialist arguments about its long-term effects, arguments that are notoriously vulnerable to counterarguments that project a set of more negative consequences as the long-term results. Since we do not believe that affirmative action bestows "preferential treatment" on its beneficiaries or imposes "costs" on white male applicants, as Dworkin does, we do not need to rely on Dworkin-type arguments that the long-term social "benefits" of these "preferences" justify imposing these "costs."

Our rationale for affirmative action also differs from social utility arguments that justify these policies on the ground that they contribute to a greater diversity of backgrounds and perspectives within academic institutions, thereby enhancing the learning process. First, "diversity" on a campus can be enhanced by admitting people from a wide variety of backgrounds and with a wide range of special talents. A commitment to "diversity" per se could justify policies that promoted the recruitment of students from abroad, from remote areas of the country, and those with artistic skills or unusual interests. While there might well be institutional reasons for, and benefits from, promoting diversity in these forms, none of these students need necessarily have suffered from the systematic effects of social and institutional forms of discrimination within the United States. Thus, many students who would provide "diversity" would not qualify for affirmative action, even though there might be other reasons for admitting them. Second, while admitting greater numbers of working-class people, women, and minorities into institutions in which they are significantly underrepresented would also increase institutional diversity in meaningful ways, we see such beneficial consequences as supplemental benefits of affirmative action rather than its central goal.

While we believe affirmative action has in fact had beneficial consequences in making many areas of work and education more integrated along class, race, and gender lines, we see these consequences as the result of treating people more equally, and not as benefits that have resulted from "imposing costs" on nonbeneficiaries of affirmative action. Our central objection to both the "compensation" and "social utility" rationales for affirmative action is that neither questions the related assumptions that affirmative action "bestows preferences" on some and imposes "costs" on others. In short, we insist that affirmative action policies that attempt to foster equal treatment do not constitute "preferential treatment" and that such attempts to undo the effects of institutional practices and criteria that privilege the capacities of some people over others are not "costs" that need to be justified by pointing to the "benefits" of the long-term consequences of these policies.

Affirmative action has been criticized on the grounds that it "stigmatizes" its participants because both they themselves as well as others regard the beneficiaries of affirmative action as "less qualified" than nonbeneficiaries. Affirmative action policies are also criticized on the grounds that they cause resentment among the "more qualified" people who are denied entry as a result of these policies and thereby forced to pay its "costs." We believe that both criticisms are often the result of failing to accurately understand the rationale for affirmative action. Furthermore, we believe that these arguments about "stigma" and "resentment" are unwittingly reinforced by those who defend affirmative action on the basis of the "compensation "or "social utility" arguments, since these arguments fail to challenge the claims that affirmative action promotes the "less qualified" and imposes "costs" on those who are "better qualified" for the positions in question. Instead they merely insist that such "preferences" and "costs" are justified either as "compensation" or as a means to promote a range of long-term goals.

Our view of affirmative action as a policy to foster equality of opportunity rejects the claim that its beneficiaries are "less qualified." We argue instead that there is good reason to believe that their capabilities are not accurately gauged or fairly evaluated by the prevailing selection criteria and procedures. Without affirmative action policies, as we see it, those who are their beneficiaries would not be given equal consideration or have their qualifications and capabilities assessed fairly. Given our rationale for affirmative action, the "stigma problem" disappears since we see nothing demeaning or stigmatizing in being given equal consideration or in being treated as fairly as one's peers. Thus, from our perspective, not only do the beneficiaries of affirmative action have no valid reason to feel "inferior," the nonbeneficiaries of it have no good reason to regard themselves as "more qualified" than affirmative action beneficiaries.

Our account of affirmative action, then, also helps to illuminate why resentment by nonbeneficiaries is unjustified. We believe that such resentment is based on the false belief that the "better qualified" are being burdened by having to bear the "costs" of "preferences" bestowed on others, a sentiment reinforced by views that see affirmative action as preferential treatment. Since we do not believe affirmative action bestows preferences, we do not think that affirmative action imposes any corresponding costs or burdens on nonbeneficiaries. On the contrary, we believe that it should be understood as an attempt to counteract a variety of procedures and criteria that work to unfairly privilege those who are middle class, white, and male. We believe that the only costs to nonbeneficiaries that result from affirmative action policies are the loss of these privileges, privileges that are the results of a lack of fairness and opportunity for others.

Neither affirmative action policies, nor fair and judicious assessment of the performance of their various beneficiaries, are the central causes of the prevailing negative stereotypes about the competencies of women, working-class people, or people of color. Critiques of affirmative action along these lines often suggest that the world was once a fairer place, which has only recently become tainted with new stereotypes about the capabilities of women or members of racial minorities as a result of affirmative action policies infusing large numbers of its "underqualified" and "unqualified" beneficiaries into American institutions. Such critiques suggest that affirmative action has exacerbated the old negative stereotypes about women and people of color which had begun to wane. In fact, however, it was racist and sexist stereotypes, and the institutional practices that worked to perpetuate and reinforce them, that made affirmative action policies necessary.

One of the ways in which racist and sexist stereotypes function is to obstruct our ability to see women and people of color as individuals. Thus, an individual woman or minority person's inadequacies can be generalized and seen as signs of the incompetence of whole groups, whereas the failures of white men remain personal limitations. Moreover, success stories involving women or minorities often tend to be interpreted as exceptions, and not as examples of the capabilities of women or people of color generally.[16] Much of the discourse on affirmative action reveals this pattern: instances of women and people of color who have failed to meet the requirements of a profession or institution are taken to be testimony to the grand failure of affirmative action policies and the incompetence of the bulk of its beneficiaries. No nuanced account is given of the possible causes of these failures. The fact that no set of admissions or promotion criteria can guarantee that everyone who manifests potential for success will in fact succeed gets lost amid anxious rumors of incompetence. Seldom dwelt upon are the numerous stories of those who have succeeded as a result of affirmative action.

As far back as the debate over the admission of minority applicants to the Davis Medical School in the *Bakke* case, little attention was paid to the success stories of people admitted as a result of affirmative action. Yet four years after the admission of the sixteen "affirmative action" candidates to Davis in

1978, thirteen had graduated in good standing, several had excelled, and one of their number had earned the school's most prestigious senior class award for "the qualities most likely to produce an outstanding physician." Much of the debate in 1978, however, presumed, just as it does now, that affirmative action's departure from the traditional admissions criteria represented a departure from objective criteria of "excellence."

There are a number of additional troublesome assumptions that underlie the stigma arguments. For example, for decades, almost all of our elite institutions and professions, as well as many blue collar career paths, were domains that permitted entry to a very small, and extremely privileged, segment of the population. Yet there were millions of equally talented individuals who, because they were working class, or women, or members of racial minority groups, were deprived of the chances to develop their talents and capabilities, which may well have exceeded those of many of their privileged white male counterparts. Rarely, if ever, in all these decades, have privileged white men who benefited from such "undeserved privileges" ever castigated themselves or publicly expressed the feeling that they were not "really talented" or "really deserving of their positions" because they had acquired them in a context that had eliminated most of their fellow citizens, including the female members of their own families, from the competitive pool. We are unaware of a body of literature from these individuals filled with anxiety and self-doubt about their capabilities and merit. Indeed, one of the unnerving effects of privilege is that it permits the privileged to feel so entitled to their privileges that they often fail to see them as privileges at all. In such a setting, it is more than a little ironic that the beneficiaries of affirmative action programs designed to counteract the effect of institutional discrimination are now expected to wear the hair-shirt of "stigma."

Many who complain about the preferential treatment they believe affirmative action accords to women and minorities in academia assume that everyone other than its beneficiaries is admitted purely as a result of merit. Yet paradoxically, policies that favor relatives of alumni and children of faculty members or donors to the university have not created a storm of legal or social controversy, or even been objected to. Perhaps this is because such policies tend to benefit predominantly white middle-class individuals. Our point is not simply to claim, however, that people who accept preferential policies that benefit middle-class whites are often outraged by "preferences" rooted in affirmative action policies. Our point is in fact a much stronger one that hinges on the profound differences between affirmative action and these other policies. Policies that favor children of alumni or donors are policies that may serve some useful goals for a particular institution, but they are genuinely "favors" or "preferences" with respect to the individuals admitted, in that such policies are in no way intended to equalize the opportunities of those thus admitted. We therefore insist on a conceptual distinction between affirmative action and policies that are genuinely tantamount to bestowing preferences.

Our point, however, is not to endorse a "purely meritocratic society" as the ideal society, but rather to highlight the reality that many existing institutional structures not only fail to function as pure meritocracies, but also serve to systematically disadvantage whole groups of people, including working-class people, women, and people of color. To those strongly committed to traditional meritocratic ideals, we suggest that when close attention is paid to the systematically disadvantaging effects of many institutional procedures, they may have reason to see affirmative action policies as conducive to their ideal rather than as deviations from it.

CONCLUSION

The intellectual confusion surrounding affirmative action transcends ideological categories. Critics and supporters of all political stripes have underestimated the significance of these policies, collaborated in equating affirmative action with "preferential treatment," and permitted important assumptions about how institutions function to lie unchallenged. We argue that affirmative action policies do not involve preferential treatment but should rather be understood as attempts to promote fairness, equality, and full citizenship by affording members of marginalized groups a fair chance to enter significant social institutions.

The fact that formal legal equality seems commonplace and obviously justified to many today should not obscure how recently formal equality has been a reality for many nor the struggles it took to make it a reality. More importantly, we should not imagine that the achievement of formal legal equality erased the consequences of centuries of inequality, making the promise of equality and full citizenship an immediate reality for those previously excluded. The institutional consequences of such historically group-based exclusions in significant domains of occupational and social life still remain. Class, race, and gender, for example, continue to deprive people of the opportunities to participate in numerous forms of association and work that are crucial to the development of talents and capabilities that enable people to contribute meaningfully to, and benefit from, the collective possibilities of national life.

Only since the latter part of the nineteenth century and the early decades of the twentieth century have some democratic political communities, such as the United States, sought to embrace the members of certain marginalized groups they had once excluded from the rights and privileges of citizenship. Only in the latter part of the twentieth century has there dawned the recognition that laws and policies that promote formal equality do not necessarily ensure substantive equality or genuine equal opportunity for all citizens to participate in all spheres of American life. In this respect, affirmative action policies are a significant historic achievement, for they constitute an attempt to transform our legacy of unequal treatment with respect to certain marginalized groups of Americans. They symbolize our political commitment to ensuring substantive participation in all domains of life for various groups of our diverse citizenry. Thus, we believe that affirmative action programs warrant a much more favorable evaluation, both as a historic achievement and in terms of their positive effects within contemporary American institutions, than they are usually accorded.

NOTES

1. *Regents of University of California v. Bakke,* 438 U.S. 265 (1978), https://supreme.justia.com/cases/federal/us/438/265.

2. Derrick A. Bell, "Bakke, Minority Admissions, and the Usual Price of Racial Remedies," *California Law Review* 67, no. 1 (Jan. 1979) 3–19.

3. Stephen L. Carter, *Reflections of an Affirmative Action Baby* (New York: Basic Books, 1991).

4. Rudolf A. Pyatt Jr., "Significant Job Studies," *Washington Post,* Apr. 30, 1985, D1–D2, cited in Tom Beauchamp, "Goals and Quotas in Hiring and Promotion," in *Ethical Theory and Business,* 4th ed., ed. Tom Beauchamp and Norman E. Bowie (Englewood Cliffs, NJ: Prentice Hall, 1993), 384.

5. Margery Austin Turner, Michael Fix, and Raymond J. Struyk, *Opportunities Denied, Opportunities Diminished: Racial Discrimination in Hiring* (Washington, DC: Urban Institute Press, 1991), 91–99.

6. Robert Blauner, *Black Lives, White Lives: Three Decades of Race Relations* (Berkeley: University of California Press, 1989).

7. Shelby Steele, *The Content of Our Character: A New Vision of Race in America* (New York: St. Martin's Press, 1990).

8. Phyllis Rosser, *Sex Bias in College Admissions Tests: Why Women Lose Out,* 2nd ed. (Cambridge, MA: National Center for Fair and Open Testing, 1987).

9. James Crouse and Dale Trusheim, *The Case against the SAT* (Chicago: University of Chicago Press, 1988).

10. Gertrude Ezorsky, *Racism and Justice: The Case for Affirmative Action* (Ithaca, NY: Cornell University Press, 1991), 72.

11. Rosabeth Moss Kanter and Barry A. Stein, "Making a Life at the Bottom," in Kanter and Stein, *Life in Organizations: Workplaces as People Experience Them* (New York: Basic Books, 1979), 176–90.

12. Lawrence A. Blum, "Opportunity and Equality of Opportunity," *Public Affairs Quarterly* 2, no. 4 (1988): 1–18.

13. Jonathan Kozol, *Savage Inequalities: Children in America's Schools* (New York: Broadway Paperbacks, 1991); Carl V. Harris, "Stability and Change in Discrimination against Black Public Schools: Birmingham, Alabama 1871–1931," *Journal of Southern History* 51, no. 3 (1985) 375–416; Harold M. Baron, "Race and Status in School Spending: Chicago, 1961–1966," *Journal of Human Resources* (1971): 3–24; Jesse Burkhead, Thomas G. Fox, and John W. Holland, *Input and Output in Large City High Schools,* vol. 2 (Syracuse, NY: Syracuse University Press, 1967); Robert L. Green and Louis J. Hofmann, "A Case Study of the Effects of Educational Deprivation on Southern Rural Negro Children," *Journal of Negro Education* 34, no. 3 (1965): 327–41.

14. Bernard R. Boxhill, "The Morality of Preferential Hiring," *Philosophy and Public Affairs* 7 (1978): 246–68.

15. Ronald Dworkin, "Why Bakke Has No Case," in *Today's Moral Problems,* ed. Richard Wasserstrom (New York: Macmillan, 1985), 138, 145–46. See also the following works by Dworkin: "Affirming Affirmative Action," *New York Review of Books,* Oct. 22, 1998 (a review of William G. Bowen and Derek Bok, *The Shape of the River: Long-Term Consequences of Considering Race in College and University Admissions,* Princeton University Press); "Is Affirmative Action Doomed?" *New York Review of Books,* Nov. 5, 1998; "Affirmative Action: Is It Fair?" *Journal of Blacks in Higher Education,* no. 28 (Summer 2000): 79–88; "Race and the Uses of Law," *New York Times,* Apr. 13, 2001; and *Sovereign Virtue: The Theory and Practice of Equality* (Cambridge, MA: Harvard University Press, 2000).

16. Luke Charles Harris, "Affirmative Action and the White Backlash. Notes from a Child of Apartheid," in *Picturing Us: African American Identity in Photography,* ed. Deborah Willis (New York: New Press, 1994).

PART THREE

———

Resistance and Transformation

The final section of the volume considers concepts, strategies, and approaches to abolish colorblindness by renovating and reimagining disciplines, institutions, and social relations. The contributors explore the relationship between knowledge production within the academy and wider forms of political and social struggle. These essays engage insights and analyses produced within a variety of "intellectual undergrounds" to uncover how race is made and contested within multiple institutional locations and contexts.[1]

In the section's first essay, Glenn Adams and Phia Salter explain how concepts in social psychology related to love, family, independence, personal development, and socialization that seem race neutral are in fact deeply dependent on racial logics. They characterize colorblindness memorably as "the cultivated disability to see the racialization of everyday life" and describe a series of interventions related to research design that can permit social psychologists to interrogate the terms of colorblindness.

In a similar vein, sociologist Aileen Moreton-Robinson shows that the broad canon of Western thought, or what she describes as the "knowledges produced by disciplines dedicated to the sciences of 'man,'" serves to discipline "the rights claims of Indigenous people." Here, the very theoretical space necessary to conceptualize Indigenous political and social life becomes attenuated by the dominant assumptions of anthropology, political science, Australian studies, and even Aboriginal studies. Moreton-Robinson argues for a new research agenda that could "investigate how White possession functions through a discourse of rights within the disciplines of law, political science, history, and anthropology on which Australian studies and Indigenous studies have relied since their formation, and examine how White possession manifests in regulatory mechanisms including legal decisions, government policy, and legislation."

The last three essays in the section investigate how countering colorblindness requires new pedagogical practices and principles. Felice Blake considers deployments of colorblindness in contemporary literary studies in relationship to a broader crisis in the humanities, evident in the relentless demand for humanists to prove the "value" of their teaching and scholarship. The corporatization of higher education has paralleled the removal of humanities-based inquiries into issues now deemed to be principally under the purview of the social sciences—discrimination, inequality, and their remedies. Blake exhumes a long history of antiracist literary and cultural study that has been deeply engaged with and critical of the social apparatus, a genealogy that will be vital to the remaking of the humanities. Like Blake, Paula Ioanide explains why the classroom continues to serve as a central site in which legacies of domination can become transformed into new imaginaries of justice. Race-and-gender-conscious frames require a radical transformation in the ways that students who identify as white construct their identities, self-perceptions, and moral bearings. Ioanide uses Race and Sexual Politics, an undergraduate course taught over seven years, as a site of inquiry, to explore the ways that race-and-gender-conscious pedagogies capable of creating "new imaginaries of justice" prevent students from evading "the moral and political responsibility fatally coupled with white hetero-patriarchal advantage" while cultivating "the desire for an aspirational yet ever imperfect praxis."

Teacher educator Milton Reynolds explains in his chapter that colorblindness promotes a mode of learning that is "conceptually impoverishing and affectively underskilling." The forms of identity and consciousness afforded to many whites within a colorblind framework are injurious to themselves and others, he explains. For Reynolds, a refusal to see or acknowledge race is neither advantageous nor ethical but instead denies students techniques, knowledge, and ways of understanding that have been forged outside dominant cultures and structures that are central to their own well-being and survival. Reynolds explores the development of promising new alternatives to "colorblind" teaching practice in the classroom environment.

This section reprises, augments, and extends a core premise of this book and the larger project from which it emerges. Research design, curricular innovation, and classroom pedagogy on campuses reflect and shape broader struggles for social justice in communities. Students, staff personnel, and faculty members come from and return to communities suffused with racialized practices, processes, and structures. The college campus itself is a racial project, a managerial training ground where racialized practices are learned and legitimated. Countering colorblindness requires the identification and development of new objects of study, but it also demands the transformation of the social relations of research by envisioning and enacting new ways of knowing and new ways of being.

NOTE

1. Stefano Harney and Fred Moten, *The Undercommons: Fugitive Planning and Black Study* (Wivenhoe, UK: Minor Compositions, 2013).

TWELVE

They (Color) Blinded Me with Science

COUNTERACTING COLONIALITY OF KNOWLEDGE IN HEGEMONIC PSYCHOLOGY

Glenn Adams and Phia S. Salter

The year 2015 was a time of campus uprisings.[1] In one of the most remarkable instances, students at the University of Missouri protested the hostile climate of campus racism, the football team refused to play, and demonstrations forced the resignation of the university president and chancellor.[2] Elsewhere in the United States, students in such diverse places as Ithaca College, UCLA, the University of Kansas, and Yale University organized to challenge the dynamics of racial domination on college campuses and to show support for the Black Lives Matter movement.[3] Beyond the United States, students across South Africa and the United Kingdom rallied around the slogan "Rhodes must fall" to challenge the slow pace of change for racial justice.[4]

The year was also a turbulent one in our home discipline of (social) psychology. Critics both inside and outside the field railed against systematic biases that cast doubt on the accumulated knowledge base of psychological science. One set of biases was a methodological sort: failures to replicate results of important studies led many observers to question the truth status of the original work and to lament the "questionable research practices" (if not outright fraud) that might have produced its biased results.[5] Another set of biases was a political sort as a group of social psychologists published an influential article claiming that the field and its conclusions deviated from objective truth in a leftward political direction.[6]

In response to these concerns about bias, psychological scientists recommended a conservative response. Some advocated affirmative action policies that would correct the purported left-leaning bias by increasing participation of politically conservative voices.[7] Many advocated conservative changes to methodological guidelines—for example, calls for greater statistical power (via larger sample sizes) to reduce the rate of false-positive results;[8] recommendations against exploratory analyses; and preregistration of experiments and hypotheses[9]—to reduce the role of researcher subjectivity in interpretation of results. Through these steps, they hoped to bring psychological science closer to the positivist ideal of positionless, unbiased observation of objective reality.

From our standpoint, the juxtaposition of campus uprisings and the perception of psychological science in crisis is not merely coincidental. Rather, the conservative backlash with regard to methods and political orientation is an expression of the white racial perspective or standpoint that informs mainstream academia and hegemonic psychological science—in other words, part of the system of racial domination against which protesters were demonstrating. From this perspective, prescriptions for greater methodological rigor and politically charged demands for politically neutral science (#allviewpointsmatter) sound suspiciously like the colorblind disciplining of race-conscious work that is the central concern of this collection.

COLORBLIND DISCIPLINING OF RACE-CONSCIOUS SCIENCE

Over our years in the field of psychological science we have observed a familiar pattern in the enculturation of aspiring social scientists. Our students often enter graduate school with some experience in social movements and activism. They frequently have an identity-conscious lens on social reality informed by broad liberal arts education and engagement with marginalized knowledge perspectives (e.g., ethnic studies, feminist studies, and queer studies). At the same time, they appreciate how good social science uses arguments based on empirical observation to advance understanding of social reality, and they aspire to apply scientific tools to illuminate and counteract inequality, injustice, and other forms of violence.

Once these students enter graduate school, they receive training in scientific discipline. This discipline teaches students that their identity-conscious perspectives are a flawed form of knowledge tainted by their particularistic biases. This discipline teaches students that their lived experience of racial subordination is a descriptively deviant condition that has distorted their perceptual apparatus, renders them suspect as scientific witnesses, and disqualifies them to comment on context-general truth about normal human experience. This discipline teaches students that their social justice activism constitutes a set of emotional investments that interfere with their ability to serve as disinterested arbiters of scientific evidence. To correct these shortcomings, students learn that they should strive to perceive reality from an objective or identity-neutral perspective free from the biases of their own identity positions. They learn that, if they decide to continue to remain active in social justice movements, they should do it on their own time and rigidly compartmentalize such activism to preserve the integrity of their scientific work. In short, scientific discipline aims to transform passionate activists for social justice into dispassionate observers of objective reality and producers of unbiased knowledge who must "un-know" the truths of racial domination that their life experience has taught them.[10]

A useful articulation of this attitude comes in a metaphor of clothing. Disciplinary training demands that researchers leave their identities on a hook at the laboratory door and exchange them for the white lab coat that animates popular imagination as the professional uniform of scientists.[11] The whiteness of the lab coat in this metaphor has two noteworthy connotations. First, it more or less deliberately connotes a sanitized absence of meaning consistent with a colorblind construction of the research process. The white coat is part of a laboratory setting designed to reflect and promote a sense of abstraction from social, historical, and material context, a privileged position or "transcendental realm where the effects of context, content, and meaning can be eliminated, standardized, or kept under control,"[12] permitting a perspective that is as close as possible to the prescriptive ideal of a "view from nowhere."[13] Second, the whiteness of the lab coat has (less deliberate) connotations of racial position. The experience of abstraction from context that it connotes is not equally characteristic of all human experience, but instead is more specifically associated with epistemic perspectives of racial power. Just as one should understand the whiteness of the lab coat as meaningful color rather than culture-neutral absence of color, so too should one understand calls for colorblind science as a thinly disguised directive for assimilation to a particular racial position rather than culture-neutral absence of racial position.

IDENTITY-CONSCIOUS PERSPECTIVES
FOR DECOLONIZING SCIENCE

As an example of colorblind ideology at work in scientific interpretation, consider a thought experiment in the influential journal *Behavioral and Brain*

Sciences, designed to demonstrate how bias against conservative viewpoints might impact scientific work. The experiment goes like this: Imagine two versions of a study where researchers use identical methods, procedures, and analyses to investigate economic disadvantage as a source of racial differences in IQ test performance. In one version, left-leaning researchers conclude that the work illuminates the role of environmental influences on intelligence. In the other version, right-leaning researchers conclude that the work illuminates the role of genetic inheritance on intelligence. From the colorblind perspective of hegemonic psychological science, one might argue (as the authors of the thought experiment do) that if left-leaning reviewers favor one version of the study and right-leaning reviewers the other, then it would constitute evidence that "extra-scientific considerations [i.e., political ideology] influence reviewers' calculus" and unfairly bias evaluation of scientific research.[14]

From an identity-conscious perspective informed by the epistemic standpoint of racially subordinated communities, the problem with this argument is that it abstracts research from its social and historical context. Both versions of the study—whether the left-leaning focus on poverty or the right-leaning focus on genetics—proceed from a White epistemic standpoint and investment in interpreting test performance differences as evidence of Black people's intellectual inferiority. People familiar with the history of scientific racism associated with the intellectual testing industry might challenge the legitimacy of the IQ test as an inherently racist tool (posing as colorblind or race-neutral) for measuring merit or ability.[15] They might view the right-leaning version of the study as particularly pernicious because of its ties to the eugenics movement, biological essentialism, and the assumption that race is a biological rather than a social construct. Yet the authors, through their hypothetical researchers, imply that this knowledge about the social and historical context of intelligence testing constitutes "extra-scientific considerations" that have no place in psychological science and hinder us from converging on the objective truth. In order to evaluate the research in a colorblind fashion, they imply that one must un-know this history of racism and pretend that the IQ test (or any other psychological measure) is a race-neutral tool.

In contrast to prescriptions for colorblindness that require scientists to leave their cultural knowledge of racial subordination on a hook by the laboratory door, we propose that an adequate approach to knowledge must proceed from a foundation of consciousness about the racial domination and colonial violence that have constituted modern society. From our perspective, calls for colorblind science are flawed because they obscure the extent to which the supposedly objective or natural standard (reasonable person, traditional methods) of social science is not race-neutral, but instead constitutes a form of racialized subjectivity. Calls for colorblind science celebrate the ideal of an objective scientific observer abstracted from social context, but they promote ignorance or unknowing of the racialized violence required for the historical production of that abstraction from context. By prescribing ways of being and knowing based on the modern experience of abstraction from context, hegemonic science actively reproduces racial domination. Identity-conscious knowledge perspectives provide a remedy for this perceptual limitation of colorblind science.

One race-conscious perspective that informs many contributions to this collection (including our own work)[16] is Critical Race Theory (CRT). As other contributors have described with greater authority, initial articulations of CRT grew out of frustration about an inattention to racial power in critical studies.[17] Conventional perspectives of critical scholarship often dismiss *race* consciousness as a form of *false* consciousness associated with tendencies of essentialism or particularization that threaten solidarity of social movements. In response, proponents of CRT contend that race consciousness is a necessary tool to illuminate the basis of hegemonic knowledge formations in epistemic perspectives associated with White racial power. Rather than the application of White-washed critical theory to a subset of phenomena with obvious connections to race relations, CRT perspectives consider the entire range of social science phenomena through an analytic lens that highlights racial power.

Another identity-conscious knowledge perspective is Decolonial Theory, which emerged as a conceptual framework for understanding the Eurocentric global modern order from the epistemic standpoint of racially subordinated communities in the Global South. In its most basic articulation, this framework emphasizes that one cannot understand modernity without consideration of its "dark side," coloniality.[18] From this perspective, Eurocentric global modernity and the individualist tendencies that constitute modern ways of being are not, as most scientists imagine them, the leading edge of human cultural progress. Instead, they are inseparable manifestations of the colonial violence and racial subordination that constituted the modern order of Eurocentric global domination.

An important focus of decolonial scholarship is the *coloniality of knowledge*.[19] Briefly stated, references to the coloniality of knowledge emphasize that the scientific research enterprise is not an unbiased reading of objective reality or identity-neutral tool wielded by dispassionate or positionless observers. Instead, it is an integral component of the modern/colonial order that reflects and reproduces racial domination. How is present-day scientific research implicated in racial domination? In one direction, the hegemonic enterprise of scientific research *reflects* racial domination to the extent that it privileges a modern epistemic standpoint, associated with the experience of abstraction from sociohistorical context, enabled by colonial expropriation of Others' wealth and productive capacity. In the other direction, the hegemonic practice of scientific research *reproduces* racial domination by interpreting complex social phenomena through the lens of a neoliberal individualist model of society (as a frictionless, free market of unfettered, free agents whose outcomes are the result of their personal choice) that obscures the role of colonial violence in the production of modern society.[20]

As a response to the epistemic (and epistemological)[21] violence of hegemonic science, identity-conscious knowledge formations provide conceptual resources, rooted in the epistemic perspective of marginalized communities, that provide the foundations for intellectual decolonization.[22] In the rest of this chapter, we illustrate strategies for intellectual decolonization in the context of two research projects.

DECOLONIZING PERCEPTION: TOOLS FOR IGNORANCE (AND CONSCIOUSNESS)

The most straightforward connection to the focus of this collection is a project that considers colorblindness as a tool for racism denial. This project takes as its point of departure a ubiquitous gap in perception, whereby White Americans tend to perceive less racism in everyday life and foundational institutions of U.S. society than do people from a variety of racially subordinated communities. Moreover, because White American racial sensibilities tend to constitute supposedly neutral standards of a "reasonable person," mainstream institutions tend to normalize and naturalize denial of racism. In other words, mainstream institutions treat perception of a nonracist or postracial society not only as a prescriptive standard for how one should see everyday reality, but also as a descriptive standard of what reality actually is. Measured against this standard, the tendency in mainstream institutions is to pathologize perception of racism: that is, to treat it as an example of paranoid delusion, unfounded concern, or a strategic move in a political game (i.e., "playing the race card").[23]

In response to this prevailing construction of group differences, an important task is to decolonize perception. Decolonial perspectives propose that the key to decolonizing thinking, feeling, and being is to shift the epistemic standpoint and consider reality from the perspective of people in racially subordinated communities. Rather than the prevailing model of the missionary intellectual who visits oppressed communities to impart expertise and "give away" scientific knowledge, this epistemic shift reflects a basis in perspectives of liberation social science.[24] Extending the liberation theology notion of a "preferential option for the poor," perspectives of liberation social science propose that one can best comprehend the human condition— including the operation of power—by treating perspectives of racially subordinated communities as a privileged site of understanding.[25] Associated with this epistemic shift are two decolonizing strategies.[26]

The Normalizing Strategy:
Racism Perception as Reality Attunement

A first decolonizing strategy is to draw upon the identity-conscious epistemic perspective of racially subordinated communities to provide a normalizing account of the patterns that mainstream perspectives portray as abnormal. In contrast to the mainstream portrayal of racism perception as unfounded concern or strategic exaggeration, the epistemic perspective of racially subordinated communities affords awareness of—that is, makes it easier to know about—the operation of racism in American society. For one thing, everyday realities of racially subordinated communities make it easier to know about racism in the present. People who inhabit these realities are not only likely to witness or experience racism themselves, but also are likely to move in social networks where other people experience racism, to get their information from news media that are attuned to the possibility of racism, to have access to (often informal) educational resources that socialize community youth about the ongoing danger and significance of racism, and to participate in cultural events that commemorate the struggle against racism.

As this last phrase suggests, everyday realities of racially subordinated communities also afford awareness about the extent and present relevance of past racism. Rather than bounded incidents that played out to their conclusion long ago, epistemic perspectives of people in marginalized communities afford awareness of the "slow violence" of racism throughout modern/colonial history.[27] One implication of this perspective is that people who know about the extent and significance of racism in the past are in a better position to understand the impact and ongoing significance of racism in the present.

Consistent with this implication, our research suggests that perception of racism in current events is associated with accurate knowledge about past racism. In this research, we observed that students at historically Black universities tended to perform better than White American students at a predominantly White institution on a true/false measure of historical knowledge. That is, they correctly identified documented incidents of past racism as true, but did not incorrectly claim that made-up incidents of racism were true. In turn, this group difference in reality attunement partly accounted for the group difference in racism perception.[28] We interpret these results as evidence that tendencies to perceive racism in American society do not reflect some pathological deviation from reality; instead, they are associated with greater attunement to reality. From this perspective, it is not surprising that people see racism in present-day society. The evidence for this conclusion is readily available for people who are sober enough to face it.

The Denaturalizing Strategy: Cultural Affordances for Denial and Ignorance

A second decolonizing strategy is to draw upon the experience of people in racially subordinated communities as an epistemic foundation from which to denaturalize prescriptions for colorblindness in hegemonic mainstream discourse. Conventional discussions take tendencies to perceive racism as a remarkable deviation from the "reasonable person" standard that requires some sort of comment or explanation. In contrast, the denaturalizing strategy of a cultural psychology analysis "turn[s] the analytic lens" and considers colorblind denial of racism as the deviant phenomenon that requires explanation.[29] Why do White Americans tend to deny something—racism in American society—that one might otherwise think obvious?

One answer to this question is certainly that various identity threats motivate White Americans to deny or avoid information about the extent of racism. Evidence of racism in U.S. society is threatening to White Americans because it calls into question their moral adequacy and the legitimacy of a system from which they derive benefit. When we use experimental techniques to temporarily neutralize these identity threats and individual motivations for colorblindness, we find that White Americans are more willing to admit the extent of racism.[30]

The other answer to this question is that White American society provides a variety of cultural-psychological tools that make it easier to deny or avoid information about the extent of racism. This is an important point that bears emphasis. Even if people set aside their identity-defensive biases and seek or weigh evidence in objective fashion, they can still fail to recognize racism where it exists—and oppose policies to address it—if the only knowledge tools at their disposal are ones that promote ignorance of racism.[31]

Our work considers one important tool for colorblind denial of racism: hegemonic representations of history. This work suggests that White Americans fail to perceive racism, in part, because they are ignorant about well-documented and consensually acknowledged incidents of past racism. Yet this ignorance of past racism is not simply the result of personal shortcomings; rather, it is a collectively cultivated, cultural product. How does society produce and maintain this ignorance?

In one investigation of this question, we compared representations of Black History Month (BHM) in racially segregated schools in the Kansas City area.[32] We observed that BHM displays in predominantly Black and Latinx schools were more likely than those in predominantly White schools to refer to historical events, especially barriers or struggles associated with the civil rights movement. In contrast, if displays in White schools included historical content, it was typically to note individual achievements rather than historical processes. Rather than explicit references to past and present racism, BHM displays in White schools were more likely than those in Black and Latinx schools to refer to themes of diversity and tolerance.

These differences in displays across schools are not accidental; rather, BHM displays realize different beliefs and desires. In a follow-up study, we observed that White American students at the University of Kansas disliked representations of BHM that referred to the history of racial domination, and they instead preferred relatively sanitized or domesticated portrayals of BHM that emphasized tolerant coexistence in diverse communities or individual achievements of African American heroes.[33] Equally important, the strength of these likes and dislikes was related to the strength of people's investment in White American identity. People who expressed a strong sense of themselves as White Americans were especially likely to prefer sanitizing BHM displays from White schools and to dislike critical BHM displays from Black and

Latinx schools. In summary, the research highlighted the extent to which representations of history in mainstream institutions are not identity-neutral reflections of fact. Instead, they are White-washed products that reflect beliefs and desires of the White American actors whose preferences disproportionately shape everyday realities.

Likewise, these differences in displays across schools are not inconsequential; rather, BHM displays promote different forms of perception and action. Results of two additional studies in the same project indicated that displays typical of White schools (which tended to emphasize diversity and achievement) were less effective than displays typical of Black and Latinx schools (which were relatively likely to acknowledge past racism) at promoting awareness of racism as a feature of present-day society.[34] In turn, because they were less effective at promoting awareness of racism, displays typical of White schools were less effective than displays typical of Black and Latinx schools at promoting support for racial justice policies. Relative to displays from Black and Latinx schools, the White-washed BHM displays typical of White schools functioned as tools for the production of ignorance, denial, and inaction.

These examples of research suggest that the "reasonable person" who informs standards of law, interpretation of scientific evidence, and resulting recommendations for policy suffers from a form of collectively cultivated ignorance about the role of racism in U.S. society. From this perspective, the cultivated inability to see the racialization of everyday life represents the colonization of perception by forces of racial power. The goal of social justice therefore requires the decolonizing of perception and knowledge not only to reveal the operation of racial power, but also to illuminate forms of perception, memory, and reason that better reflect the experience and aspirations of broader humanity. In turn, the task of decolonizing knowledge requires an active antiracism and tools for race-conscious perception that reveal the operation of racial power, rather than passive varieties of nonracialism (based in a White epistemic standpoint) that serve interests of domination by deflecting attention away from the operation of racial power.[35]

DECOLONIZING LOVE: PSYCHOLOGICAL GROWTH OR SUSTAINABLE DEVELOPMENT?

Readers of this book and people familiar with CRT will not find it surprising that ideologies of colorblindness inform scientific knowledge and broader conventional wisdom regarding the objectivity or reasonableness of statements about the role of racism in everyday society. Indeed, this stance on the role of racism is what defines the notion of colorblindness in the first place. However, an important feature of CRT is that the role of colorblind ideology in hegemonic knowledge formations is not limited to explicitly "racial" topics. Instead, perspectives of CRT emphasize that racialized knowledge forms—perhaps most profoundly White-washed conceptions of the "reasonable person" that masquerade as positionless or colorblind truth—suffuse and inform the entire enterprise of law, education, and science.

So it is that our second example of colorblind ideology in hegemonic psychological science concerns topics—love, care, and well-being—that would at first seem far removed from the topic of racialized colonial violence. For this example, we draw upon research in West African settings to critique ways in which conventional scientific wisdom reflects and reproduces habits of mind associated with individualism, an important manifestation of the coloniality of knowledge and being.[36]

To begin our discussion, we invite readers to consider a famous dilemma tale, common in many settings in the African diaspora, in which a person's mother and spouse are drowning and the person must choose whom to rescue.[37] To the extent that there is a "correct" answer to this dilemma, conventional wisdom in hegemonic science implies that the right choice is to save spouse over mother. After all, one's spouse is ideally a soulmate, the partner with whom one has chosen to build a relationship that most constitutes the modern self, touches one's authentic core, expresses one's deepest longings. Sure enough, when we presented a modified version of this dilemma to participants in the Kansas City area, the majority of participants did indeed prioritize care to spouse over care to mother.[38] Different patterns emerged when we presented the dilemma to participants in a variety of settings in the West African country of Ghana. In Accra, the metropolitan capital city of Ghana, there was no evidence of the hegemonic standard pattern, whereby participants prioritized care to spouse over care to mother. In Navrongo, a small town in northern Ghana, the standard pattern was reversed; that is, participants on average tended to prioritize care to mother over care to spouse.[39]

How is one to understand these patterns? Again, conventional wisdom in hegemonic science portrays prioritization of spouse over parent as a natural tendency of the human animal, something that well-adjusted individuals do as they transform from immature, dependent juveniles to mature, independent adults. This pattern represents a milestone of individual and cultural development as it enables people to act in accordance with principles of self-determination, indulge in self-exploration and self-expansion, and construct a social network that expresses their authentic desires (rather than accommodate themselves to connections that are merely accidents of birth). Judged against this hegemonic standard, West African tendencies to prioritize parent over spouse constitute remarkable deviations that require explanation: evidence of individual or cultural immaturity on the universal trajectory of human development.[40] In response to this pathologizing interpretation, we again apply two decolonial strategies.

The Denaturalizing Strategy: Spouse Preference as Neoliberal Growth

In this case, it makes sense to begin discussion with the second decolonial strategy: to *denaturalize* the patterns that hegemonic science portrays as colorblind, natural standards for optimal experience. Rather than a marker of normal human development, our work identifies "standard" tendencies to prioritize spouse over parent as a component of *expansion-oriented* or *growth-focused* models of well-being. These growth-focused models include such diverse features as a narrow or nuclear construction of family, dyad-oriented childcare, a construction of care as emotional support, and a "romantic" construction of true love as a form of self-expansive merging in exclusive intimacy with a partner of one's choosing. Practitioners draw upon such hegemonic scientific understandings and impose them as universal standards—for example, by valorizing maternal over community childcare or by pathologizing children's contribution to household labor[41]—without regard for cultural or historical context. In more extreme cases, policymakers draw upon these conceptions of love, relationship, and well-being (along with problematic outgroup stereotypes) to justify parent-child separation, military invasion, and other violent actions, ostensibly to liberate women and children from oppressive cultural practices.[42]

Whereas hegemonic science portrays growth-oriented ways of being as naturally superior or optimal paths to happiness, a decolonial perspective locates these tendencies in cultural ecologies of neoliberal individualism associated with Eurocentric global modernity/coloniality. These cultural ecologies promote an experience of the social world as a relatively frictionless "free market" populated by unfettered "free agents" who are at liberty (but also compelled) to choose attractive partners, avoid onerous obligations, and pursue well-being through the creation of optimally satisfying relationships. By locating hegemonic conceptions of love, care, and growth-oriented relationality in cultural ecologies of Eurocentric modernity, a decolonial analysis makes it easier to see potential drawbacks of these conceptions. In particular, it suggests that one must consider these allegedly colorblind, standard forms in terms of the dark side of modernity, coloniality. How can such apparently positive manifestations of human existence as love and growth constitute colonial forms?

In one direction, the reference to coloniality illuminates the violence that produced hegemonic forms. Rather than colorblind or racially innocent facts about the human organism, growth-oriented models of love and well-being reflect the racial domination and violent extraction that have enabled an unjustly privileged minority to pursue the neoliberal individualist project of expansive self-development, while simultaneously restricting viable options for the dominated global majority. At the very least, awareness of this history of racial violence complicates the elevation of these ways of being as a supposedly colorblind, universal prescription for love and personal development.

In the other direction, the reference to coloniality illuminates the violence that hegemonic forms continue to produce. Despite the positive connotations of "growth," these forms of relationality can expose people to considerable risks when they forgo the assurance (and obligations) of broad community for the alluring promises of personal fulfillment.[43]

Practices of narrow investment in private bonds of affection afford short-sighted personal growth at the expense of wider networks of social obligations that contribute to broader well-being. Moreover, growth-oriented models of personal development—like their counterparts in the domain of societal or economic development[44]—involve high rates of resource consumption that render them not only unavailable to most people, but also unsustainable as a long-term path. In summary, the denaturalization strategy of a decolonial analysis alerts us to the possibility that growth-oriented conceptions of love and personal development are not the leading edge of colorblind human progress; instead, these hegemonic forms reflect and reproduce the slow, crushing violence of racial (and class) domination.

The Normalizing Strategy: Parent Preference as Sustainable Relationality

The other decolonial strategy is to normalize the tendencies that perspectives of hegemonic science portray as abnormal. Viewed from this decolonial perspective, tendencies to prioritize parent over spouse reflect broader, security- or sustainability-oriented ways of being characterized by lineage models of family, socially distributed childcare, a construction of care as material or practical support, and a construction of *true love* as dutiful fulfillment of obligation. These ways of being are not (as hegemonic perspectives suggest) evidence of immaturity measured along some culturally imposed trajectory of development. Instead, they constitute healthy adaptations to cultural ecologies of social embeddedness and interdependence that promote an experience of relationality as a defining condition of everyday life. Rather than contempt, these patterns are worthy of respect.

"Yes," we can hear our scientific colleagues respond, "but which way of being best promotes optimal satisfaction?" Rather than answer the question on its own terms, a decolonial response challenges the question in the first place.[45] Rather than valorize ways of being that promote optimal satisfaction for an unjustly privileged few at the expense of the racially subordinated majority, an adequate science of global humanity must valorize ways of being that promote a secure and dignified life for all. In this respect, patterns of relationality evident in majority-world communities not only constitute viable ways of living in their own right, but also provide inspiration for imagining just alternatives to the racial violence of neoliberal individualism and Eurocentric modernity/coloniality—including the epistemic violence of colorblind science.

CONCLUSION

Here and elsewhere, the key to a more human(e) science is a process of intellectual decolonization based in identity-conscious forms of knowledge that reflect and promote the understandings and aspirations of the marginalized global majority. A practical implication of this perspective is to underscore the role of identity-conscious education in the production of critical consciousness. People who benefit from the racial violence of the status quo have a possessive investment in colorblind educational technologies that promote ignorance of facts that otherwise might be obvious.[46] The push to pack school boards with deniers of climate change, to adopt history textbooks that deny the extent of racial or colonial violence, and to defund ethnic studies programs are all recent examples of the ongoing epistemic violence of colonialism.[47]

In response to this epistemic violence, a decolonial perspective prescribes educational practices based on the ideal of *accompaniment:* ways of knowing and doing in which students, researchers, and would-be agents of change immerse themselves in the flow of everyday life and experience events with humility alongside others in the context of everyday activity.[48] Many discussions of accompaniment rightly emphasize collaboration in collective action and forms of creative expression that directly confront oppressive structures. In addition, we see modest possibilities in our professional role as teachers for a sort of vicarious accompaniment by which we educate students in knowledge traditions rooted in the epistemic perspective of people in racially subordinated communities. For example, one of us (Phia Salter) has created a course in Black Psychology as a mechanism to integrate racially subordinated perspectives into the psychology undergraduate curriculum. To be clear, the goal of this and similar initiatives is not to expose students to diversity or knowledge about racially subordinated "Others"; instead, it is to provide students with an epistemic standpoint from which to rethink the entire body of knowledge and practices that constitute hegemonic psychological science.

POSTSCRIPT

If 2015 was a time of uprising, then 2016 was a time of "whitelash" (i.e., racialized backlash),[49] epitomized by both the campaign for the United Kingdom to leave the European Union and the campaign to elect Donald Trump as president of the United States. The whitelash in these campaigns was evident not only in reactionary calls to "take back" political institutions or to "make [the country] great again," but also in a "post-truth" stance characterized by a pronounced disregard for empirical facts and the unapologetic embrace of racialized ignorance designed to manage White fragility and discomfort. The disdain for empirically grounded, expert judgment gained momentum from the remarkable failure of mainstream institutions to anticipate the success of these political campaigns. Such failure lent apparent credence to beliefs that mainstream journalists, academics, and knowledge professionals suffered from a left-leaning ideological bias that rendered them out of touch with reality. Within psychological science, the response to these developments has been to amplify the calls for colorblind science that we noted at the outset of this paper. Given this context, we thought it important to clarify two points.

First, we endorse the idea that social scientists, including those of us who work in public institutions of politically conservative states, might better engage with the diversity of communities whom our work serves and from which our students originate. This prescription is consistent with traditions of accompaniment, associated with liberation social science, that we have advocated elsewhere in this essay. The question is how to reconcile this prescription with an appreciation for the racialized ignorance that continues to inform common sense in U.S. settings. We suggest that the answer is not to un-know identity-conscious knowledge and meet people halfway, as if truth lies in a compromise between different positions. Instead, we best respect the humanity of the people concerned when we draw upon identity-conscious perspectives to illuminate uncomfortable truths, confront White fragility, and challenge investment in allegedly neutral forms of knowledge that promote White ignorance and serve racial domination.

Second, we affirm the commitment to "fighting back with sound science"[50] against the characterization of scientific knowledge as left-biased propaganda that does not merit public attention or support. Again, though, we dispute any notion that "sound science" requires us to un-know the reality of racial injustice to preserve disciplinary rigor and the integrity of scientific work. Rather than reproduce colorblind delusion, we emphasize the importance of identity-conscious knowledge to illuminate a more adequate account of empirical realities. The objective of this identity-conscious stance is not truth-free pursuit of a political agenda (characterized by fabricated "facts" and fake science), but instead to enable reality-attuned knowledge of empirical truths that hegemonic perspectives can often obscure.

ACKNOWLEDGMENTS

The Kansas African Studies Center and Oswald Family Foundation supported research in Ghana through a Graduate Fellowship in Applied Health and Development Research to Phia Salter. Conceptual development in this chapter benefited greatly from Glenn Adams's fellowship at the Center for Advanced Study in the Behavioral Sciences at Stanford University, and especially from our discussions with Alfredo Artiles, Kimberlé Crenshaw, Jean-Claude Croizet, Jennifer Eberhardt, Leah Gordon, Lani Guinier, Luke Harris, George Lipsitz, Hazel Markus, Claude Steele, and Barbara Tomlinson. A particularly important influence was a week-long seminar on colorblindness that expanded the circle of engagement to Felice Blake, Devon Carbado, Daniel HoSang, Paula Ioanide, Milton Reynolds, and ultimately (in subsequent gatherings) to other contributors to this volume. We are grateful for the generosity and inspiration of these colleagues. Throughout the process, we have benefited from critical engagement with colleagues in the Cultural Psychology Research Group at the University of Kansas.

NOTES

1. Students from at least eighty college and university campuses sent demands to their institutions calling for broader representation of Black faculty and students, curriculum that produces comprehensive racial awareness and inclusion, and other responses to institutional inequity. A collection of these demands is available at www.blackliberationcollective.org/our-demands.

2. John Eligon and Richard Pérez-Peña, "University of Missouri Protests Spur a Day of Change," *New York Times,* Nov. 9, 2015, www.nytimes.com/2015/11/10/us /university-of-missouri-system-president-resigns.html.

3. Anemona Hartocollis and Jess Bidgood, "Racial Discrimination Protests Ignite at Colleges across the U.S.," *New York Times,* Nov. 11, 2015, www.nytimes .com/2015/11/12/us/racial-discrimination-protests-ignite-at-colleges-across-the-us .html.

4. Norimitsu Onishi, "Students in South Africa Protest Slow Pace of Change," *New York Times,* Sept. 8, 2015, www.nytimes.com/2015/09/09/world/africa/student -protests-in-south-africa-highlight-dissatisfaction-with-pace-of-change.html.

5. For discussions of the replicability crisis and the issue of "questionable research practices" (QRPs), see Leslie K. John, George Loewenstein, and Drazen Prelec, "Measuring the Prevalence of Questionable Research Practices with Incentives for Truth-Telling," *Psychological Science* 23, no. 5 (2012): 524–32; Open Science Collaboration, "Estimating the Reproducibility of Psychological Science," *Science* 349 (Aug. 28, 2105): 6251, http://science.sciencemag.org/content/349/6251/aac4716; Joseph P. Simmons, Leif D. Nelson, and Uri Simonsohn, "False-Positive Psychology: Undisclosed Flexibility in Data Collection and Analysis Allows Presenting Anything as Significant," *Psychological Science* 22, no. 11 (2011): 1359–66. We agree that psychological science is full of questionable research practices, including an overreliance on studies with undergraduate students from WEIRD (i.e., Western, Educated, Industrial, Rich, and [supposedly] Democratic) cultural ecologies of Eurocentric global modernity or a near-exclusive emphasis on quantitative methodologies that strip information from participant responses and abstract them from social and historical context. However, these are not the sort of QRPs that critics have in mind. Instead, their concern is the extent to which psychologists capitalize on points of ambiguity or interpretation to see what they wanted to see in results

of the investigation rather than what was truly there. On the WEIRDness of psychological science, see Joseph Henrich, Steven J. Heine, and Ara Norenzayan, "The Weirdest People in the World?" *Behavioral and Brain Sciences* 33 (2010): 61–83. For a critique of the overreliance on quantification, see Norman K. Denzin, Yvonna S. Lincoln, and Michael D. Giardina, "Disciplining Qualitative Research," *International Journal of Qualitative Studies in Education* 19, no. 6 (2006): 769–82.

6. José L. Duarte, Jarret T. Crawford, Charlotta Stern, Jonathan Haidt, Lee Jussim, and Phillip E. Tetlock, "Political Diversity Will Improve Social Psychological Science," *Behavioral and Brain Sciences* 38 (2015): 1–13.

7. Ibid.

8. Simmons, Nelson, and Simonsohn, "False-Positive Psychology."

9. Eric-Jan Wagenmakers, Ruud Wetzels, Denny Borsboom, Han L.J. van der Maas, and Rogier A. Kievit, "An Agenda for Purely Confirmatory Research," *Perspectives on Psychological Science* 7, no. 6 (2012): 632–38.

10. On the concept of "un-knowing," see Paul Wenzel Geissler, "Public Secrets in Public Health: Knowing Not to Know while Making Scientific Knowledge," *American Ethnologist* 40 (2013): 13–34.

11. For a similar idea, see the classic work by Robert V. Guthrie, *Even the Rat Was White: A Historical View of Psychology* (New York: Harper & Row, 1976).

12. Richard A. Shweder, "Cultural Psychology: What Is It?" in *Cultural Psychology: Essays on Comparative Human Development,* ed. James Stigler, Richard Shweder, and Gil Herdt (Cambridge: Cambridge University Press, 1990), 7–8.

13. Thomas Nagel, *The View from Nowhere* (New York: Oxford University Press, 1986).

14. S.J. Ceci and W.M. Williams, "The Psychology of Psychology: A Thought Experiment," *Behavioral and Brain Sciences* 38 (2015): 21.

15. See Guthrie, *Even the Rat Was White;* also Graham Richards, *Race, Racism, and Psychology: Toward a Reflexive History* (London: Psychology Press, 1997). More specifically with respect to the IQ test, see Jean-Claude Croizet, "The Racism of Intelligence: How Mental Testing Practices Have Constituted an Institutionalized Form of Group Domination," in *The Oxford Handbook of African American Citizenship, 1865–Present,* ed. H.L. Gates et al. (New York: Oxford University Press, 2012).

16. See Phia S. Salter and Glenn Adams "Toward a Critical Race Psychology," *Social and Personality Psychology Compass* 7, no. 11 (2013): 781–93.

17. See, for example, Kimberlé W. Crenshaw, in this volume Chapter 3 and Chapter 6.

18. Walter D. Mignolo, *The Dark Side of Western Modernity: Global Futures, Decolonial Options* (Durham, NC: Duke University Press, 2011).

19. Edgardo Lander, ed., *La colonialidad del saber: Eurocentrismo y ciencias sociales—Perspectivas latinoamericanas* [The coloniality of knowledge: Eurocentrism and social sciences—Latin American perspectives] (Buenos Aires: Consejo

Latinoamericano de Ciencias Sociales, 2000), http://bibliotecavirtual
.clacso.org.ar/clacso/sur-sur/20100708034410/lander.pdf.

20. For a general treatment of these issues with respect to research, see Linda
Tihuwai Smith, *Decolonizing Methodologies: Research and Indigenous Peoples*
(London: Zed Books, 1999). For a discussion with respect to pedagogy, see Barbara
Tomlinson and George Lipsitz, "Insubordinate Spaces for Intemperate Times:
Countering the Pedagogies of Neoliberalism," *Review of Education, Pedagogy, and
Cultural Studies* 35, no. 1 (2013): 3–26.

21. See Vandana Shiva, "Reductionist Science as Epistemological Violence," in
Science, Hegemony, and Violence: A Requiem for Modernity, ed. Ashis Nandy
(Oxford: Oxford University Press, 1988), 232–56. More specifically with respect to
psychology and social sciences, see Thomas Teo, "What Is Epistemological Violence
in the Empirical Social Sciences?" *Social and Personality Psychology Compass* 4
(2010): 295–303.

22. Jean Comaroff and John L. Comaroff, "Theory from the South: Or, How
Euro-America Is Evolving toward Africa," *Anthropological Forum: A Journal of
Social Anthropology and Comparative Sociology* 22 (2012): 113–31; Rae Connell,
Southern Theory: Social Science and the Global Dynamics of Knowledge (Crow's Nest,
NSW, Australia: Allen & Unwin, 2007); B. de Sousa Santos, *Epistemologies of the
South: Justice against Epistemicide* (Boulder, CO: Paradigm, 2014).

23. For an extended discussion of this perspective, see Nia L. Phillips, Glenn
Adams, and Phia S. Salter, "Beyond Adaptation: Decolonizing Approaches to Coping
with Oppression," in Special Thematic Section on Decolonizing Psychological
Science, *Journal of Social and Political Psychology* 3, no. 1 (2015): 365–87.

24. See Enrique Dussel, *Ética de la liberación: En la edad de la globalización y de
la exclusión* [Liberation ethics: In the age of globalization and exclusion] (Mexico
City: Universidad Autonoma Itztapalapa, 1998); Orlando Fals Borda, "Science and
the Common People," *Journal of Social Studies* 11 (1981): 2–21; Ignacio Martín-Baró,
"Hacia una psicología de la liberación" [Toward a liberation psychology], *Boletín de
Psicología de El Salvador* 22 (1986): 219–31.

25. For a similar point, see George Rawick, "Radical Sociology or Marxism?
Some Comments," in *Listening to Revolt: Selected Writings of George P. Rawick,* ed.
David Roediger and Martin Smith (Chicago: Charles H. Kerr, 2010), 63–72.

26. See Glenn Adams and Phia S. Salter, "Health Psychology in African
Settings: A Cultural-Psychological Analysis," *Journal of Health Psychology* 12
(2007): 539–51; Glenn Adams, Tuğçe Kurtiş, Phia S. Salter, and Stephanie L.
Anderson, "A Cultural Psychology of Relationship: Decolonizing Science and
Practice," in *Relationship Science: Integrating Evolutionary, Neuroscience, and
Sociocultural Approaches,* ed. Omri Gillath, Glenn Adams, and Adrianne D. Kunkel
(Washington, DC: American Psychological Association, 2012), 49–70.

27. On the concept of "slow violence," see Rob Nixon, *Slow Violence and the
Environmentalism of the Poor* (Cambridge, MA: Harvard University Press, 2011).

28. Jessica C. Nelson, Glenn Adams, and Phia S. Salter, "The Marley Hypothesis:
Racism Denial Reflects Ignorance of History," *Psychological Science* 24, no. 2 (2013):

213–18. The failure to discriminate fact-based versus "fake" history is reminiscent of the failure to discriminate fact-based versus "fake" news. We suspect that these epistemic failures have roots in similar sources.

29. Adams and Salter, "Health Psychology in African Settings," 542.

30. See Glenn Adams, Teceta Thomas Tormala, and Laurie T. O'Brien, "The Effect of Self-Affirmation on Perceptions of Racism," *Journal of Experimental Social Psychology* 42 (2006): 616–26.

31. See Charles W. Mills, "White Ignorance," in *Race and Epistemologies of Ignorance,* ed. Shannon Sullivan and Nancy Tuana (Albany: SUNY Press, 2007), 13–38.

32. Phia S. Salter and Glenn Adams, "On the Intentionality of Cultural Products: Representations of Black History as Psychological Affordances," *Frontiers in Psychology* 7 (2016): 1166.

33. Ibid.

34. Ibid.

35. As an illustration of this tension, consider an empirical report that one of us published with colleagues on the topic of teaching about racism: Glenn Adams, Vanessa Edkins, Dominika Lacka, Kate Pickett, and Sapna Cheryan, "Teaching about Racism: Pernicious Implications of the Standard Portrayal," *Basic and Applied Social Psychology* 30 (2008): 349–61. Results of the research suggest that the standard approach, which locates racism in individual prejudice, is less effective at promoting awareness of racism than more sociocultural accounts—rooted in the epistemic perspective of marginalized groups—that locate racism in the structure of everyday worlds. In an evaluation of this article, an anonymous reviewer defended a colorblind approach to teaching and research: "Most social psychologists study the individual and not the society. What do we know about structural racism? It's not generally our domain of science. We cannot be blamed for teaching our science as we conduct and understand it. In any case, the goal of our research is not only to change prejudice, racism, and sexism.... But even if it is in part our goal, our real job (I think) is to teach the fundamentals of person judgment and person perception as we understand them. Whether this makes our students less or more prejudiced is not our fundamental concern." To be sure, one can take issue with the assertion here that socially responsible tolerance and appreciation for diversity are not appropriate learning goals of university education. (For an argument in support of these goals, see American Psychological Association, *APA Guidelines for the Undergraduate Psychology Major, Version 2.0* [Washington, DC: APA, 2013], www.apa.org/ed /precollege/about/psymajor-guidelines.pdf.) However, our present concern is to illuminate how the disciplinary investment in hegemonic knowledge forms both reflect and promote White domination.

36. See Nelson Maldonado-Torres, "On the Coloniality of Being," *Cultural Studies* 21, nos. 2–3 (2007): 240–70, www.tandfonline.com/doi/abs/10.1080 /09502380601162548; and Walter D. Mignolo, "Epistemic Disobedience, Independent Thought, and Decolonial Freedom," *Theory, Culture & Society* 26, nos. 7–8 (2009), http://journals.sagepub.com/doi/10.1177/0263276409349275.

37. See William R. Bascom, *African Dilemma Tales* (Paris: Mouton, 1975), 93.

38. Phia S. Salter and Glenn Adams, "Mother or Wife? An African Dilemma Tale and the Psychological Dynamics of Sociocultural Change," *Social Psychology* 42, no. 4 (2012): 232–42.

39. Ibid.

40. For versions of this pathologizing argument in Latin American settings, see Lawrence E. Harrison, *Underdevelopment Is a State of Mind: The Latin American Case* (Lanham, MD: University Press of America, 1985); also Luis D. Herrera Amighetti, L.D., "Parenting Practices and Governance in Latin America: The Case of Costa Rica," in *Developing Cultures: Essays on Cultural Change,* ed. Lawrence E. Harrison and Jerome Kagan (New York: Routledge, 2006), 21–37.

41. For an example, see Erica Burman, "Developing Differences: Gender, Childhood and Economic Development," *Children and Society* 9, no. 3 (1995): 121–41.

42. For an example, see Erica Burman, "Deconstructing Feminist Psychology," in *Deconstructing Feminist Psychology,* ed. Erica Burman (London: Sage, 1998), 1–29.

43. See Jennifer Cole, "Love, Money, and Economies of Intimacy in Tamatave, Madagascar," in *Love in Africa,* ed. Jennifer Cole and Lynn M. Thomas (Chicago: University of Chicago Press, 2009), 109–34. See also Holly Wardlow and Jennifer S. Hirsch, "Introduction," in *Modern Loves: The Anthropology of Romantic Courtship and Companionate Marriage,* ed. Jennifer S. Hirsch and Holly Wardlow (Ann Arbor: University of Michigan Press, 2006), 1–34.

44. A. Escobar, *Encountering Development: The Making and Unmaking of the Third World* (Princeton, NJ: Princeton University Press, 1995).

45. Even on its own terms, the answer to the question is not clear. For example, one can question whether the high-arousal positive affective states associated with growth-oriented patterns are inherently superior to the lower-arousal affective states associated with sustainability-oriented patterns. See Jeanne L. Tsai, "Ideal Affect: Cultural Causes and Behavioral Consequences," *Perspectives on Psychological Science* 2 (2007): 242–59. Moreover, even if the growth-oriented patterns are associated with acute spikes in optimal experience, it is not clear that they lead to sustainable levels of optimal experience either across people or within the same person over time. See Oscar N. E. Kjell, "Sustainable Well-Being: A Potential Synergy between Sustainability and Well-Being Research," *Review of General Psychology* 15 (2011): 255 66.

46. On the notion of "possessive investment," see George Lipsitz, *The Possessive Investment in Whiteness: How White People Profit from Identity Politics* (Philadelphia: Temple University Press, 1998).

47. On climate change denial, see Claire Foran, "The Plan to Get Climate Change Denial into Schools," *Atlantic,* Dec. 9, 2014. On history textbooks, see Laura Isensee, "How Textbooks Can Teach Different Versions of History," *All Things Considered,* July 13, 2015, www.npr.org/sections/ed/2015/07/13/421744763 /how-textbooks-can-teach-different-versions-of-history; also Ellen Bresler Rockmore, "How Texas Teaches History," *New York Times,* Oct. 21, 2015. On the

push to defund ethnic studies programs, see Aimee Phan, "Ethnic Studies Target of Critics, Cutbacks," *USA Today,* Feb. 6, 2012, http://usatoday30.usatoday.com /news/opinion/forum/story/2012–02–02/tucson-ethnic-studies-programs /52938952/1.

48. On the notion of accompaniment, see Barbara Tomlinson and George Lipsitz, "American Studies as Accompaniment," *American Quarterly* 65 (2013): 1–30; and Mary Watkins, "Psychosocial Accompaniment," *Journal of Social and Political Psychology* 3 (2015): 324–41.

49. Cable News Network commentator Van Jones used this word during live coverage to characterize emerging results of the 2016 U.S. election. See Josiah Ryan, "'This Was a Whitelash': Van Jones' Take on the Election Results," CNN, Nov. 9, 2016, www.cnn.com/2016/11/09/politics/van-jones-results-disappointment-cnntv.

50. This was the subject heading of a mass memorandum that Christian S. Crandall, president of the Society for the Psychological Study of Social Issues, sent to members on November 30, 2016.

_____

THIRTEEN

Toward a New Research Agenda?

FOUCAULT, WHITENESS, AND INDIGENOUS SOVEREIGNTY

Aileen Moreton-Robinson

Now post-Mabo and the "death" of terra nullius, questions lay at the feet of the Australian state. What legitimises your entry? Do you still require the consent of the natives? And if we give it to you now, what meaning will you or I give to that agreement? For who will hold the colonising state and its growing globalised identity to honour and respect our laws, territories and right to life? No one has in the past.[1]

In the above quote, Indigenous scholar Irene Watson poses questions that are almost unimaginable in the context of Australian sociology, where the discussion of "sovereignty" in modernity does not include Indigenous subjects. The "sociological imagination" has not been applied to investigate the existence of Indigenous sovereignty within both structure and agency, yet this is surely what sociology requires. C. Wright Mills coined this popular phrase, which is used as an epistemic tool to distinguish the "sociological" from the social.[2] Developing a sociological imagination means one should be able to think beyond the temple of one's familiar to examine the social world in new and unfamiliar ways. My enthusiasm for Foucault's *Society Must Be Defended* is predicated on the way in which the "unfamiliar" in his work stimulates the sociological imagination.[3]

This article is also influenced by the work of Indigenous scholars such as Irene Watson and Taiaiake Alfred, who advocate abandoning the concept of Indigenous sovereignty as it is configured in debates about Indigenous rights.[4] Raymond Williams and Patricia Monture-Angus, whose scholarship questions the epistemological basis of Western law and its application to Indigenous sovereignty struggles, also inform this piece.[5] The influence of their work has led me to consider the usefulness of Foucault's conceptual framework, as developed in *Society Must Be Defended,* for analyzing how

White possession, as a mode of rationality, functions within disciplinary knowledges and regulatory mechanisms, defining and circumscribing Indigenous sovereignty in particular ways.[6] The article considers recent work in Whiteness studies in Australia and abroad, as well as literature using Foucault's idea of the relationship between race, sovereignty, and war. It is offered as a work in progress to stimulate thinking about Indigenous sovereignty in a different way. The article begins by discussing the current literature on Indigenous rights, followed by an overview of Foucault's central ideas in *Society Must Be Defended*. The Australian critical Whiteness literature concerning Indigenous sovereignty is then outlined, and this, together with Foucault's ideas about race, war, and sovereignty, produces certain questions for future research. In conclusion, it is suggested that such a research agenda would contribute to the scope and depth of existing work on Indigenous sovereignty.

THE JUDICIO-POLITICAL FRAMEWORK

In the past three decades, questions about the status and rights of Indigenous peoples within "settler" nation-states has led to the development of a new literature within the academy across a number of disciplines such as Australian studies and Aboriginal studies, changes in domestic policy, and discussion of rights in public discourse and international law. Since the 1990s, in particular, there has been a proliferation of literature on Indigenous sovereignty and rights. This literature is often international in scope, drawing on disciplines such as law, politics, history, anthropology, and philosophy to explore issues regarding Indigenous peoples' status and rights. It has raised fundamental questions about the complexion of the democratic state and has challenged the philosophical premises of concepts such as democracy and sovereignty. Several scholars have addressed the limitations of liberalism as it applies to Indigenous sovereignty. Duncan Ivison et al. argue that a new political theory should include the acknowledgment of Indigenous difference as the essential condition of the legitimacy of the institutions and practices within which rights and resources are to be distributed.[7] Second, the universalism of liberalism and the particularism of Indigenous rights should not be perceived as mutually exclusive but rather as reference points to begin a new form of negotiation. Other work offers a range of perspectives on the political, moral, and legal rights associated with Indigenous sovereignty and agreement-making,[8] while several key legal texts have been published examining the status of Indigenous people at international law.[9]

In the Australian context, the most-cited work, *Aboriginal Sovereignty* by Henry Reynolds, charts the history of Indigenous sovereignty claims and their treatment by both law and government.[10] Bain Attwood critically extends Reynolds's work by offering a history of campaigns for Indigenous rights between the 1870s and the 1970s,[11] while Larissa Behrendt challenges the logic of formal equality by providing a clear and coherent articulation of Indigenous rights claims and the need for social justice.[12] This important and valuable literature offers detailed analyses of the racism embedded in the historical, political, and legal treatment of Indigenous sovereignty within the framework of sovereignty, rights, and law. It illustrates how Indigenous sovereignty claims have challenged conceptualizations of state sovereignty and, in a few instances, how they have worked to modify state rights through domestic and international law. The analysis of several case studies from Canada, the United States, New Zealand, and Australia provides insight into the pragmatics of exercising Indigenous sovereignty outside the realm of formal rights. In this body of scholarship, rights are perceived as being productive, enabling, and constraining, and the analysis of Indigenous rights is located within a judicio-political framework of law, rights, and sovereignty. The limitation of this literature lies in the reliance on "rights" as the cipher for analyzing Indigenous sovereignty. It does not reorient our conceptualization of power outside of a law, rights, and sovereignty paradigm to think about Indigenous sovereignty and power in different ways. Nor does this literature analyze race beyond "Indigeneity." However, it is my contention that utilizing the work of Foucault and critical Whiteness theorists to analyze the relationship between Indigenous sovereignty and state sovereignty promises to extend the scope of the existing literature.

BEYOND THE JUDICIO-POLITICAL FRAMEWORK

In *Society Must Be Defended,* Foucault offers an explanation of the development of racism and provides important insights into the mythology embedded in the history of the divine right of kings, the emergence of the theory of rights during modernity, and the establishment of what he conceptualizes as "biopower" through disciplinary and regulatory mechanisms. In these lectures, Foucault offers a genealogy of war from the seventeenth century to the present, arguing that war has been central to the development of the judicial edifice of right in democratic as well as socialist countries. He explains how the history of the divine right of kings that worked in the interests of sovereign absolutism was challenged through the work of Henri de Boulainvilliers (1658–1722), who produced a counterhistory to that of the king of France, effectively introducing the subject of rights into history. Refuting the myth of the inherited right to rule, Boulainvilliers's history of the nobility advanced the idea that, because of war, they too had rights. Having become legitimate and normalized, Foucault argues, the nobility's assertion of rights was utilized by the commoners as an impetus to the French Revolution; in this way a "partisan and strategic" truth became a weapon of war.[13] For Foucault, antagonisms, struggles, and conflict are processes of war that should be analyzed according to a grid of strategies and tactics. The relationship between the nobility, the third estate, and the king produced a form of society that became the basis of the modern nation, and war continues within new mechanisms of power. Thus politics is war by other means. The ensuing conflicts between rulers and ruled increasingly involve a relation between a superior race and an inferior race. As Foucault argues,

> The State is no longer an instrument that one race uses against another: the State is, and must be, the protector of the integrity, the superiority, and the purity of the race. . . . Racism is born at the point when the theme of racial purity replaces that of race struggle, and when counterhistory begins to be converted into biological racism.[14]

The importance of Foucault's genealogical account of rights is that it provides a new framework through which to consider how sovereignty and rights come into being through different forms of war and, more specifically, how the Indigenous subject comes into history contesting the legitimacy of sovereign right in Australia during the 1970s.

"Race" is defined by Foucault as a linguistic and religious marker that precedes the modern nation-state. While Foucault offers a genealogy of race tied to war, he does not make explicit how this conceptualization of race is tied to knowledge embedded in tactics or strategies of war. How did race play a part in the decision to go to war? How was it tied to the right to invade? These questions identify a gap in Foucault's notion of race that this project will seek to address. Foucault argues that race surfaces as a biological construct in the late eighteenth century because disciplinary knowledges came into being and regulatory mechanisms were developed to control the population. He describes this form of power as biopower, arguing that race became a means of regulating and defending society from itself. That is, war continues in modernity in different forms, while sovereignty shifts from a concern with society defending itself from external attacks to focus on its internal enemies. Race became the means through which the state's exercise of power is extended from one of "to let live or die" to one of "to let live and to make live." While Foucault acknowledges there is a relationship between biopower and colonization in *Society Must Be Defended*,[15] he does not extend his analysis of sovereignty to the colonial context. While the limitations of Foucault's work on colonization have been addressed by a number of postcolonial theorists,[16] most fail to pursue the specific ramifications of these limitations on our understanding of the issue of Indigenous sovereignty. In contrast, I believe the use of Foucault's idea of biopower to explicitly address the context of a "postcolonizing" nation will produce a new understanding of how Whiteness operates through the racialized application of disciplinary knowledges and regulatory mechanisms, which function together to preclude recognition of Indigenous sovereignty.[17]

At present there is little work that engages with power relations at the intersection of biopower, Indigenous sovereignty, Whiteness, and race. Critical engagement with some of the lectures in *Society Must Be Defended* is offered in the work of Anne Laura Stoler in *Race and the Education of Desire*.[18] Stoler takes up Foucault's idea of biopower to provide an understanding of the making of the European colonial bourgeois order in the nineteenth and twentieth centuries. While Stoler explores the role of biopower in constructing White subjectivity, she does not engage with Foucault's concern with sovereignty and war. Following Stoler, a small number of scholars have engaged specifically with *Society Must Be Defended* since its publication in English. While Brad Elliot Stone's review essay addresses the role of inferior races constituting the abnormal in contemporary race war, he does not pursue the implications of biopower's normalizing regime for Indigenous sovereignty struggles.[19] Similarly, John Marks provides an excellent overview of the philosophical and historical contexts for Foucault's text, relating it to race through a discussion of Dominique Franche's account of the Rwandan genocide.[20] However, he does not extend the connotations to engage with Whiteness and Indigenous sovereignty. Eduardo Mendieta elaborates on the implications of Foucault's work on the biopolitical state for our understanding of political rationality. He examines the relationship between "letting live" and "making live" through several historical and contemporary examples, including the death penalty, lynching, and the human genome project.[21] What his work does not address, however, is the relationship between Indigenous sovereignty and the biopolitical state. Race is discussed in this literature, but Whiteness remains invisible as a significant racial characteristic of the biopolitical state. There is also a considerable body of Australian work applying Foucault's theory of governmentality to cultural and policy texts. However, this important literature rarely engages specific issues of Whiteness and Indigenous sovereignty claims. For this reason, it is productive to bring Foucault's concept of biopower into relationship with the critical Whiteness literature.

This literature identifies Whiteness as the invisible norm against which other races are judged in the construction of identity, representation, decision-making, subjectivity, nationalism, knowledge production, and the law.[22] Warren Montag argues that, during modernity, Whiteness became an invisible norm through the universalization of humanness, which simultaneously erased its racial character and made it a universal.[23] This raises two questions: how does biopower work to produce Whiteness as an invisible norm and does it function as a tactic and strategy of race war?

Contributing to this growing literature is the work of Australian scholars who are establishing a field of Whiteness studies that engages in a variety of ways with colonization and Indigenous sovereignty.[24] In particular, the work of Alison Ravenscroft, Fiona Nicoll, and Toula Nicolacopoulos and George Vassilacopoulos considers the relationship between Indigenous sovereignty and the psychosocial and ontological realms of subjectivity, while others, such as Kate Foord, illustrate that the White fantasy of *terra nullius* and the disavowal of Indigenous sovereignty are fundamental to the narration of Australian identity and nation-building.[25]

TOWARD A RESEARCH AGENDA

The critical Whiteness literature on Indigenous sovereignty, in conjunction with Foucault's genealogy of race, leads me to ask the following questions. If sovereignty is predicated on a fiction that arises through war, how does biopower enable sovereignty to deny war through a legal fiction of *Terra Nullius?* Is the refusal to declare war itself a tactic of war? What would be useful is to consider the representation of power within the law, rights, sovereignty paradigm by approaching the relationship between Indigenous sovereignty and state sovereignty as relations of force located within a matrix of biopower. This is to identify and explicate the coexistence and mutual imbrications of a universal discourse of individual human rights and the prerogative of collective White possession that underpins the Australian national project. The specific aims of such a challenge are (1) to provide an extensive study of the emergence of Indigenous people into history as subjects of rights in the 1970s through political activism, legislative and policy change, the emergence of Australian nationalism, and media representations; (2) to trace how White possession manifests as a mode of rationality in a variety of disciplines, such as law, history, Australian studies, anthropology, Aboriginal studies, and political science from the rights activism of the 1970s to the present; (3) to extend an understanding of the terrain of sovereignty in Australia as relations of force in a war of races normalized through biopower, contributing to an understanding of how Indigenous sovereignty and its disavowal have shaped Australian nationalism. This would facilitate an exploration of the proposition that White possession is more than a right and consider how it functions to reproduce procedures of subjugation that are tied to racialized and racializing knowledges produced by disciplines dedicated to the sciences of "man."[26] In particular, we could examine how academic disciplines such as history, political science, Aboriginal studies, Australian studies, and anthropology have operated as normalizing modes of rationality that facilitate procedures of Indigenous subjugation and mask non-Indigenous investments in relations of patriarchal White sovereignty.

This is to ask: to what extent does White possession circulate as a regime of truth that simultaneously constitutes White subjectivity and circumscribes the political possibilities of Indigenous sovereignty? How does it manifest as part of commonsense knowledge, decision-making, and socially produced conventions and signs? This issue poses a series of further questions:

In what sense do rights function as tactics and strategies of race war?

How do "rights" contribute to creating bodies of knowledge and multiple fields of "Aboriginal" expertise?

What was and is the role of the human sciences (anthropology, political science, Australian studies, Aboriginal studies, etc.) in disciplining the rights claims of Indigenous people?

How does White possession of the nation function normatively within disciplines and their discourse of rights?

What are these disciplines and what truths do they produce about rights?

How and where do these truths circulate as rights claims and counterclaims?

What are their multiple forms?

Central to this is the question of how to define White possession as a concept. According to the judicio-philosophical tradition, possession is the foundation of property; it requires physical occupation and the will and desire to possess. Possession of lands is imagined to be held by the king, and in modernity it is the nation-state (the Crown) that holds exclusively possession on behalf of its subjects. Therefore possession is tied to right and power. Foucault argues that right is both an instrument of, and vehicle for, the exercising of the multiplicity of dominations in society and the relations that enable their implementation. He notes that these relations are not relations of sovereignty, and argues that the system of right and the judicial field are enduring channels for relations of domination and the many forms and techniques of subjugation. For this reason, rights should not be understood as the establishment of legitimacy but rather the method by which subjugation is carried out.[27] The limitation of Foucault's definition of right is that he does not account for the Whiteness of sovereignty, without which biopower could not function. As Stoler's work shows, racial thinking and notions of Whiteness were powerfully determinative of imperial maps that were broader than Foucault's genealogy of bourgeois identity and its biopolitics.[28]

In *Society Must Be Defended,* Foucault defines a historico-political field as a shift from a history

> whose function was to establish right by recounting the exploits of heroes or kings, their battles and wars . . . to a history that continues war by deciphering the war and the struggle that are going on within all institutions of rights and peace. History thus becomes a knowledge of struggles that is deployed and that functions within a field of struggles; there is now a link between the political fight and historical knowledge.[29]

An historico-political field is constituted by certain elements: a myth of sovereignty, a counternarrative, and the emergence of a new subject in history. The 1970s in Australia can be identified as an historico-political field in this sense because a new Indigenous subject emerged in history to challenge the myth of patriarchal White sovereignty through a counternarrative. This is not to say that Indigenous sovereignty and resistance did not exist before the 1970s; they always have. However, what distinguishes this period for investigation is the eruption of the discourse of rights and the Australian nation's exposure to Indigenous sovereignty claims through mass media and Indigenous demonstrations. Prior to the 1970s, the implicit subject of the rights discourse was the White subject, who represented the universal in human rights. This did not take account of the specificities of the rights of subjects with different embodiments, histories, and sexual orientations. The eruption of rights claims by subjects under the banner of women's and gay and lesbian liberation, as well as the fight to recognize the contribution of non-Anglo migrants, has recently been refracted through the lens of a socially conservative neoliberalism as a fractious form of identity politics. However, because these claims are made within the judicio-politico framework they paradoxically assume the legitimacy of patriarchal White sovereignty. This is in contrast to Indigenous sovereignty claims, which contested the very premise of White sovereignty. *Talkin' Up to the White Woman* argues that this distinction between non-Indigenous claims for recognition and equality within the nation-state and claims to ontological precedence and belonging is why Indigenous women's rights are not commensurable with those of White women.[30]

The eruption of the rights discourse in the 1970s was due to influences that were both global and national in character, influenced by events in the 1960s that challenged established norms, values, and social conventions. In Foucauldian terms, this represents a phase of war whereby the antagonisms, confrontations, and struggles of the 1960s became represented strategically and tactically through a discourse of rights in the 1970s. In Australia the effects were twofold: the formal assertion of Australia as an independent sovereign nation and the rights claims of subjects within its borders. Australia's formal separation from British judicial review meant that the High Court of Australia was the final court of appeal. Discriminatory legislation affecting Aborigines was revoked and our human rights were brought into a broader public discourse that encompassed racial and sexual discrimination. Simultaneously, what it meant to be an Australian was being redefined. The White Australia policy was formally abolished in 1972, and multiculturalism was promoted as Australia's new national policy.[31] Within the academy, Australian Studies centers were funded here and abroad to explore, examine, and define Australian national identity, and Indigenous studies emerged as a field of study in its own right. This raises the following questions: Did the eruption of "rights," in its many forms, produce new procedures of Indigenous subjugation? Do these procedures continue today in the remaking of Australian national identity evident in neoconservative politics, the history wars, and High Court decisions on Mabo and Indigenous native title?

My concern is not with how Indigenous sovereignty can be accommodated or included within the discourse of rights, or how they are located within an identity politics framework. Rather it is to propose that we need to investigate how White possession functions through a discourse of rights within the disciplines of law, political science, history, and anthropology on which Australian studies and Indigenous studies have relied since their formation, and examine how White possession manifests in regulatory mechanisms including legal decisions, government policy, and legislation. Critical analysis of the role of these disciplines and regulatory mechanisms in reinforcing the prerogatives of White possession should provide a significant new perspective on the politics of sovereignty in Australia.

Foucault's work on rights, race, war, and sovereignty lends itself to the analysis of legislation and legal decision-making about Indigenous sovereignty, land rights, and native title. In substantive terms this could entail the following:

- examination of anthropological models of Indigenous land tenure and their representation in legislation and court decisions;
- textual analysis of media representations of Indigenous sovereignty claims and decisions, such as land rights, native title, and reparations;
- an explication of the emergence of "Aboriginal" history and associated debates about Indigenous sovereignty;
- analysis of government policy concerning Indigenous sovereignty, land rights, and native title; and
- critical evaluation of representations of national identity and Indigenous sovereignty within Australian studies, political science, and Aboriginal studies.

This would be an innovative approach in bringing to bear upon Indigenous sovereignty in a sustained and analytic way the kinds of questions that have emerged in recent years from the rich and suggestive body of theoretical work in Whiteness and race studies in the new and interdisciplinary humanities.

As the United States pursues an imperial project of delivering democratic rights and freedoms throughout the world, a growing body of Whiteness theory in the United States has provided a counternarrative of a nation-state that continues to privilege the collective interests of White people in spite of the civil rights gains of the 1960s and 1970s. Underlying this approach is the theoretical problem central to Whiteness studies of understanding how racialized knowledge works in power relations. Understanding the complexity of power as both productive and repressive involves exploring not only disciplinary knowledges but also their regulative mechanisms and techniques of subjugation.

CONCLUSION

Applying the sociological imagination to bring together Foucault's ideas about race, war, and sovereignty, critical Whiteness studies, and Indigenous sovereignty has produced unfamiliar questions that are raised for future research. This article offers a challenge to Australian sociology to consider researching Indigenous sovereignty, exploring the way racialization works by extending the concept of "race" to denote more than just the bodies of the non-White "other." A new research agenda could extend the scope and the depth of existing work on Indigenous sovereignty, Whiteness, and race by producing analytical insights at the national level, making the Australian case central to international developments in the field. This may require Australian sociology to be more flexible with its imagination if it is to develop conceptual models that do not obscure fundamental problems with contemporary understandings of society and politics in Western countries where Indigenous sovereignty continues to exist.

NOTES

1. Irene Watson, "Aboriginal Laws and the Sovereignty of Terra Nullius," *Borderlands* 1, no. 2 (2002), www.borderlands.net.au/vol1no2_2002/watson_laws .html, para. 4.

2. C. Wright Mills, *The Sociological Imagination* (1959; Oxford: Oxford University Press, 2000).

3. Michel Foucault, *Society Must Be Defended: Lectures at the Collège de France, 1975–1976* (London: Penguin Books, 2003).

4. Watson, "Aboriginal Laws."

5. Raymond Williams, *The American Indian in Western Legal Thought* (New York: Oxford University Press, 1990); Patricia Monture-Angus, *Journeying Forward: Dreaming Aboriginal People's Independence* (London: Pluto, 2000).

6. Aileen Moreton-Robinson, "The Possessive Logic of Patriarchal White Sovereignty: The High Court and the Yorta Yorta Decision," *Borderlands* 3, no. 2 (2004), www.borderlands.net.au/vol3no2_2004/moreton_possessive.htm.

7. Duncan Ivison, Paul Patton, and Will Sanders, eds., *Political Theory and the Rights of Indigenous Peoples* (Cambridge: Cambridge University Press, 2000).

8. See, e.g., Peter Havemann, ed., *Indigenous Peoples' Rights in Australia, Canada, and New Zealand.* (Auckland: Oxford University Press, 1999); Paul Keal, *European Conquest and the Rights of Indigenous Peoples* (Cambridge: Cambridge University Press, 2003); and Marcia Langton, Maureen Tehan, Lisa Palmer, and Katherine Shain, eds., *Honour among Nations? Treaties and Agreements with Indigenous People* (Carlton, Vic.: Melbourne University Publishing, 2004).

9. See, e.g., S. James Anaya, *Indigenous Peoples in International Law* (New York: Oxford University Press, 1996); Sarah Pritchard, ed., *Indigenous Peoples, the United Nations, and Human Rights* (London: Zed Books; Leichhardt, N.S.W.: Federation Press, 1998).

10. Henry Reynolds, *Aboriginal Sovereignty: Reflections on Race, State, and Nation,* (St. Leonards, NSW: Allen & Unwin, 1996).

11. Bain Attwood, *Rights for Aborigines* (St. Leonards, NSW: Allen & Unwin, 2003).

12. Larissa Behrendt, *Achieving Social Justice: Indigenous Rights and Australia's Future* (Annandale, NSW: Federation Press, 2003).

13. Foucault, *Society Must Be Defended,* 57.

14. Ibid., 81.

15. Ibid., 60.

16. Homi Bhabha, *The Location of Culture* (London: Routledge 1994); Robert Young, *Colonial Desire: Hybridity in Theory, Culture and Race* (London: Routledge, 1995).

17. Aileen Moreton-Robinson, "'I Still Call Australia Home': Indigenous Belonging and Place in a White Postcolonising Society," in *Uprootings/Regroundings: Questions of Home and Migration,* ed. Sara Ahmed, Claudia Castañeda, Anne-Marie Fortier, and Mimi Sheller (London: Berg, 2003).

18. Ann Laura Stoler, *Race and the Education of Desire: Foucault's "History of Sexuality" and the Colonial Order of Things* (Durham, NC: Duke University Press, 1995).

19. Brad Elliot Stone, "Defending Society from the Abnormal: The Archaelogy of Bio-Power," *Foucault Studies* 1 (2004): 77–91.

20. John Marks, "Foucault, Franks, Gauls," *Theory, Culture, and Society* 17, no. 5 (2000): 127–47.

21. Eduardo Mendieta, "'To Make Live and to Let Die': Foucault on Racism," paper presented at the meeting of the Foucault Circle, APA Central Division

Meeting, Chicago, Apr. 25, 2002, www.researchgate.net/publication/262737391_
To_make_live_and_to_let_die_Foucault_on_Racism.

22. See, e.g., Karen Brodkin, *How Jews Became White Folk and What That Says about Race in America* (New Brunswick, NJ: Rutgers University Press, 1999); Kimberlé Crenshaw, Neil Gotanda, Gary Peller, and Kendall Thomas, eds., *Critical Race Theory: The Key Writings that Formed the Movement* (New York: New Press, 1995); Chris Cuomo and Kim Hall, *Whiteness: Feminist Philosophical Reflections* (Lanham, MD: Rowman & Littlefield, 1999); Richard Delgado and Jean Stefancic, *Critical Whiteness Studies: Looking behind the Mirror* (Philadelphia: Temple University Press, 1997); Richard Dyer, *White: Essays on Race and Culture* (London: Routledge, 1997); Barbara Flagg, *Was Blind, but Now I See: White Race Consciousness and the Law* (New York: New York University Press, 1998); Ruth Frankenberg, *White Women, Race Matters: The Social Construction of Whiteness* (London: Routledge, 1993); Ian Haney Lopez, *White by Law: The Legal Construction of Race* (New York: New York University Press, 1996); Cheryl Harris, "Whiteness as Property," in Crenshaw et al. (eds.), *Critical Race Theory,* 276–91; Mike Hill, ed., *Whiteness: A Critical Reader* (New York: New York University Press, 1997); Cynthia Levine-Rasky, *Working through Whiteness: International Perspectives* (Albany: State University of New York Press, 2002); Toni Morrison, *Playing in the Dark: Whiteness and the Literary Imagination* (Cambridge, MA: Harvard University Press, 1992); Birgit Brander Rasmussen, Eric Klinenberg, Irene J. Nexica, and Matt Wray, eds., *The Making and Unmaking of Whiteness* (Durham, NC: Duke University Press, 2001).

23. Warren Montag, "The Universalisation of Whiteness: Racism and Enlightenment," in Hill (ed.), *Whiteness,* 285.

24. Warwick Anderson, *The Cultivation of Whiteness: Science, Health and Racial Identity in Australia* (Melbourne: Melbourne University Press, 2002); Ghassan Hage, *Against Paranoid Nationalism* (Annandale, NSW: Pluto, 2003); Belinda McKay, ed., *Unmasking Whiteness: Race and Reconciliation* (St. Lucia: University of Queensland Press, 1999); A. Moreton-Robinson, ed., *Whitening Race: Essays in Social and Cultural Criticism* (Canberra: Aboriginal Studies Press, 2004); idem, "Possessive Logic of Patriarchal White Sovereignty"; idem, "I Still Call Australia Home"; Fiona Nicoll, *From Diggers to Drag Queens: Configurations of Australian National Identity* (Annandale, NSW: Pluto, 2001); idem, "Reconciliation in and out of Perspective: White Knowing, Seeing, Curating, and Being at Home in and against Indigenous Sovereignty," in Moreton-Robinson (ed.), *Whitening Race,* 17–30.

25. The following essays are all from Moreton-Robinson (ed.), *Whitening Race:* Alison Ravenscroft, "Anxieties of Dispossession: Whiteness, History, and Australia's War in Viet Nam," 3–16; Nicoll, "Reconciliation in and out of Perspective"; Toula Nicolacopoulos and George Vassilacopoulos, "Racism, Foreigner Communities, and the Onto-pathology of White Australian Subjectivity," 32–47; and Kate Foord, "Frontier Theory: Displacement and Disavowal in the Writing of White Nations," 133–47.

26. David Theo Goldberg, *Racist Culture: Philosophy and the Politics of Meaning* (Oxford: Blackwell, 1993), 149.

27. Foucault, *Society Must Be Defended,* 27.

28. Stoler, *Race and the Education of Desire,* 16.

29. Foucault, *Society Must Be Defended,* 171.

30. Aileen Moreton, *Talkin' Up to the White Woman: Indigenous Women and Feminism* (St. Lucia: University of Queensland Press, 2000).

31. See, e.g., Laksiri Jayasuriya, David Walker, and Jan Gothard, eds., *Legacies of White Australia: Race, Culture, and Nation* (Crawley: University of Western Australia Press, 2003); Jon Stratton, *Race Daze: Australia in Identity Crisis* (Sydney: Pluto Press, 1998).

FOURTEEN

Why Black Lives Matter in the Humanities

Felice Blake

> With current economic and world crises filling public consciousness, the crisis in the humanities pales a bit.
>
> **KATHERINE BAILEY MATHAE AND CATHERINE LANGREHR BIRZER**[1]

> These texts are becoming a way of gaining knowledge of the "other": a knowledge that appears to satisfy and replace the desire to challenge existing frameworks of segregation. Have we, as a society, successfully eliminated the desire for achieving integration through political agitation for civil rights and opted instead for knowing each other through cultural texts?
>
> **HAZEL CARBY**[2]

"I study Shakespeare; I don't do race." It's not uncommon for students who enroll in one of my courses on colorblindness to inform me on the first day of class that, as students majoring or seeking higher degrees in English, they do not "do race." It's a peculiar sensation, this feeling of being a humanities scholar committed to the study of how people process and document the human experience, on the one hand, and on the other, the discomfort of being confronted with the glaring reality of race as central to that endeavor. One might imagine that reading literature would be one of the most ideal fields for gathering invaluable insights from such an engagement with race and human experience. After all, the voices and representations of those whom policy, practice, and prejudice have labeled as threats, nonnormative, subject to exclusion, or simply as "others" pervade the creative texts featured as required readings in English departments across the United States. Critical attention to their presence and perspectives has deepened how we understand citizenship, nationalism, belonging, power, difference, and the very notion of being itself. Even still, students of literature are somehow able to hold onto the sincere belief that race-specific engagements with text analysis belong to a specialized field of study (there's modernism, the logic goes, and Black modernism), that it's particular (there's the British novel and thereafter other forms of the novel), that it implies an unsavory sociological perspective (considerations of structural oppression take away from the important attention to literariness), or that it is simply a form of identity politics that ruptures national unity. Despite my students' interest in taking a course on colorblindness, what we may describe as their defensive or self-protective articulations about whether or not they "do race" indicate how race-conscious literary studies force us to reckon with the colorblind assumptions about what literary scholars do.

This essay contributes to the discussion of colorblindness and the disciplines through an examination of the paradoxical situation of literary studies. I contend that the study of literature has adopted a multicultural stance under the sway of colorblind epistemologies. The first chapter epigraph above and my contribution to the examination of colorblindness identify the seeming disconnection between attention to the crisis facing the humanities and the crises related to economic and political calamities confronting the planet. The notion that the crisis in the humanities is unrelated to social crises outside it or that its perspectives have nothing to contribute to understanding or tackling these broader concerns is extremely troubling.

The concerns about and remedies to important issues like mass incarceration, entrenched poverty, climate change, and unending warfare, for example, are not exclusive to political and economic investigation. Indeed, documentation of the human experience must take account of the conditions *and* the perspectives sustaining such conditions into the investigation and recording of our collective struggles and how we understand or define them. To do this work, the humanities must participate fully in such public debates about structural oppression and submit its unique insights to discussion and action. But the first epigraph also suggests that the failure of the humanities to engage these debates critically has amounted to humanities-related fields' perceived irrelevance to needed preparations for living in and transforming our world.

As Hazel Carby argues in the second epigraph, reading texts by and about aggrieved populations has taken the place of creating actual relationships across difference and of agitating for political and social transformation. Carby suggests that the tendency to particularize race rather than see its structuring effect enables the maintenance of sanctioned, colorblind methodologies and of colorblind readings within humanities disciplines. While English or even literature departments in the United States would oppose the accusation of colorblindness, they are less likely to examine the underlying premises of their discipline and its hegemonic presuppositions. Such an approach does little to revitalize the discipline, to promote its relevance in public debates about racism and structural oppression, or to demonstrate its own commitment to examining how people process and document the human experience.

It isn't enough to include texts by historically aggrieved populations in the curriculum and classroom without producing new approaches to reading. Scholars like James Lee demonstrate how such inclusion without attention to the histories and structures of oppression justifies the organized abandonment of underrepresented communities.[3] If those groups are on the syllabus, isn't that an indication that we've done the work of recognizing them and including them into the consciousness of the U.S. polity? Carby's epigraph exposes a forked and rather thorny problematic that my students' attitudes about my courses on colorblindness affirm. In part, the inclusion and recognition of the works and perspectives of historically marginalized populations challenged the exclusive focus on hegemonic narratives about the nation that determined the value of whose (human) experience matters. Because the canon wars, which I discuss below, were so publicly waged in the theater of U.S. English departments, one might guess that these institutional sites would be at the forefront in responding to the necessary transformation in what counts as knowledge as well as to the critical lenses within the discipline itself. Yet the presence of aggrieved populations on syllabi and sometimes as faculty in the department may not result in the transformation of the epistemologies and methodologies for "reading" texts. If the study of ethnic literatures was once considered an antiracist technology, literary study today rarely seeks to upset the social apparatus. What Lee refers to as "managerial forms of multiculturalism" represents a compromise between the demand for inclusion and the submission to traditional manners of organizing humanities curricula, departments, and epistemologies. English departments continue to be the terrain where battles about such relevance primarily take place. The field, however, is perceived as being the least likely to produce a skill set for a salaried profession even as its practitioners struggle to conceptualize how to capitalize on its unique expertise. English therefore comes to symbolize the overall crisis of the humanities.

Because race is a structuring effect for all texts, what I describe as race-conscious reading practices challenge managerial forms of multiculturalism and colorblind epistemologies. Informed by social movements and rooted in material histories, these critical methodologies are interdisciplinary and promote public engagement. Although public opinion (and disparagement) thinks it was the gun, education was the Black Panther party's key strategy for self-defense. Educating Panther activists as well as the general public was central to the Panther program, for it enabled everyday people to engage intellectually, communally, and creatively in developing the visions of what society should and could look like. Literary scholar Doris Sommer has written extensively about how "political, economic, and emotional development depends on art" in ways that can and do shape and compel opportunities for "working constructively in the world."[4] With analyses from scholars of literature and ethnic studies, I trace the convergence between multiculturalism and colorblindness in English. I then describe in more detail how race-conscious reading practices produce new approaches and engagements with texts and the public. I conclude with a consideration of Black Lives Matter, the social movement of the 2000s and how its premises and activism interact with the unique contribution literary studies and race-conscious reading can offer to our intellectual and public engagements. Throughout I develop what a race-conscious reading practice contributes to these intellectual and activist efforts to confront our collective crises.

HOW MULTICULTURALISM BECAME COLORBLIND

> Today it's generally agreed that the multiculturalists won the canon wars.
>
> RACHEL DONADIO[5]

How does someone become a humanities-based, multiculturalist faculty member in the academy? New critiques claim that humanities education disregards mainstream cultural values and instead converts universities into indoctrination mills. There is growing concern that humanities majors receive degrees that make them unemployable and endow students with an education that puts them out of step with utilitarian culture. It is said that these disciplines fail to teach students in a manner that allows them to convey their research to the public in a meaningful or understandable way. If the multiculturalists supposedly won the first instantiation of the canon wars in the 1980s, as Rachel Donadio claims, then the demise of the humanities would seem to be the humanities' own doing, in its approach to the teaching and training of scholars. Preparing graduate students for the profession is just one place where such concerns emerge.

Because prospective faculty appointments depend on the assessment of scholars' areas of expertise and thus teaching, candidates who profess an engagement with race, gender, and sexuality indicate their training in so-called multicultural or progressive pedagogies and research. Research, teaching, and service are the trifecta of evaluation for both appointment and promotion. For example, for a mock interview, the practicing candidate has submitted job materials, such as a CV and sample syllabi, that include race and gender among his fields of research and teaching interests. As we discuss ideas about potential classes, I ask the mock candidate how his stated interest in race and gender would shape the hypothetical course under examination. After naming one or two female writers and/or authors of color, the candidate falls silent, seemingly satisfied with his answer to my question. Redirecting, I ask how the reading of those suggested texts might interact with the other material he imagines teaching. Prompted by the interviewee's obvious perplexity, another committee member moves the mock interview toward a discussion of *his* ideal course based on the specificity of the candidate's dissertation project.

Literary studies, or what we understand as the work of English departments, have at different times refused, redefined, or renegotiated the interventions that social movements produced in higher education. Expressed commitments to diversity and multiculturalism on campus and in the curriculum did not necessarily bring about the transformation of what counts as evidence in terms of scholarly literary engagement and criticism in teaching, research methodologies, and publications. For example, it is uncommon to find as required coursework for the English major survey courses on the literature of aggrieved U.S. populations. While Phyllis Wheatley, Frederick Douglass, Richard Wright, W. E. B Du Bois, James Baldwin, and Toni Morrison may now be required reading of the canon of U.S. literature, their crucial interventions about the function of literature and literary studies are less likely to be engaged critically as oppositions to the traditional development of the field and its underlying premises. Instead, Wheatley's poetry became proof of the presumed significance of European literary traditions with regard to humanity and rationality. The beauty of her literacy and writing under slavery become represented as a testament to White humanitarianism, benevolence, and instruction. The vexed issue of race and writing under structures of oppression becomes buried underneath the celebration of slave literacy in the terms of European rationality and humanity. Frederick Douglass famously challenged the relationship between racism, oratory, and national identity in "The Meaning of July Fourth for the Negro," an 1852 speech delivered to the Rochester Ladies' Anti-Slavery Society. Celebrating the national day was a revelation and reminder of "the gross injustice and cruelty to which [the slave] is a constant victim."[6] The most celebrated Black writers of the early twentieth-century New Negro era repeatedly exposed, challenged, and renegotiated the relationship between writing and public recognition, oftentimes championing Black cultural expression as a vehicle for gaining political rights.

Mass incarceration, economic abjection, and state violence in the form of civilian murder by the police continue to challenge Black political rights. Even still, the celebration of exceptional Black artists in the name of multiculturalism occurs simultaneously on college campuses across the country.[7] The representation of individual talents of color instead of critical engagement with the fundamental reimagination of the discipline of English enabled the celebration of Alice Walker at a time when the War on Drugs, hyperpolicing, prison expansion, and attacks on welfare occupied the attention of public officials and policy debates. We may have had *The Color Purple,* but did we think critically about the novel's profound concern with the vulnerability and the complexities of poor Black communities even as we championed Black creativity?

African American authors and intellectuals have always challenged the presumption of Black subordination and highlighted the role of culture and cultural artists in naturalizing such ideologies of Black inferiority and the related falsehood of white superiority. As James Baldwin observes, "A black writer in this country to be born into the English language is to realize that the assumptions on which the language operates are his enemy."[8] Baldwin suggests that the history and the praxis of the Black artist has been to create language, a new grammar, and thus a new subjectivity not rooted in the dominant terms of meaning and recognition. Toni Morrison, the first female American writer to receive the Nobel Prize for literature, also describes how U.S. literature is always marked by its own creation of a racial other. In *Playing in the Dark,* she asks how the supposed intellectual investment in the disciplinary boundaries of the field of literature mimic and legitimate the material realities of racist exploitation existent inside *and* outside the ivory tower. She interrogates the reward structure in place that enables literary scholars to achieve and advance professionally without any recognition or examination of the role of racism, colonialism, or imperialism in the formation of Western literary traditions and cultural production. Morrison argues that even "some powerful literary critics in the United States have never read, and are proud to say so, *any* African-American text. It seems to have done them no harm, presented them with no discernible limitations in the scope of their work or influence."[9] African American letters consistently examine the fundamental problematic between structural oppression and national traditions in politics, economics, society, and literature. Even a casual engagement with the most canonical texts by these writers reveals the problematic between writing, race, and structures of oppression. How, then, did the inclusion of these texts under the commitment to diversity and multiculturalism become colorblind?

The value of race and gender in the job market, as the mock candidate shows, reflects a *limited* form of engagement with and recognition of these perspectives. Such recognition was gained through the struggles commonly referred to as the canon or cultural wars of the 1970s and '80s. These struggles emerged from social movements and waged an institutional and public battle over the curriculum, methodologies, and ideologies determining the value of U.S. education. Roderick Ferguson describes how ethnic and women's movements confronted the figure of Western man and attempted to replace him with other characters and characteristics that represented the real existence of other idioms and histories.[10] This confrontation challenged disciplinary foundations and included the demand for and development of interdisciplinary fields like Black studies as well as new admissions and hiring policies.[11] Staged most prominently and symbolically in the English departments of U.S. college and university campuses, these demands inevitably meant creating a new epistemology of reading itself, the very thing that literary scholars do.

Canon wars "represent crises of political recognition that usually have galvanized proponents of the hegemonic culture against a perceived threat to that culture."[12] The very phrase "canon war" already distinguishes the progressive transformations of the 1960s from the institutional antagonisms over what education means and what purpose it should serve. In opposition to the proponents of new paths for university study, positions like Allan Bloom's *The Closing of the American Mind* argued that new directions in university education, represented by the perspectives emerging from 1960s radical movements, failed democracy and harmed students.[13] Issues related to race, gender, and sexuality for Bloom indicate a relativism that closes minds. In other words, protecting the established canon meant opposing struggles for racial, gendered, and sexual equality politically and therefore within the academy.

In addition, the preservation of the traditional canon signified a defense of the institution as a site of national identity invested in the promotion of white, heteropatriarchal normativity. Scholars like Walter Benn Michaels and Richard Rorty critiqued multiculturalism but celebrated minoritized exceptionality. Michaels promoted the notion that the trouble with diversity was its attention to difference and that such focus promoted divisions that did little to eliminate racial difference as the basis of racism itself.[14] Rorty argued specifically against ethnic or multicultural requirements for students, but conceded the value of the presence of some scholars of color. He writes:

> It is quite true that if you are a recent Ph.D. in the humanities or social sciences, your chances of finding a teaching job are very good if you are a black female and pretty bad if you are a white male. But such preferential hiring has, on balance, been a good thing for our universities. Those black females— few of whom were seen on university campuses during the first 200 years of U.S. history—include some of our leading intellectuals.

Rorty praises the individual talent, but opposes what he perceives as multiculturalism's critique of the national ethos. "Mythic America is a great country, and the insecure and divided actual America is a pretty good one" he states. "As racist, sexist, and homophobic as the United States is," Rorty believes in the overall progress of U.S. society. To proclaim the American myth a fraud, "multiculturalism cuts the ground out from under its own feet, quickly devolving into anti-Americanism."[15] Rorty's and Michaels's arguments sacrifice the reimagination of humanities education at the altar of traditional nationalism.

The canon wars thus reveal the operation of what Cedric Robinson calls a "racial regime" that proposes race "as a justification for the relations of power."[16] Racially charged language regarding Western civilization, national culture, and cultural literacy enabled a defense of the canon and opposition to 1960s movements by championing Eurocentric presumptions of intellectual value and national cohesion as universal ideals without explicit reference to gender or whiteness. Activist opposition to structural racism and sexism in *all* institutions revealed the masquerade of cultural and national histories that such references to supposedly universal and thus colorblind arguments sought to legitimate. Racial regimes, however, as Robinson argues, "are unrelentingly hostile to their exhibition," precisely because the social relations they seek to justify cannot bear up when their authority has been exposed as a forgery of history and as an oppressive definition of intellectual legitimacy.[17] As Torres-Padilla reminds us, the perceived threat to the racial status quo *is* political and mobilizes those invested in preserving the norm. In other words, the canon wars of the 1970s and '80s also functioned to produce renewed allegiances to Western man and to provide cover for the racial regime. One of the main ways this occurred was through the concession to multiculturalism and a fabricated literary history of multicultural America despite the hostility provoked by the cultural wars, which still rages just beneath the surface.

Instead of excluding the presence of nonwhite authorship from English department curricula, a practice of exclusion that held sway from the 1930s to the 1980s, formerly denied writers and texts could be included, as it were, to death. Inclusion, rather than exclusion, can also function to reproduce the racial status quo. The crisis that 1960s and '70s social movements produced in the academy was managed by commodifying and containing minority cultures under the banner of multicultural acceptance and the incorporation of certain texts and writers into the canon. As Roderick Ferguson argues, the inclusion of minority difference and culture indicates an "adaptive hegemony" or the redirection of insurgency toward normativity.[18] The state, capital, and the academy saw minority insurgence as a site of calculation and strategy. Rather than repression, institutional power produced multiculturalism as a universal and marketable good and managed difference by incorporating and disciplining it. Minority difference and culture thus become institutional objectives within and outside of college and university campuses as the academy becomes enlisted as a conduit for politics, economics, the state, and capital.[19]

Articulating a commitment to diversity in university pamphlets and websites and the creation of diversity requirements are some of the ways that campuses have adopted a defanged multiculturalism. Such diversity coursework often takes place in the humanities and especially in English departments that offer students from across the campus a *limited* introduction to the histories, culture, and perspectives of minoritized U.S. populations. For many students, these courses represent their only exposure to the critical study of race during their entire university experience. But without extending the epistemologies and methodologies gained from such scholarly engagement into the classrooms, research, and career planning students otherwise undertake, academic definitions of diversity remain segregated as tangential inquiries or narrow university demands.

Reducing multiculturalism in this way gives support to the representational fallacy that accepts language as the transparent representation of reality. Ask any undergraduate English major about what literary scholars do, and "close reading" will inevitably figure prominently in the response. Attention to the language, patterns, imagery, and so on of a text or collection of texts has been a primary agreed-upon methodology that literary practitioners teach and espouse. Close reading, however, is not colorblind or gender neutral. Perceiving the literature by people of color as merely the realist representation of reality also enables the dismissal of those very texts as uncritical. Perceiving literature that engages social reality as devoid of creativity in favor of its social justice commitments permits the dismissal of the theoretical and epistemological tensions and insights that such literature produces. The theoretical insight *and* social justice commitments of authors like Phyllis Wheatley, Frederick Douglass, Richard Wright, W. E. B. Du Bois, James Baldwin, and Toni Morrison can be readily, even if unconsciously, disregarded in favor of one's own training in English or other disciplines.[20] If diversity requirements can be fulfilled through a course on so-called minority literature, it is therefore not difficult to see how English and the humanities by extension can appear analytically distant from the public crises that compel our anxieties and consume our social, political, and economic worlds. Regulating difference in this way, wherein theoretical insights are presumed to be universal and thus race-neutral, enables the re-creation of national and cultural unity from heterogeneity. At the same time, such regulation turns attention to injustice into an aesthetic pleasure rather than critical and social engagement. Multiculturalism must necessarily be divorced from social justice organizing in order to escape the label of identity politics. "Doing race" in this way becomes possible insofar as it fails to make a difference to the normative expectations of what a literary scholar is trained to do, know, and repeat.

The unpredicted outcome of the canon wars, as waged in the humanities, has resulted in what I call "colorblind multiculturalism." As described above, colorblind multiculturalism comprises the simultaneous institutional, representational incorporation of texts by people of color and the political neutralization of their theoretical, methodological, and activist interventions. Its emphasis on difference does not address which differences make a difference and why. Its axis of margin and center occludes the axis of oppression and suppression. Colorblindness is the umbrella under which managerial multiculturalism circulates and becomes a sacrificial institutional defense. When universities articulate their commitment to diversity, they can simultaneously use that very claim to guard against accusations of racism. The presence of people of color among the faculty and in student, curricular, and administrative registers depends on the false presumption that representation alone satisfies the demands for racial, gendered, and sexual justice. As other authors in this collection point out, colorblindness has been widely embraced as a primary national value across political orientation, party lines, sectoral boundaries, and even racial identities. Most U.S. institutions are now formally organized around the untested presumption that colorblindness is the exclusive measure of a fair and just organizational practice. In seeking recognition from academic institutions, those same sites were empowered to define multiculturalism and to grant, affirm, and legitimate minoritized life and culture.[21] Recognition becomes a function of incorporation. Such institutional power extends beyond the university and interacts with public politics and crises.

The canon wars took place during an era of neoconservatism and neoliberalism. Neoliberal ideologies and policies erode the social safety net through heightened emphasis on privatization and by neutralizing social threats to the neoliberal order. As Jodi Melamed shows in *Represent and Destroy,* colleges and universities are also tasked with the training and preparation of subjects recruited into such neoliberal ways of being and knowing.[22] Melamed describes the long history of recognizing and incorporating literature by minoritized communities to demonstrate U.S. exceptionalism. Neoliberal concessions repositioned ethnic literatures as, again, minor to British literature in English departments. Most importantly, they refused, at the level of methodology, to engage the critical questions that the confrontation posed. Liberal antiracist discourses incorporate and neutralize the literature emanating from racially subordinated U.S. populations. The neutralization and marginalization of people of color and their creative work requires dismissing the traditions and epistemologies of resistance emanating from subordinated communities as well.

In the "Politics of Literature," Paul Lauter describes the devaluing of oppositional culture and the freeing of greedy impulses of free market capitalism as outcomes of the canon wars. Capital reorganizes the domains of cultural production and consumption, including higher education, in order to further its own interests and to stifle the forging of informed opposition.[23] An unappreciated crisis of the humanities is its reinforcement as "the exclusive property of those with especially large amounts of personal, cultural, or institutional capital, an apparent luxury good that proves to be intrinsically valuable."[24] Post–canon wars, literary studies have thus become more entrenched in its possessive investment in privilege. Even still, the veneer of exclusivity only thinly veils the crisis confronting the humanities and the crises in our world.

Commitment to colorblind frameworks provokes another underexamined crisis of the humanities in its inability to reach populations related to immigrant communities and people of color. English departments continue to fail to attract Black students as majors or advanced degree candidates. According to the National Science Foundation (NSF), 34,005 U.S. citizens and permanent residents received doctorates in 2014, of which 4,360 were in the humanities. Of those, 1,303 doctorates went to candidates in letters, but only 2.8 percent, or approximately thirty-six, were Black scholars (compared to 83.2 percent White doctoral recipients). While 470 candidates earned doctorates in foreign language or literature, only 1.7 percent, or approximately eight, were Black scholars (compared to 71.1 percent White doctoral recipients).[25] Such numbers indicate that most U.S. campuses proceed annually with *no* Black students (or other scholars of color) pursuing PhDs in English departments.

The price English departments have paid for the colorblind and multiculturalist incorporation of minoritized literatures has been to die in relevance. One of the major criticisms of literary education is that it does not obviously translate into professional skills one can readily trade for monetary compensation in the current service-oriented labor market. Ironically, defenders of English and the humanities argue that the skills gained from training in these fields are highly desirable and that many corporations hire employees with degrees or competencies in humanities-related fields. But in a global economy marked by corporate greed, neoliberalism, and willful ignorance about inequality, is it enough for us to be proud that our graduates get jobs, without asking which parts of their training will inform their work? Should vocational survival be the sole or primary measure of value?

The interventions made possible by social activism during the canon wars were neither fully institutionalized *nor* insignificant. To presume that they were a failure is a wishful statement uttered by their enemies. The formations of racial and gendered studies as well as the disruption of canonical hegemony are only a few of the important transformations we continue to enjoy today. Taking seriously the lessons from ethnic studies and what ethnic literatures have brought to the very conception of literary studies produces a critique of reading practices divorced from praxis. Literature cannot be added on or contained in ways separated from social purpose. We cannot separate critical analysis from social movements. Resisting such a neoliberal expectation and colorblind multiculturalism are the bases for developing a critical analysis and race-conscious reading practices. Below, I explore just how a race-conscious practice in English and the humanities in general can move toward new intellectual and social justice–based commitments and possibilities.

RACE-CONSCIOUS READING PRACTICE AND THE BLACK RADICAL IMAGINATION

Octavia Butler's 1979 novel *Kindred* tells the story of a contemporary Black woman named Dana who is repeatedly summoned back to the 1800s and the antebellum plantation where her ancestor is born. Her returns to slavery are provoked by the threat of death to the plantation heir Rufus, the future slave-owner who will father Dana's family member. Her need to save Rufus amounts to her ability to ensure her own birth, or to save herself. During one of her sojourns, she attempts to shield Rufus from one of the books she has been reading. "This is the biggest lot of abolitionist trash I ever saw," he exclaims after perusing one of Sojourner Truth's speeches. When Dana informs him that the book appears a century after the abolition of slavery, Rufus retorts, "Then why the hell are they still complaining about it?"[26]

As Rufus's comment reveals, reading Truth's speech is insufficient if analysis and social movements are separated. In Butler's neoslave narrative, a contemporary novel imitates the form conventions of the antebellum slave narrative.[27] The genre emerges with the interventions of 1960s radical historians and examines the meaning of resistance and freedom given the social movements of the long 1960s. The neoslave narrative is therefore a type of archive of social movements and the transformations they envision. The book that Rufus catches sight of foretells the end of slavery and therefore the end of his way of life. The ongoing complaints against racial injustice that Rufus so readily belittles bring attention to the processes of recovery, recognition, and reexamination of Black texts and experiences that the neoslave narrative and the canon wars provoke.

Black scholars and artists have long provided us with insight about what race-conscious methodologies are and what they can do. For example, Arturo Schomburg, writing in the context of the 1920s New Negro Movement, posited that for Black Americans "a group tradition must supply compensation for persecution and pride of race the antidote for prejudice."[28] In this sense, his essay begins by acknowledging oppression and the role of research and critical engagement in contending with racism and its erasure of Black lives and contributions. Schomburg's efforts to study Black history in opposition to the dominant perception of black inferiority lead him to conclude that Black people have been active collaborators and pioneers in the struggle for their own freedom and advancement. He challenges the notion that educated and/or successful Black Americans are 'exceptional' and thus separate from the group. Schomburg also reiterates the significance of Black collective achievement despite environing conditions and discrimination. His important essay points to the role of race-conscious methodologies for recognizing Black people as subjects rather than objects of history. He identifies the unique group identity and epistemology driving Black experience and race-conscious methodologies. Finally, Schomburg promotes research, pedagogy, and education that include Black thought and achievement and, by so doing, challenge racist oppression.

What Schomburg identified in 1925 during a period of Black insurgency and contestation of Jim Crow further illustrates the synergy between the development of race-conscious practices and social movements. The contemporary Black Lives Matter movement emerges as the latest manifestation of a philosophical practice, epistemological perspective, and activist engagement known as the Black radical tradition. To shout "Black lives matter" is to echo the latest contestation of the racial status quo and colorblind ideology. As Alicia Garza, one of the founders of Black Lives Matter, states, the formation of the movement was "a response to the anti-Black racism that permeates our society and also, unfortunately, our movements." These activists understand their work as an ideological and political intervention in a world that systematically destroys Black lives. They seek also to affirm Black people's contributions to society and our humanity even "in the face of deadly oppression." Remaining in "active solidarity with all oppressed people who are fighting for their liberation," Black Lives Matter recognizes that our destinies are intertwined and simultaneously that "when Black people get free, everybody gets free."[29] Recent calls for the dismantling of Black and ethnic studies, the delegitimization of feminist and women's studies, the opposition to queer theory, especially its attention to transgender studies and analysis, and the hostility toward related student groups should compel us to examine and articulate how race-conscious reading practices can produce critical analyses attuned to the perspectives and visions of social movements.

Black Lives Matter (and its long history within the Black radical tradition) points out new modes of literary study that help us to develop methodologies within the humanities that are better equipped to understand the worlds we live in. Students in my Colorblindness seminar, for example, think critically about the ways that race pervades the worldview that comprises literary studies. Students move from declaring that they don't "do race" to an understanding of how even that statement is racially determined by their unchallenged expectations about who and how one reads in English departments. Reading Charles Mills's *The Racial Contract* helps us to discuss what we call the "literary contract" in order to challenge the racial underpinnings limiting presumptions that organize the field. We study Black writing and the paradox of the "book" along with Homi Bhabha, Henry Louis Gates, and Houston Baker. We consider how what Lisa Lowe calls "Asian American critique" transforms Asian American literature through its embedded memories of exclusion, exploitation, and resistance.[30] We engage how Chicano literature connected writing to the formation of radical subjectivity and Jose Muñoz's notion of disidentification in the context of creative performance practices and political strategies.[31] We develop race-conscious reading practices to connect close reading to our critical discussions of discourse and power. We learn from Cedric Robinson, who reminds us that racial regimes are weakened by their own greed, collective dissent, and resistance movements. Such an approach allows us to bring our interpretation of literary language into conversation with the historical, social, and political contexts that circumscribe the field of cultural production. Students then are able to consider new propositions for engaging critically with analyses seen in their examinations of a broad range of topics from surfing to segregation, from postmodernism to white masculinity, from the post–civil rights era to the horror genre, and colorblindness as risk theory, to name a few. In this way, the course also motivates students to think critically about their own writing for and in the profession in relation to their developing commitments to social engagement and social justice. Race-conscious reading practices also help to produce critical justice discourses connected to our engagement with documenting, examining, and *shaping* human experience and social relations. These relations include the interaction between humanities faculty, the students they train, and the conscious effort to face up to the crisis confronting the field and our world.

Thinking about race-conscious reading practices also forces me to think about my own role in the university and in the classroom. I failed two students: two activist students with sketchy attendance and an inability to satisfy the course requirements. These were activists who needed information and regularly expressed their appreciation of the significance of the course, my teaching style, my compassion, the readings, the collectivity, and the experience. In over a decade of experience teaching at the university, most of the students I have had to fail were activists also grappling with extraordinary circumstances, some of them with death, others poverty. These activists always took the information and applied it to community. Most of them are still politically active as community organizers or as graduate students.

The experience presents a challenge to students and faculty. How do we reach out to students and manage our fear and theirs about what failing in academia means? The academy does not talk to or serve students who rebel against academic requirements. We need to challenge the notion that we and our students are present for indoctrination into the demands of neoliberalism. This is not to argue that we should relax such expectations or pass students along without endowing them with the necessary skills for critical analysis, argumentation, and written articulation. It is to acknowledge that there is a disconnect between our professional frustrations with the demands of the neoliberal institution and our allegiance to reproducing such standards of achievement. It's also about justice that begins with us and includes us as we transform the conditions and meaning of education and intellectual inquiry.

Activist students are also underserved. Activist students do more for progressive transformation on campus and beyond, but receive the least from the schools in which they study. These are the same students who are the most likely to be demonized, scapegoated, marginalized, and dismissed for applying their learning and experiences to campus life. They find themselves deemed as unsophisticated for their attempts to apply their education and scholarship, although the university more likely will champion the spirit of 1960s activism and 1970s counterculture or timeless student political engagement across the spectrum. The demands of neoliberalism and the desire for institutional recognition compromised the spirit of radical inquiry and intellectual vanguardism. What if our students are struggling because they are resisting the neoliberal university that always places us in a position of proving ourselves on terms we never agreed with or agreed to? They may very well be exposing our own commitments to the rules and standards of neoliberalism. When I write that I failed students, I mean that in the opposing ways that such a statement could be understood. I failed them because they didn't live up to the requirements set for passing a university course, and I failed them in developing a collective understanding about what counts for knowledge at the university and beyond its walls.

Robin Kelley, writing about the eruption of campus activism in response to the killings of Black people by the police, moves away from the desire to make the university more hospitable for Black students. As we have seen, the liberal multiculturalist strategy sought to discipline such activist energies, "not to address the historical legacies of racism, dispossession, and injustice but rather to bring some people into the fold of a 'society no longer seen as racially unjust.'"[32] Race-conscious practices that refuse the separation between intellectual and social justice work must also guide faculty/student interactions in ways that transform the classroom into a space for study and struggle and remake the humanities as well.

When I write that black lives matter to the humanities, I also intend to engage with the Black Lives Matter movement's powerful proposition about addressing those nonnormative subjects who fail to matter in revolutionary interventions, even those who don't turn in work on time. The point is also about championing those who may be perceived as "others" where we work in the institution of higher education. If we recognize the normative work of the humanities in supporting the racial status quo, as so many scholars critical of the canon wars have made clear, then we must also think about race-conscious reading practices as translating to critiques of the classroom and its formal and informal dynamics. Looking at Black Lives Matter activity across campuses throughout the United States and beyond provides examples of the energies and manifestations of our students' demands and activist and intellectual commitments. These students, often in far more vulnerable positions, have committed themselves to leaving home and developing new sites for creating a more just place to live. Our students are our greatest allies.

CONCLUSION

Admittedly, I am a junior colleague in the humanities (specifically trained in English and literature) committed to the endeavor to renew and reimagine the work that we do as literary scholars. But I am also a scholar who came to my field in the midst of police brutality and the dominant legitimation of such atrocity. During my first year as an undergraduate English major at UCLA I sat, like so many people, seemingly paralyzed in front of the television as the news broadcast again and again the sequence of Rodney King being beaten by multiple LAPD officers while even more authorities looked on without intervening. In early March I had been planning festivities for my first birthday as a university student when my attention to party planning was disrupted by the televised images in the background. I wasn't a Black studies major, but I presumed that everyone would be invested and interested in talking about the obvious disruption to the racial status quo that King's beating recognized, what the trial, the acquittal, and the uprising meant to the study of humanity in 1991–92. To my dismay, getting back to business as usual, despite our location and our course of study as scholars of literature, was the party line that was adopted in the department. For many, reading Swift or Chaucer or Milton was a reprieve from the obvious tensions that literally arrived at our campus gates.

Protagonists of the humanities and English repeatedly argue that one of the main things the related fields have to offer is the path to leading fuller, more expansive, more thoughtful, happier lives, broadening perspective and developing critical consciousness. This would also entail leading a fuller, more expansive life in relation to activism and struggle, developing commitment to community, and extending intracommunity practices and ways of being that transform and develop reading practices and the spaces where those practices develop.

Just as Rodney King transformed me and my intellectual commitments, scholars of race and ethnicity have repeatedly demonstrated how their social engagements have transformed their approach to intellectual inquiry. The canon wars, over which there has been much debate as well as transformation, emerged from precisely the type of public consciousness that provoked my engagement with literary studies. It is impossible to imagine that the transformations in academia have occurred without their provocations by social movements. The title of my essay seeks to engage that reality. In other words, I do not seek to critique literary studies simply as a means to produce a new publication, but to emphasize the necessary and existing relationship between reading practices and the cultural and political field. We read not simply to marvel at the creativity of literariness, but to do so in ways that acknowledge that power as it articulates new ways of being, knowing, and engaging. Race-conscious reading practices point us toward a reorientation and transformation of the humanities and of the university itself. A revitalized humanities studying and documenting how people process human experience would be poised to set forth a new vision of possibility.

NOTES

1. Katherine Bailey Mathae and Catherine Langrehr Birzer, *Reinvigorating the Humanities: Enhancing Research and Education on Campus and Beyond* (Washington, DC: Association of American Universities, 2004), 4.

2. Hazel Carby, "The Multicultural Wars," *Radical History Review,* no. 54 (Oct. 1992) 7–18.

3. James Lee, *Urban Triage: Race and the Fictions of Multiculturalism* (Minneapolis: University of Minnesota Press, 2004).

4. Doris Sommer, "Useful Humanism," *PMLA* 121, no. 5 (Oct. 2006): 1670.

5. Rachel Donadio, "Revisiting the Canon Wars," *New York Times,* book review, Sept. 16, 2007, www.nytimes.com/2007/09/16/books/review/Donadio-t.html.

6. Frederick Douglass, "The Meaning of July Fourth for the Negro" (1852), in *The Norton Anthology of African American Literature,* ed. Henry Louis Gates Jr. and Nellie McKay (New York: Norton, 2004), 462–73.

7. Chandan Reddy, plenary discussion, Anti-racism Inc./Works Anti-conference, University of California, Santa Barbara, May 16, 2014.

8. James Baldwin, *The Cross of Redemption: Uncollected Writings* (New York: Pantheon Books, 2010), 114.

9. Toni Morrison, *Playing in the Dark: Whiteness and the Literary Imagination* (New York: Vintage, 1992), 13.

10. Roderick Ferguson, *The Reorder of Things: The University and Its Pedagogies of Minority Difference* (Minneapolis: University of Minnesota Press, 2012), 31.

11. Ibid., 31–32.

12. Jose Torres-Padilla, "Death to the Originary Narrative! Or, Insurgent Multiculturalism and Teaching Multiethnic Literature," *MELUS* 30, no. 2 (Summer 2005): 18.

13. Allan Bloom, *The Closing of the American Mind: How Higher Education Has Failed Democracy and Impoverished the Souls of Today's Students* (New York: Simon & Schuster, 1987), 34.

14. See Walter Benn Michaels, *Our America: Nativism, Modernism, and Pluralism* (Durham, NC: Duke University Press, 1995).

15. Richard Rorty, "The Demonization of Multiculturalism," *Journal of Blacks in Higher Education* 7 (Spring 1995): 74–75.

16. Cedric Robinson, *Forgeries of Memory and Meaning: Blacks and the Regimes of Race in American Theater and Film before World War II* (Chapel Hill: University of North Carolina Press, 2007), xii.

17. Ibid.

18. Ferguson, *The Reorder of Things,* 8.

19. Ibid., 6, 8.

20. See Alison Reed, "The Whiter the Bread, the Quicker You're Dead: Spectacular Absence and Postracialized Blackness in (White) Queer Theory," in *No Tea, No Shade: New Writings in Black Queer Studies,* ed. E. Patrick Johnson (Durham, NC: Duke University Press, 2016), 48–64.

21. Ferguson, *The Reorder of Things,* 13.

22. Jodi Melamed, *Represent and Destroy: Rationalizing Violence in the New Racial Capitalism* (Minneapolis: University of Minnesota Press, 2011).

23. Paul Lauter, "The Politics of Literature—Then and Now," *The Radical Teacher* 53 (Fall 1998): 24–25.

24. Ibid., 46.

25. NSF, "Doctorate Recipients from U.S. Universities: 2014," Dec. 2015, www.nsf.gov/statistics/2016/nsf16300.pdf. Percentages for other people of color were similar or far lower.

26. Octavia Butler, *Kindred* (Boston: Beacon Press, 1979), 140.

27. See Ashraf Rushdy, *Neo-slave Narratives: Studies in the Social Logic of a Literary Form* (New York: Oxford University Press, 1999).

28. Arturo Schomburg, "The Negro Digs Up His Past," in *The New Negro: Voices of the Harlem Renaissance,* ed. Alain Locke (New York: Simon & Schuster, 1925), 231.

29. Alicia Garza, "The Herstory of the #BlackLivesMatter Movement," *FeministWire,* Oct. 7, 2014, www.thefeministwire.com/2014/10/blacklivesmatter-2.

30. See Lisa Lowe, *Immigrant Acts: On Asian American Cultural Politics* (Durham, NC: Duke University Press, 1996).

31. See Jose Muñoz, *Disidentifications: Queers of Color and the Performance of Politics* (Minneapolis: University of Minnesota Press, 1999).

32. Robin D.G. Kelley, "Black Study, Black Struggle," *Boston Review,* Mar. 7, 2016, 10, https://bostonreview.net/forum/robin-d-g-kelley-black-study-black-struggle.

FIFTEEN

Negotiating Privileged Students' Affective Resistances

WHY A PEDAGOGY OF EMOTIONAL ENGAGEMENT IS NECESSARY

Paula Ioanide

This essay proposes that a central remedy to the concealments and injustices fostered by colorblindness across the disciplines is the implementation of race-gender-sexuality–conscious methodologies, pedagogies, and curricula in higher education. If the colorblind paradigms of traditional disciplines (which are invariably entangled with hetero-patriarchal norms and assumptions) disavow and therefore perpetuate gendered racial power and domination, classroom spaces that reveal the pervasive impact of systemic gendered racism have the potential to transform students' self-concepts, worldviews, and actions. Race-gender-sexuality–conscious classrooms are critical yet challenging and contradictory spaces that help students grapple with rather than deny the ways gendered racial power structures our lives, opportunities, and actions.

This antidote to colorblindness is not as straightforward as it may seem, however. Colorblind ideologies and frames pose formidable pedagogical challenges to antiracist feminist educators that merit close examination. The first central problem produced by colorblindness is that it sees itself as the progressive response to overt expressions of white supremacy. In other words, dominant ideologies in the post–civil rights era generally equate being a "good" nonracist with adopting colorblind frames and evading open discussions about race, gender, sexuality, and power. This formulation is particularly true for advantaged students (white, male, heterosexual, wealthy, or a combination of these and other identity attributes) at predominantly white, liberal colleges and universities in the United States.[1] For them, the process of embracing race-gender-sexuality–conscious methods, frames, and histories is not simply a matter of undoing ignorance. It is a process that requires a reconstitution of the entrenched moral, emotional, and embodied geographies established by colorblindness. These embodied geographies have taught advantaged students that discussions about gendered racism are socially unacceptable. As a result, directly engaging race-gender-sexuality–conscious topics often feels like a visceral, embodied violation of what it means to be "good." If colorblindness has ingrained the idea that the "good" nonracist is someone who avoids talking about gendered racial identity and power so as not to be perceived as discriminatory, becoming someone who views and negotiates the world through race-gender-sexuality-conscious frames requires working against advantaged students' core identities, moral assumptions, and embodied instincts.

A second problem is that colorblindness teaches advantaged students that race, gender, sexuality, class, and other structures of power are irrelevant to their life chances, opportunities, and choices. Colorblind ideologies myopically restrict gendered racism to individual acts of bigotry and overwhelmingly deny the ways policies and practices continue to structure people's opportunities and vulnerability to premature death along gendered racial lines. Advantaged students are peculiarly persuaded by the supposed "irrelevance" of race, gender, sexuality, and class precisely because their unearned gendered racial privileges and opportunities safeguard them from experiences of discrimination. Moreover, the core mythologies of colorblindness persuade advantaged students that the gender-specific exploitation and exclusion of people of color is a thing of the past and has no bearing on present social inequalities. As such, colorblind ideologies cultivate emotional economies that teach advantaged students to remain detached, dissociated, or indifferent to gendered racism. Since a majority of advantaged people do not acknowledge or grapple with the fact that they receive unearned, automatic advantages because they are white, male, heterosexual, and/or wealthy (and deny that these privileges are fundamentally tied to the disadvantages experienced by people of color, women, queer people, and/or poor people), they view gendered racism as a peripheral issue that does not affect their lives. Even when advantaged students hear painful testimonies of discrimination, they tend to experience affective dissociation, indifference, or sentimentality. Since colorblindness and hetero-patriarchy have normalized the idea that advantaged students are "good" people because they do not see color, gender, sexuality, or class differences, they do not see themselves as agents of white racism, sexism, and/or homophobia. For them, these oppressions tend to be provincialized as "special-interest" problems that affect people of color, women, and/or gender-nonconforming people but have nothing to do with their political and personal choices. By contrast, race-gender-sexuality–conscious frames challenge advantaged students to dismantle these affective structures and to feel personally implicated in systemic oppression and responsible for racial and gender justice.

I argue that these emotionally charged investments in the "goodness" of colorblindness or the "irrelevance" of gendered racism deepen advantaged students' resistances to receiving and integrating race-gender-sexuality–conscious knowledge. Indeed, students already exhibit generalizable resistances to learning across various disciplines and topics. Despite being presented with vast amounts of empirical, historical, and testimonial evidence, students often display a staunch refusal to rescind beliefs and ideas formed in their narrow sociocultural environments. Put differently, exposure to sound evidence, even in seemingly "objective" disciplines like math and physics, routinely fails to lead to learning.[2] Advantaged students' resistances to accepting and integrating the evidence offered by race-gender-sexuality–conscious curricula, however, are of a different caliber. These resistances are at once more prevalent and more unshakable because the stakes of rescinding colorblind frames are palpably higher. Students are not merely being asked to accept established facts that pose no observable threat to the ways they move about the world (e.g., the law of special relativity in physics); rather, they are being asked to recognize that the hard facts of systemic gendered racism require them to demolish and reconstitute their worldviews and self-concepts. Race-gender-sexuality–conscious curricula demand that advantaged students work against a lifetime of lies that have masqueraded as truths. They ask advantaged students to switch from being blind to gendered racial hierarchies to being vigilantly attuned to them. These race-gender-sexuality–conscious curricula invite students to acknowledge that many of their advantages and opportunities are fundamentally linked to the disadvantages of others. They guide advantaged students to see that we are all inescapably implicated in and responsible for collective outcomes. They compel students to acknowledge that the democratic processes, rights, and opportunities we often take for granted were largely struggled for and implemented because oppressed people sacrificed their blood, sweat, and tears through collective action. For students who have been taught all their lives to think of themselves as autonomous individuals whose opportunities are rooted in strokes of luck, hard work, or merit, such relational ways of understanding oneself require a formidably difficult emotional and intellectual undertaking that has beautiful long-term rewards but feels highly threatening in its initial and short-term stages.

The putative moral "goodness" of colorblindness and/or the supposed "irrelevance" of systemic gendered racism in the post–civil rights era also leads many educators to adopt pedagogical and methodological approaches that avoid, negate, or suppress the tangible realities of oppression inside and outside the classroom. Educators who use these teaching tactics essentially pretend that the histories of race, gender, sexuality, class, and other inequalities have no bearing on their subject, disciplinary training, methodologies, and classroom dynamics. Like advantaged students, educators who regularly deliver race-gender-sexuality–blind curricula want to avoid experiencing the discomforts, anxieties, insecurities, or fears conjured by open discussions about gendered racial power and inequalities. As I will show below, the regularity with which educators avoid, negate, and/or suppress the structural realities of gendered racism in the world, across the disciplines, and in the classroom exacerbate the discriminatory practices colorblindness supposedly seeks to avoid.

This essay argues that race-gender-sexuality–conscious educators must do more than contest advantaged students' ignorance. To teach effectively, they must also address advantaged students' resistances to *receiving and integrating* the hard facts of gendered racism. In other words, race-gender-sexuality–conscious curricula must employ strategies that contend with the emotional and affective dimensions of learning. Rather than assuming that advantaged students' exposure to the hard facts of gendered racism will lead to knowledge integration, I begin with the presumption that most advantaged students will dismiss, deny, or falsify information that does not affirm their existing self-concepts and beliefs about race, gender, sexuality, class, and other axes of power.[3] I suggest that antiracist feminist pedagogues must engage such staunch resistances to learning using teaching strategies that openly acknowledge and attend to advantaged students' embodied emotional geographies.[4] Finally, I claim that it is not enough to show advantaged students how they are implicated in perpetuating oppression. This approach often leads to forms of affective paralysis that are rarely useful to the praxis of dismantling gendered racism. To change the orientation of advantaged students' emotions, beliefs, and practices, we must posit alternative ways of being, doing, and belonging, or what might be called pathways toward restructuring the self-concepts propagated by colorblindness.[5]

Because such resistances are most acutely expressed by advantaged students, this essay focuses on outlining pedagogical strategies that effectively negotiate their tenacious defenses. Disadvantaged students demonstrate similar levels of miseducation about the history of systemic gendered racism. But their experiences with discrimination create points of cognitive and emotional receptivity to antiracist feminist knowledge that are generally absent in advantaged students. Though disadvantaged students' receptivity to antiracist feminist knowledge is certainly not automatic or inevitable, their resistances tend to be motivated and structured by factors that are quite distinct from those of advantaged students. As such, disadvantaged students' defense mechanisms would require a separate analysis.

In the first section, I briefly explain why advantaged students tend to dismiss, deny, or falsify the evidence of gendered racism (without necessarily knowing why). Next, I outline strategies that cultivate affective receptivity and knowledge integration in race-gender-sexuality–conscious courses through what I call the pedagogy of emotional engagement. In the final section, I identify pedagogical tactics that not only fail to produce genuine knowledge integration but also potentially increase students' explicit and/or implicit expressions of gendered racism.

My claims regarding the primacy of affect in knowledge integration processes are based on pedagogical lessons I've learned from three general fields of inquiry. First, they come from teachers and mentors I've encountered who are deeply effective in fostering genuine learning, and who changed my own emotional and intellectual paradigms as a student. Second, they are informed by lessons I've learned while teaching race-gender-sexuality–conscious courses over the past ten years. Through many failures, experiments, challenges, and transformative experiences in the classroom, I came to see that engaging advantaged students' affective responses to both curricular content and interpersonal classroom dynamics increases the likelihood that they will critically interrogate their belief systems, worldviews, identities, and political practices. Third, my arguments are grounded in social psychology, neuroscience, and educational research that identifies strategies for diminishing both explicit and implicit forms of gendered racism.[6]

WHY ADVANTAGED STUDENTS DISMISS IRREFUTABLE EVIDENCE

I turn to scan the students' faces. The white students have sunk in their chairs. Their bodies show signs of anxiety, confusion, shame, or stoic indifference. They have just learned how systemic racism endows white people in the United States with automatic, unearned advantages. They are confronted with the historical fact that these advantages were won through violent and everyday forms of racial exclusion and exploitation. Rationally, they know now that, whether they like it or not, they are implicated in systemic racism. Emotionally, this knowledge is causing profound conflicts in their embodied geographies. The emotional corollaries attached to their self-concepts of work, merit, worthiness, and moral goodness require significant remapping in light of what they've learned. Affectively, they tend toward refusal, denial, disavowal, guilt, shame, paralysis, and silence. They are afraid of being called racist. They are afraid of being responsible. They are afraid of saying the wrong thing. They are afraid that everything they thought they knew is based on a mountain of lies. They are afraid of what they don't know. They are afraid to admit their desire not to know more.

The students of color in the class look pissed. They are enraged that the web of systemic racial discrimination in housing, education, health, transportation, and criminal justice is much more extensive than they thought. They personalize the ways these systemic disadvantages have impacted their families, their opportunities, their health, and their life chances. They are thinking of all the times people of color have been blamed for their poverty and social status when all this time their disadvantages were created by design. They are ashamed that they, too, bought into dominant explanations. They are thinking about all the times they derided themselves for their failures without realizing that the cards were stacked against them. They are trying to figure out what their hard work in college is worth in a system that is set up to ensure white people's advancement over theirs. Their anger is mixed with relief. They now have a language for things they have sensed and felt all their lives; why their high school teachers and counselors had low expectations of them; why their neighborhoods are segregated and high schools underfunded: why they were at once racially fetishized and ridiculed by their peers in white suburban schools; why their parents told them that they had to work twice, three times as hard. They want the white students to acknowledge their unearned privileges. They want to know if the white students give a crap about what we just learned. They want to know if the white students will stand up to gendered racism. Their gazes and inquiries are met with white silence and fearful looks.

These reactions and emotions make the classroom space feel like something is about to burst. My introductory ethnic studies class tends to be one of the most racially, ethnically, and gender-mixed spaces students will experience at our predominantly white college. The diversity of students' backgrounds and perspectives guarantees that they will engage the curriculum in vastly different ways. Rather than performing myself as a distanced, rational authority, I am about to delve into the murky and difficult terrain of students' complex affective reactions to what they've just learned. I am reluctant. Engaging emotion takes me far from my comfort zone. I do it anyway. I know that if I am to facilitate genuine learning, I must delve into the work of emotion.

Contrary to the perception that students who are exposed to good evidence and argumentation about gendered racism will shift their beliefs, I have learned that the affective structure that undergirds what Charles W. Mills has theorized as the "epistemology of white ignorance" is deeply resistant to learning.[7] This affective structure is highly selective about the information it accepts. Indeed, its general function is to accept evidence only insofar as that evidence does not threaten advantaged students' core beliefs and self-concepts. In addition, the affective structures of hetero-patriarchal whiteness falsifies, skews, or hallucinates evidence about gendered racism in order to extinguish intuitively perceived threats to self-identity. As Gary Olson and Lynn Worsham claim, "We do not observe the world and then believe what we see. We have beliefs and then observe or hallucinate the truth of our beliefs in our observation of the world. In this case, 'believing is seeing.'"[8] Marshall Alcorn calls this tendency to dismiss, falsify, or hallucinate information that otherwise seems irrefutable as the "desire not to know."[9] He describes a process where students initially recognize information, but if that information fails to confirm their intimately held beliefs or if it triggers negative affects like fear, anxiety, or the need to dissociate, students intuitively proceed to dismiss, contain, or falsify the information they initially recognized.[10] Long before Alcorn, social psychologists, and neuroscientists theorized the affective structures of denial, James Baldwin identified the egregious social costs produced by white people's denials using hauntingly similar terms. In "My Dungeon Shook," Baldwin tells his nephew that rather than undertake the work of acknowledging their role in perpetuating gendered racism and their responsibilities for redressing it, white Americans tend to default to a position of not wanting to know. "This is the crime of which I accuse my country and my countrymen, and for which neither I nor time nor history will forgive them, that they have destroyed and are destroying thousands of lives, and do not know it and do not want to know it."[11]

Why do advantaged students tend to avoid, dismiss, or falsify information that, to others, seems irrefutable? In their analysis of how the mind works, neuroscientists and social psychologists have shown that "much of the content of our life is organized unconsciously along emotional principles. New information that introduces significant conflict within an existing emotional/feeling system is not integrated with the reasoning resources of the brain."[12] The mind's emotional structures tend toward what Laurie Rudman calls "self-partisanship." This self-partisanship (developed through a person's emotionally inflected social experiences and ideological influences) has a dual function. First, it motivates people to ward off perspectives, evidence, and facts that threaten their "implicit self-esteem"—a composite of experiences, beliefs, values, group identifications, and other factors that is reflexively defended without a person necessarily knowing why.[13] When people feel that their self-esteem or group identity is attacked, they are often motivated to "derogate a target outgroup as a way of recovering positive self-regard or ungroup regard."[14] In other words, the emotional tendency is to blame others rather than engage in self-examination and self-critique. This is because self-partisanship generally leads people to favor those who belong to their racial, gender, and/or sexual orientation group more than those deemed outsiders. Even if at a conscious level they express the desire to be egalitarian, implicit bias studies show that people tend to uphold preconscious biases that favor their in-group.[15] Importantly, in-group bias, particularly at implicit levels, is more pronounced in people who belong to advantaged, socially valued groups than those who belong to disadvantaged ones.[16]

Although the affective structure of self-partisanship is operative in a number of domains, it is amplified in the race-gender-sexuality–conscious classroom precisely because the knowledge, methods, frames, and histories of systemic gendered racism stand in stark contrast to the normative beliefs, presumptions, and ideas of colorblindness. The more dissociated students are from the experiences, evidence, and testimonies of gendered racism, the more fearful, threatened, indifferent, or anxious they tend to feel when they confront these historical realities and narratives. As a result, advantaged students' self-partisanship in race-gender-sexuality–conscious courses often manifests as a silent resistance to integrating the hard facts of systemic gendered racism and/or as an aggressive contestation of the material presented.

When I taught my first ethnic studies course in graduate school, I was impatient with advantaged students who resisted or challenged the evidence I was presenting. Taking a condescending or sarcastic tone, especially toward white male students who openly expressed their racism and/or sexism, I would show them exactly why their reasoning was faulty. I would overwhelm them into conceding that their views were unsubstantiated. I would adopt a confrontational attitude. I thought it was my job to make them see their discriminatory attitudes and to show others in the class that this would be prohibited. But when that class ended, a student's comments on the course evaluation forced me to have a profound confrontation with myself. They wrote that I made students feel stupid, talked over students, and acted like a know-it-all. They noted that this made them feel like they shouldn't even come to class.

That student made me admit something to myself that I had buried deep in the recesses of my mind. My condescension, my clever use of rational argumentation and factual evidence, my sarcasm, my patronizing or confrontational attitude was really a way to conceal my own insecurities, incompleteness, and lack of certainty both as a teacher and as a self-professed white antiracist feminist. I had engaged in one of the most typical modes of white feminist disavowal: I hoped that by policing and judging other advantaged students' racism, sexism, or homophobia, I would prove my exceptionalism as a "good, enlightened antiracist feminist." I did this despite knowing at a rational level that there was no way for me to escape being implicated in systemic gendered racism and reaping the automatic benefits of whiteness and gender normativity. I did this despite knowing that my private struggles with hetero-patriarchy were far from the feminist ideals I espoused. That is to say, even inside myself, I could see how my affective logics struggled against what I knew to be reasonably true.

My self-examination led me to seriously question my motivations for using certain pedagogical tactics. Rather than performing "pedagogical authority" and "good antiracist feminism," I sought to develop tactics that fostered greater affective and intellectual receptivity to learning in myself and in my students. Rather than engage in a pedagogy that sought to ideologically convert my students, I had to begin engaging in the uncertain pedagogical process of respecting students' widely divergent points of entry into race-gender-sexuality–conscious knowledge. I also had to allow and foster students' autonomy to accept, integrate, or reject the evidence and arguments presented in class. At the most basic level, this meant that I had to openly admit my own vulnerabilities, incomplete knowledge, and ongoing struggles with antiracist feminist thought and praxis in the classroom. It meant admitting that I didn't have all the answers, and that the intersectional dynamics of oppression created complex political responses that were often counterintuitive. Surprisingly, the more I did this, the more students—both advantaged and disadvantaged—were willing to share their own hesitations, insecurities, fears, and anxieties in relation to what they were learning.

I began exploring what Michalinos Zembylas calls "strategic empathy" for my students' emotional and intellectual struggles. This pedagogical tactic "refers to the willingness of the teacher to make himself/herself strategically skeptical (working against his/her own emotions) in order to empathize with the troubled knowledge students carry with them, even when this troubled knowledge is disturbing to other students or to the teacher."[17] In order to negotiate advantaged students' affective resistances, I had to work against my own instincts to judge, condemn, correct, suppress, negate, or avoid their ignorant responses to the evidence presented. I had to have "strategic empathy" for the fact that most advantaged students had been inculcated in the popular myths of colorblindness for seventeen to eighteen years prior to taking my class, and that undoing those frames would take time. I had to remind myself that colorblindness had made advantaged students believe that they were the "good," exceptional people who tried to avoid being discriminatory so long as they did not engage in overt expressions of bigotry, and that learning to see the monstrous scale of systemic gendered racism would take time. I had to have "strategic empathy" for the fact that open discussions about gendered racism were an experiential anomaly for a majority of advantaged students, some of whom had never engaged people of color and/or queer-identified people in conversations about discrimination until they sat in my class. In a systematic effort to conceal the ongoing significance of gendered racism in the present, colorblind ideology had socialized my advantaged students to accept a delusional sense of reality that proliferated social alienation and severed interpersonal and interdependent connectivity.

This did not mean that I conceded the validity of advantaged students' racist, sexist, or homophobic remarks. It did not mean that I stopped teaching the historical realities of hetero-patriarchal racial capitalism in the United States. It did not mean that the classroom was transformed into a group therapy session where students' feelings are divorced from their unequal power relations and differentiated vulnerabilities to suffering. But it did mean that I began to openly engage advantaged students' affective responses (however ignorant, angry, guilt-ridden, shamed, or indifferent) with the kind of patience my own formative teachers had once shown me. It meant pausing and asking students to acknowledge, engage, and discuss their emotions, particularly in those moments when their affective reactions were clearly inhibiting them from learning and listening. It meant asking for deep clarification about ideas and feelings during contentious moments between advantaged and disadvantaged students. I noticed that the more I asked advantaged students to be self-reflective during those moments when they were most resistant to learning, the more they took ownership over their learning processes and engaged in self-directed modes of critical examination.

THE PEDAGOGY OF EMOTIONAL ENGAGEMENT

Educators can easily default into authoritarianism or adulation. As Alcorn argues, in the former case, students are quickly intimidated into regurgitating the instructor's views even if they have not genuinely accepted them. In the latter, students' idealization of their instructor motivates them to suppress their own emotional and intellectual conflicts in order to please the teacher. While authoritarian teaching avoids emotions and conflict through intimidation and dictation, adulation for a charismatic teacher forestalls learning because students fail to develop their own relationship to critical inquiry. At various points in my teaching career I have fallen into both of these dynamics and must constantly remind myself that if my teaching becomes didactic, self-serving, or emotionally unconflicted, it is not likely to cultivate student learning. Rather than intimidating, seducing, or coercing students into accepting what I have come to believe, I had to "develop a mode of research and inquiry responsible to the emotional complexity of thought."[18] I call this process the pedagogy of emotional engagement.

In race-gender-sexuality–conscious courses, expressions of affect and emotion tend to run high. For this reason, it is important to theorize how we might engage the work of emotion in order to produce the outcomes we desire, namely to reduce implicit and explicit expressions of gendered racism and to cultivate positive identifications with racial and gender justice.

Recent studies in social psychology have increasingly clarified the significance of affect in reducing expressions of racial bias. For example, Laurie Rudman et al. gauged whether a seminar on prejudice and conflict taught by a Black male professor reduced white students' self-reported (explicit) and automatic (implicit) biases. "As a result of learning, engaging in (sometimes heated) discussions, and keeping a journal documenting instances of bias (including their own), seminar students were expected to increase their awareness of prejudice, and also their motivation to counteract biases in themselves."[19] At the beginning of the study, seminar students (eighteen of whom were white, nine Black, and three other) were no less prejudiced than a control group of students (ten white, three Black, and four other) who did not take the seminar. Only white students' changes in explicit and implicit bias were evaluated.[20] The results showed that cognitive learning processes were correlated with reducing explicit forms of gendered racial bias in white students, while affective processes were critical to reducing implicit biases. Put differently, although affective and cognitive processes are interdependent, reductions in explicit forms of gendered racism do not necessarily lead to reductions in preconscious, automatic, and embodied ones. Instead, "implicit changes covaried with affective variables, including favorable attitudes toward the professor and, in the case of implicit stereotyping, pro-social contact with out-group members."[21]

Noticing the significance of affective processes to reducing implicit forms of bias and stereotyping in white students, Rudman et al. focused on clarifying which affective variables reduced implicit anti-Black attitudes and beliefs. Were implicit biases reduced simply because the class was taught by an African American male professor? Were they reduced because of the interracial contact fostered by the class? Were they reduced because of the subject matter explored in the class? Or was a combination of affective processes involved in all these factors?

In a subsequent experiment, Rudman et al. showed that implicit racial bias remained unchanged among white students who took a class with the same African American male professor but whose subject matter did not explore prejudice and conflict.[22] They therefore concluded that the subject matter of the class was central to cultivating affective processes that diminished implicit expressions of gendered racism. Their findings suggested that positive affects (e.g., liking the professor, developing friendships with classmates) and/or a reduction in negative affects (e.g., experiencing less anxiety or fear as a result of long-term interracial engagement) are correlated with a reduction in implicit bias and stereotyping. White students "who evaluated the professor and the course favorably, or who reported making friends with out-group members during the seminar, also showed less automatic prejudice and stereotypic beliefs over time." Additionally, students who "reported feeling less threatened by out-group members as a result of seminar participation also showed reduced implicit prejudice and stereotyping."[23] Rudman et al., echoing Alcorn and neuroscientists, conclude that "emotional reconditioning may be an effective means of reducing automatic biases" in white students.[24]

The implications of these findings are quite remarkable. They suggest that both race-gender-sexuality–conscious knowledge (a largely cognitive process) *and* what I call the pedagogy of emotional engagement (a largely affective process) are central to reducing expressions of gendered racism. Teaching tactics that effectively engage students' affective and emotional reactions entail developing the habit of asking students to consciously examine their resistances to antiracist feminist curricula, their resistances to hearing each other, and their resistances to examining themselves. The pedagogy of emotional engagement involves pausing to make students' existing beliefs objects of inquiry exactly in those moments when affective logics seek to protect those beliefs most ardently. It asks students to reflect on their emotional attachments to particular values, principles, and ways of being. It invites advantaged and disadvantaged students to openly scrutinize fears of losing friendships and familial bonds, chances toward economic and professional mobility, and physical safety as a result of aligning with antiracist feminist praxis. Although the pedagogy of emotional engagement has no hard and fast rules, it is rooted in the counterintuitive proposal that the more educators foster emotional openness and relinquish affective rigidity, the more students will adopt self-reflective attitudes toward their resistances to learning.

As I make this argument, I realize that educators may view the work of engaging advantaged students' resistances and emotions to be unjustly burdensome and unwarranted. Numerous scholars and activists of color have understandably expressed impatience for white people's fragile or reactionary emotional responses to the factual reality that they are beneficiaries of unearned racial advantages or to the moral demand to redress gendered racism.[25] While people of color are getting killed, violated, or exploited, white people are worried about feeling uncomfortable about their privilege and fearful of losing advantages? Similarly, many feminists and queer critics claim that it is not their job to deal with men's and heterosexuals' privileged emotional tantrums. These critics demand that advantaged people take responsibility for both self-examination and the emotional by-products of confronting their sexism and homophobia. Why would educators, particularly those who are themselves marginalized, take on the additional labor of dealing with advantaged students' emotions? Given that educators in antiracist feminist curricula already take on disproportionate amounts of labor to mentor and sustain marginalized students and faculty (not to mention themselves), asking them to attend to advantaged people's affective reactions and cultivate "positive" affective experiences in the classroom seems obscene.

Still, educators rarely have the option to extract themselves from these problems, as they might outside the classroom. In principle, they can choose to dismiss, ignore, suppress, negate, or avoid the affective responses raised by advantaged students in favor of attending to the oppressions and emotions of disadvantaged students. But as I demonstrate in the next section, this comes at a price. Pedagogical tactics that negate, suppress, and avoid advantaged students' existing beliefs, stereotypes, and emotions will likely increase students' explicit and/or implicit forms of discrimination. To be clear, the pedagogical practice I'm arguing for—one that openly acknowledges and negotiates advantaged students' affective resistances and discriminatory responses—does not mean emotionally coddling advantaged students by avoiding discomfort, anxiety, fear, confrontation, and contention in the classroom. On the contrary, it means asking students to critically reflect on resistances and emotions that are always already there. Nor does it mean that educators should feel responsible for how advantaged students react or that they should strive to protect students from guilt, shame, anger, fear, anxiety, or other difficult emotions. While Rudman et al. suggest that "positive" affects and the reduction of "negative" affects are correlated with stereotype and prejudice reduction, it is important to remember that these outcomes represent students' cumulative and composite affective evaluation of a course on prejudice and conflict that included many moments of contention, disagreement, and emotional turmoil.

Indeed, even confrontational pedagogical tactics are more likely to reduce implicit and explicit forms of gendered racism than those that avoid, negate, or suppress students' emotions and existing beliefs. Though some studies have shown that hostile attacks on a person's self-esteem or group identity can increase discrimination against out-groups,[26] Alexander Czopp et al. showed that confronting a person about their discriminatory comments can stimulate emotions resulting in stereotype and prejudice reduction. Across three experiments, Czopp et al. correlated the experience of "negative affect directed toward themselves (e.g. guilt and self-criticism)," or what they term "Negself," to decreased levels of prejudice and stereotyping. They note that "participants who experienced greater Negself in response to a confrontation of bias provided fewer stereotypic responses in a subsequent situation."[27] Thus, when advantaged students experience negative emotions of guilt, shame, anxiety, or fear because their discrimination is challenged through interpersonal encounters and/or the course material, they are potentially undergoing processes that are conducive to both learning and the reduction of gendered racism.

Czopp et al. acknowledge that self-negating affects are more likely to occur in low-prejudiced individuals who are self-motivated to be nondiscriminatory. By contrast, "more prejudiced individuals find their prejudiced responses acceptable and appropriate and are consequently less motivated to change or control such responses." In short, to the extent that people are either "unaware of their prejudiced responses or are unmotivated to change such responses," [28] pedagogical strategies that evoke self-negating affects may not operate successfully. In other words, a person's emotional state, their investment in protecting their self-concept or group esteem, and their motivation to control their prejudice are all contributing factors in whether a person is more or less likely to engage in self-examination and to change discriminatory views and practices. [29] Although educators can never control advantaged students' defensive responses, motivations, or emotional states, understanding and negotiating these variables increases the likelihood that instructors will develop transformative pedagogical strategies that encourage students' identification with gender and racial justice.

If colorblindness teaches advantaged students to remain affectively detached and dissociated from the problems perpetuated by systemic gendered racism, race-gender-sexuality–conscious courses challenge them to restructure their identities, worldviews, relationships, and practices through both emotional work and knowledge. Indeed, when learning about state-sponsored white racist violence, gendered and racially discriminatory policies in housing, education, and employment, and the ways these systemic patterns continue to affect the present, advantaged students testify to experiencing feelings of guilt, shame, cynicism, self-conflict, and responsibility. If they concede the interconnected nature of systemic oppression, advantaged students have a difficult time remaining dissociated and detached from the racist, sexist, and/or homophobic discourses and actions of their advantaged peers. These affective and emotional experiences can feel overwhelming to students who are rarely asked to link their lives, choices, and actions to what they are learning in the classroom. Yet these emotional and intellectual experiences also have the potential to deepen advantaged students' commitments to racial and gender justice, to resituate how they see their families' and friends' participation in systemic oppression, and to struggle over how they might reconstitute their self-concepts and worldviews in light of the historical and contemporary realities of gendered racism.

UNWITTINGLY INCREASING STUDENTS' EXPLICIT
OR IMPLICIT GENDERED RACISM
—AND WHAT WE MIGHT DO INSTEAD

Commonly used pedagogical approaches in higher education tend to mirror the principles of colorblind ideology. Because colorblindness teaches people to avoid, fear, and/or remain indifferent to conversations about gendered racism, educators tend to avoid, negate, or suppress discourses, questions, and interpersonal confrontations that openly highlight hierarchies of power. Significantly, these teaching tactics do not produce neutral results. Rather, they exacerbate students' explicit and implicit discriminatory biases.

Traditional disciplines tend to default into a generalizable avoidance of race-gender-sexuality–conscious methods, frames, and content. Educators who use this approach essentially pretend that the histories of race, gender, sexuality, class, and other inequalities have no bearing on "universally" applicable subjects or on classroom dynamics. Like advantaged students, educators who regularly deliver race-gender-sexuality-class–blind curricula want to avoid experiencing the discomfort, anxiety, insecurity, or fear evoked by matters that they deem peripheral to most students' education. The authors in this collection astutely articulate the negative effects of these avoidance tactics at disciplinary, methodological, and curricular levels. But it is important to note that these tactics not only affect people's ideological frames; they also impact their reflexively embodied geographies.

In one study, Michael I. Norton et al. showed that the more white students were encouraged to behave in colorblind ways, the more they displayed negative nonverbal behaviors and emotions toward Black people (anxiety, unfriendliness, less effective communication of emotion).[30] Similarly, Jacques-Philippe Leyens et al. demonstrated that white students who were told to behave in colorblind ways toward a Black photographer experienced greater anxiety and appeared less friendly.[31] Leyens et al. "proposed that the cognitive effort and uneasiness associated with inhibiting biased responses in the colorblind condition led participants who typically do not express high levels of prejudice toward Blacks to appear less open and friendly with a Black person."[32] Finally, tactics that aim to suppress salient identity attributes like race have also been shown to increase stereotype activation.[33] Thus, instructors who default to colorblind, gender-blind, and sexuality-blind approaches are not only reinforcing the mythology that avoiding these topics diminishes discrimination; they are actually helping to increase negative nonverbal behaviors toward disadvantaged students.

When educators are forced to deal with expressions of discrimination in the classroom, they often resort to using two other detrimental teaching tactics: negation or suppression. These approaches essentially tell students to stop stereotyping or making discriminatory statements without exploring the emotional and intellectual causes of these biases or their effects.

Early in my teaching career, my desire to mitigate advantaged students' epistemic violence in the classroom led me impulsively to use negating or suppressive tactics. In a class addressing affirmative action, a white woman had expressed resentment over a diversity program that gave fifty high-achieving students of color scholarships at our predominantly white institution of six thousand. She was angry that her white identity denied her eligibility for "diversity" scholarships. Though we had covered the extensive history of white advantages in higher education, legacy admissions, and wealth building at the exclusion of people of color, she displayed an insistent affective refusal to integrate the evidence of the course. I methodically negated the white woman's stereotypical comments with evidence. Having no intellectual defenses against my comments, she eventually broke down in tears. Afterward, I did not go and comfort her. But I noticed that several students, including many students of color who had argued with her in the class discussion, undertook the labor of comforting her.

Today, I know that the manner in which I engage the advantaged students' stereotypes and ignorant comments may be more important than the intellectual arguments and evidence I offer. If I berate students for their ignorance, I risk backing them into a corner of intuitive, emotional self-defense. That student, and other advantaged students in the class, will likely never reveal what they really think again out of fear of being judged or punished. If students feel attacked or shamed, particularly by the authority who holds power over them, they might experience negative self-directed affects that foster self-examination; but they might also reflexively dismiss anything the course offers and increase their discrimination toward disadvantaged people.

My confrontational manner and dismissive tone may have unwittingly burdened disadvantaged students in the class. Students of color may feel morally conflicted about contributing to a white woman's tearful breakdown, even if they intellectually disagree with her viewpoint. White people have the ability to *emotionally* constitute themselves as "aggrieved subjects" precisely in those moments when their *intellectual* arguments prove entirely baseless. But not everyone can read this sophisticated leap from the cognitive to the affective. My negating manner may have displaced the emotional labor of caring for the white student onto disadvantaged students, who rarely receive similar types of care in response to their emotions. Worse, I modeled a behavior that encourages students to believe that shaming white people is a good way to challenge gendered racism. Subsequent experience has taught me that this punitive approach tends to produce affective and interpersonal impasses that make the cross-racial, collaborative transformation necessary for dismantling institutional racism difficult, if not impossible. Shaming students, whether out of hurt, defensiveness, or my own egotistical motivations to prove my "antiracist, feminist exceptionality," methodologically replicates the very oppression I seek to dismantle.

At the same time, I cannot allow advantaged students' stereotypes and ignorant comments to stand as if it they are valid claims. Nor am I interested in coddling their "fragility" to the point of suppressing discomforts, anxiety, or fears that are clearly there.[34] And should my consideration of advantaged students' affective logics trump what other students in the class, particularly disadvantaged students, might be feeling? How might an educator attend to students' disparate affective responses to the white woman's ignorant comment on affirmative action?

Cognitive behavioral psychologists have shown that telling people what *not* to do, particularly if these expressions are coupled with negative affects like anger or condescension, generally reinforces and strengthens negative behaviors. Studies conducted by Bertram Gawronski et al. show that telling students to stop stereotyping activates normative stereotypes in their mind with greater force and increases the reflexive quickness with which they make stereotypical associations. Participants who were asked to repeatedly say "no" to common stereotypical associations (negation training) displayed an increase in both stereotype activation and automatic evaluations (the speed at which people make stereotypical associations without having time for conscious deliberation).[35] Other studies similarly show that telling people to stop being racist, or to become aware of their racism, has some impact on diminishing explicit bias, but it does not change implicit, preconscious, or automatic forms of gendered racism.[36]

By contrast, positing alternative associations and mental images can motivate people to shift their thoughts, emotions, and behaviors.[37] If we take this lesson to the classroom, we see that positing new associations about marginalized groups enables the creation of new neural and ideational pathways. Gawronski et al. confirmed this when they showed that affirmation trainings—saying "yes" to counterstereotypic associations and showing no response to stereotypic pairings—led to a decrease in both stereotype activation and automatic evaluations.[38]

In my class about the model minority myth, an Asian American male student claims that because Asian families work hard, value education, and commit less crime, they are more successful than Black people. Inside I wince, but I have now learned to calmly acknowledge that the student is articulating a common belief about Asian Americans. Rather than asking students to suppress or negate the stereotypes they already hold, I openly acknowledge them without confirming their validity. My method for diminishing students' stereotype activation, and by extension their expressions of discrimination, involves offering rich, detailed histories that create new associations, visions, and images in students' minds that complicate their perceptions and engender new emotional pathways. Referencing key passages from Claire Jean Kim's *Bitter Fruit, Who Killed Vincent Chin?,* and Robert Lee's *Asian Americans in Popular Culture,*[39] our class works through complex Asian American histories, regressive immigration policies, and discriminatory practices against Black Americans that reveal the reductive nature of the model-minority stereotype. I intentionally craft space for students to share testimonies and arguments about the model-minority myth without asking anyone to speak on behalf of their racial/ethnic group. I know that these emotionally inflected testimonies are crucial to engendering what psychologists call "individuation processes" that effectively diminish the power of stereotypes.[40] Student stories introduce complex personal attributes that unravel reductive and simplistic stereotypes based on singular aspects of identity. As Galen V. Bodenhausen argues, "Attending to multiple aspects of a target's identity simultaneously should give rise to more complex, integrated (i.e., personalized) impressions that are less likely to be dominated by unwanted mental associations."[41]

The value of using intersectional methodologies to foster individuation processes and stereotype reduction is conspicuously clear here. Complicating what Cathy Cohen describes as traditional single-identity-based politics and "single-oppression frameworks"[42] through antiracist queer and feminist narratives diminishes the power of hegemonic associations and problematizes simplistic in-group/out-group divides that reinforce implicit and explicit forms of gendered racism. For example, when students read Helen Zia's *Asian*

American Dreams, they are encouraged to grapple with multiple axes of oppression and resistance as she critiques both her father's patriarchy and white racism.[43] When we discuss Zia's work, Asian American women and other women of color often open up about their personal struggles against familial forms of patriarchy. But they also speak to the ways they face racial discrimination on campus as well as sexism from men of color and white men. Asian American students explain the enormous pressures of being associated with "positive" or "exceptional" stereotypes. Women-of-color students hold tensions that not only disallow simplistic narratives about race but also potentially create new points of identification among their peers through what psychologists call "perspective-taking."[44] Studies have shown that being exposed to complex perspectives through interpersonal contact tends to diminish in-group/out-group divides, though these interactions also tend to produce greater benefits for advantaged students than disadvantaged students.[45] Interestingly, weakening stereotype activation and in-group/out-group divides through perspective-taking in our classroom has the potential to impact intergroup relations beyond the classroom. Changes in advantaged students' perceptions resulting from the new associations and emotional pathways they develop in class will likely extend to how students perceive marginalized groups in the world at large.[46]

Finally, it is critical that antiracist feminist curricula do more than offer systemic analyses of oppression. The consequences of failing to include histories of antiracist feminist resistance to oppression are emotionally and intellectually dire. When I was developing my first syllabus in graduate school, I outlined reading after reading of how oppression worked. Because this knowledge had been critical to my own development, I thought it was important, especially for advantaged students, to know the extensive record of American racial violence, exploitation, and policy-based exclusion. When I brought it to my mentor for review, she laughed and said, "What do you want to do here, Paula? Tell these folks that oppressed people just sat idly by while they were being oppressed?" My face fell. In my effort to highlight the atrocities of white supremacy, I had failed to structurally integrate oppressed people's agency in my syllabus. I had failed to show that people's collective struggles for racial and gender justice had often forced hetero-patriarchal racial capitalism's structure to shift, collapse, and reinvent itself.

Later, I realized that integrating examples of antiracist feminist resistance in my courses was not only critical for documenting oppressed people's agency and resilience; it was critical for fostering new visions of being, acting, and relating in the world, and for countering the epistemologies and ontologies of colorblindness and hereto-patriarchy. Without the alternative value systems posited by traditions of resistance, advantaged students could not see why they should relinquish their monetary advantages, risk their social and familial bonds, or break their habits of interracial social alienation and dissociation. Without these alternative visions, oppressive systems appeared insurmountably powerful and inevitable. Without positing principles where people are valued more than property, and collective interests are foregrounded over individualist hoarding and self-aggrandizement, even disadvantaged students reached the cynical conclusion that their only option was to conform to normative standards and compete to move up in social and economic hierarchies.

The long record of oppression cultivated a deep sense of affective defeat and hopelessness about change in my students. But when this oppressive record was put in dialectical and dialogical relationship to the equally resilient record of resistance, advantaged and disadvantaged students were empowered to believe that they too could create identities, modes of being, and sites of belonging based on principles of dignity, interdependence, social and spiritual connection, and honest self-examination. They saw that past resistance struggles had been difficult, fraught, and full of contradictions and conflicts. But these examples also offered them aspirational ideals for building more equitable worlds and social relations. Most importantly, these resistant struggles motivated many students to consider shifting from affective resistances to reflective thought, to the imperfect and always incomplete praxis of social justice.

NOTES

1. Throughout this essay, I will use the awkward phrase "advantaged students" to refer to people whose group identity automatically endows them with unearned advantages. These advantages yield concrete monetary rewards (e.g., white people are automatic beneficiaries of the cash value of prime mortgage loans routinely denied to people of color) or social rewards like being automatically favored for certain jobs (e.g., men are more likely to be hired in police, fire, and construction). But advantages can also be automatically produced from the *absence* of discrimination (e.g., heterosexual people are less vulnerable to physical violence compared to those who identify as LGBTQ). These advantages are correlated with racial, gender, class, sexual orientation, and other aspects of identity. At the same time, advantages are

mitigated when one or more attributes of a person's identity makes them vulnerable to systemic disadvantages (e.g., Black men's gender advantages are mitigated by their racial disadvantages).

2. Marshall Wise Alcorn, *Resistance to Learning: Overcoming the Desire-Not-to-Know in Classroom Teaching* (New York: Palgrave Macmillan, 2013).

3. Paula Ioanide, *The Emotional Politics of Racism: How Feelings Trump Facts in an Era of Colorblindness,* Stanford Studies in Comparative Race and Ethnicity (Stanford, CA: Stanford University Press, 2015).

4. Psychologists, psychoanalysis, and neuroscientists generally define "emotions" as feelings that have concrete definition (sadness, anger, joy, excitement, etc.). By contrast, "affect" can represent instinctual, embodied energy of either a positive or negative quality that often lacks concrete definition or a relationship to a clear object (e.g., anxiousness without knowing exactly what's causing the anxiety). Affect is also more likely to operate unconsciously. Though the two are related, throughout this essay I use "emotion" to refer to concretely defined feelings and "affect" to refer to embodied responses, processes, and logics that are often performed unconsciously and/or lack clear definition.

5. In saying this, I realize that my arguments are implicated in the dangers of recentering hetero-patriarchal whiteness, and thereby reifying the power of the very object I seek to critique. I nonetheless proceed to develop these ideas because anti-racist feminist educators can rarely avoid the problem of advantaged students' refusals and spend a great amount of emotional labor dealing with it both inside and outside the classroom. It is understandable why educators, particularly feminist educators of color, might want to "give up" on advantaged students and instead channel their energy toward students who show a willingness to learn. Holding these reservations, my hope is that learning to understand and better navigate advantaged students' affective logics ultimately offers sustenance to educators committed to the long struggle of social justice.

6. Whereas explicit forms of gendered racism are gauged through self-reporting measures and therefore suggest some level of cognitive awareness, implicit forms are evaluated through tests that do not allow time for conscious deliberation or intent. Thus, implicit gendered racism manifests in preconscious, automatic, and reflexive ways.

7. Charles W. Mills, "White Ignorance," in *Race and Epistemologies of Ignorance,* ed. Shannon Sullivan and Nancy Tuana (Albany: State University of New York Press, 2007).

8. Gary Olson and Lynn Worsham, "Rhetoric, Emotion, and the Justification of Belief," in *Postmodern Sophistry: Stanley Fish and the Critical Enterprise,* ed. Gary Olson and Lynn Worsham (Albany: State University of New York Press, 2004), quoted in Alcorn, *Resistance to Learning,* 1.

9. Alcorn, *Resistance to Learning,* 2.

10. Ibid., 3.

11. James Baldwin, "My Dungeon Shook," in *Collected Essays* (New York: Library of America, 1998), 292; first published as "A Letter to My Nephew," *The Progressive,* Jan. 1, 1962.

12. Alcorn, *Resistance to Learning,* 19.

13. Laurie A. Rudman, "Social Justice in Our Minds, Homes, and Society: The Nature, Causes, and Consequences of Implicit Bias," *Social Justice Research* 17, no. 2 (June 2004): 137, https://rutgerssocialcognitionlab.weebly.com/uploads/1/3/9 /7/13979590/rudman2004sjr_1.pdf.

14. Nilanjana Dasgupta, "Mechanisms Underlying the Malleability of Implicit Prejudice and Stereotypes: The Role of Automaticity and Cognitive Control," in *Handbook of Prejudice, Stereotyping, and Discrimination,* ed. Todd D. Nelson (New York: Psychology Press, 2009), 273.

15. For examples, see Pamela M. Casey, "Helping Courts Address Implicit Bias: Resources for Education," National Center for State Courts, 2012, http://ncsc.con-tentdm.oclc.org/cdm/ref/collection/accessfair/id/246; Dan-Olof Rooth, "Automatic Associations and Discrimination in Hiring: Real World Evidence," *Labour Economics* 17, no. 3 (June 2010): 523–34, https://doi.org/10.1016/j.labeco.2009.04.005; Shannon Sullivan, *Revealing Whiteness: The Unconscious Habits of Racial Privilege* (Bloomington: Indiana University Press, 2006).

16. Marginalized groups also tend to explicitly favor their in-group, but in implicit tests, marginalized people show more complicated results. According to implicit association tests, while about half of African Americans indicate implicit biases for their in-group, another half show implicit bias for whites. Explanations for this have to do with the ways cultural processes encourage those who are in marginalized identities to identify with high-status groups even if they do not belong to them. For research on Black Americans' and other marginalized groups' implicit biases, see Robert W. Livingston, "The Role of Perceived Negativity in the Moderation of African Americans' Implicit and Explicit Racial Attitudes," *Journal of Experimental Social Psychology* 38, no. 4 (July 2002): 405–13, www.sciencedirect .com/science/article/pii/S0022103102000021; Theodore R. Johnson, "Black-on-Black Racism: The Hazards of Implicit Bias," *Atlantic,* Dec. 26, 2014, www .theatlantic.com/politics/archive/2014/12/black-on-black-racism-the-hazards-of-implicit-bias/384028; "Project Implicit FAQs," https://implicit.harvard.edu /implicit/faqs.html.

17. Michalinos Zembylas, "Pedagogies of Strategic Empathy: Navigating through the Emotional Complexities of Anti-racism in Higher Education," *Teaching in Higher Education* 17, no. 2 (Apr. 2012): 114, https://doi.org/10.1080/13562517.201 1.611869.

18. Alcorn, *Resistance to Learning,* 44.

19. Laurie A. Rudman, Richard D. Ashmore, and Melvin L. Gary, "'Unlearning' Automatic Biases: The Malleability of Implicit Prejudice and Stereotypes," *Journal of Personality and Social Psychology* 81, no. 5 (2001): 858, http://myfootballcoach .net/bias/Unlearning Automatic Biases The Malleability of Implicit Prejudice and Stereotypes.pdf.

20. Because advantaged groups are assumed to present the highest levels of explicit and implicit discrimination, the majority of social psychology research on prejudice and bias focuses on their self-reported and affective responses. While this

is understandable, it creates a major vacuum in understanding how marginalized groups internalize, negotiate, or respond to oppression, and how cultural processes shape their explicit and implicit preferences. Clearly, more research needs to be done on the complexity of marginalized people's psychology in oppressive regimes.

21. Rudman, Ashmore, and Gary, "'Unlearning' Automatic Biases," 861.

22. Ibid., 863.

23. Ibid., 864.

24. Ibid., 866.

25. Robin L. Hughes, "Dear Critical White Scholar and Colleague," *Huffington Post,* June 4, 2017, www.huffingtonpost.com/entry/dear-critical-white-scholar-and-colleague_us_59347797e4b00573ab57a4aa; Afua Hirsch, "I've Had Enough of White People Who Try to Deny My Experience," *Guardian,* Jan. 28, 2018, www .theguardian.com/commentisfree/2018/jan/24/white-people-tv-racism-afua-hirsch; John Metta, "I Don't Discuss Racism with White People," *PopularResistance.org,* July 13, 2015, https://popularresistance.org/i-dont-discuss-racism-with-white-people.

26. Dasgupta, "Mechanisms Underlying the Malleability of Implicit Prejudice and Stereotypes," 273.

27. Alexander M. Czopp, Margo J. Monteith, and Aimee Y. Mark, "Standing Up for a Change: Reducing Bias through Interpersonal Confrontation," *Journal of Personality and Social Psychology* 90, no. 5 (2006): 798–99, http://citeseerx.ist.psu .edu/viewdoc/download?doi=10.1.1.138.462&rep=rep1&type=pdf.

28. Ibid., 785.

29. For a longer discussion of these factors, see Dasgupta, "Mechanisms Underlying the Malleability of Implicit Prejudice and Stereotypes," 273–75.

30. Michael I. Norton et al., "Color Blindness and Interracial Interaction: Playing the Political Correctness Game," *Psychological Science* 17, no. 11 (2006): 949–53, http://journals.sagepub.com/doi/abs/10.1111/j.1467-9280.2006.01810 .x?journalCode=pssa.

31. J.-P. Leyens et al., "Expressing Emotions and Decoding Them: Ingroups and Outgroups Do Not Share the Same Advantages," in *From Prejudice to Intergroup Emotions: Differentiated Reactions to Social Groups,* ed. D. M. Mackie and E. R. Smith (New York: Psychology Press, 2002), 139–51.

32. Galen V. Bodenhausen, Andrew R. Todd, and Jennifer A. Richeson, "Controlling Prejudice and Stereotyping: Antecedents, Mechanisms, and Contexts," in *Handbook of Prejudice, Stereotyping, and Discrimination,* ed. Todd D. Nelson (New York: Psychology Press, 2009), 127, discussing Leyens et al., "Expressing Emotions."

33. Rudman, Ashmore, and Gary, "'Unlearning' Automatic Biases," 857.

34. Robin DiAngelo, "White Fragility," *International Journal of Critical Pedagogy* 3, no. 3 (May 16, 2011): 54–70, https://libjournal.uncg.edu/ijcp/article /viewFile/249/116.

35. Bertram Gawronski et al., "When 'Just Say No' Is Not Enough: Affirmation versus Negation Training and the Reduction of Automatic Stereotype Activation," *Journal of Experimental Social Psychology* 44, no. 2 (March 2008): 119, www

.researchgate.net/publication/222668002_When_Just_Say_No_is_not_Enough_
Affirmation_versus_Negation_Training_and_the_Reduction_of_Automatic_
Stereotype_Activation.

36. Dasgupta, "Mechanisms Underlying the Malleability of Implicit Prejudice
and Stereotypes," 277.

37. Kai Sassenberg and Gordon B. Moskowitz, "Don't Stereotype, Think
Different! Overcoming Automatic Stereotype Activation by Mindset Priming,"
Journal of Experimental Social Psychology 41, no. 5 (2005): 506–14.

38. Gawronski et al., "When 'Just Say No' Is Not Enough."

39. Claire Jean Kim, *Bitter Fruit: The Politics of Black-Korean Conflict in
New York City* (New Haven, CT: Yale University Press, 2000); *Who Killed
Vincent Chin?,* a *POV* documentary, first aired July 16, 1989, www.pbs.org/pov
/whokilledvincentchin; and Robert G. Lee, *Orientals: Asian Americans in Popular
Culture* (Philadelphia: Temple University Press, 1999).

40. Bodenhausen, Todd, and Richeson, "Controlling Prejudice and
Stereotyping," 121.

41. Ibid.

42. Cathy J. Cohen, "Punks, Bulldaggers, and Welfare Queens: The Radical
Potential of Queer Politics?" in Still Brave: The Evolution of Black Women's
Studies, eds. Stanlie M. James, Frances Smith Foster and Beverly-Guy Sheftall (New
York: The Feminist Press, 2009), 244.

43. Helen Zia, *Asian American Dreams: The Emergence of an American People*
(New York: Farrar, Straus & Giroux, 2001).

44. Bodenhausen, Todd, and Richeson, "Controlling Prejudice and
Stereotyping," 121.

45. Richard J. Crisp et al., "Imagined Intergroup Contact: Theory, Paradigm,
and Practice," *Social and Personality Psychology Compass* 3, no. 1 (Jan. 2009): 8,
www.researchgate.net/publication/227658981_Imagined_Intergroup_Contact_
Theory_Paradigm_and_Practice.

46. Bodenhausen, Todd, and Richeson, "Controlling Prejudice and
Stereotyping," 121.

SIXTEEN

Shifting Frames

PEDAGOGICAL INTERVENTIONS IN COLORBLIND TEACHING PRACTICE

Milton Reynolds

> These "innocent people" are trapped in a history they do not understand, and until they understand it, they cannot be released from it.
>
> JAMES BALDWIN[1]

In a few short words, James Baldwin encapsulates a social and psychological phenomenon that has preoccupied my thoughts for many years. My first conscious recollection of this behavior was during the sixth grade. We had moved across the San Francisco Bay from Martinez, California, a working-class town with a multiracial population where my family and I were known and trusted members of the community, to San Carlos, a largely white and affluent suburb where I instantaneously became highly apparent, a visible visitor. I became a raisin in a bowl of rice overnight.

My attendance in middle school, as I now know, was part of a much larger process of desegregating San Carlos, a suburban enclave nestled on the peninsula, roughly equidistant between San Francisco and San Jose. It had formerly existed as a sundown or near-sundown town, which was clearly evidenced by the disquieting lack of diversity. The term "sundown town" refers to cities, towns, or neighborhoods that are purposefully all white. Discriminatory laws, violence, and intimidation were traditionally used to exclude other racial groups.[2] My family and I became the sixth African American family to enter, joining the Allan, Olive, Patterson, Jerrie, and Bonds families. I recollect only a few Latino classmates and even fewer Asian peers. There was no language to mark this conspicuous difference: colorblindness ruled the day.

Years later, once I entered the educational profession, the patterns of interaction I had witnessed as a child continued, as did my curiosity about them.

The fact that I entered the profession at all was a shock to many. My trajectory through the educational system certainly wasn't smooth. I began my freshman year of high school as a promising student with a full complement of Advanced Placement courses. By my junior year I had been expelled. The psychological toll of navigating the evasions and denials of colorblindness extinguished my desire for learning and obliterated the relevance of schooling. Interrupting the patterns that I had witnessed, endured, and on occasion withered under as a student became a primary intellectual preoccupation of mine.

Comprehending teachers' motivations for investment in colorblindness is essential to the development and ultimate adoption of alternative practices. If we stand any chance of reclaiming schools, which too often function as primary sites of colorblind socialization, we must first invert the gaze to fully understand teachers' motivations. In the absence of such understanding, efforts to redeem teachers' practice are often futile. The intent of this chapter is to offer educators alternative approaches.

My former position, as a senior program associate for Facing History and Ourselves, an international educational nonprofit organization, provided me access to a variety of different educational contexts. Designing and delivering workshops and seminars while providing direct support to educators, schools, and school districts were all aspects of my daily routines. The organization hosts an award-winning website that houses a wide range of teaching resources, including "Race and Membership in American History: The Eugenics Movement." This text played a prominent role in situating the professional development work with schools within a broader historical context.[3] Schools are increasingly reaching out, in some cases being sued into action, as the failures of colorblind practice become more evident. These dynamics have created opportunities for sustained engagement with educators and development of a range of different interventions.

It may feel more comfortable, or dare I say "natural," for some to see racialized educational outcomes as rooted in the children themselves, their caregivers, culture, or class background. The dominant culture's misperception that "colorblindness equals justice" encourages many teachers to feel they are effective in their job if they pretend not to notice color and make no explicit mention of race in their course lessons and curricular goals. Study after study, however, shows that this colorblind approach does not work, that it leads students to learn little and to respond to challenges with evasion, denial, and anxiety. Fundamentally, such thinking ignores the fact that today's inequitable outcomes are the product of systems, structures, and policies that are animated by the discredited yet relentlessly pervasive ideology of eugenics, a belief system we have yet to fully own or confront.

In recent years, an increasing body of research has demonstrated the relationship between cognitive and affective domains of learning. These findings, when considered in concert with a consistent pattern of negative educational outcomes for students of color in particular, provide a theoretical warrant for interrogating colorblind practice itself as the source of harm and disjunction. Schools are primary sites of colorblind production and socialization; consequently, engaging educators and educational institutions in confronting these practices is essential.

Colorblindness in education produces a pattern of harmful social and cognitive consequences that are detrimental to students and teachers alike. "Conceptual impoverishment" and "affective under-skilling" are the terms I now use to describe the problematic outcomes that accrue as a result of investment in these teaching practices.

CONCEPTUAL IMPOVERISHMENT

Conceptual impoverishment refers to a pattern of learned outcomes that distorts the way people understand and make meaning of the world they inhabit. Denied access to specific information, students formulate belief systems that fail to account for the significant role race plays in structuring opportunities and outcomes. Like doing math without all the variables, one's best efforts will never render a correct proof.

In my experience, these outcomes result from a particular set of teacher-driven behaviors. Teachers who embrace colorblindness tend to skip over troubling moments in American history, misrepresenting them entirely or downplaying their significance. They may present historical moments as redemptive tales of a continual forward progress that is disconnected from precedent events, historical context, or the violent resistance and backlash often occurring in the wake of such advances. As addressed in previous chapters, deprivation of such contextual knowledge promotes a misunderstanding of social hierarchy as natural, reflecting racial or identity-based deficiencies. In essence, colorblind knowledge fosters ignorance by intentionally abstracting historical events from the systems and structures of power and subjugation that produce these outcomes.

Two examples of such impoverishment I've often encountered are the Dunning School narrative of Reconstruction, which depicts Blacks after the Civil War as unfit for freedom and incapable of self-governance rather than as victims of racist violence and repression,[4] and the "tired Rosa" myth that portrays Rosa Parks as an isolated, unknowing individual who unwittingly touched off the Montgomery Bus Boycott rather than as an active and informed agent of her own liberation.[5] These erasures serve to inflate white agency and deny people of color and other marginalized groups their own.

In other cases, the experiences and contributions of other racialized groups are entirely absent from conversations. Students in fourth-grade classes in California build models of mission buildings in a curriculum that might never connect the mission system to the genocidal practices that accompanied it. Defining the experience of Indigenous Californians as genocidal is a fairly recent occurrence among many scholars, but that finding likely remains absent from classrooms where Indigenous students will be blindly coached to celebrate their people's holocaust.[6]

Recent battles over ethnic studies in Arizona and fights over the Advanced Placement history curriculum in Colorado and Oklahoma speak to the politically contested nature of historical narratives.[7] Continued controversy over the history to be presented in textbooks produced in Texas and, more recently, in California offer examples of this ongoing skirmish to determine whose experiences matter and what history is deemed relevant or "fit" to be considered for inclusion.[8] Textbook history is often presented as a series of static facts rather than as contested narratives that, by nature, are reflective of political power struggles that mirror an evolving understanding about the past.[9]

Ultimately, conventional practices and historical frames based on avoidance of the hurts of history rob students of their agency. This sort of abstraction encourages people to think about the practice of democracy as an individual act rather than something done in the service of the collective. If the challenges we face as a society are rooted solely in individual choices, we can only be accountable for our own behavior, destined to a planktonic existence, helpless against the tides of change. However, when students understand inequality and injustice as the outgrowth of systems, structures, and ideology that produce such outcomes, they can channel their civic energy toward confronting and reforming these institutions, ideas, and ideologically driven practices.

Helping educators "see race again" demands surfacing the history of eugenics. Without access to the history of eugenics, the formation of whiteness as normative is concealed, rendering all else suspect and visible. This intervention is, in essence, a process of historical revision. Reclaiming this history is necessary to counter conceptual impoverishment, as it is the selective erasure of this particular history that makes identifying patterns of cause and effect within history difficult. Knowledge of eugenics helps illustrate how race is produced, how past investments in notions of "fitness" and fundamental differences in the human family have been codified by law and buttressed through social practice and convention.

The term "eugenics" refers to a scientifically based, ideological movement dedicated to the reification of race. It is the wellspring of scientific theories used to construct taxonomies of difference within the human family and to legitimate the subjugation of different groups. Eugenics played a central role in shaping the modern concept of nationhood, in addition to informing groups' positions within nations. Utopian in nature, eugenics' primary goal was "race betterment." National health was assumed to be a function of biological or racial "fitness." Schools and other institutions actively promulgated the message of "race betterment." Accordingly, anyone exhibiting traits deemed to be dysgenic or "unfit" was considered a threat to the nation, something to be protected against.

Exposure to the heretofore untaught history of eugenics is a powerful linchpin of the historical revision process, and serves several purposes. Knowledge of eugenics can assist educators in tracing the origins of many ethnic notions back to their sites of production. It illuminates the purposes they originally served, and facilitates deeper understanding of the enduring social, political, and economic legacies of these ideas in relationship to the context out of which they emerged. Many teachers are mortified when first exposed to this history. The sense of outrage and embarrassment that often materializes in the wake of this exposure can, however, be channeled into intellectual curiosity and facilitate shifts in practice that align intentions with effective practice. The notion that we don't know what we don't know is leveraged to foment self-reflection.

Access to this history can help educators connect eugenic ideology and its influence with the structures and institutions that produce racialized outcomes. This can be particularly provocative as they discover that they are themselves likely, if unwitting, participants in practices that forward eugenic objectives. The persistence of racial tracking, the use of standardized testing, and high rates of suspension and expulsion—particularly among students of color and students with disabilities—serve as evidence that students historically marked as "unfit" by eugenicists continue to be defined as such by today's educational institutions.

Engaging honestly and accurately with history requires making whiteness visible within the context of educational settings. The presentation of whiteness as the "normative state" contributes to racialized dynamics within school settings. More often than not, educators begin to question why they weren't exposed to this history during their time as students or in their teacher education courses, which often leads them in turn to question what else might be lurking in the shadows.

That a movement so widespread and central to understanding both historical and current patterns of social stratification and injustice has been, until recent times, effectively expunged from the nation's historical memory or transposed onto studies of Nazi Germany only aids and abets processes of affective distancing and historical abstraction. Erasure and deflection make it difficult, if not nearly impossible, to resist effectively or confront the legacies of eugenics. Many such legacies—standardized testing, ability tracking, and differentiated curricula among them—are hidden in plain sight.

Reclaiming this history as an American phenomenon and examining the greater international reach of this movement can catalyze complex systemic analyses that directly counter the conceptual impoverishment produced by colorblind socialization. It can enliven a sense of critical civic agency. For example, presenting ideas from then-esteemed educational thought leaders from the past, such as Stanford's Lewis Terman and Ellwood P. Cubberley, forces educators to grapple with their own assumptions about intellect and the nature of learning. In our studies, we explore statements like this by Terman:

> It is interesting to note that . . . [these cases] represent the level of intelligence which is very, very common among Spanish-Indian and Mexican families of the Southwest and also among Negroes. Their dullness seems to be racial, or at least inherent in the family stocks from which they come. The fact that one meets this type with such extraordinary frequency among Indians, Mexicans, and Negroes suggests quite forcibly that the whole question of racial differences in mental traits will have to be taken up anew and by experimental methods. The writer predicts that when this is done there will be discovered enormously significant racial differences in general intelligence, differences which cannot be wiped out by any scheme of mental culture.[10]

Such exposure illuminates the continuity between eugenic ideology and its centrality in the development of educational practices and policies both past and present. Eugenicists believed intellect to be fixed and ascribed along lines of race, class, and gender. Unexamined notions of racialized ability or belief in such ideas continue to inform how resources are allocated within education and to whom.

In another of the paragraphs that we study, Cubberley draws out the implications of eugenicist assumptions:

> We should give up the exceedingly democratic idea that all are equal and that our society is devoid of classes. The employee tends to remain an employee; the wage earner tends to remain a wage earner. . . . One bright child may easily be worth more to the National Life than thousands of those of low mentality.[11]

I have never met an educator who entered the field intending to damage children; yet without access to this history we might all be complicit in enacting policies that, by their very nature, forward exclusionary and eliminationist objectives that are ultimately antidemocratic.

Examining the impact of eugenic constructions of intellect can be particularly evocative for educators, and often unsettles the foundations of their fundamental beliefs. The history of IQ testing and its relationship to standardized testing helps teachers understand that standardized assessments represent far more than objective markers of ability, merit, or academic fitness. With such background knowledge, high-stakes testing and other educational reforms can be more easily apprehended as political and economic incursions made in response to rapidly changing demography and other societal shifts. The current use of standardized tests mirrors the use of these tools to segregate and marginalize students of color and disabled students in the early twentieth century. Similarities in the patterns of use also suggest these tests are still being used to sequester resources for those deemed more "fit."

In the mid and late 1960s, physicist William Shockley and psychologist Arthur Jensen resurrected the idea of intellect as hereditary endowment.[12] Richard Herrnstein and Charles Murray's *Bell Curve* followed in 1994, a book that sold nearly half a million copies within several months of publication, suggesting that these notions are still germane.[13] I have heard teachers utter such thoughts on more occasions than I care to recount.

Knowledge of eugenics allows teachers to connect seemingly disassociated ideas, events, or social outcomes they might otherwise have attributed to other factors. As they come to grasp the depth and scope of America's eugenic past they can begin to reconsider the contemporary salience of these ideas. Accessing the history of eugenics in America can facilitate a shift from framing race as "people" toward an understanding of race as an ideological belief system that assigns value and worth to groups of people. This reframing helps lower defensiveness and provides access to a more historically accurate understanding of race, one that is also more civically and intellectually generative. Comprehension of eugenics illuminates the "masks" of colorblindness and reveals the strategy animating its "moves." With access to eugenic history, race can no longer be considered peripheral, relegated "to the past," or viewed as something primarily rooted in the body. This curriculum offers an impenetrable defense for accusations of playing "the race card." This conceptual revision enables people to understand how specific markers of identity—race, gender, class, presumed sexual normativity, and disability—become designations of "fitness" or lack thereof. The concept of intersectionality becomes more accessible with knowledge of this history, as does the possibility of forming communities of solidarity across too often siloed liberation struggles.

This conceptual shift allows people to penetrate the shroud of colorblindness. As people become aware of how this ideology gets translated into institutional practices and policies, systems and structures of power can be more effectively explicated. The historical illumination of schools as eugenic institutions of racial stratification and subjugation also reveals them as potential sites of contestation and struggle.

Educational policies that allocate resources such as highly skilled teachers, school funding, teaching resources, and facilities along historical lines that predictably and systematically disenfranchise particular groups can be considered as targets that invite confrontation and revision. Historically informed interventions can supplant costly, ineffective, and unsound practices predicated on deficiency framing.

Teachers' predispositions toward the classroom can be examined, refurbished, and replaced over time with practices that develop civic and cognitive competencies rather than erode them. Shifts in historical understanding help elucidate more plausible explanations for the current state of affairs than can be generated within a colorblind worldview.

The consistent employment of historical thinking skills such as cause and effect, historical perspective taking, and change/continuity help to demonstrate the ways eugenic thought continues to influence social, economic, and educational policy.

Affective under-skilling is a term I developed to describe the predictable patterns of social anxiety, agitation, evasion, and consternation that emerge in conversations regarding race among people who have been socialized to be colorblind. These patterns seem to be most evident among, though not entirely exclusive to, people who identify or might be identified as white.

I have never heard an educator of color or any other person of color declare themselves to be colorblind. That is not to suggest that some might not subscribe to this belief, but I have not met them. I surface this to suggest that investment in colorblindness appears to be directly connected to teachers' racial identity within the context of the classroom.

Some of my earliest insights into affective under-skilling came when I was doing equity and diversity work as one of two principal partners of CoAction, an equity-focused consulting firm. We used a form of Bohnian dialogue as the basis for our work on communications.[14] We also relied on practices like the Crossing the Line activity, which had become, and still remains, a staple of equity work.[15] As a way of elucidating issues of power and privilege, the activity (also known as the Power Walk) has participants advance forward or backward from an initial shared starting point in response to a series of questions related to different aspects of identity. Generally speaking, those in the nontarget group move forward, reflecting privilege, while those in the target group move backward, communicating an absence of power. Those for whom the prompt is not relevant stay stationary.

However, I was concerned that some of the activities, even rendered as skillfully as possible, still seemed to generate among the participants, white males in particular, unintended consequences. At times, the dissonance of the interactions seemed too much for some participants to countenance. Though infrequent, these expressions of duress, which ranged from flight responses to vociferous pushback, raised concerns for me and provoked a host of additional questions. Clearly, something deep was at play.

One of the earliest pieces that helped me understand what I was observing, and which ultimately shifted the focus of my work, was Claude Steele's "Thin Ice: Stereotype Threat and Black College Students," published in the August 1999 edition of the *Atlantic*.[16] The article, investigating the performance gap between equally well prepared African American college students and their white counterparts, posits the idea that these differences, rather than being a function of heredity or preparation, may reflect the consequences of African American students laboring under negative stereotypes about their cognitive ability. The concept of stereotype threat provided me with a lens that enabled me to see connections across the patterns I was observing and among the questions I was raising.

The interactions I was witnessing among white participants in the Power Walk reminded me of the feelings of threat or rejection I often felt as a student, when conversations regarding civil rights or police violence I understood to be common and legitimate at home were rebuffed in the classroom. Steele's work provided me with language to describe what I had felt, as well as what I was observing. It also offered a framework around which to reform my practice.

I've chosen to focus my work primarily on addressing the impact of colorblind practice on people who identify or are identified as white. This focus reflects the demographic composition of our current teacher population and recognizes the historical reality that full membership in American society has always been associated with being identified as white or "performing whiteness" well enough to pass as such. This focus brings into relief patterns of differential racialization and the subsequent impact on identity development, which are the very understandings colorblind practice attempts to elide.

Due to a host of factors, the composition of our teaching corps is not likely to transform overnight, necessitating this focus on white teachers. The elementary and secondary educator workforce is overwhelmingly homogenous (80 percent white in public schools).[17] Education leaders are also predominantly white. In the 2011–12 school year, only 20 percent of public school principals were people of color.[18] Many if not the majority of younger teachers were likely socialized in colorblind classrooms themselves.

Inverting the gaze of research and focusing on the role of white teachers and white identity in creating classroom environments is an important interruption of historical trends that tend to define the persistence of unequal outcomes as being rooted in the deficiencies of the children, their caregivers, communities, culture, or class background. Most approaches to disparate racial outcomes in schools fail to consider how the identity of white teachers, laboring under stereotype threat in diverse classrooms, may be contributing to this pattern.

Robin DiAngelo's concept of "white fragility" is useful in understanding this dynamic. Her work offers the following observation:

White people in North America live in a social environment that protects and insulates them from race-based stress. This insulated environment of racial protection builds white expectations for racial comfort while at the same time lowering the ability to tolerate racial stress, leading to what I refer to as White Fragility. White Fragility is a state in which even a minimum amount of racial stress becomes intolerable, triggering a range of defensive moves. These moves include the outward display of emotions such as anger, fear, and guilt, and behaviors such as argumentation, silence, and leaving the stress-inducing situation. These behaviors, in turn, function to reinstate white racial equilibrium.[19]

The term "racial equilibrium" refers essentially to the state of colorblindness, in which all individuals are assumed to have the benefit of being seen as individuals, equally endowed with agency, opportunity, resources, and access to the levers of power of society. I've only recently become acquainted with DiAngelo's work, but her concept of white fragility effectively describes the patterns of educator behavior I have observed and worked to disrupt. Her work provides additional evidence of affective under-skilling. In an educational Faustian bargain, comfort is often confused with safety. It is the pursuit of comfort rather than comprehension or confrontation that begets affective under-skilling. Teachers' efforts to avoid being perceived as racist or to avoid any potential conflict with or among students may actually create the very conditions they hope to obviate.

Students who resist out of psychic self-protection or principled resistance are often disciplined or banished from those spaces.[20] Surfacing questions and perspectives that exist as normative elements of the discourse at home become violations of protocol, marking the offender as "unfit" for the environment. Disparate rates of suspension and expulsion, in most cases for little more than angering an adult, serve as additional evidence of the need for reform.[21] Students should not have to make the decision of whether to capitulate to an imposed and potentially destructive social norm or risk being sanctioned for resisting, especially when there are alternatives.

Colorblind conditioning encourages investment in a series of rhetorical contortions and other behaviors in service of creating the impression that one does not see color. Likely self-protective, these commitments may be best understood as by-products of reductively defining racism as the domain of "bad people" expressing "antiquated" attitudes. These exculpatory narratives are reductive, supplanting more civically fruitful and affectively informed understandings of the world. Emancipatory frameworks of understanding give way to constrictive and limiting conceptions and increasingly indefensible stances. In this sense, the very purpose of engaging in meaning-making is divorced from its civic utility.

Regardless of intent, investment in these behaviors is maladaptive. Among the skills that appear to be truncated are the ability to hold dissonance in mind, the ability to honor multiple perspectives, and the capacity to consider context, causation, change, and continuity over time. Such intellectual and pedagogical investments can produce other problematic outcomes as well.

Students of color in these spaces are forced to perform whiteness as a condition of full membership. Those who learn to do this may gain a higher degree of membership, but it is always tenuous and contested. Success may also come at the expense of developing a coherent and strong sense of identity. For white students, this homogenization of expression may come at the expense of developing a critical racial perspective and diminish opportunities for cross-group solidarity. Students of mixed ethnic heritage are confronted with unique challenges in navigating such spaces.

Regardless of whether this investment is motivated by good intention, lack of other options, or self-protection, these norms rob educators who choose to embrace them of opportunities to know differently and to broaden their understanding of the world they inhabit. Such commitments in approach also impose this same debilitating practice on students inhabiting these spaces. The tendency to universalize experiences or pretend "everyone is the same" obfuscates both important historical realities of group experience and contemporary lived experience.

These lived realities need to be recognized for many students to see their time in school as legitimate or relevant. Failure to do so deprives all students of opportunities to develop critical cognitive, social, and civic competencies, skills necessary to function in an increasingly diverse society. Those navigating conversations from a subaltern position are subject to having their experiences and perspectives invalidated, diminished, or denied altogether. Those in more privileged positions retreat into dominant frames at the expense of understanding a more expansive palette of lived experiences.

Whitney Dow's Whiteness Project has become a useful tool for elucidating the impact of colorblind practice on students' identity development with educators. One element of the project, a series of interviews conducted with millennials in Dallas, Texas, provides a fascinating window into such experiences.[22] These interviews, at times painfully, reveal the conceptual limitations and psychological consequences for students steeped in colorblind learning spaces. The range and number of participant interviews also reveal the social and intellectual benefits of students being encouraged to confront difference and its nature of construction.

In these interviews, distinct differences in use of verbal language can be observed. The body language of the interview subjects is also quite telling of the facility some have for navigating these conversations, a facility others lack. The patterns also suggest that these differences aren't random, but rather reflect a function of opportunities to engage in such exchanges. The physiological and often unconscious manifestation of discomfort in these exchanges is important for teachers to observe, as these behaviors echo the cues to which students often react. The pedagogical choices explored later in this chapter are designed to help teachers circumvent this aspect of under-skilling, such that their own body language isn't too disruptive to the classroom environment while they are developing the capacity to actively engage with difference.

THE ROLE OF PEDAGOGY

Understanding that malice is not required to create differential outcomes helps educators to recognize that good intentions alone are not sufficient to create equitable and inclusive learning environments. Good intentions in the absence of effective practice may in fact exacerbate the challenges we face. Identifying the consequences of colorblind practice and relating them to specific classroom behaviors and other dilemmas educators face helps them to reclaim a sense of agency in relationship to these outcomes.

Too often, colorblindness privileges comfort in the classroom. Such norms impede a teacher's ability to make that classroom safe and inclusive for all students. Comfort and safety are not the same. Rooted in patterns that avoid recognition of difference, a teacher's norms often become universalized, failing to take into account that there are alternative ways of being, knowing, and creating community. Notions of safety require intentional recognition of difference and the valuing of such differences as assets to learning, not simply things that need to be managed.

The practices and behaviors associated with colorblind teaching generate cues that erode the safety of students of color and other marginalized students whose identities mark them as "others" or "visible visitors" in the classroom. Students' awareness and interpretation of these cues can trigger a threat response, simultaneously stifling or silencing these voices or rendering them unimportant. Students often withdraw from the learning as they invest more cognitive resources in self-protection. This silencing narrows the scope and depth of classroom conversation and exploration, limiting everybody's ability to make meaning of the world in a more complex way

Our larger societal patterns of racial spatialization make the loss of opportunities to connect across various divides in the classroom all the more consequential.[23] The infrequency of exchanges related to difference, coupled with the goal of avoiding recognition of those differences, heightens the affective load for those engaged. In the absence of such exchanges, understandings of interdependence, connectivity, and shared interest give way to tribalism, fear, and defensiveness. Civic imagination languishes and democracy remains stillborn. All the more reason that educational institutions, though increasingly segregated, must be places where these exchanges take place.

A number of teachers cling to colorblindness out of self-protection in diverse classrooms. The daily navigation of borders—literal and psychological—heightens anxieties for many teachers, and they often retreat into colorblind practice to avoid these challenges. In fact, such actions only make matters worse.

An important step before offering alternative practices is to confront the idea that racism or differential racial outcomes must be the result of intention or malice, or a tendency to frame such outcomes as reflecting solely individual behaviors, choices, and attitudes. It is essential to destabilize the notion that colorblind practice without explicit negative intention is a defense against the accusation of racism. Recent research on implicit bias has proven to be a useful tool, as it suggests that we are all susceptible to observing and reproducing patterns of racial bias.[24]

Our tendency to notice difference, assign meaning to those differences, and think and engage differently toward those perceived as different is a trait we all exhibit. It is important, however, that this behavior not be used to retreat from personal responsibility. Recognition of these patterns of behavior helps to deepen our comprehension of the ways colorblind socialization thwarts interrogation of the broader consequences such patterns generate.

PEDAGOGY AND THE IMPORTANCE OF TEACHER PRACTICE

When facilitating this work, the objective is not to control what participants feel but, instead, to create a context or a container in which the participants will be allowed to access a broader range of emotions in the process of learning, and to hear a wider range of perspectives from their colleagues. Ultimately, the goal is for them to construct knowledge together in hopes the experience will embolden them to do the same with their students.

I've found it useful to model the use of specific pedagogical practices with teachers and take time to explicate each strategy upon conclusion of the session, shedding light on structure and intention. These teaching strategies are primarily presented as mechanisms for democratizing voice and eliciting higher levels of participation. More active involvement in the learning process provides students additional time to develop the skills of discourse and civic engagement. Such student-centered strategies additionally function as safeguards teachers can rely on as they increase their own level of comfort with exposure to counter or alternative narratives that will likely emerge as orchestration of classroom interactions shifts from the teacher to the students. By shifting the classroom locus of control away from being teacher-centered toward more student-centered approaches, teachers' often unconscious expressions of discomfort are less likely to interfere with the ability of students to be in discussion. Developing a more student-centered classroom implies trust, an essential component for developing identity-safe learning spaces.

These tools facilitate deeper investment in the learning process by surfacing connections between content and issues relevant to participants' lives. These tools allow people to have authentic exchanges and model real-time interactions that embrace a fuller range of lived racial experience. The felt experiences and outcomes are significantly different from colorblind conversation that attempts to skirt these issues, predictably falling into patterns of dominant discourse and power relationships.

TITRATING DISSONANCE AND DEMOCRATIZING VOICE

Racial stressors such as engaging openly about issues of difference often result in defensive behaviors. This is especially true in environments where colorblind practice has been normative or when working with people who have been socialized in colorblind environments. Teachers' primary role as arbiter of classroom norms necessitates they develop the ability to navigate such conversations.

Affective under-skilling is a function of social conditioning rather than something innate. As with any skill, through practice and expanded knowledge, conversations that used to provoke a sense of threat become less threatening and ultimately become normative. There are some specific pedagogical practices I find beneficial to the process.

The practices I employ most frequently encourage participants to work in pairs or small learning constellations no larger than three or four participants. They tend to emphasize deep listening, inquiry over advocacy, and building upon each other's thoughts, and provide structure to speaking roles. Strategies like Save the Last Word for Me and Learn to Listen, Listen to Learn require participants to number off and observe an ordered protocol for speaking.[25] Constructivist in nature, both of these strategies focus on expanding understanding of the content by building on the shared knowledge of the group and democratizing voice, so that no one voice or perspective dominates the exchange.

Another useful strategy is titled Big Paper: Building a Silent Conversation.[26] This is particularly useful when dealing with a provocative text or imagery that one anticipates will generate strong reactions. For this activity, primary source documents are affixed to large papers that are then placed on walls or tables. Participants are asked to gather in groups, no smaller than two but no larger than five, in front of a specific document that they will analyze in silence, using only writing utensils to communicate. The facilitator leads participants through a guided explication of the document, beginning with simple observation of the words or imagery that draws attention and culminating in a full deconstruction of the document. The entire process is done in silence. Once explication is done, the participants are encouraged to circulate and comment on the other big papers—again, in writing and in silence. The silence helps prevent participants from making distracting or evasive comments, which often occurs when one's schema is disrupted or when experiencing emotional discomfort, often in service of avoidance. Before breaking the silence, participants are asked to return to their initial document to view any contributions left by others during the gallery walk. Once silence is broken, the conversation is usually lively.

Implementing such strategies engenders conversation that is often much deeper than it would have been otherwise. Such conversations also tend to reflect a more balanced and representative understanding of the content. Valuing a broader range of perspectives requires learning how to listen to others without interrupting, negating, minimizing, or inserting a dominant narrative. Traditional classroom norms tend to reinforce dominant narratives at the expense of understanding other perspectives, insights, or ways of knowing. The structured listening and speaking opportunities also help participants learn to hold dissonance that might otherwise be mitigated by speaking over, misdirecting the conversation, or challenging those surfacing alternative viewpoints.

Because participants know they will have an opportunity to speak, they can hold their thoughts rather than asserting them immediately or at the expense of a traditionally marginalized voice. Often, by the time one's turn comes, their thought process has shifted as a function of hearing other perspectives. Additionally, people's thinking is often affirmed and supported by their colleagues' offerings.

Regular use of these kinds of strategies allows students opportunities to practice listening for meaning, as opposed to listening for the purpose of advocacy. Consistent implementation of these student-centered approaches enhances engagement and models the idea that knowledge is co-constructed, often becoming the normative mode of engagement.

As many of our revered national institutions are coming under increased scrutiny, with calls for systematic reform, education should be at the top of the list. Glaring patterns of racially inequitable outcomes that are national in scope suggest we are systematically underdeveloping vast swaths of our nation's human capital. While the difference is commonly called an "achievement gap," Gloria Ladson-Billings has looked at the many ways schools are set up to fail students of color and calls it an "educational debt."[27] Business as usual is untenable; we must find more effective alternatives.

Developing innovative approaches to engage with difference will become increasingly necessary in order to support and fully develop a progressively diverse student population. Essentializing narratives that frame inequity as reflecting biological limitations stifle agency and render the significant challenges we face as educators outside our domains of influence. Ultimately, they have proven to be ineffective.

IDENTITY SAFETY AND THE ROLE OF THE EDUCATOR

Dorothy Steele et al.'s original investigation of Identity Safety theory is the framework I have used to develop my practice and have offered to teachers to replace colorblindness or other maladaptive frameworks. The ability to cultivate inclusive and safe learning environments with great predictability relies almost exclusively on this theory, which was first tested in the Stanford Integrated Schools Project (SISP).[28]

Initiated in 1998, SISP was an attempt to determine whether and how educators could create classroom environments that would mitigate or eliminate the impact of negative stereotypes on the academic performance and sense of belonging of students of color. Fortunately, the project was able to demonstrate that this could indeed be accomplished.

The SISP research project identified a set of factors that when considered as a set of interdependent and consistently present practices can reduce the impact of identity threat. The four domains of practice are

1. *Child-Centered Teaching,* characterized by classroom autonomy, listening for students' voices, teaching for understanding, and a focus on cooperation;

2. *Cultivating Diversity* characterized by diversity as a resource, a challenging curriculum, high expectations, and academic rigor;

3. *Classroom Relationships* characterized by teacher warmth, teacher availability to support learning, and positive student relationships;

4. *Caring Environments* characterized by emotional and physical comfort, which are promoted by teacher skill and attention to prosocial development.[29]

The SISP research was conducted on primary-grade students, but I have found this framework to be especially useful in working with educators, and specifically white teachers working in racially diverse settings, due to their lower ability to tolerate racial stress.

My early participation in the project enabled my involvement in developing the observation instrument and testing its reliability. Early involvement also meant participation in a number of the classroom observations, follow-up work with members of a teaching cohort composed of teachers we observed during the research project, and eventually assisting a revision of the New Teacher Induction Program, in concert with the study's findings in the district where the research was conducted. To date, it is among the most valuable learning experiences of my life.

I've sustained my engagement with these ideas over the past several years in my work with teachers. These principles, made visible by pairing particular pedagogical practices with the strategic use of history, offer an alternate approach for educators. Strategic use of history refers to illuminating the historical moments and social and legal practices that demonstrate how race is constructed. This expanded awareness primes educators to better receive a broad range of perspectives, insights, and experiences, especially those dissimilar from their own that emerge from conversations in increasingly diverse classrooms.

CONCLUSION

The United States possesses a history of brutal violence, subjugation, and genocide that has never been confronted by any meaningful form of transitional justice process. Providing educators access to this history is an act of transitional justice. Historical illumination has the potential to catalyze a deliberate and historically informed process of reforming educational institutions. Transforming their purpose as eliminationist and stratifying structures toward becoming engines of democratic agitation, uplift, and collective endeavor is the work we must implement. In the absence of sustained, intentional confrontation with our past eugenic embrace, our institutions remain wedded to their original objectives. As our student population increasingly consists of communities that eugenicists' aspirations were designed to protect against, the failure to reform schools presents a looming crisis. Comprehensive and meaningful school reform feels even more distant in the wake of recent events, but there are pragmatic and effective ways to engage and support educators who represent the front lines of a battle for our nation's future.

A teacher will touch thousands of students' lives over the course of a career. Offering teachers alternative approaches to colorblindness can have a dramatic and lasting effect on their practice and in turn on the lives of students. Shifts in population demographics continue to evolve, as do reactions to these changes. If we are to make this experiment in participatory interracial democracy work, we must recognize schools themselves as primary sites of racial formation and colorblind knowledge production. Prioritizing schools as critical sites of intervention and reform will be necessary to foster the tectonic shifts needed to counter the pervasive and increasingly detrimental consequences of colorblind socialization.

NOTES

1. James Baldwin, *The Fire Next Time* (New York: Dial Press, 1963), 8.

2. James W. Loewen, *Sundown Towns: A Hidden Dimension of American Racism* (New York: New Press, 2005), 4–5.

3. Facing History and Ourselves National Foundation, Inc. Brookline, Massachusetts, "Race and Membership in American History: The Eugenics Movement," www.facinghistory.org/books-borrowing/race-and-membership-american-history-eugenics-movement.

4. Eric Foner, *The Story of Emancipation and Reconstruction* (New York: Vintage Books, 2006), xx.

5. Herbert Kohl, "The Myth of Rose Parks 'the Tired': Teaching about Rosa Parks and the Montgomery Bus Boycott," *Multicultural Education* 1, no. 2 (1993): 6–10.

6. Benjamin Madley, *An American Genocide: The United States and the California Indian Catastrophe* (New Haven, CT: Yale University Press, 2016), 1–15.

7. See, for example, Edwin Rios, "Arizona Republicans Banned Mexican American Studies—the Fight Is Now Back in Court," *Mother Jones,* July 2, 2017, www.motherjones.com/politics/2017/07/arizona-republicans-banned-mexican-american-studies-the-fight-is-now-back-in-court; Terry Tang, "Judge Blocks Arizona Ethnic Studies Ban He Found Was Racist," Associated Press, Dec. 28, 2017, www.usnews.com/news/best-states/arizona/articles/2017-12-28/judge-blocks-ban-on-ethnic-studies-in-tucson-school-district; Sara Ganim, "Making History: Battles Brew over Alleged Bias in Advanced Placement Standards," CNN, Feb. 24, 2015, www.cnn.com/2015/02/20/us/ap-history-framework-fight/index.html; Charles Lane, "What the AP U.S. History Fight in Colorado Is Really About," *Washington Post,* Nov. 6, 2014, www.washingtonpost.com/blogs/post-partisan/wp/2014/11/06/what-the-ap-u-s-history-fight-in-colorado-is-really-about; Heide Brand and Jon Herskovitz, "Oklahoma Is Trying to Ban AP US History," Reuters, Feb. 18, 2015, www.businessinsider.com/r-oklahoma-lawmakers-aim-to-halt-advanced-placement-history-course-2015-2.

8. Gail Collins, "How Texas Inflicts Bad Textbooks on Us," *New York Review of Books,* June 21, 2012, www.nybooks.com/articles/2012/06/21/how-texas-inflicts-bad-textbooks-on-us.

9. Derrick P. Aldridge, "The Limits of Master Narratives in History Textbooks: An Analysis of Representations of Martin Luther King, Jr.," *Teachers College Record* 108, no. 4 (2006): 662–86, https://zinnedproject.org/materials/martin-luther-king-jr-narrative-critiques.

10. Lewis M. Terman, *The Measurement of Intelligence* (Boston: Houghton Mifflin, 1916), 91–92.

11. Ellwood P. Cubberley, *Public Education in the United States: A Study and Interpretation of American Educational History* (Boston: Houghton Mifflin, 1919), https://archive.org/stream/publiceducationi032029mbp/publiceducationi032029mbp_djvu.txt.

12. William Shockley, *Shockley on Eugenics and Race: The Application of Science to the Solution of Human Problems,* ed. Roger Pearson, with a preface by Arthur R. Jensen (Washington, DC: Scott-Towsend, 1992).

13. Richard Herrnstein and Charles Murray, *The Bell Curve: Intelligence and Class Structure in American Life* (New York: Free Press, 1994).

14. David Bohn, *On Dialogue* (London: Routledge, 1996).

15. Crossing the Line activity is described at https://my.vanderbilt.edu/vucept /files/2014/08/Crossing-the-Line-Activity.pdf.

16. Claude M. Steele, "Thin Ice: Stereotype Threat and Black College Students," *Atlantic* 284, no. 2 (Aug. 1999): 44–54, www.theatlantic.com/magazine/archive /1999/08/thin-ice-stereotype-threat-and-black-college-students/304663.

17. Based on data from the U.S. Department of Education, National Center for Education Statistics, Characteristics of Public Elementary and Secondary School Teachers in the United States: Results from the 2015–16 National Teacher and Principal Survey (Aug. 2017) https://nces.ed.gov/pubsearch/pubsinfo .asp?pubid=2017072rev.

18. U. S. Department of Education, The State of Racial Diversity in the Educator Workforce (July 2016) https://www2.ed.gov/rschstat/eval/highered/racial-diversity /state-racial-diversity-workforce.pdf.

19. Robin DiAngelo, "White Fragility," *International Journal of Critical Pedagogy* 3 (2011): 54–70.

20. Tony Fabelo et al., Breaking Schools' Rules: A Statewide Study of How School Discipline Relates to Students' Success and Juvenile Justice Involvement (New York: Counsel of State Governments Justice Center, July 19, 2011), ix–xii, http:// knowledgecenter.csg.org/kc/system/files/Breaking_School_Rules.pdf.

21. Ibid.

22. Whitney Dow, "Whiteness Project," KUDOS Design Collaboratory, www .whitenessproject.org.

23. George Lipsitz, "The Racialization of Space and the Spatialization of Race," *Landscape Journal* 26, no. 1 (2007): 12–16.

24. Jennifer L. Eberhardt, "Imaging Race*,"* *American Psychologist* 60, no. 2 (Feb.–Mar. 2005): 181–90.

25. The specified teaching strategies and others are available at the Facing History and Ourselves Resource Library, www.facinghistory.org/resource-library /teaching-strategies. Save the Last Word for Me, www.facinghistory.org/resource-library/teaching-strategies/save-last-word-me; Learn to Listen, www.facinghistory. org/resource-library/teaching-strategies/learn-listen-listen-learn.

26. "Big Paper: Building a Silent Conversation," Facing History and Ourselves Resource Library, www.facinghistory.org/resource-library/teaching-strategies /big-paper-silent-conversation.

27. Gloria Ladson-Billings, "From the Achievement Gap to the Education Debt: Understanding Achievement in U.S. Schools," *Educational Researcher* 35, no. 7 (Oct. 2006): 3–12, www.montgomeryschoolsmd.org/uploadedFiles/departments /clusteradmin/equity/educational debt.pdf.

28. Dorothy Steele et al., "How Identity Safety Improves Student Achievement," unpublished ms., Stanford University, 2007. See also "Identity Safe Classrooms: An Interview with Dr. Dorothy Steele," www.youtube.com/watch?v=o4hkbRYCpgI.

29. Dorothy M. Steele and Becki Cohn-Vargas, *Identity Safe Classrooms: Places to Belong and Learn* (Thousand Oaks, CA: Corwin, 2013), 6–8.

CONTRIBUTORS

GLENN ADAMS is a professor in the Department of Psychology and director of the Cultural Psychology Research Group at the University of Kansas. The enduring focus of his work is the power of marginalized knowledge to reveal and counteract the epistemic violence associated with white supremacy.

FELICE BLAKE is a faculty member of the English Department at the University of California, Santa Barbara. She has published work on contemporary racism, culture, and resistance in *Al Jazeera, Ethnic and Racial Studies,* and *SOULS: A Critical Journal of Black Politics, Culture, and Society.*

DEVON W. CARBADO is associate vice chancellor of BruinX for Equity, Diversity, and Inclusion and the Honorable Harry Pregerson Professor of Law at UCLA School of Law. He teaches constitutional criminal procedure, constitutional law, Critical Race Theory, and criminal adjudication. Carbado writes in the areas of employment discrimination, criminal procedure, constitutional law, and identity. He is the author, with Mitu Gulati, of *Acting White? Rethinking Race in "Post-Racial" America* (Oxford University Press, 2013) and coeditor of several volumes, including *Race Law Stories* (Foundation Press, 2008), with Rachel Moran; *The Long Walk to Freedom: Runaway Slave Narratives* (Beacon Press, 2012), with Donald Weise; and *Time on Two Crosses: The Collective Writings of Bayard Rustin* (Cleis Press, 2003), with Donald Weise.

KIMBERLÉ WILLIAMS CRENSHAW, professor of law at UCLA and Columbia Law School, is a leading authority in the area of civil rights, Black feminist legal theory, and race, racism, and the law. She is the founding coordinator of the Critical Race Theory Workshop, and coeditor of the volume *Critical Race Theory: Key Documents That Shaped the Movement* (New Press, 1996). Crenshaw is cofounder and executive director of the African American Policy Forum, a gender and racial justice think tank and a leading voice in calling for a gender-inclusive approach to racial justice interventions. She spearheaded the Why We Can't Wait campaign and coauthored the reports *Black Girls Matter: Pushed Out, Overpoliced, and Underprotected* (2016) and *Say Her Name: Resisting Police Brutality against Black Women* (2016).

LEAH N. GORDON, Lewis-Sebring Visiting Associate Professor of History and American Studies at Amherst College, holds a joint PhD in history and education from the University of Pennsylvania. A historian of the twentieth-century United States, Professor Gordon has particular interests in intellectual history, the history of education, the relationship between social science and social policy, and ideas about race, class, and inequality in modern America. Professor Gordon's first book, *From Power to Prejudice: The Rise of Racial Individualism in Midcentury America* (University of Chicago Press, 2015), received the 2016 Linda Eisenmann Prize from the History of Education Society.

LUKE CHARLES HARRIS is former chair of the Department of Political Science at Vassar College (2001–4), where he teaches American politics, constitutional law, and Critical Race Theory; and cofounder and program director of the African American Policy Forum (AAPF). An expert in the field of Critical Race Theory, Harris has authored a series of influential articles on questions of racial and gender equality.

DANIEL MARTINEZ HOSANG is an associate professor of ethnicity, race, and migration and American studies at Yale University. He is the author of *Racial Propositions: Ballot Initiatives and the Making of Postwar California* (University of California Press, 2010) and coeditor, with Oneka LaBennett and Laura Pulido, of *Racial Formation in the Twenty-First Century* (University of California Press, 2012).

PAULA IOANIDE is a mother, teacher, scholar, and prison abolition organizer who strives to counter the social and spiritual ills produced by gendered racial capitalism. An associate professor of comparative ethnic studies at Ithaca College, Ioanide focuses her research on the emotional dimensions of racism and the spiritual depravity of white domination. Ioanide is the author of *The Emotional Politics of Racism: How Feelings Trump Facts in an Era of Colorblindness* (Stanford University Press, 2015) and is coeditor of a forthcoming anthology on the appropriation of antiracist discourses titled *Antiracism Inc./Antiracism Works* (Punctum Books).

LOREN KAJIKAWA serves as associate professor of ethnomusicology and musicology at the George Washington University's Corcoran School of the Arts and Design. His teaching and research explore the intersection of race and music in the twentieth and twenty-first centuries, and he is author of *Sounding Race in Rap Songs* (University of California Press, 2015). He serves as coeditor for the Tracking Pop Series at the University of Michigan Press and as editor of the *Journal of the Society for American Music*.

GEORGE LIPSITZ is professor of Black studies and sociology at the University of California, Santa Barbara. His publications include *How Racism Takes Place* (Temple University Press, 2011), *The Possessive Investment in Whiteness: How White People Profit from Identity Politics* (Temple University Press, 2006), and *A Life in the Struggle: Ivory Perry and the Culture of Opposition* (Temple University Press, 1995). He won the American Studies Association Angela Y. Davis Prize for Public Scholarship in 2013 and the Bode-Pearson Prize for Career Distinction in 2016.

Lipsitz is chair of the board of directors of the African American Policy Forum and chair of the board of directors of the Woodstock Institute.

MARZIA MILAZZO is an interdisciplinary scholar and assistant professor of English at Vanderbilt University. Her forthcoming book, *Colorblind Tools: Global Technologies of Racial Power,* traces the racial technology of colorblindness from the Americas to South Africa, and from the colonial to the contemporary era, to argue for the centrality of colonialism to present-day racial formations and call attention to the longevity, insidiousness, and power of colorblind rhetoric as a key tool of white supremacy. Her articles have appeared in *Journal of Commonwealth and Postcolonial Studies, The Global South, Research in African Literatures, Journal of International and Intercultural Communication,* and *Journal of Applied Philosophy.*

AILEEN MORETON-ROBINSON is a Geonpul woman from Minjerribah (Stradbroke Island), Quandamooka First Nation (Moreton Bay), in Queensland, Australia. Prior to her appointment as professor of Indigenous studies at Queensland University of Technology she was an Australian Research Council postdoctoral fellow at the Australian Studies Centre, University of Queensland. Previously she taught sociology at Queensland University of Technology, women's studies at Flinders University, and Indigenous studies at Griffith University and the University of South Australia. Her book *Talkin' Up to the White Woman: Indigenous Women and Feminism* (University of Queensland Press, 2000) was short-listed for the New South Wales Premier Literary Awards and the W. E. H. Stanner Award.

UMA NARAYAN is professor of philosophy and Andrew Mellon Chair at Vassar College. She is the author of *Dislocating Cultures: Identities, Traditions and Third World Feminism* (Routledge, 1997) and coeditor of *Reconstructing Political Theory: Feminist Perspectives* (Pennsylvania State University Press, 1997), with Mary L. Shanley; *Having and Raising Children: Unconventional Families, Hard Choices, and the Social Good* (Pennsylvania State University Press, 1999), with Julia Bartkowiak; and *Decentering the Center: Postcolonial and Feminist Challenges to Philosophy* (Indiana University Press, 2000), with Sandra Harding. She regularly offers courses on contemporary moral issues, social and political philosophy, and feminist theory in the philosophy department.

MILTON REYNOLDS is a San Francisco Bay Area–based career educator, antiracist activist and educational consultant. His civic investments have been devoted to disability rights, environmental justice, juvenile justice reform, law enforcement accountability, and youth development. He serves on the board of Literacy for Environmental Justice, an environmental justice and youth development nonprofit committed to addressing the legacies of environmental racism in southeast San Francisco, and on the advisory board of the Paul K. Longmore Institute on Disability at San Francisco State University.

DWANNA L. MCKAY (MVSKOKE) is a sociologist and assistant professor of Indigenous studies at Colorado College. Robertson's research focuses on the reproduction of social inequity through institutionalized race, ethnicity, and gender processes, particularly for Natives. Her work has been published in *American Indian Quarterly, American Indian Culture and Research Journal, Sociology of Race and Ethnicity Journal,* and the *European Sociological Review.* Robertson's current research projects include the examination of authenticity policing within Indigenous communities, an investigation of Indigenous women faculty's experiences in predominantly white and patriarchal institutions, and a book project analyzing the character of self-employment among women of color.

PHIA S. SALTER is an associate professor of psychology and Africana studies at Texas A&M University. She utilizes cultural-psychological and Critical Race perspectives to inform her work on collective memory, social identity, and systemic racism. She is an interdisciplinary scholar whose work draws upon diverse methodologies to integrate social psychological science with connections to real-world social issues. Phia earned her BS in psychology from Davidson College and her PhD in social psychology from the University of Kansas.

BARBARA TOMLINSON is professor of feminist studies at the University of California, Santa Barbara. Her research interests include rhetoric and feminist politics, Critical Race Theory, and intersectionality. Her publications include *Undermining Intersectionality: The Perils of Powerblind Feminism* (Temple University Press, 2018), *Feminism and Affect at the Scene of Argument: Beyond the Trope of the Angry Feminist* (Temple University Press, 2010), and *Authors on Writing: Metaphors and Intellectual Labor* (Palgrove Macmillan, 2005). She has recently published articles in *Signs, Feminist Theory, Meridians, American Quarterly,* and *Social Identities,* and coedited a special issue of the *Du Bois Review.*

INDEX

Abinake people, 98

abolitionists, repression of, 130–31

Aboriginal studies, 267, 302

the academy: activist students as not served by, 322–23; boundaries between civil society and, transcending, 2; demography of, generally, 47; and "epistemology of ignorance," 47; institutional reforms, 1960s/70s movements for, 11–13, 75–76, 313–14; and the media, 107; and methodology of Indigenous researchers, 93–94; neglect of pervasive patterns of segregation and subordination, 47; powerblindness as rewarded in, 176; as racial episteme, 11. *See also* disciplines; universities

accompaniment, ideal of, 285, 286

achievement gap/performance gap: "educational gap" as conceptual framework vs., 368; equal educational opportunity and, 228, 233–34; and stereotype threat, 360–61

ACT tests, 252

Adams, Glenn, 267, 375

affect, definition of, 348n4

affective learning: and need to interrogate colorblind practice, 354; as reducing implicit biases, 337–39, 349–50n20. *See also* pedagogical interventions in colorblind teaching practice—affective under-skilling and need for; race-gender-sexuality–conscious

classrooms—affective resistances of advantaged students

affirmative action: overview, 154, 246–47, 263–64; assessment of capabilities, equal opportunity in, 251–56, 257; as attempt to "level the playing field," 252; *Bakke* decision as removing racial justice as foundation of, 67–68; campaign against, 129, 146n6, 238; campaign against, as against antidiscrimination law in general, 41; claimed as damaging for Black people, 120; class and, 248–51, 263–64; and contradiction of defending race-blind merit alongside color-conscious departure from it, 71; diversity as distinguished from, 259; "diversity" programs and liberal ambivalence as undercutting, 54; equality of opportunity as promoted by, 251–56, 260–61, 262, 263–64; formal legal equality as not erasing need for, 263–64; gender and, 248–50, 263–64; global colorblindness and demonization of, 107, 108–9, 116–23; imperfections of, 251, 256; legacy students contrasted with, 262–63; and meritocracy as myth, 254, 262–63; in moral equivalency with segregation, 135–36, 149n26; multiple criteria of inclusion utilized in, 247–50, 256; patterns of exclusion as shaping, 248–49; potential for success, assessment of,

affirmative action *(continued)*
255–56; privilege of white males and,
262; stereotype threat as disrupting
campaign against, xii; successes of,
261–62; tort-based compensation
compared to, 256–57; veteran benefits
contrasted with, 257–58. *See also* U.S.
Supreme Court—affirmative action
—MISCONCEPTIONS ABOUT: overview,
246–47, 263–64; "costs imposed" on
nonbeneficiaries, 258–59, 260–61;
middle-class Blacks as not suffering
from discrimination, 249–50; poor
and working-class Blacks as not benefiting from, 250; as "preferential
treatment" creating "reverse discrimination," 251; as "preferential treatment"
justified as compensation, 251, 256–58,
259, 260; as "preferential treatment"
justified on grounds of social utility,
258–59, 260; race as only basis of, vs.
gender and class affirmative action
programs, 247–50; as stigmatizing
participants, 260–63; "unqualified"
people, 120, 255–56, 257, 260, 261–62;
unsolved social problems blamed on,
251
Africa: colonial proxies for local rule in,
193; Ghana, and dilemma tale, 281–82;
as "outside history," 9
African American Policy Forum (AAPF),
x, xii
African Americans: and classical music,
exclusion from, 160–62, 164; environmental racism and, 36; gay rights
advocacy as marginalizing, 214, 215–16,
218–19, 222n33; intraracial conversations among, and Obama campaign,
133; municipal takeovers by states as
disproportionately affecting, 43; music
of, as devalued, 159–61, 162–63, 167,
171n8, 172n16, 173n28; My Brother's
Keeper initiative and, 137–43, 149–
50n34; narrative of family failure as
principle site of racial inequality, 138,
140, 141–42, 149–50n34; one-drop
racialization rule for, 91, 118; racial
binarism and, 119; white racial framing

theory and, 1–3n27, 91–92. *See also*
Black people; killings of Black people
African National Congress (ANC), 116,
120
aggregation, unjust, research design as
producing, 13
Aikin, Scott F., 185, 188, 189
Alcoff, Linda Martín, 180
Alcorn, Marshall, 333, 337, 338
Alfaro, Olmedo, 10; *El peligro antillano en
la Amèrica Central,* 112
Alfred, Taiaiake, 293
Algonquian people, 96
alien land laws, 31
American Civil Liberties Union (ACLU), x
American Enterprise Institute, 238
American Indian Movement (AIM), 98
American Musicological Society,
172–73n27
Andersen, Margaret, and Patricia Hill
Collins, anthology introduction,
189–93, 198n41
anthropology: and affirmative actions
policies, demonization of, 116–17;
emphasis on particularity and difference in, 8; and epistemic whiteness,
construction of, 46; origins in white
supremacy of, 5, 7, 8; and "primitive"
civilizations, 5; and scientific theories
of racial difference, 7; state of nature,
46; White possession as reinforced by,
267, 302–3
anthropos. See humanitas vs. *anthropos*
antidiscrimination laws: black women as
"impossible subjects" of, 202–3, 210–11;
portrayed as special preferences for
Blacks and "reverse racism" against
whites, 41. *See also* affirmative action;
colorblind intersectionality—sex
discrimination law
Anzaldúa, Gloria, 182–83
Arizona v. U.S. (2012), 38
Asian Americans: and affirmative action,
247; critique of Asian American literature, 321; environmental racism and,
36; model minority myth, 345–46
Asian immigrants, policy of U.S. toward,
26, 31

assemblages, 204–5

Attwood, Bain, 295

Australia: as historico-political field (1970s), 300–301; national project of, 299, 301–2; and native title, 302; and the sociological imagination, 293, 303; White Australia policy, 301. *See also* Indigenous sovereignty

Australian studies, 267, 301–2

autonomous individual: and contracts, 45; economics as based in, 8; and language, 9; and the "other," fear of, 9–10; rights and responsibilities theories and, 45

Baker, Houston, 321

Bakke decision (1978), xii, 67–68, 82n35, 247, 261–62

Baldwin, James, 311, 312, 316, 352; "My Dungeon Shook," 333

Behavior and Brain Sciences (journal), 273–74

Behrendt, Larissa, 295

Bell, Derrick, 60, 63, 69, 248

Bhabha, Homi, 321

bias: colorblindness as solution to, 66–67; implicit vs. explicit, 337–39, 340, 349–50n20; in-group, 334, 349n16

Biko, Steve, 122

biology: and Collins's argument on social construction of race and gender, 185–87; conquest as justified by, 5–6; and legitimized racism against Native Americans, 88; race as biological concept, 7, 18n18, 46, 115, 296–97; research design as based in, 7, 13–14; white demographics of scientists, 47. *See also* research design

biopower. *See* Indigenous sovereignty— and biopower (disciplinary knowledges and regulatory mechanisms)

Birzer, Catherine Langrehr, 307

Black cultural expression: and significance of Black collective achievement, 320; as vehicle for gaining political rights, 311–12. *See also* literature/cultural studies—the canon, presence of aggrieved populations in

"Black exceptionalism" argument, 92

blackface, 87, 89

Black History Month (BHM), 279–80

Black Lives Matter movement: campus uprisings in support of, 271; formation of, 320; and literary studies, 310, 320–21, 323; music departments in era of, 162–63

Black middle class: creation of, 250; discrimination and, 249–50

Black Panther party, 310

Black people: income differentials by race, 105–6; West Indian, 10, 112. *See also* African Americans; Black women; killings of Black people

Black Power movements: and equal opportunity, 225, 237; and systemic and institutional racism, 229

Black radical tradition, and race-conscious reading practices, 320–22

Black rights portrayed as special preferences/"reverse racism" against whites: of affirmative action, as misconception, 251; antidiscrimination laws, generally, 41; colorblind proponents' claims for, 33; contradiction in defending affirmative action against claims of, 71; desegregation programs and, 35, 37, 41; fair employment laws and, 38, 41; Jim Crow era judicial interpretations, 29–30; students' race consciousness in Harvard Law School protest framed as, 64, 66–67; and uninterrogated meritocratic baselines, 54; voting rights protections and, 39, 41. *See also* affirmative action—misconceptions about; desegregation

Black Scholar, The, 12

Black Studies programs: calls for dismantling of, 320–21; establishment of, 11, 313; as foundational framework vs. subfield, 12; as transdisciplinary, 74

"Black tax," 122

Black women: and grooming standards for hair, 211–12; historical masculinization of, 209, 211; as "impossible subjects" of antidiscrimination law, 202–3, 210–11; and increasing unspeakability to frame theoretical and political interventions

City University of New York, 248

Civil Rights Act (1866), 28, 29, 42, 45

Civil Rights Act (1875), 29

Civil Rights Act (1964), 37, 227

colonialism (continued)
of history, 8, 9, 178; violence of, projection of white guilt about, 46. See also Indigenous sovereignty; modern/ colonial order and racial domination
colorblind intersectionality: overview, 154, 200–201, 205, 220; definition of, 201; nonwhiteness as the racial modifier of differences, 210–11, 213; and whiteness as unarticulated racial default, 201, 209–13, 215–20, 222n23. See also intersectionality; white feminist powerblind critiques of the concept of intersectionality
—GAY RIGHTS ADVOCACY: overview, 201; African Americans as marginalized in, 214, 215–16, 218–19, 222n33; analogizing race to sexual orientation, 213–15; "Don't Ask, Don't Tell" military policy, 213–18; gay as "the new straight," 219, 220; gay as "the new white," 219–20; and "Gay is the New Black" frame, 218–20, 223n44; and imperative to be gay like a white heterosexual man, 213, 215–18, *217*, 219–20; marriage equality, 218–20, 223n44; and whiteness as unarticulated racial default, 215–20
—SEX DISCRIMINATION LAW: overview, 201; "equal burdens" test and, 206, 208, 209; formal equality approach and, 206, 208, 209, 212; hair and, 211–12; and imperative to be female like a white heterosexual woman, 208, 213; *Jespersen v. Harrah's Operating Co.* (2004), 205–13; normative gender imperative and, 205–9; *Price Waterhouse v. Hopkins* (1989), 205–6; *Rogers v. American Airlines* (1981), 212; and sexual orientation, 211; and whiteness as unarticulated racial default, 209–13, 222n23
colorblindness: overview, ix–x, 13–14; and black subordination as a thing of the past, 218–19, 359; and "blindness" as metaphor of impairment, 4; claimed to be a recent product of the civil rights movement, 25, 52; as default position for social justice, 3–4, 12, 317, 353; defini-

tions of, 13, 106, 175, 280; effect on social justice, studies contesting, 4, 342–43, 344; and equal education opportunity, interpretations of, 224–26, 230, 238; as exculpating white responsibility for status of people of color, 106, 226; "goodness" of, as evasion of open discussions of gendered racism, 237–38, 329, 330, 336, 362–63; international terms for, 106, 116, 126n43; and "irrelevance" of gendered racism, 328–29, 330; liberal/conservative/radical conceptions of, 53, 54, 66–67, 71; as never fully embraced by moderates and liberals, 129; as personal disclaimer, 2, 15; in postracialism's trajectory, 129, 137, 144; racial epithets as socially unacceptable, 90, 93; turn to, 12–13; white supremacy as preserved via, 30, 40. See also Black rights portrayed as special preferences/"reverse racism" against whites; Critical Race Theory (CRT); differences, elision/transcendence of; disaggregation of knowledge; global colorblind discourse; multiculturalism; neutrality and colorblindness; postracialism in the age of Obama; psychology—colorblind ideology and; racial nonrecognition; racial recognition vs. racist subordination as the problem to be solved
—AS HISTORICAL POLITICAL PROJECT: overview, 25–26; and civil rights era, 33–36; and Constitutional support for the slave system, 27; and epistemology of disavowal, 106; European conquest and, 25; Jim Crow segregation and, 28–33, 42; reversals of cause and effect and, 26; the Roberts Court and, 35, 36–44
colorblind racism: coded language used to discriminate in, 90; as covert vs. overt racism, 85–86, 101n3; defined as racial inequality resulting from nonracial dynamics, 85; and inequalities perceived as personal/cultural faults of people of color, 86, 93; legitimized racism against Native Americans and,

86, 88–89, 92–93, 100; systemic racism and, 92–93. *See also* proxies for race

color consciousness. *See* race consciousness

Columbus, Christopher, 88, 98

Columbus Day, 87, 89, 98–99

community: as model for well-being, vs. growth-focused models, 282–84, 291n45; music initiatives based in, 168–69, 173nn35–36

community control of schools, 230, 231

Connerly, Ward, x, 129, 146n6

conquest, and white supremacy, 5–6, 176

contracts: Civil Rights Act (1866) and right to pursue, 28; Locke's free autonomous subject and, 45

Cooper, Anna Julia, 11

cosynthesis, 204–5

Countering Colorblindness across the Disciplines project: array of formalized and informal interventions for, 16–17; background of, ix–xi; goals and objectives of, xiii, 1, 47–48; history of, xi–xviii; retrenchment discourses and need for, 145–46; as transcending boundaries between the university and civil society, 2; as transdisciplinary, xiv–xv, 1–2

covert vs. overt racism: colorblindness and, 85–86, 89, 101n3; and differences in expression and function of overt racism, 85; hate groups and, 86, 101n3; Native Americans and, 86–87, 89, 99. *See also* colorblind racism; legitimized racism (overt racism)

Cox, Oliver Cromwell, 55, 83n61, 148n24, 229, 232

credit scoring and worthiness, 26, 32, 42, 43

Crenshaw, Kimberlé Williams, xii–xiii, 21–22, 375; as a founder of Critical Race Theory, xi, 14, 184; on colorblindness, 24, 31, 35–36, 125n16; on foundational imperative for change, 15–16; and intersectionality, 182–83, 200, 202, 204, 213, 222n23; on race consciousness, 109; on seemingly race-neutral policies, 43

criminal justice system, racial disparities in, 38, 139

Critical Legal Studies (CLS), 53, 72, 75

Critical Race Theory (CRT): ambivalence of civil rights establishment toward, 53–54, 72; canon of, 69–70; Countering Colorblindness project and, xiv; Crenshaw as a founder of, xi, 14, 184; intersectionality as undertheorized within, 200, 201–2; and the law as constructing social categories, 204; migration across disciplines of, 55; and perspective/life experience and intellectual work, 64, 71; and racial position as foundation for all topics, 15, 281. *See also* racial nonrecognition

—HISTORY OF: overview, 52–54, 73–74, 78–79; conservative character of law discipline and rise of, 74–75; as dynamically constituted, 57; forerunners of, 74, 83n61; and frame misalignment, 55–56, 70, 72; and liberal reform, limits of, 56–57; and "New Developments in CRT" (first workshop), 57–59, 72–73, 83n55; and rationality of law, skepticism of, 77–78, 83n66; and retrenchment, the law on frontlines of, 76–79; second workshop (Buffalo, NY), 73, 83nn58–59; temporal opportunity and, 75–76; and tradition of critiques of the academy, 55, 80n13. *See also* Harvard Law School protest (1982), and history of CRT

Crossroads Project, 169, 173n36

Crouse, James, 252

Cubberley, Ellwood P., 357, 358

culture, "high art," 158–59. *See also* popular culture

Cumming v. Richmond Board of Education (1899), 30

Cuneo, Michele de, 104n39

Czopp, Alexander, 340–41

Darwin, Charles, 46

Davis, Angela, 182–83, 184

Davis, Jordan, 138, 141–42, 150n36

Davis Medical School. *See Bakke* decision

Decolonial Theory, 275–76. *See also* identity-conscious perspectives informed by the epistemic standpoint of racially subordinated communities—and intellectual decolonization

decolonization: as emancipatory process, 100; strategic concessions necessary to, 93

dehistoricization: conceptual impoverishment of colorblindness and, 354–55; legitimized racism and, 86, 89–90; in psychology, colorblind ideology and, 273, 274, 275, 276

Delgado, Richard, 58, 69, 70, 72

democracy: imperial project of U.S. as delivering, 303; as individual vs. collective acts, colorblind frame and, 355; pedagogical interventions for democratizing voice, 365–66, 367–68

demographics: of the academy, generally, 47; Black students in English departments, 318; "diversity" solutions not addressing faculty, 54, 62; of Harvard Law School, 59–60; student diversity, commitments to, 54, 62, 65, 82nn34–35, 156, 259; of teachers, 361

Derek, Bo, 212

desegregation programs: benefits for Blacks as "unfair impositions" on whites/"reverse racism," 35, 37, 41; campaign against, generally, 238; Coleman Report used to support, 231; local autonomy and, 34–36; and myth of Blacks as "unfit for freedom," 33–34; Roberts Court and dissolution of, 31, 36–37, 119, 120, 224

Detroit, *Milliken v. Bradley* (1974), 34–35

DiAngelo, Robin, 361–62

differences, elision/transcendence of: and affective under-skilling, 363; and dominant particulars masquerading as universals, 3; as foundational to colorblindness, 106; as mechanism for occluding social injustice, 3; and otherness as threat to ideal egalitarianism, 3; subfield paradigm and, 12; universal human condition/interchangeability and, 2–3; white feminist powerblind critiques of the concept of intersectionality and, 179–80, 194

disabilities, people with: and "blindness" metaphor in "colorblindness," 4; and eugenics, 356–57, 358, 359

disaggregation of knowledge, 6, 13–14

disciplines: agenda-setting power of, 225, 226; architecture of universities and, 46–47, 155; contemporary commitments to scientific racism in, 10–11; demography of, 47; destructive disaggregation and, 13–14; either/or vs. both/and perspective in, 176, 198–99n43; epistemic whiteness and, 13, 46; false aggregation and, 13; formal and informal strategies of critical interdisciplinary work, 16–17; foundational imperative for change in, 15–16; as generative source of important work, 46; migration of concepts across, 46; migration of knowledge for purposes never intended, 225; origins in white supremacy of, 5–11, 78; and powerblindness, training for, 176; and propagation of colorblind doctrines, 108; as racial episteme, 11, 15, 44–45; racial gatekeeping in, 74; reforms in 1960s/70s, 11–13, 75–76; silencing of voices in, 44–45, 50n45; subfield paradigm and disavowal of white supremacist origins, 12–13; tradition of critiquing, 55, 80n13. *See also* academy, the; Indigenous sovereignty—and biopower (disciplinary knowledges and regulatory mechanisms); interdisciplinarity; transdisciplinarity; universities; white supremacy—disciplinary engagement and complicity with; *specific disciplines*

discourse, as constructing and producing reality, 177

discrimination: and disaggregation of knowledge, 14; educational inequality and, 229–30; in-group bias, 334, 349n16; middle-class Blacks as spared from, as misconception, 249–50; military exclusion, analogizing sexual orientation to race and, 213–15; overt racial recognition not requirement for, 26; private, Jim Crow era and protection of, 29; racial nonrecognition as narrowing definitions of, 14–15; societal, as relieving institutions of respon-

sibility, 136, 149n27. *See also* Black
rights portrayed as special
preferences/"reverse racism" against
whites; colorblind intersectionality—
sex discrimination law; colorblindness;
employment discrimination

disidentification, 321

diversity: accompaniment and, 285, 286;
affirmative action undercut by, 54; as
distinguished from affirmative action,
259; faculty recruitment not valued in,
54, 62; as guard against accusations of
racism, 317; racial retrenchment and
decreasing importance of, 62; racial
retrenchment and hope for vehicle of,
67–68; of students, commitments to,
54, 62, 65, 82nn34–35, 156, 259. *See also*
multiculturalism

divine right of kings, 295–96

Doane, Woody, 109

Donadio, Rachel, 310–11

Douglass, Frederick, 311, 316; "The Meaning of July Fourth for the Negro," 312

Dow, Whitney, Whiteness Project, 353–54

Drake, St. Clair, 232

Dream Unfinished, The: A Symphonic
Benefit for Civil Rights, 169

drug war, sentencing differentials in, 26

Du Bois, W. E. B.: in the canon, and disregard of social justice commitments of,
311, 316; as forerunner of CRT, 83n61;
in opposition to colorblindness, 50n45;
in opposition to the academy's complicity with racial domination, 11, 55,
74, 80n13, 148n24; and systemic/
institutional racism, 229, 232; on
whiteness, 44

DuBruyn, Lemyra, 98–99

Dunning School, Reconstruction narrative of, 355

Dworkin, Ronald, 258–59

economics: and biology as justification for
conquest, 5–6; and class vs. racial
disparities, claims for, 120–22; and
epistemic whiteness, construction of,
46; methodological individualism and,
46; neglect of pervasive patterns of

segregation and subordination in
society, 47; and propagation of colorblind doctrines, 108; "public choice"
paradigm, 8; and the universally interchangeable rational and self-interested
acquisitive subject, 8, 13, 46. *See also*
income and wealth; neoliberalism;
poverty

education: accompaniment and, 285, 286;
as Black Panther party's key strategy,
310; defunding of, 164; funding of
Black school districts, differential in,
255; high-stakes testing in, 26; in identity-conscious forms of knowledge,
284–85; as locus in 1960s/70s struggle
for racial justice, 11–12, 75–76; migration of CRT into, 55; neglect of pervasive patterns of segregation and subordination in society, 47; precollege
advising of minority students, differential in, 255; and propagation of colorblind doctrines, 108; school choice and
vouchers, 238; STEM subjects discour-
aged for minority students, 255; teacher
tenure opposition, 238. *See also* equal
educational opportunity; pedagogical
interventions in colorblind teaching
practice

Egypt, humanities and study of, 8

Elementary and Secondary Education Act
(1965), 227

Emanuel, Rahm, 139; "Becoming a Man"
program of, 138

emotional work. *See* race-gender-sexuality–conscious classrooms—pedagogy
of emotional engagement

emotions, defined, 348n4

empathy, 168, strategic empathy of educators, 335–36

empire. *See* colonialism

employment, occupational mobility of
Black middle class, 250

employment discrimination: overview,
254; conscious and unconscious stereotyping, 254; cumulative adverse
effects of, 254; and educational inequality, 229, 230, 238; interviews, job
evaluations, and recommendations

employment discrimination *(continued)* and, 253–54; layoffs and, 253; middle-class Blacks and, 249; Obama initiative as silent on, 140; "old boy network" and, 253; qualifications, assessment of, 255–56; recruitment practices and, 253–54, 256; resume assessment and, 253; Roberts Court dissolution of standards, 31, 37–38; standardized tests and, 252–53. *See also* affirmative action; colorblind intersectionality—sex discrimination law

Enlightenment, the, 44

environmental racism, 36

epistemic whiteness, 13, 44–45, 46, 210

equal educational opportunity: overview, 224–27, 237–38; ambiguity of the term, 225, 232, 238; colorblind interpretations of, 224–26, 230, 238; community control and, 230, 231; compensatory education, 230, 231, 232–33; rejection of ideal of, 225, 236–37; as right of citizenship, 225

—COLEMAN REPORT ON: overview, 226–28; achievement gaps and, 228; blame the victim mentality supported by, 229–30; community control efforts attacked in, 230; and deficiency paradigms (attributes of communities), 228, 230; diverse range of policies calling on, 231; inequality among adults as naturalized in, 228; as methodologically individualistic, 228; question addressed by, 227; racial power (political and economic contexts) as elided in, 229–30, 231, 237–38; racist causality (discrimination) as obscured in, 229, 231; reduced investments in schooling of poor and minority students legitimized in, 230; socioeconomic status and, 230; sociological traditions as ignored in, 228–29, 230; statistical methods of, 231, 236; systematic and institutionalized racism as obscured in, 228–29, 230, 237, 242n23; teachers attacked in, 242–43n27; and test scores, 230

—CRITIQUES OF AND ALTERNATIVES TO COLEMAN REPORT: and achieve-ment gaps, 233–34; blaming the victim avoided in, 236, 237; and causal significance of systemic and institutionalized racism, 232–33, 236, 238; and community control, 233; and compensatory approaches, 233–34; as countering colorblindness, 231–32; and danger of believing the problem is solved, 238; and educationalization (asking schools to solve problems in isolation), 235–36; and racial power (political and economic contexts) as causal, 233, 234–35, 236, 238; and racist causality (discrimination), 233–34, 236; redistributive policies and, 235–36; and statistical research, 236

equal opportunity: affirmative action as promoting, 251–56, 260–61, 262, 263–64; as enduring political ideal, 225; formal legal equality as not ensuring, 263–64; and Lyndon Johnson's call for equality, 225; liberalism as infused with ideal of, 225; as rationalizing white supremacy, 225, 237

ethnic studies programs: ambivalence of civil rights establishment toward, 53; calls for dismantling of, 320–21, 355; establishment of, 11; as foundational framework vs. subfield, 12; as most diverse environment on predominantly white campuses, 332–33; neoliberalism as neutralizing and marginalizing, 317–18; and orientation toward racial power and inequality, 76; as transdisciplinary, 74

ethnomusicology, 165. *See also* music departments

eugenics: confronting colorblind pedagogies and, 353–54, 355–59, 370; definition of, 356; educational policies and, 359; educator complicity with, 356–58; as expunged or transposed from U.S. history, 355–57; and "fitness" or lack thereof, 356–57, 359; and "highbrow"/"lowbrow" as terms, 158; and identity markers becoming designations of "fitness" or lack thereof, 359, 370; and intelligence/IQ testing, 7, 274, 357–58; intersectionality in context of, 359; persistence of influence of, 10–11, 18n18, 353–54, 359; and race as ideological construction, 358–59; racial tracking, standardized testing, and high rates of suspension and expulsion as current policies connected to, 356–57; and schools as institutions of racial stratification and subjugation, 359; and whiteness as "normative state," 355–56, 357. *See also* scientific racism

Europe: immigrants from, 115; "new racism" as term for colorblindness in, 106; positioned as center of modern progress, 6

evolution, 46

Facing History and Ourselves, 353; "Race and membership in American History: The Eugenics Movement," 353

faculty: careers of, as issue for literary studies/humanities, 309, 310–11, 313, 318; demographics of, 47, 59–60; "diversity" solutions not addressing, 54, 62; minority law professors, need for, 60–61, 64, 68. *See also* Harvard Law School protest (1982), and history of CRT

family failure as site of racial inequality, narrative of, 138, 140, 141–42, 149–50n34

FBI, COINTELPRO, 131

Feagin, Joe, 91–92, 100

Federal Housing Act (FHA), 32

Feder, Lester, 159

femininity. *See* gender

feminist studies: and colorblindness, 109, 181; delegitimization of, 320–21; as discursive technologies of power, 180, 205; and hegemony-seeking disciplines, allegiance to, 180; incorporation of difference and, 179–80; interdisciplinarity of, 179–80; narratives of history of, 179–80; universal woman of, 2; and use of disciplinary power, 179–80; workshops to build feminist legal theory, 73. *See also* intersectionality; white feminist powerblind critiques of the concept of intersectionality

Fenstermaker, Sarah. *See* West, Candace, and Fenstermaker

Ferguson, Missouri, 139, 141

Ferguson, Roderick, 11, 16–17, 313, 315

Fineman, Martha, 73

Fink, Robert, 162

Foord, Kate, 298

foreign policy: Alternative Course and interrogation of, 69; origins in white supremacy of, 7

formal-race unconnectedness, 115

Foucault, Michel, 180; *Society Must Be Defended,* 293–94, 295–98, 300, 301, 302, 303

Fourth of July, 89

frame alignment, 55–56

France, and universal principles, search for, 6

Franche, Dominique, 297

Frankenberg, Ruth, 15

Frazier, E. Franklin, 229, 232

freedom, myth of Blacks as "unfit" for, 33–34, 355

French Revolution, 296

Freyre, Gilberto, *Casa-grande e Senzala,* 111, 112, 113

Fry, Peter, *A persistência de raça,* 117

Garner, Eric, 139

Garza, Alicia, 320

Gates, Henry Louis, 132, 321

Gawronski, Bertram, 344–45

gay rights advocacy. *See* colorblind intersectionality—gay rights advocacy; LGBTQ people; sexual orientation

gender: affirmative action based on, 248–50, 263–64; college admissions test differentials, 252–53; Collins's argument about social construction of, 185–87; conscious and unconscious stereotypes of, 254, 261; eugenics and, 359; hair and, 206; interview process and, 254; makeup and conformity to, 206, 207–8, 209; normative femininity, sex discrimination law and, 205–9; normative masculinity, gay rights advocacy and, 214, 215–16, 218, 219–20; resume assessment and, 253; whiteness as, 209–11

the law as abstract and neutral, 68; school's defense of meritocratic academic standards for faculty candidates, 62, 63, 64–65, 66, 68, 81n32; school's offering of three-week minicourse as answer to student demands, 63, 67, 82n37; and social change, slowness of legal education to respond to, 64–65; and student diversity aggressively advanced by Harvard, 62, 65, 82nn34–35; student-organized Alternative Course as illuminating, 68–70; student protest of dearth of minority law classes and faculty, 60–62, 81n25; students' conflict with the civil rights establishment, 70–71; students' critique of traditional criteria as unjustified preferences, 62–66, 82nn35–36; students' race consciousness framed as "reverse discrimination," 64, 66–67; Third World Coalition (TWC) and, 64, 67, 68–69, 70, 81n25, 82n37

Harvard music department, 171n6

Hawaii, 6–7

health care, white demographics of professionals in, 47

Hegel, G. W. F., and white supremacy, 9, 10

Hemmings, Clare, 179–80, 183

Heritage Foundation, 238

Herrnstein, Richard, and Charles Murray, *The Bell Curve,* 358

heterosexuality: sex discrimination law as presupposing, 211; "straight" identity as distinguished from, 219

"highbrow" vs. "lowbrow" culture, 158

hip hop, 160, 161, 162, 165, 166, 172n16

history: and affirmative actions policies, demonization of, 116–17; the archive as structured in dominance, 44–45; and biology as justification for conquest, 5–6; W.E.B. Du Bois's critique of, 55; as foreclosing understanding of race as structuring force within, xv, 47; representations of, as promoting racism, 279–80; textbooks controversies, 355; White possession as reinforced by, 267, 302–3

Hitler, Adolf, 98, 173n31

Home Owners Loan Corporation, 32

hooks, bell, 182–83

Hoover Institute, 238

Hopkins, Anne, 205–6

HoSang, Daniel Martinez, xi, 170, 376

housing discrimination: and inequality of education, 229, 230, 238; lending policies and, 32, 43, 229, 230

humanitas vs. *anthropos*: construction of, as gendered enterprise, 181; and managerial logic of the colonial matrix, 8–9, 178; powerblindness and, 181; and white feminist powerblind critiques of the concept of intersectionality, 193, 194; women classed as *anthropos,* 181

humanities: calls for dismantling minoritarian studies, 320–21; careers in, as issue, 309, 310–11, 313, 318; crisis in, 308, 309, 310–11, 318; development of critical consciousness as goal of, 324; and difference as margins/center vs. domination/oppression, 8, 317; and disciplinary complicity with white supremacy, 5–11; and elision of difference, goal of, 2–3; and epistemic whiteness, construction of, 46; and fear of engulfment by a threatening social aggregate, 46; as foreclosing understanding of race as structuring force within, xv; and foundational imperative for change, 15; private interiority of the individual as emphasis in, 14, 46; and transdisciplinarity, xv; and universals, false aggregation of humanity into, 8. *See also humanitas* vs. *anthropos*; literature/cultural studies; music departments; philosophy

Hung, Lyiis, 173n36

Huntington, Samuel P., 18n18

Hurston, Zora Neale, 11

identity-conscious perspectives informed by the epistemic standpoint of racially subordinated communities: and coloniality of knowledge, 175–76; Critical Race Theory (CRT) as, 275; Decolonial Theory as, 275–76; education in, and production of critical consciousness,

identity-conscious *(continued)*
284–85; empirical studies as illuminated by, 286; and IQ test performance
thought experiment, 274; and racialized ignorance, combating, 285–86; of
students, colorblind enculturation
against, 272–73
—AND INTELLECTUAL DECOLONIZA-
TION: overview, 276, 284–85; denaturalizing strategy: cultural affordances
for denial and ignorance, 278–80;
denaturalizing strategy: spouse preference as neoliberal growth, 282–83; love
and, 280–84; and missionary vs. liberation social science, 277; normalizing
strategy: parent preference as sustainable relationality, 283–84, 291n45;
normalizing strategy: perception of
racism as reality attunement, 277–78,
289–90n28; perception and, 276–80
"identity politics": multiculturalism
engaged with social justice seen as, 316;
rights discourse seen as, 301
Identity Safety theory, 368–70
immigration, fear of, and Anglo-Saxon
cultural gerrymandering, 158
immigration policy: Brazil and, 115; and
construction of whiteness, 26; and
legitimized racism, 90; origins in white
supremacy of, 7; racial profiling, 38
imperialism, origins in white supremacy
of, 6–7, 10
income and wealth: and Black middle
class, rise of, 250; and "Black tax," 122;
differentials by race, 105–6, 121–22;
inherited wealth, Black lack of, 122;
inherited wealth, white land ownership
and, 31, 121–22; inherited wealth,
whiteness as, 164. *See also* economics;
neoliberalism; poverty
India, humanities and study of, 8
Indians. *See* Native Americans
Indigenous dispossession: erasure of, via
assumed legitimacy of the nation, 45;
of Native Americans, 88–89, 92, 95,
355; systematic treaty violations, 27;
terra nullius legal principle and, 25. *See
also* Indigenous sovereignty

Indigenous peoples: as "people without
history," 6, 9; women's rights, as not
commensurable with those of white
women, 301. *See also* Indigenous dispossession; Indigenous sovereignty;
legitimized racism (overt racism
against Native Americans); Native
Americans (Indians, Indigenous
peoples)
Indigenous sovereignty: overview, 293–94;
and historico-political field, 300–301;
judicio-political framework, current
literature of, 294–95; racism and, 295;
and the sociological imagination, need
for, 293, 303; and subjectivity, 298, 299,
300–301; *terra nullius* and the disavowal of, 298
—AND BIOPOWER (DISCIPLINARY
KNOWLEDGES AND REGULATORY
MECHANISMS): and colonial bourgeois
order, 297; establishment of, 295,
296–97; political rationality and,
297–98; race and war and, 296–97,
298; rights discourse and, 295–96,
299–303; and whiteness as invisible
norm, 298; White possession and, 267,
297, 298–303
Indigenous studies, 267, 301–2. *See also*
Indigenous sovereignty; legitimized
racism (overt racism against Native
Americans)
individualism: colorblindness as emphasizing, 14, 86, 115, 355; racism as personal
aversion, 4, 115, 117, 143, 290n35. *See also*
autonomous individual; methodological individualism; neoliberalism
inequality: and differentially situated
individuals and groups treated as
though they are equal, 30–31, 40,
42–44, 136; as increasing, 23–24;
intraracial, as tool to silence the reality
of white dominance, 120–21; narrative
of family failure as principle site of, 138,
140, 141–42, 149–50n34; objectors to,
castigated for identifying differences, 3;
perceived as personal/cultural faults of
people of color, 86, 93. *See also* equal
educational opportunity; equal oppor-

Kajikawa, Loren, 153, 376

Kamel, Ali, *Não somos racistas: Uma reação aos que querem nos transformar numa nação bicolor,* 107, 108–9, 110, 113, 115, 116–19, 120, 121–23

Kant, Immanuel, and white supremacy, 9, 10, 46

Kelley, Robin D. G., 170, 323

Kennedy, Anthony, 119, 120

Kennedy, Duncan, 81n25

Kerner Commission (1968), 229

killings of Black people: by civilians, 137–38, 141–42, 149n31, 150n36; by police, 45, 105, 139, 141, 323

Kim, Claire Jean, 23; *Bitter Fruit,* 345

King, Deborah K., 182–83

King, Martin Luther Jr., 32–33; and complaint vs. dream, 149n30; manipulative quotation of his words, 33, 34; and universal messages of equality and dignity, 135

King, Rodney, 324

knowledge production: hegemony-seeking vs. subjugated knowledges, 180, 184; whites as managing conditions of, 178–79

Kozol, Jonathan, *Savage Inequalities,* 238

Kun, Josh, 170

labor market segmentation: New Deal exclusions based on, 32; as proxy for race, 31, 36

labor protests, police killings and, 105

Ladner, Joyce, 55

Ladson-Billings, Gloria, 368

land ownership: alien land laws (prohibition of Asians), 31; private mortgages excluding Blacks, 32, 43; and white wealth accumulation, 31, 121–22. *See also* property

Lang, Clarence, 47

language and languages: coded, of colorblind racist frame, 90; and discursive limits on complex processes, 204; legitimized racism against Native Americans expressed via, 86; of Native Americans, appropriation by federal government, 88; pure/impure and the

autonomous self, 9; racial epithets, 86, 90, 93

Latinx people: and affirmative action, 247; credit scoring and, 43; fatherlessness and, 138; racialized as Mexicans, 90, 102n14; racial profiling of, 38, 139; voting rights and, 39

Lauter, Paul, "Politics of Literature," 317–18

law: colorblindness as perpetuating errors of, 45; colorblindness in, as policy choice of judges, xii; conservative character of, and evolution of CRT, 74–75; Critical Legal Studies (CLS), 53, 72, 75; and epistemic whiteness, construction of, 46; history of disciplinary contestation in, 74–75; intent to discriminate, xv; Law and Society movement, 75; Legal Realism, 75; methodological individualism and, 46; neglect of pervasive patterns of segregation and subordination in society, 47; precedents (*stare decisis*), 40, 45; rights-bearing subject of, 13, 46; and social categories, construction of, 204; and transdisciplinarity, xv; White possession as reinforced by, 267, 302–3. *See also* colorblind intersectionality—sex discrimination law; Harvard Law School protest (1982); Indigenous sovereignty; legal education; postracialism in the age of Obama; racial nonrecognition

Lawrence, Charles, 14, 69, 70

Lazarsfeld, Paul, 227

Lee, James, 309

Lee, Robert, *Asian Americans in Popular Culture,* 345

legal aid/legal services, 66

legal education: and activist orientation of students of 1970s/80s, 75–76; "diversity" programs and, 54, 62; and the law as abstract, neutral principle vs. inherently political, 68, 78; rhetorics of institutional defense and, 54. *See also* Harvard Law School protest; law

legitimized racism (overt racism against Native Americans): overview, 22,

85–88, 99–101; appropriation of Indigenous culture, 88, 89, 90, 97; colorblindness as relying on, 111; colorblind
racism and, 86, 88–89, 92–93, 100;
definition of, 86; erasure of historic
context and, 86, 89–90; historic specificity against Indigenous Peoples, 90;
internalized oppression and, 88, 97–98,
100, 101n10; as invisible, 86–87,
99–101; language use and, 86; and
media misrepresentations, 87–88, 89,
97; methodology of study of, 93–94;
and other marginalized peoples,
acceptance of, 87, 89; other racialized
groups as subjected to, 90, 102n14; as
overt, 86–87, 89, 99; playing Indian
and, 87, 89, 97–98, 104n48; protest of
by individuals and groups, reaction to,
89; racial epithets, continued use of, 86,
90, 93; racial power and, 88, 90, 99;
racism defined for, 88; "savagism discourses and," 96, 97; and social character of the U.S., 89; sports teams and,
89; systemic racism and, 88, 100; white
denial of, 89; and whiteness, normative, 90; white supremacy and, 95–96
—AND THEORIES OF RACE AND
RACISM: overview, 90–91; colorblind
racism theory, 92–93, 100, 103n30;
racial formation theory, 91, 92, 100;
white racial framing theory, 91–92,
100
—THEMES OF: overview, 94; celebrating
genocide, 98–99; dirty squaw or sexy
maiden, 96–97, 104n39; lazy, drunk,
casino-rich Indians, 94–96; playing
Indian, 87, 89, 97–98, 104n48
lending policies, discriminatory, 32, 43,
229, 230
lesbians, as marginalized in white feminist
history, 179–80
Levine, Lawrence, 158
Lewis, George, 173n28
Leyens, Jacques-Philippe, 342
LGBTQ people: community-based music
initiatives and, 169, 173n35; lesbians as
marginalized in white feminist history,
179–80; opposition to queer theory/

transgender studies, 320–21; whiteness
as intersectionally unmarked for, 210.
See also colorblind intersectionality—
gay rights advocacy; sexual orientation
liberalism: citizen subject of, 2; defined,
225; Indigenous sovereignty and, 294.
See also universals
libraries, 47
Lincoln, Abraham, 29, 45
Lipset, Seymour Martin, 227
Lipsitz, George, xi, xii–xiii, 21–22, 161, 168,
170, 376–77
literacy tests, 26, 28
"literary contract," 321
literary criticism: lack of exposure to
African-American texts in, 313; by Toni
Morrison, 55
literature/cultural studies: and Black
students, lack of, 318; careers in, as
issue, 309, 310–11, 313, 318; "close reading" as methodology of, 316; and crisis
in humanities, 308, 309, 310–11, 318; as
foreclosing understanding of race as
structuring force within, xv; metadiscursive paradoxes of colorblind texts,
122; migration of CRT into, 55; the
novel and the universalizing subject,
9–10; primitives, representation of, 6;
social movement interventions as
ignored in, 311; structural oppression as
ignored vs. engaged with, 308–10,
311–13, 316, 319; textual contradictions
created via suppressing of race as
category of analysis, 110, 118–19, 122.
See also global colorblind discourse;
race-gender-sexuality–conscious
classroom
RACE-CONSCIOUS READING
PRACTICES: overview, 310; and activist
students, support for, 322–23; Black
Lives Matter movement and, 310,
320–21, 323; canon expansion as revealing need for, 309, 315–16, 319; critical
justice discourses produced through,
321–22; methodologies, 321–22; the
neoslave narrative and, 319; social
movements and development of, 319–
21, 323–25

—THE CANON, PRESENCE OF
AGGRIEVED POPULATIONS IN: colorblind methodologies and readings as
enabled by, 308–9; colorblind multiculturalism resulting from canon wars,
309–10, 312–19, 323; critical interventions of such authors, as ignored,
311–13, 316; and cultural war to protect
the established canon, 313–15; diversity
requirements as limiting engagement
with, 315–16; and inclusion as function-
ing to reproduce the status quo, 315;
neoliberalist corporatization of education and, 317–18; and new approach to
reading, need for, 309, 315–16, 319;
reading texts as substitute for relationship building and social activism,
308–9
local autonomy as colorblind principle,
34–36
Locke, John: South Carolina constitution,
9; and white supremacy, 9–10, 45
loitering laws, 28
Lopez, Ian Haney, 26, 31, 42
Louisiana Separate Car Act, 30–31
Louisville, KY, desegregation program
dissolved in, 36–37, 119
love, decolonizing, 280–84
Lowe, Lisa, 321

McCall, Leslie, "The Complexity of Intersectionality," 177, 182–84, 196n19,
197n23. See also white feminist powerblind critiques of the concept of
intersectionality
MacLean, Nancy, 8
Maggie, Yvonne, 107
makeup: gender conformity and, 206,
207–8, 209; and white women's entry
into the workplace, 208
Malcolm X, 32, 44
Maliseet people, 96
Maré, Gerhard, Declassified: Moving
beyond the Dead-End of Race in South
Africa, 108–9, 110, 113–14, 115–16, 117,
119–23
market, minorities' status rationalized as
product of, 226

marks, John, 297
Marshall, David, 46–47
Martin, Trayvon, 137–38, 139, 141–42,
149n31
Marxism: and colorblindness, 109; universal worker of, 2
masculinity. See gender
math: white demographics of mathematicians, 47. See also research design
Mathae, Katherine Bailey, 307
Matsuda, Mari, 14
Maya-Aztec civilizations, 8
Mbeki, Thabo, 118
Mbembe, Achille, 126n43
media: and fatherlessness scripted as
primary cause of society endangerment
of Black males, 142; and frame of
"reverse discrimination," 67; and gay
rights advocacy, 216, 217; and global
colorblindness, 107; and Indigenous
sovereignty, 299, 302; overt racism
against Native Americans in, 86; and
postracialism in the Obama era, 141,
142, 146n4, 147n13, 148n21; support
for de facto coup in Brazil, 106
Meinhold, Keith, 216, 217, 220
Melamed, Jodi, Represent and Destroy, 317
Melville, Sam, 173n36
Mendieta, Eduardo, 297
merit: overview, 22; baselines of, as naturalizing maldistribution of opportunity, 54; conservative/liberal commitment to, 71; as contradiction in
defenses of affirmative action, 71; myth
of meritocracy, 254, 262–63; as off-
limits mechanism of racial power, 68;
as sanitizing racial power, 71; as social
construction, 71. See also Harvard Law
School protest
Merton, Robert, 227
methodological individualism: and Coleman Report, 228; definition of, 46; in
disciplines, 46; statistical research
design and, 7–8
Mexican Americans: environmental
racism and, 36; immigration policy
and, 26; and intermarriage claimed to
end racism, 114–15

Mexicans: legitimized racism and, 90, 102n14; "mestizo" privilege and, 114–15

Michaels, Walter Benn, 314

Michigan, efforts to limit affirmative action, 129

Mignolo, Walter D., 8, 177–79, 194

Milazzo, Marzia, 10, 22, 377

military: "Don't Ask, Don't Tell" policy, 213–18; veterans, 257–58

Miller, Teresa (Terri), 58, 72

Milliken v. Bradley (1974), 34–35

Mills, Charles, 44, 45, 47, 109, 333; *The Racial Contract*, 321

Mills, C. Wright, 293

minority scholarship: in legal education, and CRT formation, 68–70; racial gatekeeping and, 74; subfield paradigm as marginalizing, 12

miscegenation: as barred by law, 26, 42; and hair type vs. skin color as characterizing slavery, 186; as "overcoming" racism, claim for, 110, 111, 113, 114–15; and "pure" music, white supremacist desire for, 159

modern/colonial order and racial domination: neoliberal individualist tendencies as manifestation of, 275, 282–83; scientific research enterprise as integral component of, 275–76. *See also* identity-conscious perspectives informed by the epistemic standpoint of racially subordinated communities

modernization theory, 46

Mohanty, Chandra Talpade, 182–83

Montag, Warren, 298

Montgomery Bus Boycott, 355

Monture-Angus, Patricia, 293

Moraga, Cherríe, 182–83, 191–92

Moreton-Robinson, Aileen, 23, 25, 267, 377

Morris, Aldon, 55–56

Morrison, Toni, 15, 55, 311, 316; *Playing in the Dark*, 312–13

Morris, Quentin, 169

mortgage lending, 32, 43

Moynihan, Daniel Patrick, Moynihan Report, 227, 228

multiculturalism: colorblind, as resulting from canon wars, 309–10, 312–19, 323;

national identity viewed as threatened by, 314–15

multidimensional analysis: held to have inherent advantages over intersectionality, 204–5; and white feminist appropriation of black feminist intellectual production, 181, 185, 188, 197n23

municipalities: corporatization of, 43; and My Brother's Keeper initiative, 141; privatization of services in, 43; state government takeovers of, 26, 43

Muñoz, Jose, 321

Murray, Charles, 18n18

Murray, Charles, and Richard Herrnstein, *The Bell Curve*, 358

Muscogee people, 94–95

music departments: overview, 153, 155–57; building architecture as reflecting classical focus of, 155; colorblindness and, 158, 161–62, 163; community-based initiatives and, 168–69, 173nn35–36; conventions of music instruction/standards of excellence and, 157, 161–62, 165, 168–71; and curricula, 165, 168, 169–71; and empathy, 168; and exclusion, culture of, 157–62, 164–65, 171n8, 172n16, 172–73n27; financial pressures on, 165–66; founding of, generally, 158, 160, 171n6; interdisciplinarity and, 169–70; material resources of, 165; musical racism permeating, 160–61; and popular music, dangers of, 160; and popular music, politics of inclusion of, 165–67, 172–73nn27–28; as privileging white European and American male composers, 156–58, 160; publicity and brochures for, 156, 157–58; segregation and, 160; solutions to inclusivity problem/confronting the legacy of white supremacy, 157, 167–71, 173nn35–36; student diversity, initiatives to increase, 156; systemic racism and, 156, 163–66, 167–68. *See also* classical music

My Brother's Keeper (MBK), Obama initiative, 137–43, 149–50n34

Narayan, Uma, 154, 377
Nascimento, Abdias, 118, 125n26; *Brazil: Mixture or Massacre?*, 111–12
National Association of Music Education, 160
National Labor Relations Board, 32
nation-states: assumed legitimacy of, 45; eugenics and modern concept of, 356; multiculturalism seen as destructive to identity of, 314–15; possession held by, 300. *See also* sovereignty; white nationalism
Native Americans (Indians, Indigenous peoples): and covert mechanisms of colorblind racism, 86; dispossession of lands and resources of, 88–89, 92, 95, 355; environmental racism and, 36; erasure of, in colorblind classroom, 355; federal "benefits" (reimbursement), 95; federal Indian policy, 90, 91, 101n5; "friendlies" as colonial proxies among, 193; and genocide, 88, 92, 98–99, 355; population of, 91, 92; poverty and, 86, 95–96, 99; racial epithets continued to be used against, 86, 90, 93; racialization of, 91–93, 103nn20–21,27,30; suicide rates among youth, 99; as term, 101n5; in urban vs. rural environments, 93, 103n31; and "vanishing Indian" trope, 92; violence and sexual assault against women, 104n39. *See also* Indigenous peoples; legitimized racism (overt racism against Native Americans)
Nattrass, Nicoli, and Jeremy Seekings, *Class, Race, and Inequality in South Africa*, 120–21
neoliberalism: activist students and resistance to, 322–23; and corporatization of higher education, 165–66, 317–18; individualist model of society, scientific research as utilizing, 276, 282–83; individualist tendencies, and violence of racial subordination, 275, 281; indoctrination of students into, 322; "neoliberal asset-stripping," 177, 182; power-blindness as cultivated in, 176; and privilege, investment in, 318; rights

discourse seen as identity politics under, 301; social safety net as eroded by, 317
neoslave literary form, 319
Nettl, Bruno, 155, 157
neutrality: contestations of, 78; interview process assumption of, 254
neutrality and colorblindness: overview, xiv–xv; and disparate effects on differentially situated persons, 43; and public image of Obama, 132; of research design, 7; white racial sensibilities held to constitute neutrality, 276
New Haven, CT, fair employment law, 37–38
New Left, 236–37
New Negro Movement, 312, 320
new racism. *See* colorblindness
Newspeak ensemble, 169, 173n36
New Teacher Induction Program, 369
Newton, Huey P., 237
Nicolacopoulos, Toula, 298
Nicoll, Fiona, 298
Nok civilization, 8
nonracialism. *See* colorblindness; South Africa
Norton, Michael I., 342
Nri civilization, 8
Nuttall, Sarah, *Entanglement*, 113

Obama, Barack: "A More Perfect Union" speech, 133–37, 148n22, 149n25; My Brother's Keeper (MBK) initiative, 137–43, 149–50n34. *See also* postracialism in the age of Obama
Obasogie, Osagie K., 4
objectivity, as supporting the racial order, 78, 226, 274–75
O'Connor, Sandra Day, 149n27
Olson, Gary, 333
Omi, Michael, 91–92, 100
opportunity-based egalitarianism. *See* equal educational opportunity; equal opportunity
O'Reilly, Bill, 138, 139, 141, 143
Oriental Studies, 8
Orwell, George, 37

otherness: and difference, elision of, 2; as
justification of white supremacy, 5–6;
as justifying differential treatment,
147–48n18; rhythm as associated with,
171n8; as threat to ideal egalitarian
future, 3
Otoe people, 97
Oyo Benin civilization, 8

Panama, and white nationalism, 10, 112
*Parents Involved in Community Schools v.
Seattle School District No. 1* (2007), 35,
36–37, 40, 41, 119, 120, 224, 238
Parker, Charlie, 173n28
Parks, Rosa, 355
Parsons, Talcott, and Kenneth Clark, *The
Negro American,* 229
Patterson, Orlando, 186, 187
pedagogical interventions. *See* literature/
cultural studies—race-conscious
reading practices; pedagogical interventions in colorblind teaching practice; race-gender-sexuality–conscious
classrooms
pedagogical interventions in colorblind
teaching practice: overview, 268,
352–54, 370–71; and cognitive and
affective domains of learning, 354; and
"educational debt" vs. "achievement
gap," 368; and schools as primary site of
colorblind production and socialization, 354, 359; white educators as audience for, 360, 361–62
—AFFECTIVE UNDER-SKILLING AND
NEED FOR: anxieties of educator and,
362, 365; body language and, 364; and
comfort as confused with safety, 362,
364; definition of, 360; and difference,
elision of, 363; educators' white racial
identity and, 360; and identity development of students, 363–64; language use
and, 364; malice as not required to
create differential outcomes, 364, 365;
racism as reductively defined and,
362–63; relevance of school as issue in,
363; resistance of students of color to,
362; as social conditioning vs. innate
characteristic, 366–67; stereotype

threat and "performance gap" of Black
students, 360–61, 369; truncated skills,
363; unequal outcomes as rooted in
deficiency paradigm, 359, 361, 365;
white fragility and, 361–62
—CONCEPTUAL IMPOVERISHMENT
AND NEED FOR: and abstraction of
historical events from context, 354–55;
and agency of students, 355; and alloca-
tion of resources, 358, 359; definition of,
354; and eugenics, reclaiming the
history of, 353–54, 355–59, 370; historical thinking skills and, 359; and individual acts vs. collective action, 355;
intelligence and IQ testing and, 357–
58; tracking, standardized testing, and
high rates of suspension and expulsion,
356–57, 358, 362; and whiteness as
norm, 355–56, 357, 363
—PEDAGOGICAL APPROACHES: body
language of educator, 364; creation of
context/container, 365–66; democratizing voice as goal in, 366, 367–68;
diversity as a resource, 369; educator as
arbiter of classroom norms, 366–67;
good intentions alone as insufficient
and may exacerbate challenges, 364–
66; higher levels of participation, 366,
367–69; identity-safe learning spaces,
366, 368–70; interpersonal exchanges
related to difference, 365, 369; prosocial
development, 369; safety of marginalized students, 362, 364–65; structured
listening and speaking opportunities,
366–67; student-centered classroom,
365–66, 369
—PEDAGOGICAL STRATEGIES: Big
Paper: Building a Silent Conversation,
367–68; Crossing the Line/Powerwalk,
360, 361; Learn to Listen, Listen to
Learn, 367; Save the Last Word for Me,
367
Peller, Gary, 14
Penha, Roberto, 105
Penobscot people, 94
perception, decolonizing, 277–78,
289–90n28
perspective-taking (technique), 346

Pewewardy, Cornel D., 97

Pezão, Luiz, 105, 106

philanthropy, xv

Phillips, Stephanie, 58, 72

philosophy: and biology as justification for conquest, 5–6; and epistemic whiteness, construction of, 46; as foreclosing understanding of race as structuring force within, xv; migration of CRT into, 55; and white ignorance, theory of, 109. *See also* affirmative action

photo identification cards, 26, 43

phrenology, 158. *See also* eugenics

physical and natural sciences: and theories of racial difference, 7. *See also* research design

Plessy v. Ferguson (1896), x, 30–31

Pocahontas, 96

police brutality: killings of Black people, 105, 139, 141, 323; Rodney King beating and uprising, 324

political science: and biology as justification for conquest, 5–6; and epistemic whiteness, construction of, 46; migration of CRT into, 55; origins in white supremacy of, 6; White possession as reinforced by, 267, 302–3. *See also* affirmative action

poll taxes, 26, 28

popular culture: and braided hairstyles in sex discrimination cases, 212; and colorblindness considered a virtue, 24; "high art" defined against, 158–59; and legitimized racism against Native Americans, 87, 97–98; and migration of concepts from academic disciplines, xv

popular music: Afro-Diasporic influence on, 162, 167; black music, devaluation of, 159–61, 162–63, 167, 171n8, 172n16, 173n28; canons of, 162; "high art" of classical music defined against, 158–59, 167, 173n28; inclusion in music departments, politics of, 165–67, 172–73nn27–28; music education and "dangers" of, 160. *See also* classical music; music departments

Posner, Richard, 207–8

postracialism in the age of Obama: overview, 128–29; and Blackness made palatable by its disassociation with racial complaint, 133, 134, 147–48n18–19; and Civil Rights Movement distorted into special interest politics, 135–36; colorblindness and trajectory of, 129, 137, 144; colorblindness as rebranded/repackaged in, 134, 136–37; and "common sense," 129, 142; as instructive guide for racial others, 135, 137; marketability brought by Obama as symbol, 129, 143; media and, 141, 142, 146n4, 147n13, 148n21; and "misunderstanding" between races, 134–35, 148n24; My Brother's Keeper (MBK) initiative, 137–43, 149–50n34; and other nonwhite groups, 134, 148–49n18, 148n21; and private-public partnerships, 138–39, 140–41; and punitive outcry prompted by Obama's comment on Henry Louis Gates's arrest, 132; and race as closed chapter, 131, 137, 147n13; and race consciousness of Obama campaign, 132–33; and "race neutrality" of Obama, 132, 133; and racial grievances placed on par with white anger and anxieties, 135–36, 149n25; and racial grievance, turn away from, 128–29, 130–31, 133, 149n30; and racial power as an after-effect of the past, 136, 137, 149n27; and retrenchment, rhetorical frames of, 129; and silencing of structural racism, 136, 139–40, 141–44, 149n27; as ushered in by election of Obama, 128–29, 146n4; white nationalist backlash following, 144

"post-truth" era, 285–86

poverty: "Black tax," 122; Brazil and, 121–22; Native Americans and, 86, 95–96, 99; South Africa and, 115, 120–22; as unsolved, as blamed on affirmative action, 251. *See also* economics; income and wealth; neoliberalism

Powell, John, 159–61, 170; *Rhapsodie Nègre*, 159

Powell, Lewis F. Jr., xii

powerblindness: definition of, 175–76. *See also* white feminist powerblind critiques of the concept of intersectionality

precedents (*stare decisis*), 40, 45

Price Waterhouse v. Hopkins (1989), 205–6

"primitive" civilizations: designation of, 5–6, 8–9; music and, 158–62, 171n8, 172n16; precolonial Europe and stratification of, 171n4; representation of, 6, 46

prison reform, community-based music initiatives and, 173n36

privilege: "mestizo," Mexicans and, 114–15. *See also* pedagogical interventions in colorblind teaching practice—affective under-skilling; race-gender-sexuality-conscious classrooms—affective resistances of advantaged students; white privilege

professional schools: and affirmative action, 248. *See also* education; law

property: differentials in ownership of, 121–22; differentials in protection of, 45; whiteness and classical music as related forms of, 163–65; whiteness as, 163–64; White possession defined via, 300; white privilege claims couched as rights of, 33. *See also* land ownership

proxies for race: education, 36; income, 36; labor market segments, 31, 36; nationalities and continents as, 26; naturalized citizenship, 31; rhythm, 171n8; in Roberts Court era, 42–43; school district lines as, 34

PSAT/NMSQT tests, 252

psychology: colorblind suppression as increasing negative nonverbal behaviors, 342–43; and epistemic whiteness, construction of, 46; implicit vs. explicit biases, 337–39, 340, 349–50n20; in-group bias, 334, 349n16; intentionality of racism, xv; methodological individualism and, 46; migration of CRT into, 55; negation vs. affirmation training, 344–45; neglect of pervasive patterns of segregation and subordination in society, 47; perspective-taking, 346; self-negating affects, 340–41; self-partisanship, 334; stereotype threat, xii, 360–61, 369; and teaching about racism as individual prejudice vs. structural, 290n35; and tradition of critiquing disciplines, 55; and universal principles, 13. *See also* identity-conscious perspectives informed by the epistemic standpoint of racially subordinated communities

—COLORBLIND IDEOLOGY AND: overview, 267; and abstraction of research from context, 273, 274, 275, 276; and conservative backlash with regard to methods and political orientation, 271–72, 285–86; and denial of racism, 278–80; enculturation of students into, 272–73; and objective standard (reasonable person) as form of racialized subjectivity, 274–75, 276, 281; and pathology, perception of racism as, 276–78; as racial position vs. culture-neutral absence of racial position, 273; and thought experiment about IQ test performance, 273–74; and whiteness as a "view from nowhere," 273

—RESEARCH PRACTICES: overview, 287–88n5; demands for politically neutral science, 271–72, 285; extra-scientific considerations negated in, 274; failures to replicate studies, 271–72; as integral component of racial domination, 275–76; and neoliberal individualist model of society, 276

public policy: Coleman report and, 229; and the colorblind imperative, 3–4, 23, 31, 45; colorblindness as default position for racial justice, 4; interdependent relationship of university with, 4; and migration of concepts from academic disciplines, xv, xvi; white subject as normative standard in, 12

Puerto Ricans, 228

queer theory, opposition to, 320–21

race: in binary opposition with class, 6; as biological concept, 7, 18n18, 46, 115, 296–97; Collins's argument about social construction of, 185–87; colorblind racism theory, 92–93, 103n30; epithets for, 86, 90, 93; eugenics and construction of, 358–59; hair as constitutive of, 186, 212; modern nation-state as preceded by, 296–97; "race card," 276–77, 359; racial formation theory of, 91, 92, 100; racializing terms, nonwhite people as marked by, 90; as reduced to racial identity, 136; sexual orientation analogized to, 213–15; as socially constructed, 91, 103n20; social reality of, 103n20; as synonymous with skin color (formal-race unconnectedness), 115; and war, Foucault on, 296–97; white racial framing theory of, 91–92. *See also* proxies for race

race-based remedies for race-bound problems: Civil Rights Act (1866) as, 28, 29, 42, 45; difficulty of pursuing under colorblind imperative, 3, 5, 23–24, 35–36; and need for collection of racial data, 117; postracial industry of, as silent on systemic and structural racism, 141–43. *See also* identity-conscious perspectives informed by the epistemic standpoint of racially subordinated communities; literature/ cultural studies—race-conscious reading practices; pedagogical interventions in colorblind teaching practice; race–gender–sexuality–conscious classrooms

race consciousness: of collective white advantage, marked as illegitimate, 24–25; deployed by whites as explanation for inequalities, 25; deployed to affirm the claim that race doesn't matter, 131; and hierarchy, acceptance of, 109; Obama campaign and, 132–33

race-gender-sexuality–conscious classrooms: overview, 268, 327; vs. "-blind" curricula, 330; cognitive learning processes as reducing explicit biases, 337–39, 349–50n20; disadvantaged

students' receptivity vs. resistance to, 330–31, 332, 335–36, 347; explicit vs. implicit biases, defined, 348n6; positionality of educator as antiracist feminist and, 335–36, 344; and white fragility, 343–44

—AFFECTIVE RESISTANCES OF ADVANTAGED STUDENTS: believing is seeing, 333; definition of "advantaged students," 327, 347–48n1; desire not to know, 333; dismissal of irrefutable evidence, 329, 330, 331–37; dissociation and detachment from effects of gendered racism, 328, 341; epistemology of white ignorance and, 333; "goodness" of colorblindness as evasion of open discussions of gendered racism, 237–38, 329, 330, 336; in-group bias and, 334, 346, 349n16; "irrelevance" of gendered racism, 328–29, 330; self-partisanship and facts that threaten self-esteem, 334

—PEDAGOGICAL TACTICS THAT FAIL: adulation of charismatic teacher, 337; authoritarianism, 334–36, 337, 343; avoidance of discussing gendered racism, 336, 340, 342–43; "-blind" curricula, 330, 342–43; confrontational attitude, 334–36, 340–41, 343, 344; emotional labor of disadvantaged students and, 343–44; as increasing expressions of gendered racism, 340, 342–43, 343–44; negation and suppression, 343–45; shaming students, 343, 344

—PEDAGOGY OF EMOTIONAL ENGAGEMENT: affective learning processes as reducing implicit biases, 337–39, 349–50n20; as creating pathways to restructuring self-concepts, 330, 341, 348n5; as deepening commitment to social justice, 341; definition of, 337; emotional labor of educator in, 333, 339–40, 348n5; emotions vs. affect, definitions of, 348n4; evoking self-negating affects, 340–41; fears, open scrutiny of, 339; fields of inquiry informing, 331; interpersonal contact, 346; intersectional methodologies/ multiple axes of oppression, 345–46;

outcomes desired for, 337; outcomes of, as cumulative and composite, 340; patience and, 336, 339; perspective-taking, 346; positing new associations, 344–45; resistance, integration of examples of, 346–47; self-reflection, asking for, 336–37, 339, 340; strategic empathy of educator in, 335–36

racial classification: of African Americans, 91, 118; collection of data, importance of, 117, 129; global colorblindness and demonization of, 113–14, 116–22; government role in, 91; of Native Americans, 91–93, 103nn20–21,27,30; racial power produced and perpetuated by process of, 178

racial data, collection of: assaults on, 129; as necessary to combat systemic and structural racism, 117

racial democracy. *See* Brazil; colorblindness

racial discrimination: conscious and unconscious stereotypes and, 254, 261; employment and, 249–56; funding of Black school districts, 255; interview process and, 254; precollege advising, 255; recruitment policies and, 253–54, 256; resume assessment and, 253; standardized testing and, 252–53; STEM subjects, discouragement of, 255. *See also* racism

racial nonrecognition: and "blindness" metaphor of "colorblindness," 4; definition of, 14; logic of formal equivalence used in, 31; as reducing the ways racism takes place to the use of racial classification, 14; as restricting remedial uses of race while narrowing definitions of discrimination, 14–15. *See also* colorblindness

racial power: as after-effect of the past, postracialism and, 136, 137, 149n27; as causal of unequal educational opportunity, 233, 234–35, 236, 238; Coleman report as eliding, 229–30, 231, 237–38; contrasted with liberal notions of discrimination, 66–67; legitimized racism and, 88, 90, 99; merit and, 68, 71; racial classification as producing, 71; racial classification as producing,

178; "remainder" of, at center of liberal institutions, 71

racial profiling, 38

racial recognition vs. racist subordination as the problem to be solved: overview, 23–24; Dr. King's words manipulated to support, 33, 34; European conquest and, 25; explicit recognition as not required for racial subordination, 26; as foundational fiction of colorblindness, 33; global colorblindness and, 116, 117; and harms done by de jure segregation, 41–42; Jim Crow era and interpretation of laws for, 29; as reversing cause and effect, 26. *See also* colorblindness

racial regimes: the canon wars as revealing, 314–15; colorblindness as serving, 30, 40; definition of, 40; powerblind and colorblind discourses as part of, 176; as unstable truth systems, 176; as weakened by their own greed and resistance movements, 321; of white supremacy, 29, 40–41, 43–44

racism: definition of, 88; and Indigenous sovereignty, 295; literary studies and perpetuation of, 312–13; "slow violence" of, 278, 283. *See also* Black rights portrayed as special preferences/"reverse racism" against whites; colorblind racism; discrimination; environmental racism; individualism; institutional discrimination; legitimized racism (overt racism against Native Americans); scientific racism; systemic and structural racism

radical subjectivity, 321

Ravenscroft, Alison, 298

Rawick, George, 50n45

Reagan administration, 76

Reconstruction, 11, 28, 29, 42, 355

Reddy, Chandan, 219

Regents of University of California v. Bakke (1978), xii, 67–68, 82n35, 247, 261–62

regulatory mechanisms. *See* Indigenous sovereignty—and biopower (disciplinary knowledges and regulatory mechanisms); law research design: overview, xiv–xv; biological basis of, 7, 13–14; destructive disaggregation produced by, 13–14; facile aggregation produced by, 13; false aggregation produced by, 13; as favoring individual prejudice vs. collective power (methodological individualism), 7–8; origins in white supremacy of, 7–8. *See also* psychology—research practices; statistical research

retrenchment of race reform: and "diversity," decreasing importance of, 62; and diversity, hope for vehicle of, 67–68; and need for Countering Colorblindness Project, 145–46; and rise of CRT, 75, 76; white nationalism, re-legitimization of, 144–45. *See also* desegregation; postracialism in the age of Obama

"reverse racism". *See* Black rights portrayed as special preferences/"reverse racism" against whites

Reynolds, Henry, *Aboriginal Sovereignty,* 295

Reynolds, Milton, 268, 377

Ricci v. DeStefano (2009), 37–38, 40, 41

Rice, Lisa, 43

Rigg, Kate, 173n36

rights discourse: emergence of, in modernity, 295–96; eruption of, in 1970s, 301–2; and gender, sexual orientation, and non-Anglo migrants, 301; Indigenous sovereignty and, 295–96, 299–303; as neoliberal "identity politics," 301; and rights as producing methods of subjugation, 300, 302; White possession and, 300–303

Roberts, John, 36, 38, 39–40, 224

Robertson, Dwanna, 22, 377–78

Robinson, Cedric, 17n4, 40, 43, 50n45, 176, 314–15, 321

rock music, 160, 162, 165, 166, 172–73n27

Rodrigues, Wesley, 105

Rodriguez, Gregory, *Mongrels, Bastards, Orphans, and Vagabonds,* 114–15

Rogers, Renee, 212

Rogers v. American Airlines (1981), 212

Rome, ancient, 8

Roosevelt, Franklin, 32

Rorty, Richard, 314

Rosser, Phyllis, 252

Roth, Stephen A., 34

Rousseff, Dilma, 106

Rudman, Laurie, 334, 337–39, 340

rule of law, as reinforcing structures of power, 53, 77–78

Said, Edward, 15

Salter, Phia S., 267, 378

Sandoval, Chela, 182–83, 184

SAT tests, 252

Scalia, Antonin, 38, 39, 41

Schoenberg, Arnold, 166

Schomburg, Arturo, 320

school-to-prison pipeline, 140

scientific racism: and classical music, 158; commitment to, 7; in contemporary academy, 7, 10–11, 18n18; as historical context constituting "extra-scientific considerations," 274; and IQ testing, 7, 274, 357–58; race as biological concept in, 5–6, 7, 46. *See also* eugenics

scientism, as complicating racist causality, 226, 237

Seattle, WA, desegregation program dissolved in (*Parents Involved* decision), 35, 36–37, 40, 41, 119, 120, 224, 238

Seekings, Jeremy, and Nicoli Nattrass, *Class, Race, and Inequality in South Africa,* 120–21

segregation: and Black History Month displays, race differential in, 279–80; and demography of the academy, 47; Jim Crow laws, 28–33, 42, 163, 215; and local autonomy as colorblind principle, 34–35; in moral equivalency with affirmative action, 135–36, 149n26; and myth of Blacks as "unfit for freedom," 33–34; in the north, 32–33, 34–35; residential, as limiting access to employment, 140; residential, educational inequality and, 229, 230; separate but equal, 30–31. *See also* desegregation; equal educational opportunity

self-concepts, restructuring, 330, 341, 348n5

self-negating affects, 340–41

self-partisanship, 334

self-reflection by students, eliciting, 336–37, 339, 340

sex discrimination law. *See* colorblind intersectionality—sex discrimination law

sexual assault: Native American women as subject to, 104n39; in slavery, 111–12, 125n26

sexual harassment, employment grooming policy and, 207

sexual orientation: analogized to race, 213–15; in employment discrimination, 211; eugenics and, 359; and rights discourse, 301. *See also* LGBTQ people

Sharpton, Al, 130, 138, 143, 146–47n8

Shelby County v. Holder (2013), 38–40

Shockley, William, 358

Simpson, O.J., 147–48n18

slavery: abandonment of slaves following manumission, 115; archive of, as structured in dominance, 44–45; in Brazil, 111–12, 115, 125n26; Constitutional protections for, 27, 45; Constitutional reversal of, 29, 42, 45; hair type vs. skin color as characterizing, 186; humanism and justification of, 9–10; literary studies' treatment of, 311–12, 319; John Locke and rationales for, 9–10, 45; as most egregious consequence of racialization, 92; and myth of Blacks as "unfit for freedom," 33–34, 355; neoslave narratives, 319; sexual assault and, 111–12, 125n26

Small, Christopher, 168–69

Smith, Barbara, 182–83, 184

Smith, David, 214

social contract theory, 45

social justice: colorblindness as default position for, 3–4, 12, 317, 353; effectiveness of colorblindness to produce, as contested, 4, 342–43, 344; pedagogy of emotional engagement as deepening commitment to, 341. *See also* differences, elision/transcendence of; social movements

social media, and legitimized racism, 97

social movements: academic reform (1960s/70s), 11–13, 75–76, 313–14; campus uprisings for racial justice (2015), 271, 287n1; canon/culture wars as emerging from, 313; enculturation of students against, 272–73; and eruption of rights discourse, 301; literary studies as ignoring reforms wrought by, 311; neoslave literary form and, 319; and race-conscious reading practices, development of, 319–21, 323–25. *See also* Black Lives Matter movement; Black Power movements; Civil Rights Movement

social sciences: colorblind assumptions of, as legitimizing inequality, 226; and disciplinary complicity with white supremacy, 5–11; private interiority of the individual as emphasis in, 14; and transdisciplinarity, xv; and universal principles, search for, 6; white demographics of professionals in, 47. *See also* anthropology; political science; psychology; sociology

Social Security Act, racist effects of, 26, 32

sociology: and affirmative actions policies, demonization of, 116–17; and biology as justification for conquest, 5–6; Chicago School of, 148n24, 228–29, 232; and epistemic whiteness, construction of, 46; as hegemony-seeking discipline, 180, 184; neglect of pervasive patterns of segregation and subordination in society, 47; origins in white supremacy of, 6, 55; political economic approaches, 228–29, 230; and propagation of colorblind doctrines, 108; race relations school of, xv, 134–35, 148n24, 180; the sociological imagination, 293, 303; status attainment school of, 229; and tradition of critiquing disciplines, 55; and white subjects' disclaiming complicity with racism via colorblind tropes, 15

Sommer, Doris, 310

South Africa: and affirmative action, demonization of, 108–9, 120–22; campus uprisings in, 271; and

education and racism as individual prejudice vs., 290n35; racial formation theory as missing persistence of, 91; research design as ignoring, 7–8; societal discrimination as not responsibility of, 136, 149n27; tangible material benefits for white people under, 105–6, 117, 121–22, 164–65; and white racial framing, theory of, 91–92. *See also* eugenics; institutional discrimination

Talisse, Robert, 185, 188, 189
Tawantin-suyo civilization, 8
tax policies, 43
Teixeira, Aloísio, 107
Temer, Michel, 106
Terman, Lewis, 357
terra nullius, 25, 298
Texas, textbooks of, 355
Thanksgiving, 87, 89
Third World Coalition (TWC), 64, 67, 68–69, 70, 81n25, 82n37
Thomas, Clarence, 75
Thomas, Kendall, 57, 73
Thompson, Charles H., 232, 234–35, 236, 238
Till, Emmett, 142
Title VI, organized efforts to attack, 129
Tomlinson, Barbara, 153–54, 205, 378
Torres-Padilla, Jose, 315
transdisciplinarity: Black and Ethnic Studies programs and, 74; Countering Colorblindness across the Disciplines project and, xiv–xv, 1–2. *See also* interdisciplinarity
Trubek, David, 72
Trump, Donald: and "post-truth" stance, 285–86; and whitelash, 285; and white nationalism, 22, 79, 144
Trusheim, Dale, 252
Truth, Sojourner, 319
Ture, Kwame, and Charles Hamilton, *Black Power,* 32, 117, 225, 237

unemployment rates, 115
unions, 253
United Kingdom: Brexit campaign, 285; campus uprisings in, 271

United States: founding of, and legitimized racism against Native Americans, 88–89; imperial project of delivering democratic rights around the world, 303; income differentials by race, 105–6; Indian policy of, 90, 91, 101n5; and universal principles, search for, 6

universals: and aggregation, 13; the autonomous self and, 9–10; and colorblind pedagogy, 342; and disaggregation, 6, 13–14; dominant particulars masquerading as, 3, 178; economics and, 8; human condition/interchangeability, 2–3; of human rights, and whiteness as invisible norm, 298, 301; Indigenous sovereignty and, 294; as logic ignoring asymmetries and inequalities, 136; and music instruction, 161–62; the novel and, 9–10; search for principles of, and complicity with white supremacy, 6, 13; as structured on solidarities of sameness vs. dynamics of difference, 14. *See also* differences, elision/transcendence of

universities: activist students, better support for, 322–23; affirmative action and, 248–49; architecture of buildings for disciplines, 46–47, 155; Black students, rise in numbers of, 250; campus protests of building names, 10; campus protests of participation in slave economies by, 10; demographics of faculty, 47; as management training ground for racialized practices, 268–69; market-based ideologies' role in setting priorities of, 165–66; music programs as serving elite interests in, 157, 164; open admissions programs in, 248; perception of racism as associated with knowledge of past racism, 278; and relevance, reorientation toward, 17; underrepresentation of Black students in, 107; uprisings for racial justice on campuses (2015), 271, 287n1. *See also* academy, the; disciplines; diversity; Harvard Law School protest (1982)
University of California: Los Angeles, 271, 324

University of Kansas, 271
University of Missouri, 271
University of Oregon, 160, 171n6
University of Texas, 82n33
urban crises, 229
urban planning, 47
U.S. Constitution: fugitive slave clause, 26, 27; Indians as racialized in, 103n27; John Locke and drafting of, 45; New Birth (Lincoln), 29, 45; slave trade protection clause, 27; three-fifths clause, 26, 27
—AMENDMENTS: Thirteenth, 29–30, 45; Fourteenth, 29, 45, 119; Fifteenth, 28, 29, 45
U.S. Supreme Court: abandonment of principles long held by, 40; equal protection reduced to racial nonrecognition, 14–15
—AFFIRMATIVE ACTION: *Adarand Constructors, Inc. v. Peña* (1995), 149n26; *City of Richmond v. J. A. Croson Co.* (1989), 149n27; *Regents of University of California v. Bakke* (1978), xii, 67–68, 82n35, 247, 261–62
—EMPLOYMENT, RACE, AND GENDER DISCRIMINATION: *Price Waterhouse v. Hopkins* (1989), 205–6; *Ricci v. DeStefano* (2009), 37–38, 40, 41
—IMMIGRATION LAW, *Arizona v. U.S.* (2012), 38
—PUBLIC ACCOMMODATION DISCRIMINATION: Civil Rights Act (1875), 29; *Civil Rights Cases* (1883), 29–30, 41, 45; *Plessy v. Ferguson* (1896), x, 30–31
—SCHOOL DESEGREGATION: *Brown v. Board of Education of Topeka* (1954, 1955), 33–35, 36, 53, 148n22, 224, 225, 228, 232; *Cumming v. Richmond Board of Education* (1899), 30; *Milliken v. Bradley* (1974), 34–35; *Parents Involved in Community Schools v. Seattle School District No. 1* (2007), 35, 36–37, 40, 41, 119, 120, 224, 238
—VOTING RIGHTS: *Shelby County v. Holder* (2013), 38–40; *United States v. Bhagat Singh Thind* (1923), 31

vagrancy laws, 28
Vassilacopoulos, George, 298
veterans, 257–58
violence: of empire, projection of white guilt about, 46; Native American women as subject to, 104n39; neoliberal individualism and, 275, 281; "slow," of racism, 278, 283. *See also* sexual assault
Virginia, Racial Integrity Act (1924), 159
visual impairments, 4
Vitalis, Robert, 6
Vorenberg, James, 59–62, 67, 81n19, 82n37, 83n58
voting rights: Fifteenth Amendment and, 28; grandfather clauses to limit, 26, 28; literacy tests limiting, 26, 28; photo identification, 26, 43; poll taxes limiting, 26, 28; poor whites and universal franchise, 28; reduction of polling places, 39; Roberts Court dissolution of, 31, 38–40, 49n29; selective enforcement of vagrancy and loitering laws limiting, 28
Voting Rights Act (1965, amended 1975, 1982, 2006), 129; preclearance clause invalidated, 38–40, 49n29

Wagner Act, 26, 32
Walker, Alice, *The Color Purple,* 312
Walser, Robert, 156
War on Poverty, 225, 227
Watkins, Perry, 216
Watson, Irene, 293
Wells, Ida B., 11
West, Candace, and Sarah Fenstermaker, "Doing Difference," 177, 185–87, 188–93, 198–99nn41,43. *See also* white feminist powerblind critiques of the concept of intersectionality
Western subject, 8
West Indian Blacks, and white nationalism, 10, 112
Wheatley, Phyllis, 311–12, 316
white feminist powerblind critiques of the concept of intersectionality: overview, 153–54, 175–77; and allies, adoption of imaginary, 190–92, 193, 194; appropria-

white possession: biopower and Indigenous sovereignty and, 267, 297, 298–303; definition of, 300

white privilege: accrued during era of legal discrimination, 163; couched as property and states' rights issues, 33; as empowerment to ignore the legacy of discrimination, 163–64; entitled attitude toward, 262; and gay rights advocacy, 215, 219; and white feminist powerblind critiques of the concept of intersectionality, 187–88, 193, 194

white subject: continued status as representative political figure, 45; as default Western subject, 8; disclaiming complicity with racism via colorblind tropes, 15; as normative standard/"reasonable person," 12, 274–75, 276, 281; as universal in human rights, 298, 301

white supremacy: collective agency central to, as disavowed, 46; colorblindness as means of preserving, 30, 40; equal opportunity concept as rationalizing, 225, 237; global colorblindness as upholding, 106–7, 108–9, 112, 117, 122–23; as racial regime, 29, 40–41, 43–44; and refusal to see the humanity of people of color, 25, 168. *See also* conquest; Indigenous dispossession; race; slavery; white nationalism

—DISCIPLINARY ENGAGEMENT AND COMPLICITY WITH, 5–11, 78; and silencing of alternative sources, 44–45, 50n45; turn to colorblindness and, 12. *See also* eugenics; Indigenous sovereignty—and biopower (disciplinary knowledges and regulatory mechanisms); research design

Who Killed Vincent Chin? (documentary film), 345

Will, George, 146–47n8

Williams, Patricia, 23, 41, 73

Williams, Raymond, 293

Williams, Robert, 27

Wilson, James Q., 18n18

Winant, Howard, 91–92, 100

Wisconsin Law School, 83n55

women: Native American, violence and sexual assault against, 104n39; rights of white women as not commensurable for Indigenous women, 301; in slavery, sexual assault against, 111–12, 125n26. *See also* Black women; colorblind intersectionality—sex discrimination law; feminist studies; sexual assault; sexual harassment

women's studies programs, 11, 182, 320–21

Woodson, Carter G., 11, 148n24

working-class white men, in affirmative action programs, 248–50

Worsham, Lynn, 333

Wright, Jeremiah, 134–35

Wright, Richard, 311, 316

Wynter, Sylvia, 8

Yale University, 271

Yellow Brave Heart, Maria, 98–99

Young, Whitney, 232; *To Be Equal,* 226, 232–33, 234, 235–36, 238

Zembylas, Michalinos, 336

Zia, Helen, *Asian American Dreams,* 345–46

Zimmerman, George, 139, 149n31

Zuberi, Tufuku, 15, 55, 176–77

Made in the USA
San Bernardino, CA
08 March 2020

65443978R00263